Our Glorious Dead

Malmesbury and the Great War 1914-21

Charles Vernon

Malmesbury Civic Trust

Published by
Malmesbury Civic Trust
Chalcourt, Dark Lane, Malmesbury, SN16 0BB

Printed by
Antony Rowe
Bumper's Farm Industrial Estate, Chippenham, SN14 6LH

Front Cover: The Field of Remembrance laid outside the
Abbey by the Royal British Legion, November 2007.

ISBN 978-0-9536692-2-6

Introduction and Acknowledgements

Having picked up this book you will, I hope, be provoked to ask a couple of questions (at least) - why such an apparently inappropriate title for this subject and didn't the war end in 1918?

Britons of 1918 were proud of the men who went to war, they did not think, as later generations tended to, that lives had been needlessly sacrificed - the fallen were venerated. The 'lions led by donkeys' idea is a modern invention. In fact the British Army of 1918 was the main instrument that had comprehensively beaten the much vaunted German Army and in the final months was expelling it from the territory seized four years before. Our war dead were held in high esteem which is reflected in the words *To Our Glorious Dead* at the head of the panels on the Triangle memorial.

The war against Germany ceased at the 11th hour of the 11th day of the 11th month of 1918. However the Versailles Peace Treaty was not signed until 28th June 1919 and not ratified until 10th January 1920. Other battles continued - the Allies had started fighting the Bolsheviks in the summer of 1918 and did not withdraw from Russia until September 1919. In fact Britain remained in a state of war until an Order in Council was issued on 31st August 1921. The Commonwealth War Graves Commission regard the same date as the cut-off for deaths related to the Great War. But the main reason for ending this book in 1921 is because our main memorial was completed that March and the first Armistice ceremony was held there later that year.

This book has grown exponentially - my original idea was to tell the story of those who died. It quickly became evident that many more from Malmesbury fought abroad and a greater number supported the war effort from home (the town always seems to 'punch above its weight') so that important elements of the story would be missed without expansion. This would help to put the efforts of those who made the supreme sacrifice into context.

I owe a huge debt to many people who have assisted the production of this work. First Derek Tilney must be mentioned, Chairman of Malmesbury's Royal British Legion branch. It is fortunate that he started researching the men from our town who died many years ago - he was able to get personal reminiscences no longer available due to the inevitable consequence of the passage of time. He has made all of his information available to me. You will note that I have relied to a great extent on material from our local newspapers. At the time the Devizes or Wiltshire Gazette, the North Wilts Herald and the Wilts & Gloucester Standard all provided coverage of our town with different emphases. I am extremely grateful to the present editors of the Gazette & Herald and the Wilts & Gloucester Standard for permission to utilise this material. These archives were made available from the new Wiltshire and Swindon History Centre in Chippenham which I can wholeheartedly recommend for anyone researching local history.

Personal data has been more difficult to find and here I must thank: Leonard Ing (for information about his uncle Dick Exton and distant cousin Henry Poole), Malcolm Salter (his grandfather Frederick Salter), Dave Ashford (Frank Woodward), Jamie Lester (Albert & Stanley Lester), Colin Lockstone (Sharland Lockstone), Gerald Willis (Herbert Willis), Nigel & Sue Kirkman (Walter Bond), Julie Jowitt (Leslie Carey), Yvonne Gunstone (John Brickell) and Sara Crabb (United Reformed Church). Photographs were also a problem and my thanks go to the newspapers, the Athelstan Museum, John Bowen, Leonard Ing, Dave Ashford, Michael Adye and a number of internet sites listed below.

The National Archives at Kew have an impressive collection of records which are easy to access - I have used their war diaries and service records in particular. Much is available online from www.nationalarchives.gov.uk . They have formed a partnership with a family history organisation which has all of the censuses, military service records and army pension records at www.ancestry.co.uk. Ancestry have also combined with the Western Front Association to provide online copies of the medal card records. The Commonwealth War Graves Commission has an excellent website www.cwgc.org.uk. The Commission does a marvellous job looking after the thousands of cemeteries and hundreds of thousands of war graves worldwide. The Naval and Military Press (publishers of very useful reprinted historic military books) have made available online details of *Soldiers Who Died in the Great War* (www.military-genealogy.com). For information about the British Army during the Great War, www.1914-1918.net cannot be bettered. I am grateful that the Museum of the Rifles, successors to the Wiltshire Regiment, the Wardrobe (www.thewardrobe.org.uk), has transcribed their war diaries. Most of the maps have been taken from the Official History of the Great War, Military Operations France and Belgium. Originally published in 14 volumes with accompanying Appendices and Maps between 1922 and 1949 these were reprinted by the Imperial War Museum and Battery Press during the 1990s and can still be found in specialist bookshops (or ordered from the Library). I have spent many hours in Malmesbury Library using their free internet access and have tracked down many obscure books through them. I must commend the staff and facilities as invaluable resources.

The 81 individuals who are described are either commemorated or buried in Malmesbury. During my research I found many others who might have been commemorated here. For example *Soldiers Who Died* lists more than 120 men who were either born or resident in this town when they enlisted. Several of those included in this book are not in that list due to incomplete records. Some of these 'extras' came from nearby villages, others had moved away and should be commemorated where they lived. Any men who might have been remembered here are mentioned in Part One and their names have been included in the Index.

Some explanation about the organisation of the text is required. Direct quotations from newspapers, letters, war diaries etc. are typed in italics and are given verbatim - so mistakes such as wrong names and misspellings ought not to be mine! In Part Two individual biographies appear chronologically in order of death. The name, rank, service number, age and unit is given in the first paragraph. This is followed by cause of death (note that Died means either accidental death or as a result of disease), date of death, where the body is buried and where the person is commemorated. Next comes a description of the cemetery or foreign memorial, followed by the life story including a description of his unit's activities. These stories, with a brief introduction to each year, provide an outline of the progress of the war. I have done my best to provide as much detail as possible but some entries are short due to lack of information whereas others have had to be edited.

Once again I have to thank my wife, Val, for her excellent editorial skills resulting in fewer errors and much improved presentation as well as for her indulgence in agreeing to holiday solely to visit many war cemeteries. These trips have enabled us to visit most of the graves of Malmesbury men in France and Belgium. The Imperial War Graves Commission, as it was then known, offered the next of kin the opportunity to add a personal inscription at the foot of the gravestone. This was supposed to cost 7s. 6d. which must have put off many families, although such debts were not pursued. Where there is such a family inscription the wording is given. All of the gravestones in Malmesbury Cemetery have them.

I thought it was important to publish this book to coincide with the 90th anniversary of the war's end. After having made that declaration I discovered that the 1911 census would have been very helpful to track the young men's pre-war careers. Also one man remains a mystery - Private J. Kerr who is commemorated at the Triangle. Just before publication an article in the Gazette and Herald brought some fresh ideas but no definite identification. If I can solve this last puzzle it may be necessary to have an updated edition in a few years time!

Charles Vernon   October 2008

Contents

Part One
Malmesbury; the War and its Aftermath

The Volunteers go off to War 1914-15

Britain was well prepared for war but unfortunately not for the war that it was drawn into on 4th August 1914. The traditional bulwark of our defence, the Royal Navy, was still the strongest in the world although new technology in the form of the Dreadnought put our supremacy under pressure. The Kaiser had begun an arms race and our budget constraints caused difficulty. However the main threat lay on the continent where our loose alliance with the French and Russians meant that land forces would be more important in the coming struggle.

The British Army organisation was based on a system designed by Lord Cardwell in the 1880s. He reorganised the infantry, the basic fighting soldiers, into regiments mostly comprising two battalions (the army structure is described at the end of Part One). One battalion would serve overseas and would be kept up to strength in peacetime by the other battalion at home. This led to the home based unit being under-strength and needing to be brought up to establishment by reservists in the event of war.

Mr. (later Lord) Haldane was charged with modernising the Army after being appointed as Secretary of State for War in 1905. He introduced a General Staff and created the Territorial Force. The Regular Army was organised to provide an Expeditionary Force of six Divisions of all arms and one Cavalry Division in addition to the Empire's garrison. Each Division comprised three Infantry Brigades each of four Battalions with divisional mounted troops, artillery, signal service, supply & transport train and field ambulances.

The normal term of Regular service was 12 years, 7 with the Colours and 5 in the Reserves. After completing this obligation Reservists could sign on for another 4 years. Most Reservists were paid 6d. per day compared to a Regulars' 1s. 1d. Their role was to fill out the Regular Army units and provided about 60% of those who went to France. Each Reservist had an Identity Certificate which was his authority to draw his quarterly pay. It also contained full instructions as to where and when he should report on mobilisation. Attached was a rail warrant for the journey from his home to the Depot and a money order for 3s. subsistence. He was to proceed as soon as he learned of mobilisation through posters or the press.

Special Reservists were the successors of the old Militia. They received 6 months training on joining and had to complete one month's training per year during their 6 years of service. They were paid the same as Regulars whilst in uniform with another £4 a year in bounties. Most Specials were organised into Reserve units but specialists like drivers were not required to carry out any military training. The strengths of the components of the Army on 1st August 1914 were;

Regular Army	247,432
Reserve	145,347
Special Reserve	63,933
Territorial Force	268,777

Regimental Depots received the Reservists, armed, clothed and fed them until despatched to their units. They were also responsible for mobilising the Special Reserve units. To avoid confusion these would not be mobilised until the 4th day. The process of mobilising them was not automatic but done by sending out individual notices normally by post. Depots were also responsible for looking after soldiers who were under 19 and not eligible for overseas service or those who were medically unfit.

The part-timers of the Territorial Force, formed in 1908, were responsible for home defence. The antecedents of this body were the Yeomanry, citizen cavalry formed originally in 1794 during the Napoleonic wars and the Rifle Volunteers resulting from another scare about

French invasion in 1858. The new structure was to provide 14 Divisions supported by 14 Yeomanry Brigades. Haldane had intended the Territorials to reinforce the Regulars after six months' training following mobilisation. Lord Kitchener, appointed Secretary of State for War on 5th August, had a low opinion of the TF and at the outset of war some units were sent to the Empire to replace Regular Army units on garrison duty including 4th Battalion Wiltshire Regiment. He did not trust them to form the basis of the volunteer 'Kitchener' New Armies which were very chaotic at the start. However by the start of 1915 more troops were urgently required and both TF and New Army units had to be sent overseas.

The final component was the National Reserve not included in the totals above. This was initiated by private enterprise in 1910. Organised by the Territorial Force County Associations it was composed of former soldiers who were no longer official Reservists but *would be able to render assistance in time of grave national emergency*. There were two classes, one to reinforce Regular Army units, the other to fill vacancies in the Territorial Force. They were under no obligation but numbered around 215,000 extra potential soldiers.

So what was the situation in North Wiltshire? At the outbreak of war the Duke of Edinburgh's (Wiltshire Regiment), a Regiment being an administrative rather than fighting formation, had 4 Battalions – two Regular (1st in Tidworth, 2nd in Gibraltar), one Special Reserve (3rd to provide reinforcements for the Regular battalions, based at the Regimental Depot in Devizes) and one Territorial Force (4th, Headquarters at Fore Street, Trowbridge with 8 Companies based at 23 or more Drill Halls, the closest to Malmesbury being D Company at Chippenham and H Company at Swindon).

Aside from the Silk Mill where the workforce was predominantly female, Malmesbury was reliant on agriculture for employment. Farming had been depressed for more than a quarter of a century and it is not surprising that many local men had enlisted in the armed services well before the war for an assured wage and keep. Malmesbury was also a centre for citizen soldiers having formed one of the first Troops of the Royal Wiltshire Yeomanry during the Napoleonic War and in 1914 was home to a detachment of C Squadron which had its headquarters in Chippenham. In the 1908 reorganisation the need for more supporting arms led

As the Mayor reads the proclamation outside the Cottage Hospital at the Market Cross the Yeomanry are paraded in front of him with the Ammunition Column to the right of the picture (Athelstan Museum)

Men of the Royal Wiltshire Yeomanry from Malmesbury at Annual Camp, Pyt House, Tisbury in 1914. (Moonraker)

to A Company of the 2nd Volunteer Battalion Wiltshire Regiment, originally raised in 1860, becoming 3rd Wessex Brigade Royal Field Artillery Ammunition Column. A new drill hall was built to accommodate this unit in Bristol Street at the junction with Bremilham Road. This is now Holford Rise to the west of the junction. The town was also host to A Company (Malmesbury) Wiltshire National Reserve, commanded by Colonel Charles Napier Miles of Burton Hill House who had served in the 1882 Egyptian and the 1899-1901 South African Wars.

The War Office started preparations before war was declared. On 29th July 1914 all army leave was stopped. Those on leave were recalled to barracks and over the next few days other precautionary steps were taken. On 4th August after German troops invaded Belgium, our government sent an ultimatum demanding that the troops be withdrawn and if no satisfactory reply was received by midnight Britain would consider itself at war. At 11 a.m. that

The Ammunition Column's Drill Hall after it had been bought by Reg Adye and turned into a garage. (Michael Adye)

morning the King's Proclamation for mobilisation had been signed, although the War Office did not send out the telegrams putting it into effect until 4.40 p.m.

Regimental Depots swung into action having had time to prepare all of the notices to be posted to individual Special Reservists. On 5th August the Regular Reservists began to arrive and after kitting out were dispatched to the Regular Battalions. At the same time the unfit and those under 19 were returned from those battalions to the Depots. As soon as the Regulars had been dealt with, the Special Reservists were mobilised and once their units were complete they moved to their war stations. In the case of the 3rd Wiltshires this was Weymouth. The mobilisation plan for assembling the Expeditionary Force and sending it to France had been thought out by General Sir Henry Wilson, Director of Military Operations at the War Office 1910-1914. It, like the plans of the major belligerents, was based around railway timetables because of the huge amount of men and materials to be transported. Britain also had the complexity of crossing the Channel. However the scheme ran like clockwork and the fighting troops began arriving in France on 13th August.

In Malmesbury as the Regular Reservists departed, the Territorials mobilised. The Yeomanry went to Chippenham whilst the Ammunition Column collected in their Drill Hall. The Devizes Guardian of 14th August reported;

The week at Malmesbury has been marked by a considerable reduction of the troops quartered in the town, most of the men of the Wilts R.F.A. Ammunition Column having left for a war station. The first party, consisting of 30 non-commissioned officers and men, with 24 horses and 4 waggons, left by train on Thursday under the command of Lieut. Godwin. Those were followed on Saturday night by 51 non-commissioned officers and men, 54 horses and 8 waggons. Capt. A.L. Forrester was in command, and with him were Lieut. J.D. Gouldsmith and Second Lieut. Pym. All the Malmesbury men and all except two from Tetbury have now left, those remaining comprising the Small Arms Ammunition Section, under the command of Lieut. Cooper.

On Friday 7th August Colonel Sir Audley Neeld, commander of the Wiltshire National Reserve, instructed the Malmesbury Company to hold a recruiting meeting. In the absence of both the Commander, Col. Miles and the Secretary, Mr. J.G. Bartlett, Sergeant Major Joe Moore (owner of the Bell Hotel) arranged this in Cross Hayes. From there they marched to the Old Drill Hall near the water tower at Abbey House where they were addressed by Colonel C.R. Luce who had commanded the Rifle Volunteers but was now aged 85. First volunteers for Class 1 were called for, they would join the Regular Army if required and had to be aged under 42 years of age. 24 men stepped forward but only 22 enlisted. Then those prepared to join the Territorials (without an obligation to serve overseas) in Class 2 were asked for, those aged up to 55 for Sergeants and up to 50 for Corporals and below - 23 volunteered for this including Sergeants E.F.E Edwards and H. Young.

The army required a large number of horses, vehicles and other equipment before they could depart for war. Colonel W.W. Turnor of Pinkney Park was appointed the local Remount Officer, assisted by William Rich of West Hill and Peter McGregor MRCVS. Mr. Rich commented that it was a matter of utmost difficulty to purchase suitable horses and many local farmers had their horses requisitioned. Captain Rennie of Oaksey Park was doing similar work in the district. The Stroud Brewery's motor lorries and drivers had been called upon to assist the military. The Post Office reported that so many of their men were reservists that they were having difficulty making deliveries.

The first local war related fatality occurred on Thursday 27th August. Private James Idle, aged 23 from Bolton, of the 5th Battalion the Loyal North Lancashire Regiment Territorial Force was struck and killed (*literally cut to pieces*) by an express train on the main line near Rodbourne. The train was the Bristol to London non-stop express, said to be the fastest train in England. He slipped on the wet sleepers and was unable to get out of the way. After an inquest he was buried at Hullavington.

On Wednesday 2nd September 24 Class 1 National Reservists received notices requiring them to report to Devizes that Friday. 19 of them paraded at the Old Drill Hall at 2.15 p.m. to hear speeches made by the Mayor and Joe Moore before being marched amidst a cheering crowd led by the Town Band to catch the 2.55 p.m. train. They were: Sergt. W. Kaynes, Ptes. T.H. Bowman, J. Clark, H. James, W. Johnson, T. Jones, A. Pike, A.H. Stevens, A. Strange, E. Thornbury, W. Tugwell, H. Wilcox, R. Bridges (Corston) and W. Jones (Milbourne), all late of the 2nd Wilts Volunteers; Trooper A.G. Angell, late of the Royal Wilts Yeomanry; Ptes. A. Bailey, J. Bond, F. Fry and J. Grey, late of the 3rd Wilts. Ptes. Johnson, Stevens and Thornbury were all veterans of the South African War. Two of them (Angell & James) were destined never to return. G. Brownett (ex 1st Gloucesters), Private Barnes and W. Shaw (both ex 1st Wilts) left separately.

The pressure for new recruits continued. The Mayor arranged a meeting at the Old Drill Hall on Tuesday 8th September at 6.30 p.m. to be addressed by George Terrell M.P. and Harold Gorst, prospective Liberal candidate for North Wiltshire. The two politicians were touring the towns in the area to rally support. Councillor Farrant asked that employers close their businesses at 6 p.m. that evening until the meeting was over, in order that every adult should have the opportunity to attend. So many people turned up that the meeting had to be moved into the open air at Cross Hayes. Major R.H. Steward, commander of the Wiltshires' Depot at Devizes, attended and announced that Sergeant H. Young of Gloucester Road had been appointed as local recruiting sergeant. After the speeches they went to the Old Drill Hall and enlisted 51 young men. Railway warrants were provided for sixteen who wished to join Kitchener's Army.

The 51 were; James Anderson, F. Bailey, B. Bishop, Daniel Bishop, Frank Bishop, R. Bishop, H. Blackford, Charles Bond, Cyril Bond, F.J. Burgess, James Carey, R. Clark, W.J. Clark, E. Curtis, J. Edwards, R. Exton, H. Goodfield, W. Heal, F. Jefferies, Harry Jefferies, Frank King, Samuel Lewis, Fred Liddington, G. Oram, E. Paul, G.H. Paul, Ralph Peer, E. Peters, F.W. Pike, Val. Pike, Wilfred Pike, Charles Pinnell, T. Pinnell, W. Poulton, G. Ratcliffe, A. Read, L. Reeves, Cecil Rich, R. Saunders, W. Savine, R.T. Sawyer, S. Sealey, S. Selby, W. Selby, Arthur Sheall, Arthur Stevens, William Thompson, E. Thornbury, C. Wakefield, Elton Whittaker and Mark Wilkins. Captain A.L. Forrester appealed for men who understood horses to join the Ammunition Column which was then at Amesbury. W. Heal, Ralph Peer, E. Peters, T. Pinnell, L. Reeves and Cecil Rich (all of Lea), G. Ratcliffe (Garsdon), A. Read and E. Whittaker (Corston), R. Clark (Filands) and W. Savine and M. Wilkins (Malmesbury) offered themselves for that unit. Another nine of the town's volunteers from this group were to die in action.

These volunteers arrived at Devizes when the depot was overrun by recruits. The 5th Battalion, the first of Wiltshire's Kitchener units, had been quickly filled and by 10th September it was reported that the 3rd Battalion had a strength of 2000 and that the 6th Battalion was nearly full. This had happened because the Duke of Cornwall's Light Infantry had sent 600 recruits from Bodmin. It was then intended to enrol surplus numbers and after one day send them home, to be called up when required. They would receive 3s. 6d. per week and be given 10 days notice of their recall. But this measure could not cope with the rush. Recruitment in Ireland proved to be difficult at this time. Both the Ulstermen and the Nationalists at first refused to support the war due to the furore over Home Rule. Following the passage of an Act granting devolved government after the war John Redmond, the Nationalist leader threw his weight behind the recruiting drive in a speech on 20th September. Unfortunately by then steps had been taken to provide extra manpower which included sending men from Devizes, with many Malmesbury men amongst them, to Ireland.

There was still a great enthusiasm to join up. The following report appeared in the North Wilts Herald;

PATRIOTIC ARDOUR – As an example of patriotic ardour and self-sacrifice Mr. Joe Moore, of the Bell Hotel related an incident which occurred a day or two ago. A young man had offered himself as a recruit for the Army and after being medically examined was rejected owing to his having varicose veins. The doctor who tested him informed him that an operation would be necessary to remove the veins. This in no way damped the would-be soldier's ardour, for on his return to Malmesbury he at once called upon Mr. Moore and asked him if he could oblige with a ticket for Bristol Infirmary. He told Mr. Moore all that the doctor had said, and the genial landlord of the Bell Hotel was so touched by the lad's plucky determination to undergo the necessary operation that he went to some trouble to procure a ticket of admission to the Infirmary, and cordially wished him the best of luck. "That young fellow's pluck in facing the ordeal of an operation," said Mr. Moore, "only shows how seriously he was in his efforts to serve his country; and such conduct is, I believe, typical of the general spirit throughout the Empire. Can the Kaiser win against this? I don't think!" One wonders how that young man fared at the front.

Another seventeen young men were sent from Malmesbury on 9th September. The Herald said that their send-off was no less hearty than that of those who went previously. The Mayor addressed them as follows;

He was pleased to see so many Malmesbury young men ready to serve their country, and they were, he hoped, going to do their duty with credit. He counselled them to remember always the first duty of a soldier was obedience and attention to orders. He put before them the example of the men of Nelson's time, who acted up to the famous signal from the great Admiral. The duty of England was done well, with the result that there was peace for a hundred years from the time of Trafalgar (applause). "Now do your share," said his worship, "you men will have the opportunity of shooting Germans (several voices: "We hope so, sir"). I hope you will do your duty and come back with credit to yourselves and Malmesbury" (applause). After another speech from the Deputy Mayor, J.A. Jones, the men marched off to the station singing popular choruses and were seen off by a large crowd. This was the most unfortunate group to volunteer, most of them were to be sent to the Curragh, join Irish regiments and many did not survive the war.

The first batch of Class 2 National Reservists left Malmesbury on Friday 10th September for the 4th Battalion's Drill Hall in Trowbridge. Eighteen men, middle-aged with previous service in the forces, reported to the Old Drill Hall the previous evening where they were greeted by their Commander, Colonel Miles, Sergeant Major Moore, the Mayor and other Councillors. The names were: A. Bailey, H. Barnes, James Bishop, Joseph Bishop, W. Bishop, James Box, W. Brown, M. Fry, H. Grant, T. Jefferies, S. Kite, P. Lomax, T. Ody, H. Phelps, J. Porter, G. Savine, W. Selby and W. Woodward.

The first newspaper report of a local soldier being wounded appeared on 2nd October. Private Frank Hinder, a native of Malmesbury of the 1st Wiltshires, had been wounded in action in France and was being treated at a base hospital. He had been called up as a Reservist from his job as a Sherston postman. The same edition reported another death on the railway. Private Arthur Croston, 26, a Preston shuttlemaker, of 4th Battalion the Loyal North Lancashire Regiment Territorial Force was struck by an express train at 5.45 p.m. on 28th September at Brinkworth. The inquest held in the village on 1st October heard that he left a widow (in delicate health) and two children. Another accident occurred just one week later when Private Robert Rosebottom aged 20 of 5th Battalion of the same regiment was knocked down and run over by a goods train at Hullavington. He was more fortunate in that he survived but Dr. Moore had to amputate his right foot in the Cottage Hospital. A couple of weeks later it was decided to replace the Territorials with National Reservists on this guard duty.

At the beginning of November the Mayor received a letter from the Devizes and District Recruiting Committee asking him to use his best endeavours to recruit more young men. Councillor Farrant told the Borough Council that it was a pity that 30 men recruited locally recently were sent to the Royal Munster Fusiliers at the Curragh rather than serving with the Wiltshires, Wiltshire should find its own men and Ireland should do the same (hear, hear). It was felt that Sergeant Perry, the old Volunteers' instructor, who was retired like Sergeant Young, already recruiting, could assist if the War Office communicated with him. Mr. Bartlett thought that young men did not realise how much depended on them coming forward and that many unmarried young men were walking about on Saturday nights.

The Ammunition Column left town for Swindon at the beginning of December. The last 50 were seen off from the station by a large crowd of well wishers with a band playing British Grenadiers and Auld Lang Syne. It was suggested that they were destined for foreign parts.

Other Territorials had already departed - the 1/4th Battalion Wiltshire Regiment embarked at Southampton for India on the 9th October, followed by 2/4th Wiltshire Battalion (formed in October from a few officers and non commissioned officers from the 1/4th and new recruits) on the 12th December. The latter comprised 29 officers with 816 rank and file, leaving 2 officers and 370 men behind to form the nucleus of another battalion. By the turn of the year four Companies of National Reserve, each 3 officers and 117 men strong, were on railway duties.

The year ended on a sad note with the death of Private George Grey being confirmed on 17th December. On the 23rd a memorial service was held in the Abbey attended by a large congregation including the new Mayoress, Mrs. Adye, Councillors, family and between twenty and thirty soldiers. The vicar, Canon McMillan, expressed the hope that the town would erect a memorial so there would be a permanent record of the bravery of Malmesbury men. It was a bitter-sweet time for other families. Many soldiers not yet overseas were given leave, many of them from Ireland, whilst others prayed for their menfolk in harm's way.

Units of the Wiltshire Regiment were by now spread around the world – 1st and 2nd Battalions with the BEF, 3rd (Special Reserve) at Weymouth, 1/4th Territorial Force in India , 2/4th TF shortly to arrive there, 5th (Service) at Cirencester, 6th (Service) at Basingstoke, 7th (Service) at Marlborough and 8th (Service) at Weymouth. The elements of the Royal Wiltshire Yeomanry were stationed in these places; 1/1st in Sussex and 2/1st at Chippenham and Calne.

1915

The Mayor, Alfred Adye, had announced in November that he wished to compile a Roll of Honour listing all those from the town who had answered the Country's call. This was published on 1st January 1915 and amended over the following few weeks. The final version was:

OFFICERS

The Malmesbury officers are:-
> Capt. J. Luce R.N. H.M.S. "Glasgow"
> Major L.E. Morrice D.S.O. 1st Royal Warwick Regiment.
> Major R. Clark R.G.A.
> Surgeon-Capt. A. Heaton, R.A.M.C.
> Capt. A.L. Forrester, 3rd Wessex Brigade, R.F.A.
> Capt. E.M.S. Mackirdy.
> Lieut. J. Pitt, Leicesters
> Midshipman John Morrice R.N.

EMPLOYERS' LIST

Messrs Adye & Hinwood, Bacon Factory –
> Pte H. Goodfield, Kitchener's Army

Mr. B. de Bertodano, Cowbridge House –
> H. Steele, Royal Naval Reserve
> E. Thornbury, Kitchener's Army

Board of Guardians –
> Sergt. Major G.F.V. Fenton, Royal Wilts Imperial Yeomanry
> Pte. H. James, 6th Wilts (National Reserve)

Mr. F.W. Ball, baker, High Street –
> Pte. F.G. Ball, A.S.C.
> Sergt. Thomas Clark, R.F.A.
> Bombardier A. Stancombe, R.F.A.

Messrs. Bowman & Golding, builders, Holloway –
> Trooper F. Bowman, Royal Wilts Imperial Yeomanry
> Pte. J. Clark, 6th Wilts (National Reserve)
> Pte. J. Ponting, 4th Wilts (National Reserve)

Mr. C. Buhrer, sculptor -
> Trooper C. Cullen, Royal Wilts Imperial Yeomanry.

Mr. W.B. Carter, Arches Farm -
> Gunner F.J. Jones, R.F.A.

Charlton Estate (Lord Suffolk) -
  Gunner W. Exton, Wilts Battery, R.F.A.
  Driver H. Hudson, Wilts Battery R.F.A.
  (A large number of Lord Suffolk's men have enlisted from the village of Charlton)
Corporation -
  Pte. G. Grey, Wilts Regiment (Killed).
  Pte. A. Pike, National Reserve.
  Driver Frank Poole, Wilts Battery, R.F.A.
Mr. J.D. Curtis, High Street -
  Pte. G. Jobbins, 4th Wilts.
Mr. F. Day, butcher. Market Cross -
  Driver R. Paginton R.F.A.
Messrs. Duck & Co, Cross Hayes Brewery -
  Pte. H. Jefferies, Kitchener's Army.
Messrs. Edwards & Son, coach builders. Holloway -
  Pte. D. Bishop, Royal Munster Fusiliers.
  Corpl. W. Clark, Royal Wilts Yeomanry.
  Pte. E.W. Curtis, 6th Leinsters.
  Pte. P. Lomax, 6th Wilts (National Reserve).
  Pte. W. Pike, Royal Munster Fusiliers.
Emery's confectioneries, High Street –
  Pte. W.H. Boulton, 4th Wilts
Mr. S. Fisher, coal merchant -
  Driver G. Reynolds, R.F.A.
Gas Company -
  Corpl. M.B. Clark, R.F.A.
Mr. W. Gladwin, farrier -
  Corpl. Shoeing Smith, F. Golding, R.F.A.
Messrs. Harrison & Co, tailors -
  Pte. J. Porter, 2nd Class, National Reserve.
Mr. A.E. Hays, plumber, Triangle -
  Pte. H. Barnes, 4th Wilts (National Reserve).
  Pte. W. Woodward, National Reserve.
Messrs. Hays & Smith, Gloucester Road –
  Pte. H. Blackford, Kitchener's Army.
Mr. T. Henry, Southville –
  Driver R. Jones, R.F.A
Messrs. Hughes & Son, Ingram Street –
  Sergt. S. Selby, Royal Munster Fusiliers.
India & China Tea Co., High Street –
  Gunner A. Stancombe, R.F.A.
Mr. E. Jones, jeweller, High Street –
  Pte. Arthur Phelps, 4th Wilts
Messrs. Jones' Motors, High Street –
  Pte. Cyril Bond, Royal Munster Fusiliers.
Mrs. H. Jones, King's Arms Hotel –
  Pte. L. Fry, 2nd Class, National Reserve.
Messrs. W. & E. Lockstone, grocers, Oxford Street –
  Pte. A. Lewis, Bristol Battalion, 12th Gloucesters
  Quarter-Master-Sergeant J. Lockstone, Hants Battery R.F.A.
Colonel C.R. Luce, Holcomb –
  Pte. J. Edwards, Kitchener's Army.
  Pte W. Selby, 2nd Class, National Reserve
Mrs. W.H. Luce, The Knoll –
  Sergt. W. Kaynes, 6th Wilts (National Reserve).
  Pte. J. Anderson, Kitchener's Army.
Malmesbury Coal Co. –

Pte. T. Jones, 5th Wilts (National Reserve).
Pte. T. Pincott, National Reserve.
Pte. H. Wilcox, 6th Wilts (National Reserve).
Mr. J. Moore, Bell Hotel –
Pte. H. Phelps, 2nd Class, National Reserve.
Pte. F. Young, 6th Wilts.
Mr. J. Mortimer, The Dairy, High Street –
Pte. S.E. Lewis, 6th Royal Munster Fusiliers.
Messrs. F. Newman & Sons, grocers. High Street –
Trooper R.G. Newman, Royal East Kent Mounted Rifles.
Pte. V.G. Newman, 5th Gloucesters.
Messrs. Pike & Son, plasterers –
Pte A. Strange, 6th Wilts (National Reserve).
Pte. E. Thornbury, 4th Wilts (National Reserve).
Sir Richard Pollen –
Driver John Taylor, A.S.C.
Mrs. M. Ponting, builder, Park Road –
Pte. F. Bush, 1st Wilts.
Pte. T. Grant, Royal Engineers.
Pte. W. Johnstone, 6th Wilts, (National Reserve).
Trooper G. Oram, 2nd Life Guards.
Messrs. J.E. Ponting & Sons, High Street –
Pte. J. Bishop, 4th Wilts.
Pte. W. Bishop, 4th Wilts.
Pte J. Carey, 6th Leinsters.
Pte. W. Clark, Royal Dublin Fusiliers.
Gunner R. Pear, 3rd Wessex Brigade, R.F.A.
Gunner J. Pike, 3rd Wessex Brigade, R.F.A.
Pte. W. Rymell, Kitchener's Army.
Pte. H. Weeks, Royal Marines.
Gunner M. Wilkins, 3rd Wessex Brigade, R.F.A.
In addition the firm have F.E. Ponting, section leader, Red Cross Detachment:
W.W. Ponting, National Reserve: A.J. Ponting, Assistant-Scoutmaster, King
Athelstan Troop B.P. Boy Scouts: and H. Iles, Red Cross Detachment – all doing
useful service locally.
Mr. H. Poole, Bloomfield House -
Gunner A. Beasant, Wessex Brigade R.F.A.
Pte. F.E. King, 6th Munsters.
Post Office -
Pte. J. Bowman, 2nd Wilts (prisoner of war).
Pte. T.H. Bowman, 6th Wilts (National Reserve).
Pte F.A. Hinder, Wilts Regiment (prisoner of war).
Pte. J. Paginton, 1st Wilts.
Pte. G. Peters, 1st Wilts (prisoner of war).
Gunner J. Sellwood, Royal Horse Artillery.
Messrs. Ratcliffe & Son, Foundry –
Pte. E. Ratcliffe, A.S.C.
Sergt. G. Vanstone, R.F.A.
Mr. Tom Rich, butcher. High Street -
Pte. A.G. Angell, 6th Wilts (National Reserve).
Pte. F.J. Burgess, Kitchener's Army.
Trooper H. Cordy, Royal Wilts Yeomanry
Mr. W. Rich, posting stables -
Bombardier W. Oram R.F.A.
Driver W. Poole, R.F.A.
Roman Catholic Presbytery-
Pte. W. Brown, National Reserve.

Secondary School -
    Gunner J.H. Tugwell, R.F.A.
Messrs. Shuttleworths Ltd. -
    Pte. F. Liddington, Kitchener's Army.
    Corpl. G.H. Paul, Kitchener's Army.
Messrs. Stroud Brewery Co -
    Pte. A.H. Stevens, 6th Wilts (National Reserve).
Thompson's outfitters. High Street -
    Gunner A.E. Cluley, R.F.A.
Mr. A. Watts, saddler, Gloucester Street.
    Trooper D. Pike, Royal Wilts Yeomanry.
Mr. W. Woodman, grocer, Triangle –
    Sergt. W. Buckland, Wilts Regiment
    Pte. E. Dunsby, Kitchener's Army.
    Pte. W.C. Lewis, Bristol Battalion, 12th Gloucesters.
    Pte. M. Price, Bristol Battalion, 12th Gloucesters.
    Pte. W. Selby, Kitchener's Army.
    Sergt. W.H. Wilkins, Wilts Regiment (wounded)
    Pte. D. Whittaker, 1st Wilts.
    Pte. C. Wood, 1st Wilts.
    (Selby was the only one employed by Mr. Woodman since the war started, the others being his old "boys.")

UNATTACHED

Pte. B. Agg, 2nd Wilts.
Pte. G. Allsop, 3rd Wilts.
Pte. A. Bailey, 4th Wilts.
Pte. F. Bailey, 6th Wilts (National Reserve).
Pte. F. Baker, 1st Norfolks.
Pte. W. Baker, 5th Oxford & Bucks L.I.
Gunner M.J. Barnes, R.F.A.
Pte. W. Barnes, Wilts Regiment
Pte. C. Bishop, 1st Wilts (wounded)
Pte. F.T. Bishop, 6th Leinster Regiment.
M. Bishop, C.P.O., H.M.S. "Eskimo".
Pte. D. Blackford, National Reserve.
Pte. C. Bond, 6th Leinster Regiment (invalided).
Pte. J. Bond, 6th Wilts (National Reserve).
Pte. Fred Boulton, Wilts Regiment
Pte. Arthur Brown (Castle Inn licensee), Wilts Regiment
L-Corpl. J. Brown, Wilts Regiment (in hospital Manchester).
Pte. G. Brownett, 2nd Gloucesters.
Pte. A. Buckland, Coldstream Guards
Sergt. W. Buckland, Wilts Regiment.
Driver W. Bush, R.F.A.
F. Carey, R.N. H.M.S. "Blake".
Trooper A. Clark, Royal Wilts Yeomanry.
Driver M. Clark, R.F.A.
Pte. R. Clark, 2nd Class National Reserve.
Tom Clark, 2nd Canadian Contingent.
Driver Reginald Clark, R.F.A.
Corpl. W. Clark, R.F.A
Driver J. Collar, R.F.A.
W. Collar Signaller, H.M.S. "Suffolk".
F. Deadman R.N., H.M.S. "Conqueror".
Pte. A. Drew, Royal Engineers.
Trooper F. Drew, Royal Wilts Yeomanry.

Pte. H. Ellis, Wilts Regiment (wounded).

Pte. G. Elsip. Kitchener's Army.

Corpl. R. Exton, Munsters.

Trooper H.J. Farrow-Alexander, West Kent Yeomanry.

Pte. P. Fry, London Teachers' Battalion.

L-Corpl. C. Gale 3rd Wilts.

Pte. H. Grant, 4th Wilts.

Pte. J. Grey, National Reserve.

Pte. R. Grey, Kitchener's Army.

Pte. W. Harris, Army Cycling Corps.

Gunner E.V. Jefferies, R.F.A.

Gunner H.C. Jefferies, R.F.A.

A.E. Jones R.N., H.M.S. "Southampton".

Gunner F. Jones, R.F.A.

Pte. W.E. Jones, National Reserve.

Sergt. S. Kite, National Reserve.

W. Lester H.M.S. "Hercules".

Driver E.E. Lewis, R.F.A.

Pte. E.S. Lockstone, 2nd Wilts (in France).

Pte. Long 1st Devon Regiment (wounded).

Trooper T. Luce, Shropshire Yeomanry.

F. Lumsley, Royal Horse Artillery.

Trooper R. Matthews, Royal Wilts Yeomanry.

Pte. T. Ody, 4th Wilts (National Reserve).

Pte. A. Paginton, 2nd Wilts.

Pte. T. Paginton, 1st Wilts (wounded).

Gunner Palmer, R.F.A.

Gunner E. Peters, R.F.A.

E. Pike AB., H.M.S. "Irresistible".

Pte. F. Pike, Kitchener's Army.

Trooper H. Pike, Royal Wilts Yeomanry.

Pte. Joe Pike, Wilts Regiment

Pte. Richard Pike, Wilts Regiment

Pte. C. Pinnell, Royal Munster Fusiliers.

H. Pitt, Royal Navy.

Pte. H. Poole, Wilts Regiment.

Pte. A. Porter, A.S.C.

Pte. E. Porter, 5th Wilts.

Pte. J.A. Porter, Royal Engineers.

Pte. R. Price, Royal Dublin Fusiliers.

Pte. W. Price, 12th Gloucesters.

Trooper W.H. Reeves, Royal Wilts Yeomanry.

Pte. A. Rymell, Kitchener's Army.

Pte. G. Savine, 2nd Class National Reserve.

Pte. H. Sawyer, Kitchener's Army.

Trooper A. Seeley, Royal Wilts Yeomanry.

Driver A. Shellum, R.F.A.

Trooper H. Shingles, Royal Wilts Yeomanry.

Driver Sivell, R.F.A.

Bombardier H.H. Smith, R.F.A.

Pte. A.H. Stevens, National Reserve.

G.B. Stooke, R.N., H.M.S. "Warrior".

Trooper H. Taylor, Royal Wilts Yeomanry

Corpl. Shoeing-Smith G.H. Thompson, R.F.A.

Pte. W. Thompson, Kitchener's Army.

Pte. W. Thornbury, 1st Wilts (wounded).

Pte. H. Tinley, London Teachers Battalion.

H. Tugwell, A.B., Royal Fleet Reserve.
Pte. W. Tugwell, National Reserve.
Pte. S.W. Wakefield, 1st Wilts.
Pte. W.E. Wakefield, 2nd Wilts.
Gunner J. Wallington, Royal Marine Artillery.
Pte. A. Wheeler, 1st Wilts (invalided).
Pte. Tom Wilkins, 1st Wilts.
Pte. J. Willsdon, Royal Marines, H.M.S. "Nottingham".
Gunner F. Woodward, R.F.A.
Pte. G.A. Woodward, 4th Wilts.

Five members of the Malmesbury Fire Brigade are serving out of a total of ten men. Those are F. Bowman, J. Clark, E. Thornbury, A. Strange and J. Ponting. Fireman Thornbury served in the South African War to which campaign the Brigade sent four men. The record is a good one considering the size of the Brigade.

Another 39 men from Charlton and 16 men from Brokenborough were also listed. When published the only confirmed fatality was Private George Grey and his name was placed at the top. The completed Roll contained 208 names from the town and this compares with the total populations recorded at the time of the 1911 census of: Malmesbury Borough 2,656; Westport & St. Paul Without 996; Brokenborough 388; and Charlton 468. At that time the county's population was 286,822.

The Wilts and Gloucester Standard of Saturday 16th January reported the following items from that week's meeting of Malmesbury Town Council: since the last meeting two townsmen had yielded their lives for their country - George Grey of Westport was killed in action and at the New Year Midshipman John Morrice only son of Major and Mrs. Morrice of the Priory had been lost with H.M.S. Formidable; there had been a collection of £2 5s. in the Electric Picture House, Town Hall for the purchase of cigarettes for the Wiltshire Regiment at the front - 7,000 cigarettes had been forwarded; the local roll of honour had been placed in the hands of the Town Clerk.

Capt. John Luce R.N., commander of H.M.S. Glasgow, became a Companion of the Honourable Order of the Bath for his part in the Battle of the Falkland Islands. At 8 a.m. on 8th December a squadron of British warships including the Battlecruisers H.M.S. Invincible and Inflexible were in the harbour at Port Stanley when the German squadron they were seeking, comprising S.M.S. Scharnhorst, Gniesenau, Dresden, Leipzig and Nurnberg, came into sight. Whilst the battlecruisers dealt with the armoured cruisers Scharnhorst and Gniesnau, British cruisers engaged the other three ships. Glasgow, a light cruiser with a higher speed than

H.M.S. Glasgow, Captain John Luce's ship. (firstworldwar.com)

other ships, was able to slow the Leipzig which allowed the larger H.M.S. Cornwall to finish her off. The Mayor sent Capt. Luce a congratulatory telegram.

By the Spring of 1915 the enthusiasm to join the services was waning. Sergeant Young sent off about 30 recruits in February and the small number meant that some of them were reported in the papers – James Player, Abbey verger and H. Barnes, carpenter, both joined the Royal Engineers. The 7th Wiltshires marched around the district in early March. By the time they reached Malmesbury only 7 young men had enlisted. The Army Service Corps advertised in April for butchers and bakers.

One Malmesbury family came in for particular praise in their war effort;

A PATRIOTIC FAMILY – Mr. Charles Bailey, of the Triangle, Malmesbury, is a proud man to-day, for he has five sons in H.M.'s Forces, two of whom have been in engagements and wounded, one being wounded twice. Charles is in the London Rifles; Frederick is in the 2nd Wilts, has been invalided home for wounds, but has recovered and returned to the scene of hostilities; William is also in the 2nd Wilts, has been wounded, recovered, gone back to the front, and has been wounded a second time; Francis is in the Norfolks, and James is in the Bedfords. Thomas, a member of the Boy Scouts, has joined the Volunteer Training Corps as bugler; and Mr. Bailey's son-in-law, George Phelps, is with the 3rd Wessex Brigade in India. The two first named have put in seven years' service; George Phelps was in the Coldstream Guards and served three years in the Boer War, receiving two medals and seven bars.

A short time afterwards the proud father received the following;

Privy Purse Office,
Buckingham Palace, S.W.
8th June 1915

Sir, - I am commanded by the King to convey to you an expression of His Majesty's apprecia-tion of the patriotic spirit which has prompted your five sons to give their services at the present time to the Army.
The King was much gratified to hear of the manner in which they have so readily responded to the call of their Sovereign and their country, and I am to express to you and them His Majesty's congratulations on having contributed in so full a measure to the great cause for which all the people of the British Empire are so bravely fighting.
I have the honour to be, Sir, your obedient servant,
  F.W. Ponsonby
  Keeper of the Privy Purse

Unfortunately by the time this letter was received news had reached Mr. Bailey that Jim had been badly wounded and was in hospital at Boulogne. His parents asked if they could visit him and were denied permission – in fact he died shortly afterwards. Within a few months Frederick had also been killed.

At the beginning of June the Old Corporation met with Albert Bailey, the Warden, presiding. Matthew Thompson, Chairman of the trustees of King's Heath, proposed that no young commoner who was fighting should be disqualified from taking up his rights on the ground of him not being a householder. He went further; *I venture to suggest that any young man who is a citizen and resident of the ancient borough of Malmesbury, and who has gone forth with his life in his hands for the protection of the realm, of which Malmesbury is an important part, even if cannot show by his pedigree that he is entitled to the rights, I for one would make such young men, provided they have lived here, freedom of the borough for their services for going forth like our forefathers went against the Danes (applause). Their reward from the Old Corporation should be that they should be made entitled to the rights.* The original motion was carried unanimously but the modification to extend rights to all soldiers was withdrawn.

W.G. Perry, Scoutmaster of the Malmesbury King Athelstan Troop of Boy Scouts reported the following voluntary enlistments from his old boys: Fred Bowman and Claude Cullen (Ser-geant), Wilts Yeomanry; Aubrey Heal, Harold Hudson, James Palmer and James Tugwell

(Corporal) all of Wilts Battery, R.F.A. India; H. Wilson, Canadian Contingent; Sidney Selby, Sergeant, Royal Munster Fusiliers; Arthur Phelps, Charlie Price, 4th Wilts; Stanley Hudson, A.S.C.; V.S. Jobbins, Stephen Pettifer, H.C. Scott, Percy White, all Kitchener's Army; Frank Wheeler, Royal Fusiliers; Walter Carter, Royal Flying Corps; Bradley Bartlett, R.N. (Wireless); Harold Bonner, 3rd Wessex, R.F.A.; Alec Taylor, Gloucestershire Regiment; Jack Willsdon, R.M.L.I.; H. Bishop, West of England Bantams; Claude Alec Perry, Army Ordnance Corps.

Voluntary enlistments were not keeping pace with the replacement of casualties and the first step taken by the Government was the National Registration Act 1915 which passed into law on 15th July. Under it, local authorities were required to provide a census of all men and women aged between 18 and 65 with details of the trades in which they were employed. The Town Council split the Borough into 12 areas and appointed a voluntary enumerator for each. The mammoth task of collecting this data was completed in the middle of September. Despite the supposed plethora of those avoiding service, staff shortages now caused several grocers' shops including Adye's, Farrant's and Long's to close for lunch.

Recruiting continued to be of concern although the Wilts Regimental Depot reported that 82 enlistments per week at the beginning of October had risen to 93. Locally recruiting was progressing slowly with E.T.L. Lucas, who worked for W. Jones, hairdresser, High Street, volunteering for the A.S.C. at the end of October. Nationally on 11th October 1915, Lord Derby - who had played a major part in raising volunteers, especially for the King's (Liverpool) Regiment - was appointed Director-General of Recruiting. He brought forward a programme five days later, called the Derby Scheme, for raising the numbers. Using the census information from National Registration various categories of worker would be 'starred' to indicate that they were vital to the war effort. Every 'unstarred' man of military age, 18-40, would be sent a letter exhorting him to enlist. All were invited to voluntarily register and be called up for service in batches by age. The last day of registration was to be 10th December 1915. Recruits were given a day's pay and a khaki armlet emblazoned with the royal crown to avoid the attentions of 'white-featherers' and recruiting sergeants. However there were hiccups in the scheme;

WHY NOT STARRED? – Recruiting is progressing very favourably here, but we doubt if one recipient of Lord Derby's letter would be passed even if he presented himself. We refer to Private Ernest Gleed, of Holloway Terrace, who, as our readers know has had both his legs blown off in the trenches! That he should be asked to "consider his position" is absurd, and it forms a humorous comment upon the statement at the recruiting committee yesterday that all unstarred men must be vigorously canvassed, as the starring had been carefully done by an important committee. Mr. F.E.N. Rogers, Agricultural Commissioner, in the speech reported elsewhere, stated that the starring had been done by officials of the Labour Bureau, which would better explain the receipt of the letter by Mr. Gleed.

Later Mr. Gleed was presented to the King and Princess Mary. Local ladies, *who prefer their names not to be mentioned,* arranged for him to be taught boot making and repairing. He set up in business at his home in Holloway which readers of the Gazette were exhorted to patronise. He was also presented with a tricycle, purchased from Ratcliffe & Sons for the sum collected, £33 8s. 6d.

In November Mr. J.D. Curtis, the Honorary Secretary to the Recruiting Committee reported that the Scheme was making satisfactory progress. However in some instances canvassers met men with the famous challenge of "wait and see". The starring created anomalies, for example an agricultural labourer was unstarred whilst a cattle-man was starred. So the Borough and Rural District Councils set up a joint Appeals Tribunal. The Town appointed Colonel C.N. Miles, Mr. J.G. Bartlett and Mr. R.C. Warner and the R.D.C. appointed Sir R.H. Pollen and Mr. F.E. Bates. At their first meeting Col. Miles was appointed Chairman and M.H. Chubb clerk. When the Derby Scheme closed 900 men in the Malmesbury Union area had responded which was thought to be an excellent result. The Standard gave details of how the scheme operated locally;

MALMESBURY AND THE ENLISTMENT.- Under Lord Derby's scheme about 300 men have enlisted up to date in the Malmesbury sub-area, including a large proportion in the married groups. The offices are at the Y.M.C.A. Hall, Sergeant Young being in charge, assisted by Sergeant Jarvis and Sergeant Topps (Tetbury). Dr. Hosegood is the surgeon, and he has the assistance of Dr. R.C. Pitt and Dr. Heaton. It is believed that a large number of starred men (who did not receive Lord Derby's letter) are holding back on the erroneous supposition that they need not come forward, but in view of Lord Derby's final appeal that it is the duty of every man to come forward (the question of their being indispensable to their masters being a point for the local tribunals to settle), the falseness of their position should be at once apparent. It appears that instances could be multiplied of young men who happen to be starred making the fact their excuse for non-enlistment. This being the last week, it is possible the returns will be considerably increased, and certainly the gravity of the general situation demands it.

As implied by the numbers (300 reported in the Standard but 900 by the end) there was a last minute rush to sign up, replicated across the country. The Y.M.C.A. Hall was in Cranmore House at the Market Cross and was later turned into a hospital ward.

Corporal Shoeing-Smith Bert Thompson, who had transferred to 2/6th Hants Battery from the Ammunition Column, wrote telling of life in India;

The newspapers are not so good out here as they are in England, and by the time we get the papers from home they are about a month old. There is a big Y.M.C.A. here, and it is very well patronised. They have two three-quarter-size billiard tables, a reading room, and a writing room, and a refreshment room, where we can go and get a good supper. We have had it very wet here lately, as it is the monsoon, or rainy season, but I think this is the last week of it, and then we get another three months of colder weather. Last Saturday a half of our battery (the left section) commenced its duties as movable column. We had to pack our kits and have everything ready in case of an alarm, if there was any trouble with the natives, etc., so that we should be ready to move off quickly, till the rest of the troops in the station could be got ready. On Saturday we had to parade in full marching order, and be inspected by the Colonel. There was also a squadron of the 7th Hussars, two companies of infantry, a squadron of the 27th Native Light Cavalry, a squadron of the 22nd Native Lancers, an Ambulance Corps, a Camel Corps and a Mule Corps, with machine guns, etc. It was a fine sight to see all the different uniforms, etc., but the worst of it was that it was raining in torrents. It is a very rough country round about the station, but it is reckoned one of the best for artillery training in India. There are bridges and fields like in England, but it is like one vast plain covered in places with hills of rock, bushes, palm-trees, rice-fields, native villages, deep gulleys and ditches, and barrack cantonments, etc. The houses the poorer class native live in are wretched hovels, which in England we should think not fit for a pig-sty. I have seen some different sights since I have been out here, and I should never have believed some of the habits of the natives, and the way they dress, etc., if I had not seen it. I see in the papers I got from home that there have been a lot of casualties amongst the Malmesbury men. I noticed a good few of them were very young, and had not joined up very long.

Recruitment did not improve and the first four Groups of Derby men received their call up papers before Christmas – not exactly a festive gift! At the end of 1915 the battalions of the Wiltshire Regiment were scattered around the world – the 1st and 2nd with the BEF in France, 3rd at Weymouth, 1/4th and 2/4th in India, 3/4th (Reserve Battalion for Territorial Force formed in March 1915) at Bournemouth, 5th amongst the last troops in Gallipoli, 6th with the BEF, 7th in Salonika and 8th (Reserve Battalion for New Army units) at Wareham. The 1/1st Yeomanry were with the BEF, 2/1st at Canterbury and 3/1st (a Reserve unit formed during the year) at Tidworth.

Conscripts join the fray 1916-18

The year started with Parliament considering the Military Service Bill which would introduce conscription. Passed into law before the end of January, all men aged between 18 and 41 on 15th August 1915 were deemed to have enlisted on 2nd March 1916. There were four grounds for exemption:

> if engaged in work or training important to the national interest;
> if serious hardship would accrue to the individual, due to exceptional personal circumstances;
> ill health or infirmity; or
> conscientious objection.

The date of birth determined the Class in which each man was placed (volunteers under the Derby Scheme joined Groups of the same number as the Classes now described). Class 1 were single men born in 1897, i.e. 18 years old, Class 2 1896 and so on to Class 23 1875. Married men were in Classes 24 (1897) to 46 (1875). These numbers also applied to those enrolled under the Derby Scheme and from them Groups 2 to 5 had to report for duty at the end of January, Groups 6 to 13 before the end of February, with the rest, other than the 18 year olds, the next month. The first conscripts who joined in March were sent to France as replacements for casualties on the Somme four months later.

During the early months of the year many men appealed against their call up before the Malmesbury District Tribunal, part of the 750,000 appeals heard nationally in the first six months. Very few of them were completely exempted, most gained between one and six month's exemption and some of these re-applied after that period. A typical example was reported at the end of March;

A MOTHER'S APPEAL – Mrs. B. Jackson, 16, High Street, attended to support the appeal for exemption of her son, Percy G. Jackson, who managed an outfitting and boot business. If he went the business could not be continued as the other assistants had joined the Army, and it was now worked solely by him and a school-boy who helped after school hours. Her son also had an estate agency. Mrs. Jackson said she was too ill to manage the business herself. She had failed to find a suitable assistant. The business was obviously not one that a woman could manage.
The Chairman suggested that the business might be closed as Mrs. Jackson was very well off, and every man was wanted.
Mrs. Jackson: Why should my business be closed?
The Chairman: It is not a national necessity.
Mrs. Jackson urged, however, that it was, for working men must have clothes and boots. Besides, there would be the loss to the Government of taxes, etc., which would ensue. It was a physical impossibility for her to manage to manage the business herself, at her age and in her condition of health.
The Tribunal having considered the case, the Chairman said: We do not see that there is any serious hardship; you can very well manage without him. We give you one day, which means two months – he will go on May 29th.
Mrs. Jackson: You say I can very well manage? I am very much obliged to you for your good opinion of me.

Baldemiro de Bertodano of Cowbridge House frequently appeared on behalf of his employees – a carter, his chauffeur, butler, groom and electrician. He complained that he *could drive five or six coaches and horses through the Act.* At the hearing regarding the electrician, Richard Bishop, Mr. de Bertodano threatened to leave the country but did not do so. Another feature of the Tribunals was appeals by Recruiting Officers against individuals being placed in starred occupations. Many of these succeeded.

Detailed casualty lists in the North Wilts Herald had become fewer and in May published some of the last to be listed on a regular basis. The list concentrated on the Wiltshire Regiment and amongst the many names of those wounded were two men from Malmesbury, Lance Corporal R. Liddington and Private E.E. Rymell.

Following the Battle of Jutland on 31st May H.M.S. Lion was amongst the ships needing major repairs in a dockyard. Most of her company were given leave including Charles Bishop who spoke to a reporter from the North Wilts Herald;

HOME FROM THE FIGHT.
Malmesbury Marine's Story.

Private C.M. Bishop, Royal Marine Light Infantry, son of Mr. and Mrs. W. Bishop, Burnivale, Malmesbury, is home on leave. The young soldier, who has been in the Marines about three years, was in the recent naval battle off the coast of Jutland. To our Malmesbury representative he gave a vivid account of the great clash of steel in the North Sea, when it is to be hoped, the German Navy received its quietus for many a day to come.

The ship on which Bishop was serving was in the forefront of the battle. The first shot fired was at 4.55 p.m., and except for a brief interval the guns were spitting forth destruction until 11 p.m. By that time the remnant of the German Fleet, divided into two parts, had fled into the night, many of them burning or smouldering hayricks.

Pte. Bishop and the crews of the Fleet were eager to meet the foe, and, although the encounter turned out to be a "hot time," now that it is over they are more anxious than ever to come to grips with the German Navy to avenge their shipmates who died fighting so gallantly for the honour of the King and old England.

Pte. Bishop's father is in the Wilts National Reserve on home defence duty, and he also has a brother serving in the 22nd Battalion Welch Regiment.

James Paginton who had frequently written home from the trenches had been discharged from the Army in February 1916. He had joined the Wiltshire Regiment in 1903 at the age of 18 for a twelve year term, three with the Colours and nine on the Reserve. He had been mobilised on 5th August 1914 and when his original term came to an end it was extended for a year in accordance with the conditions of service. However the Military Service Act 1916 only exempted men still serving or in the reserves, so he became liable for call up. In July he appealed to the Tribunal;

"DONE HIS BIT."

James Paginton (30), married, Blick's Hill, Malmesbury, rural postman, was the next appellant. He said he had served 13 years in the Army, including a year and a half in the trenches in France. He received his discharge on the termination of his service on February 22nd last. He asked for exemption as he thought he had already "done his bit" for his country.

The Recruiting Officer made favourable comments on the appeal. The young man had three brothers at present in the Army.

Colonel Sir Audley Neeld said appellant went through the thick of the fighting all the time. Appellant said he went out with the Wilts Regiment and saw fighting from Mons onwards until his discharge. He now had a permanent appointment as postman, having returned to his former employment. He had five brothers – four were serving and one was rejected.

Mr. Bartlett: A very good record indeed.

Appellant further stated that he had got married since his discharge. That was before the new Military Service Act came in. He did not think he would be called up again, but that, having done his bit, he would settle down.

Sir Audley Neeld described appellant as "a very good chap."

Asked if he would join the Volunteers, appellant said he did not know whether the postal authorities would allow him to do so.

Mr. Warner: We think you would attract others to join who have done nothing.

Mr. Bates: You would be a great help to us and we should be honoured by having you in the Corps. If you can join we shall be very pleased if you would do so.

Appellant, who was exempted until January 1st, promised to enquire whether he would be permitted to join the Volunteer Training Corps.

Even before notification of the casualties from the Somme battles arrived, the town had received notification of five deaths in a short time and the Wilts and Gloucester Standard on 15th July reported a memorial service;

MEMORIAL SERVICE AT MALMESBURY.
FIVE FALLEN HEROES.

A service in memory of five young townsmen who have lost their lives through wounds or sickness in the war was held at the Abbey Church, Malmesbury, on Sunday evening, an exceptionally large congregation being present, including many relatives of the deceased. The service was conducted by the Vicar (Canon C.D.H. McMillan), assisted by the Rev. F.W. Nicklin (curate). The ordinary form of service was followed up to the third collect, after which the Vicar led a special intercession service.

A large laurel wreath resting on the Union Jack, was place in front of the altar rails. Within the wreath was a printed card containing the names of the five heroes: Private A.J. Lewis, 12th Battalion Gloucester Regiment; Seaman Ernest Pike, H.M.S. Russell; Private Charles Wood, bandsman and stretcher-bearer, Wilts Regiment; Gunner John Henry Wallington, Royal Marine Artillery, H.M.S. Queen Mary; and Trooper Reginald George Newman, Royal East Kent Mounted Rifles.

Canon McMillan said the five young men had passed into the unseen in various ways. Alfred John Lewis, 12th Battalion Gloucester Regiment, after being engaged in the fighting on the plains of Flanders, passed away from illness in hospital in France. Ernest Pike, able-seaman, whom so many remembered as a singularly winsome lad, full of activity and animal spirits, and who developed into the ideal British seaman, was lost while on his way home by the sinking of H.M.S. Russell. Two of the lads they thought of at that service once led the praises as singers in the choir. Private Charles Wood, bandsman and stretcher-bearer, was the next. It was very pathetic to record his death; for he was present in that church when they last had a similar service in memory of others who had died in this war. He was killed in action when engaged in his work of mercy as a stretcher-bearer. Surely no "passing hence" could be more heroic and suitable than whilst succouring the wounded in the very mouth of hell and passing from such surroundings into peace and rest? John Henry Wallington, gunner, R.M.A., passed away in the great sea fight in the treacherous North Sea, with the sinking of the Queen Mary. Then in Egypt there passed away in hospital Reginald George Newman, trooper in the Royal East Kent Mounted Rifles. He was there, like so many others, ready to do his duty, ready to be sent where the authorities decreed, but illness, due probably to climatic conditions, overtook him and death claimed this young life so full of promise. All these had died for their King and country – they died for us – and the lesson he wanted to learn and which he wanted to teach them was that behind that great and supreme sacrifice there lay a reason, a reason which they must learn and a behest which they must obey if they were to see happier days.

The same paper had the first news of deaths on the Somme;

THREE MORE MALMESBURY LADS KILLED.

Although not yet official, the news has been received by a letter from Private Jones to his wife at Milbourne, and corroborated by a letter from Private Ernest Thornbury to his wife, that in the great advance three more Malmesbury lads were killed on July 2nd. They belong to the Wiltshire Regiment, and their names are Privates George Angell, son of Mrs. Angell, late school mistress, of Westport; William Savine, a son of Mr. George Savine, of the Horsefair; and Frederick Shaw, whose mother also resides in the parish.

It later transpired that William Savine had been wounded, he survived the war.

The Town Council decided that it was not appropriate to mark the second anniversary of the outbreak of war. However on 4th August the North Wilts Herald printed the toll taken from the local men who were serving their country. Amongst the dead it included Private Long of the Devonshire Regiment and Private W.J. Roberts of the Australian Imperial Force, neither of whom appear on our memorials. Walter Roberts' death was reported in the same edition as follows;

Pte. Walter James Roberts, of the Australian Imperial Force, youngest son of the late Mr. John Roberts and of Mrs. Roberts, of the XXX Inn, Malmesbury, has lost his life in the fighting in France. He was mortally wounded on Saturday and died the same day. A chaplain wrote to Mrs. Roberts a most sympathetic letter describing her son's death and his burial on Sunday.

The deceased soldier, who was 27 years of age, had been in Australia, and, like so many sons of the Empire, he joined up out there. Much sympathy is felt for Mrs. Roberts in her bereavement.

The Roll of Honour continued (remember this did not include wounded who had recovered and returned to the front);

PRISONERS OF WAR

Pte. J. Bowman, Wilts Regiment.
Pte. F.A. Hinder, Wilts Regiment (wounded).
Pte. G. Peters, Wilts Regiment.
Pte. Saunders, Wilts Regiment.

WOUNDED

Sergt. F.H. Bailey, Wilts Regiment.
Corpl. W. Bailey, Wilts Regiment.
Pte. R. Bailey, Wilts Regiment.
Sapper H. Barnes, Royal Engineers.
Pte. F. Bishop, Leinster Regiment.
Pte. A. Brown, Wilts Regiment.
Pte. E. Curtis, Leinster Regiment.
Pte. J. Edwards, Royal Dublin Fusiliers.
Pte. W. Elsip, Wilts Regiment.
Pte. A. Emery, Wilts Regiment.
Pte. E. Gleed, Gloucester Regiment.
Pte. H. Goodfield, Royal Munster Fusiliers.
Sergt. W. Kaynes, Wilts Regiment.
Pte. S. Lewis, Royal Munster Fusiliers.
Pte. T. Paginton, Wilts Regiment.
Pte. R. Pike, Wilts Regiment.
Pte. C. Pinnell, Royal Munster Fusiliers.
Sapper J. Player, Royal Engineers.
Pte. E.E. Rymell, Wilts Regiment.
Pte. W. Rymell, Wilts Regiment.
Pte. W. Savine, Wilts Regiment.
Pte. E. Strange, Wilts Regiment.
Pte. G. Thornbury, Royal Munster Fusiliers.
Pte. C. Wakefield, Wilts Regiment.
H. Tugwell, R.N.R. (Hood) Battalion.

It is very probable that there are others besides those in the above list. Malmesbury is, for its size, paying a high price, but is content to have a share in the great sacrifice for King and Empire.

The following week the Herald had two interesting items;

RECRUITING OFFICER'S PREROGATIVES – In the course of the proceedings of the Malmesbury Tribunal on Wednesday Mr. M. Thompson said he wished to ask Col. Sir Audley Neeld why Col. Sir George Helm elected his prerogative in the way he did, exempting certain young men in Malmesbury on his own account without those ever having to appear before the Tribunal - Col. Sir Audley Neeld said the Recruiting Officer had the right to appeal against any decision of the Tribunal – The Clerk said the Recruiting Officer was perfectly at liberty to act on his own responsibility. Mr. Thompson protested against that, as he considered that in some cases it was a slight to the Tribunal. Sir Audley Neeld said the Recruiting Officer had a prerogative to exempt a man without going to the Tribunal at all. Mr. Thompson: - If that is the case, I think it a very bad one. – The Clerk said they could always ask the Recruiting Officer to reconsider his decision, especially when they had special knowledge of local cases.

And;

Malmesbury Notes

Few small towns, or large either, have a better war record than Malmesbury. It was always a good recruiting ground for the Wilts Regiment, whose plucky deeds have won for them a worldwide fame. It follows as a matter of course that townspeople are immensely fond of their soldier heroes, and generally speaking think nothing too good as a reward for their self-sacrificing valour. It is with all the more surprise, therefore, that we hear a whisper that some of our boys who have been broken in the present war are being none too well treated. One particular case we have in mind is of a miserable pittance having been doled out to a partially-disabled soldier with a wife and family – an allowance which is an insult to a brave man and a woman none the less brave. At the Tribunal employers complain that they cannot get men "for love or money." This may be true of able-bodied man, but by all accounts there is some labour, such as can be done by partially disabled soldiers, going a-begging in Malmesbury. One would have thought that men who had sacrificed everything save life itself in the great war would not be lost sight of for a moment. Why is there no organisation on the spot equipped for the defence of our men broken in the war? Such an organisation should be searching out those heroes and restoring their station to at least what it was before the war.

Although the intention of this book is to tell the stories of those who died in the war it must be remembered that many more suffered grievous injury as a piece in the Herald of 1st September testifies;

WAR CASUALTIES – Official news has been received that Pte. Samuel Walter Wakefield, of the Gloucestershire Regiment, third son of Mr. Samuel Wakefield, of West Street, was seriously wounded on August 22nd. He was shot in the arms, legs and right eye, and now lies in hospital at Rouen. Pte. Wakefield, who is only 20 years of age, was previously in the Wiltshire Regiment and saw fighting at Mons. He was invalided owing to frostbite, but recovered sufficiently to re-join the Army. Perhaps Samuel's strong desire to return to the front might have been due to the death in action of his elder brother William in October 1914.

Another of the early volunteers returned in circumstances he would not have wished for as reported by the Wilts and Gloucester Standard;

MALMESBURY MAN'S GOOD WAR RECORD.- Private William Edward Tugwell, of the Wiltshire Regiment (who volunteered for the front with the first men of the National Reserve), has returned home after nine months in Leeds Hospital. He served six months in France, and was wounded by shrapnel in the thigh at Loos, and is now discharged, through permanent unfitness for further active service, with a certificate of good conduct. We understand that he is to be recommended for the Military Medal because, after receiving his wound, he continued under fire to carry water to many of his wounded comrades on the field of battle. Private Tugwell belongs to Malmesbury, where he was born.

Although the casualty reporting system seems to have improved since the early days of the war, mistakes were still made. One such was reported on 27th October. One wonders whether there was confusion between John and Cyril Bond who were in different battalions but whose records were held in the same office;

WRONGLY REPORTED KILLED
Good News for Malmesbury Soldier's Parents
By an error on the part of the military authorities the parents of Pte. John Bond, 16, Burnivale, Malmesbury, were last week notified that he had been killed in action. To the indescribable joy of the family, however, yesterday morning a letter was received by the father from the Officer in Charge of Records, Dublin, as follows: "I have to acknowledge receipt of your communication of the 20th inst. relative to your son 17504 Pte. Bond, Dublin Fusiliers, and to acquaint you in reply that the report of death sent to you was in error, the mistake being caused by the confusion of the same name being on the base casualty list. Regret is expressed for the natural pain and anxiety caused you by this report, and I am to inform you that your son is alive and well and serving with the —— Battalion Royal Dublin Fusiliers, Expeditionary Force _____ H.J. Cooney, Captain. October 24th 1916.
Mr. and Mrs. Bond are naturally full of joy and thankfulness at the good news. They had received countless messages of sympathy in their supposed loss, which would have been their second bereavement, as they have already lost one son. Their many friends will now have cause to congratulate them on the fact that their son is alive and well. Pte. Bond will

have the rare experience of reading his obituary notice and his name in the "North Wilts Herald" roll of honour, where these appeared last week. At a service in the Westport Congregational Church the congregation, after the receipt of the first erroneous message from the War Office, showed their sympathy by standing when the name of the soldier was announced as that of one who had sacrificed his life. Now the mourning is turned to joy for the relatives and friends.

Another death of a serviceman with a connection to the town appeared in the Herald of 24th November;

MALMESBURY COLONIAL'S SON KILLED – In a letter to Mr. Charles Pike, of Kingswall, Mr. L. Gwilliam, a Malmesbury man resident in New Zealand, states that his son, Pte. H.B. Gwilliam, of the New Zealand Army, has died of wounds received in action. Mr. Gwilliam, who left this country many years ago, is head gardener to the Premier of New Zealand, Mr. W.F. Massey, and, during the latter's stay in England is living in the Premier's residence in Wellington. There are still many in Malmesbury who remember Mr. Gwilliam, and their sympathy will go out to him and Mrs. Gwilliam in their bereavement. This is another of the many instances of the sons of Malmesbury, who, from the far colonies, have made sacrifices for King and Empire. At home or abroad they are always, as ever in the past, ready to prove their loyalty and patriotism. Mr. Gwilliam in his letter bitterly denounces those responsible for the war and blames the Christian Churches for their lethargy in permitting the dominance of militarism. As in England, the food pirates, he says, are active, though apparently not so extortionate as here. Butter in New Zealand is 1s. 9d. per lb., bread 5d. a loaf, meat 6d. to 10d. per lb., and bacon 1s. 3d. per lb. Those prices, he declares, show the profiteers to be foes as formidable to the people as the Germans.

At the end of the year the battalions of the Wiltshires were spread around the world as follows; 1st and 2nd with the BEF, France, 3rd at Weymouth, 1/4th and 2/4th in India, 3/4th at Bournemouth, 5th in Mesopotamia, 6th in France, 7th in Salonika and 8th subsumed into 8th Reserve Brigade at Wareham. The Yeomanry were based; 1/1st BEF, 2/1st had become part of 10th (Wiltshire and North Somerset) Yeomanry Cyclist Regiment at Ipswich and 3/1st still at Tidworth.

1917

The Army Council issued further instructions to Tribunals about the calling-up of agricultural labourers. It was emphasised that great care had to be exercised in connection with recruiting those employed in food production. Whilst some parts of the country had an unnecessarily strong complement of farm labourers of military age other areas had been denuded of them. It was suggested that exemption could be given to a certain proportion of labourers that are surplus to requirements on the understanding that they would transfer to areas with a shortage.

The Herald had a curious item in its edition of 16th February (see the story of Henry Newman in Part Two);

A DISCLAIMER – Mr. F. Newman, grocer, High Street, Malmesbury, wishes it to be known that the man named Newman, of the Royal Engineers, residing at Lower High Street recently proceeded against as an absentee from the Army was in no way related to him. Mr. F. Newman, as is well known locally, has lost two sons in the war, and his third son is still serving in the R.F.A.

Towards the end of April news reached the town of three deaths of soldiers connected with the town. Major Henry Molyneux Paget Howard, 19th Earl of Suffolk and 12th Earl of Berkshire of the Royal Field Artillery was killed in action on the 21st. He had married Miss Marguerite Hyde Leiter of Washington, U.S.A. in 1904 and they had three sons. He had helped raise and commanded the Swindon battery of the Wessex Brigade, Royal Field Artillery. He went with them to India on the outbreak of war. Anxious to see action he transferred to a R.F.A. unit which was in Mesopotamia where he was killed by an enemy shell. On 5th April Private H. Tugwell who had been born here was killed in action with the Wiltshires. His parents had moved to Maidenhead and he is commemorated there. Battery Sergeant Major W.J. Bullock also died the same day. He married Agnes Edwards, sister of E.F.E. Edwards, in Malmesbury in August 1915 and had earned the Military Medal for gallantry but had been unable to collect it before he died. His widow was presented with the medal in October. None of these men are commemorated in Malmesbury.

One young man who later became the owner of a garage in the High Street was awarded a high honour;

BRAVE FLYING OFFICER.
Malmesbury Lady's Brother.
WINS MILITARY CROSS.

The King has conferred the Military Cross upon Lieutenant E.S.T. Cole, Royal Flying Corps. The young officer – he is only 22 years of age – is the youngest brother of Mrs. Edward Jones, of High Street, Malmesbury, and has performed some wonderful feats in the air in battling with Hun aviators. His relatives have been informed that he has brought down at least nine enemy aeroplanes and two balloons. A few days ago, he had a terrible fight with a notorious German aviator – a captain – and succeeded after a sharp duel, which began 12,000 feet up, in bringing his man down in flames after shooting him through the heart. Lieutenant Cole, who was in Malmesbury on leave recently, is one of the most promising of flying officers and will probably make an even better name for himself than he enjoys at present. Mrs. Jones is to be congratulated on having so gallant and distinguished a brother. It is hoped that the best of good fortune will attend him in his hazardous exploits.

Some conscripts were clearly not as keen to serve in the Army as the volunteers had been. Private Greening of Brokenborough first appeared before Malmesbury Magistrates as an absentee in March. He again went absent from Swindon on 7th May and was arrested at Willesley. Brought before the Justices charged with being absent and stealing a jacket he was remanded to await an escort back to his unit. A few days later he appeared again;

ASSAULTING THE POLICE.
Soldier Sentenced at Malmesbury.
"AN ABSOLUTELY WORTHLESS FELLOW."

AT A SPECIAL POLICE COURT AT Malmesbury on Tuesday – before Mr. T.L. Hinwood and the Mayor (Mr. M. Thompson) – Pte. Albert Edward Greening, of the 16th (T.W.) Battalion, Worcester Regiment, stationed at Swindon, was charged with being an absentee and also with assaulting P.C. A. Stone whilst in the execution of his duty.
P.C. Stone, stationed at Hullavington, deposed that on Monday at 5 p.m. he was on duty cycling near the railway station, Hullavington, when he saw prisoner walking alone on the road towards Malmesbury. Witness asked him if he had a pass permitting him to be absent from his regiment, and he replied, "I have not got any pass." He refused to explain how he came to be there and would not give his name. When told by witness that he would be taken to Malmesbury he said, "I shan't come." Eventually, however, witness persuaded him to accompany him, and they proceeded along the road in the direction of Malmesbury. They had not gone far when the prisoner suddenly stopped and said, "I shan't go any further." With that he struck witness a blow on the cheek, and as witness was putting his bicycle down on the roadside prisoner rushed at him again, and he fell on his back, prisoner on top showering more blows on his face and chest. Witness recovered and threw him over into the road, holding him until he consented to continue the journey quietly, and then conducted him to Malmesbury.
Asked if he had any questions to put to the witness, prisoner said, "It is no good me saying anything at all."
Supt. Witt said prisoner was brought to the police station at 7.15 p.m. on Monday, P.C. Stone bearing marks of the assault. Prisoner said he understood the charge. In reply to witness' question as to how he came by the mark on his face he said it was where the constable struck him, but, as the magistrates could see, the mark was not that of a blow, but grave-rash through prisoner falling when he attacked the constable.
Prisoner: It is a blow, not a bump.
The Chairman, in sentencing prisoner, said: You were treated very leniently when you were

here before and handed back to an escort, and every consideration was given to you; but you have abused the kindness and consideration of the Court and repeated your absence. In addition to that you have seriously assaulted the constable. The Bench will always support the police in the execution of their duty. The constable did his duty, which is an unpleasant one very often, and brought you to the police-station. For the assault you will have to go to Gloucester gaol for three months' hard labour, and on the expiration of that you will be handed over to an escort.

Supt. Witt said he had communicated with the prisoner's commanding officer, who stated that prisoner was absolutely good for nothing, and was to be court martialled on Wednesday morning for the offence for which he had recently been brought before the Bench. The train service did not permit of an escort being sent this time. There was no doubt that the prisoner was an absolutely worthless fellow.

The Mayor expressed agreement with Mr. Hinwood's remarks. He was sorry prisoner had not more sense, and hoped that when he came out of prison he would become a good man.

Prisoner, who enlisted in Cardiff last September, had been before the Bench twice previously for being an absentee and for theft.

The number of appeals against conscription did not seem to diminish. In June the Tribunal heard 66 cases and the newspaper headline was "Poor Day for the Army" as only two final dates were handed down. One of these was George Young, 42 and single of Burton Hill. He told the panel that he was the last photographer in the town and although this was not work of national importance he was very busy. Other photographers, Francis Summers and Edgar Basevi had previously appealed on a couple of occasions each and but their exemptions had ended on 31st March and 1st June respectively. Mr. Young had attested under the Derby scheme but had been rejected as unfit. However on being examined again he was passed for Class C2 (fit for home service labour units). He was exempted until 1st August.

In early June news was received of the death of another son of a man living in Malmesbury who was not later commemorated locally;

Mr. W.J. May, of Caer Bladon, Malmesbury, has received news of the death of his younger son, Private Phil. Tierney May, of the London Scottish. Private May, who was 28 years of age, lived at Plymouth, where his father formerly resided, and left to join the London Scottish last year. He had been in France since January 12th. He was wounded on May 12th – exactly a year and a day since he joined – and at the Base hospital it was found necessary to amputate his right arm. Recovery, however, was not possible, and he died on Whit-Monday. He was brother of Mr. W.E. May, the local Excise officer. To Mr. W.J. May the father, the shock of losing his gallant son has been great, and to him and Mr. W.E. May will go out a large measure of sympathy from all who know them. Private May was married, and his wife re-sides at Plymouth. Her sorrow is overwhelming, but she, too, has the solace of genuine sympathy from a host of friends, and the more abiding memory of a brave husband who made the supreme sacrifice for his country.

War reports formed a large part of the reported news but only a few items related directly to Malmesbury such as;

A WAY THEY HAVE IN THE ARMY. – We learn that a local professional artist after several vain attempts to obtain employment as a munition worker – although he took an expensive course of training and became qualified for the work – joined the Army. He was subjected to a four days' "trade" test, and out of a large number of applicants was told that he had qualified for a certain class of Army work in which his art experience was essential. Instead, however, of utilising his exceptional talents in that direction – he is an artist to his finger-tips – he was drafted away to another depot and put to trench-digging. The latest news of him is that he has been promoted to a post of assistant-cook! Meanwhile his business is closed down with a loss of hundreds of pounds in the family, and the country is deprived of his services in his profession – services which, we are told, are urgently needed to help win the war.

A SERGEANT KILLED. – Official news has been received that Sergt. Daniel Johnson, South

Wales Borderers, second son of Mr. George Johnson, High Street, Malmesbury, was killed in action on July 26th. The late sergeant, who was 41 years of age in June, had served 10 years in the Army, nearly six years of which he had spent in India; and he also went through the South African Campaign. Returning to civil life, he settled down at Ebbw Vale, where he was employed in the steel works. He joined the National Reserve and enlisted voluntarily soon after the war started, the chaplain who wrote to the family stated that the Major was killed on the same day as Sergt. Johnson, and both were buried in the same cemetery. Much sympathy I felt for the widow and four young children in their bereavement, as well as for Mr. George Johnson and his other children. Mr. George Johnson has still two sons serving – Pte. William Johnson, Wilts Regiment, who also fought in the South African War and has seen a lot of fighting in France, and Pte. Robert Johnson, Wilts Regiment, who is home on agricultural work. Another son, James, is in a munition works at Ebbw Vale.

Although his parents could have put Daniel's name on our war memorial they obviously felt that he would be more appropriately remembered in his adopted home in South Wales.

Another letter appeared from Sergeant William Bailey telling how he had been wounded for the fifth time;

"OVER THE TOP."
Malmesbury Sergeant's Experience.
Sergt. W.E. Bailey, Wilts Regiment, son of Mr. and Mrs. Charles Bailey, Triangle, Malmesbury, is in the Royal Hospital, Sheffield, wounded for the fifth time. Mr. and Mrs. Bailey sent five sons to the Army. Two – Sergt. F. Bailey and Pte. James Bailey – have been killed in action. From the following letter which was received by the parents from Sergt. W. Bailey, it will be seen that the latter was in the thick of recent fighting near Ypres. He was exceedingly fortunate in escaping with his life. It is hoped that he may soon recover and return home.
"At last I have arrived in England safety. I could not write to you before as we have been moving about almost every day since I got wounded. In the first place I am going on grand – I sent you a couple of postcards to let you know I was A1. Well, on July 28th we went up to our assembly place on the right of Ypres and in the rear of our front line, of course. There we stayed for a couple of nights, and I might say it was not too pleasant; between the gas shells and the ordinary shells, which were rather heavy at times, we had several gassed there. On the third night we went into an advanced trench; that is, in front of our front line. Well, we stayed there until morning, and then we went over at the time appointed. Then the guns opened fire, and over we went. The bombardment was the best I have ever witnessed and the most peculiar; the sky was lit up with all kinds of Verey lights. It was a treat to watch it, but we had no time for watching fireworks, for we were over and advancing like the devil. During our advance there were many strong points held by the Germans; but these were taken very easily – we simply threw bombs in them and passed on,, leaving others to deal with 'John.' A little further ahead was our objective, but all at once 'John' opened fire on us with a machine-gun, and if had not been for 'John' having the wind up and shooting wide, he would have had us all. We were nearly on top of him, so of course, down we went for a bit. I had no bombs left, so could do nothing. We had to outflank that gun, and in doing so he had me through the left arm, and I knew it too. I was only in the battle for about two hours, and quite long enough, too, for me. On coming back 'John' had still another go, but he did not touch me again. Before coming back I must say we had only lost a few up till then, hardly any killed. I have rather a nasty arm, and the bone being fractured makes it ache a good bit. I came over on the steamship ——, and landed at Dover, taking train from there, arriving here after an eight hours' journey."

Another family with not only all the sons serving in the forces but with daughters in harm's way had some anxiety;

AN OMINOUS MESSAGE.- On Wednesday Mrs. Jones, of 44, Foundry Road received a letter, undated, from her son, Private Bernard Jones, Durham Light Infantry, serving in France. There was written on the back of the envelope a message to the effect that the letter was found in a dug-out and forwarded to Mrs. Jones by the finder, who was, presumably, an officer. To Mrs. Jones the message seems ominous, and she fears that her son is among the missing, as she has not heard from him for some time. The finding of the letter in such circumstances, and the fact that no further news has been received, lead her to fear the worst: but it is sincerely hoped that her son is alive and well. Mr. and Mrs. Jones have had five sons serving in the present war. Of one – Driver Reginald Jones, Royal Field Artillery – they have received tidings that he is seriously ill in hospital in Mesopotamia. Another, Fred, is in the Canadian Machine Gun Corps. Two other sons have been killed. Bernard had been suffering from shell shock and trench feet, but had returned to the firing line after recovering. He is only 19 years of age and joined the Army 18 months ago. To add to their grave anxiety Mr. and Mrs. Jones are awaiting news of their two daughters, who, with their families, were living near Halifax, Nova Scotia, the scene of the recent catastrophic explosion. Few homes have been overshadowed with such tragic sorrow as that of Mr. and Mrs. Jones, and it is sincerely hoped that they may soon have the comfort of better news. Whatever the future has in store for them they have the proud knowledge that their sons, have one and all, played a heroic part in fighting for their country. The catastrophic explosion referred to was when the S.S. Mont Blanc, a French ship laden with munitions accidentally exploded in the harbour causing widespread devastation and many deaths.

At the end of November notice was received that Sergeant J.H. Mackett, a former resident of the town, had been killed in Palestine. When his father died in 1905 Jack had come to live with his uncle L. Gore in High Street, Malmesbury. He played with the Town football team from 1911 to 1913. He worked for the County Council in Trowbridge and being in the Territorials went to India shortly after the outbreak of war. He is not commemorated here.

On the 13th December the Gazette reported that they thought the prospect for further recruitment was limited;

BARREN OF RESULTS.- The Tribunal sat for two hours on Tuesday, but without gaining a single recruit for the Army. It is patent that the area is a purely agricultural one, and that men must be kept to cultivate the land. Still, as a member of the Tribunal remarked, if units for H.M. Forces cannot be obtained from agricultural occupations, what is the use of summoning members of the authority week after week listening to the same tales – more or less accurate – of farmers who cannot spare their employees if the land has to be cultivated and food produced, involving, not only the loss of valuable time to the members – who cheerfully give their services – but journeys of farmers to Malmesbury (from 6 to 18 miles return), with the attendant expenses and loss of energy on the land. We re-echo the sentiments. What is the good? – If these workers are needed on the land, why not give them certificates from the War Agricultural Committee and save the Tribunals and the employers all this waste of time and money? We may be reminded that the decision is invariably "subject to substitution," but, how often are these substitutes provided by the military? And if they cannot be provided, why add the proviso? How often has the Malmesbury Tribunal met with barren results for the Army.

However the year ended with a shorter list of appeals. The dictum now was that "in the national interest every available man is required for military service." As a result the cases heard were appeals by the Recruiting Officer against individuals who had previously been given conditional exemption. Most were granted exemption to April and only one was given the option of appealing when this period expired.

At the turn of the year the Wiltshire battalions were distributed as follows; 1st and 2nd in France, 3rd at Sittingbourne, 1/4th in Palestine, 2/4th in India, 4th (Reserve) (the renamed 3/4th) at Larkhill, 5th in Mesopotamia, 6th (amalgamated with the 1/1st Royal Wilts Yeomanry in September) in France and 7th in Salonika. The 2/1st Yeomanry had been reconstituted and were at Frinton and Clacton and the 3/1st had become part of the 3rd Reserve Cavalry Regiment at Aldershot.

1918

The work of the Tribunals continued with the medical standards being dropped so that men previously rejected were now called up. The Board of Trade was seeking more ways in which women could be substituted for men in the workforce. It was estimated that there were still one and a half million women with industrial or commercial experience who could yet be called upon. It was pointed out that two thirds of these would be married and over 35. A new National Registration Act came into force which required all boys to register as soon as they became 15 and tightened the regime further. The Act gave unlimited power to abolish exemption.

Another Malmesbury man lost his life on 24th January. Private Arthur John Bull, only son of Fred James Bull who lived in Back Hill, aged 33 had enlisted in the Wiltshire Yeomanry in 1915 but was transferred to the 6th Wiltshires. He was killed by the bursting of an artillery shell and is buried in Fifteen Ravine, Villers Plouich close to Harry Shingles. Arthur's widow, Kate, lived in Shipton Moyne so he is commemorated there and not in Malmesbury.

On 29th March the Tribunal considered an appeal from the recruiting officer to reclassify F.H. Summers, one of Malmesbury's photographers, who was working in a munitions factory in Melksham. The Mayor was outraged and said; "Are we going to act like the Germans, and tear up our decision like the proverbial piece of paper?" The appeal was refused. Within a month this case was referred to the County Appeal Tribunal as the Gazette reported on 25th April;

At the Wilts Appeal Tribunal at Trowbridge on Friday, the Marquess of Bath presiding, the National Service authorities applied for the withdrawal of the exemption granted by the Malmesbury Tribunal to Francis Herbert Summers, formerly carrying on the business of a photographer and bookseller, at 31, High Street, Malmesbury, now described as a rubber worker in the employ of the Avon India Rubber Company Ltd., at Melksham. A similar application was made to the Malmesbury Tribunal, but was refused on the ground that the man having taken up work of national importance as requested, upon which he was given exemption, he should be given a further term, having regard to his grade, and that he was 40 years of age. – Respondent: I was 40 19 months ago. – The case for the appellants was that the man holds the M.A.R.O. (Munitions) certificate which protected him as long as it was operative, consequently he did not require both forms of exemption. – In reply to the Chairman, the respondent said he was given exemption 14 months ago on the ground of financial hardship – a one-man business. He was in B1. He had been in his business as a photographer and stationer for 20 years at Malmesbury. In view of the conditional exemption recommended by the Recruiting Officer at Chippenham, he made arrangements to close down his business. It was closed, but he had retained a hold on the property and a large stock which was still there. He then took up work of national importance, first at Swindon, then at the Rubber Works at Melksham. – Lord Bath said that he did not see what advantage it was to the respondent to be in the Rubber Works; he understood that his object in not going into the Army was to keep the business going. – Respondent said that was impossible. – Lord Bath: What was the object of your exemption? – Respondent: That I might be able to keep my stock and premises. If I went into the Army I should have to sell out. – Lord Bath: But you would get compensation, would you not? – Captain Morley said he could make application to the Civil Liabilities Committee. – Lord Bath: I should think you would be no worse off than in the Avon Rubber Works or at Swindon. – Asked the question, respondent said he removed from Swindon to Melksham in September last. – The Acting Clerk said the man could not appeal again if this certificate were withdrawn. – Captain Morley: He could on domestic grounds, but not occupational grounds. – Lord Bath said if the Court withdrew the exemption the man should not be damaged. He made a note of the case. The Court would withdraw the Tribunal's exemption, and the man would rely on the M.A.R.O. certificate. If that were withdrawn, he would still have the right to appeal on domestic grounds. The military appeal would therefore be granted.

The Malmesbury Tribunal had written to the War Office protesting that men were being taken from the land to munitions factories and aerodromes which made food production difficult. This was raised in the Commons by George Terrell, our M.P. The Secretary of War replied saying that the matter had been forwarded to the Minister for National Service.

At the beginning of April the annual financial report was presented to the congregation of the Abbey. The Vicar took the small attendance as evidence that the parishioners were sure that parochial affairs were in good hands. Canon McMillan proposed a motion of gratitude to those who had given their lives for their country and stated that 16 names had been added to the roll of honour since last Easter; *The first name was of one who was not actually resident in the parish, but it was a name dear to every one of them – Lord Suffolk. In May came the news of the death of Second-Lieut. Edmund John Hibbard; in June Pte. Arthur Edward Bishop, Pte. Henry Thomas Reeves and Gunner James Sellwood; in August Pte. William Emery; in September Pte. Archibald James Perry; in October Pte. Roland Weeks; in November, Gunner Joseph Thompson and Rifleman Frank Deadman; in December Second-Lieut. Harold Jones and Pte. Colin Bishop; in January Pte. Leslie James Carey and Pte. Percy Wood; and in April the Rev. Emlyn H. Davies and Pte. James Hibbard. It was very pathetic that the first name and the last should be those of two brothers – the brothers Hibbard. Theirs was the third family in the town to lose two sons. The war had come home to every-one, and he felt that the least the Church could do was to record its sense of gratitude for those who had laid down their lives and to record such an expression as that of the resolu-tion.*

At the beginning of April the death in action was reported of Pte. Fred Bailey, Wilts Regiment, a man with a wife and four children, who was formerly employed at Halcombe where his sister was in service. His name is not included on our memorials. Also Mrs. L.G. Pope died, widow of Private Thomas Pope, A.S.C. who had died in November 1917. She was 28 years old and had been in poor health for some time. She was the daughter of Harry Goulding of Burnivale.

Attempts to motivate the populace to support the war effort continued as reported in 4th May's Gazette;

VISIT OF WAR CINEMA.- The motor van now touring the district visited Malmesbury on Friday night and "pitched" in the Cross Hayes. Hundreds of people and children congregated, and, as darkness gathered, listened with interest to the story of the war, the aims and ambitions of our unscrupulous foe, the imperative need to destroy the burglar of Europe, with fervent appeals for every man to come forward and do something for his country – from the lips of a capable lecturer of the "John Bull" type. The lecture was applauded. About 9 p.m. the operators in charge proceeded to throw on the huge screen the finest set of pictures relating to the war, on land and sea and others depicting various kinds of war work ever seen here. The sight of the heavy guns in action, the tanks moving forward to the attack, the bonny boys in and marching to the trenches, brought home for the mind with realistic force the greatest tragedy of modern times. Many fine glimpses of H.M. King George reviewing his navy, with Sir David Beatty, were included and a sight of the smart sailor boys marching and saluting the King as they passed the Royal stand – sailors whose worth Zeebrugge has written in letters of gold – evoked hearty cheers from the onlookers. Munitions, hospital work, limb-making for the limbless provided an interesting series, and at the close some clever pictorial appeals for the financial help of the working man whose war savings loaned to the State would help to "down" Kaiserism once and for all, made people realise the value of the last mite in turning the scales of justice in favour of John Bull and Co.

Morale required lifting as casualty reports streamed in;

A PRISONER OF WAR.- Pte. Henry Wilcox, Wilts Regiment, husband of Mrs. Wilcox, of Horsefair, is reported to be a prisoner of war in German hands. He was an old Reservist and joined up when the war started.

REPORTED MISSING.- Pte. Frederick Hinder, R.M.L.I., whose wife and three children live at 36, St. John Street, is reported missing. He and his father between them were over 50 years in the service of the late Lord Estcourt at Estcourt, Shipton Moyne.

It would seem that the protests of Malmesbury and elsewhere had been heeded when a new scheme was introduced to retain in civil life men of military age who were engaged in the import, production or distribution of food. The first cases considered by the Malmesbury Tribunal were those of Mr. W.C. Pocock, manager for Mr. H. Farrant grocer in the High Street and Frederick Day, butcher at Market Cross. However they were only exempted until 1st

September.

One result of the lowering of medical standards was that some individuals had to be discharged from the forces as they really were unfit. One such was Edgar Basevi who had been called up to the Royal Engineers but had been transferred to the Royal Air Force. During his service he suffered from poor health and so was discharged in June.

A lot of anxiety arose from the major German attacks that started on 21st March and carried on until July. Because the enemy advanced far into the Allied lines it was some time before it was known whether missing loved ones had been killed, wounded or captured. Even when good news arrived there was scepticism about its accuracy;

TWO BROTHERS TAKEN PRISONER.- Mrs. Brown, of Bristol Street, heard several weeks ago that her two sons, Charlie and George, were missing. During the past week she has received news from each of them. George saying he was all right. The father, Pte. W. Brown, Wilts Regiment, is serving in Ireland. Below we append the letter written from Germany on May 3rd from Lce.-Corpl. Charlie Brown. Reading between the lines, it is probable that the letter was dictated by the young soldier's Hun captives. Apart from the natural disinclination on the part of the son to send any news likely to worry his mother, there is reason for believing that the phrase in the letter, "We are getting on fine here" and "We get plenty of food," were Hun inspired. the letter ran: "My dear mother, - Just a few lines to let you know I am all right, although I am in hospital with a bit of a wound in the face. I have not been allowed to write till now, so I expect you have been worrying about me, but my wound is nearly well now and I expect I shall soon be discharged from hospital. Have you heard anything about George? I have not been able to get any definite news about him. All that I could find out about him was that nearly all his company were taken prisoners. Let me know if you have heard from him. We are getting on fine here; we are not allowed to go far, but we walk about in the park and we get plenty of food. When you write back to me you must not put in any news about the war. Don't send any parcels until you hear from me again, as I don't expect I shall be here long enough to get an answer; but write a letter and put two packets of Woodbine in, as that is the only thing we cannot get. Well, dear mother, I hope this letter will relieve your mind. I shall have to wait till the end of the war now before I see you all again, so I hope it will not be much longer. I must close now, so remember me to all from loving son – Charlie."

The Tribunal hearing on 9th July brought about the dramatic resignation of the Mayor, Councillor Matthew Thompson, from the panel. One of the early cases was Albert May of High View House, 47, an auctioneer's clerk, with one son in the Army and another in a low medical category temporarily exempted. His appeal was refused. Another case heard was that of H.C. Woodham, aged 35 married with seven children employed by the Stroud Brewery Company as a maltster, tiler and plasterer. The Company representative said that Woodham carried out repairs to more than 25 tied houses in the summer and worked as a maltster in the winter. There were 1,560 sacks to malt in Malmesbury which would take three months – they did not ask for total exemption but just sufficient to complete the task. The Tribunal confirmed that he would be called up on 1st August but would not be asked to leave Malmesbury until a fortnight later. The Mayor was uneasy about the Tribunal's decisions that day as he felt that men of Mr. May's age should not be asked to go before younger men. He said he had to resign from the committee. Although his health was not good the chief reason was that he could not agree with men of 47 to 51 being taken away from important work in the national interest only to be employed as navvies. Only the week before he had seen a party of older men put into the Army equipped with pick-axes, shovels and barrows doing navvies' work. At the next meeting of the Town Council, the Mayor explained the reason for his resignation but no-one could be found to fill the vacancy.

By August the crisis on the Western Front was over and what was later known as the 100 days Advance to Victory had begun. However there was no lessening in the number of casualties. In September Alfred and Martha Gale heard that their grandson, Private Alfred John Gale of the Royal Marine Light Infantry had been killed in action in France on 25th August, aged 21. He had joined up in August 1917, having been a railway worker at Highworth station, and had been at the front for four months. After the grandparents died his name was added to their headstone in Malmesbury Cemetery but not either having been born or lived here he is not included on any other local memorial. Other casualty reports continued to arrive, not always accurate;

AN INCORRECT REPORT.- The report in last week's issue that Driver R. Sealy, R.F.A., son of Mr. Marcus Sealy, Triangle, had been killed, was, it has now been ascertained, incorrect. Mr. Sealy on Wednesday received a letter from a chaplain in France which stated that Driver Sealy, though seriously injured, was quite cheerful and looked forward to being removed to England shortly. It is a coincidence that Corporal George Sealy, Machine Gun Corps, another son of Mr. Sealy, is in hospital in the same ward "gassed." He is progressing favourably. Another son is also in the same neighbourhood serving in the Royal Engineers.

Just before the war ended it was announced that Colonel R.H. Luce, C.B., C.M.G., M.B., F.R.C.S., Territorial Force Reserve had been promoted to temporary Major-General with effect from 19th September. He had served with distinction throughout the war and had been one of the last to leave Gallipoli when the evacuation took place.

The report of the war's end was rather stilted, one can only hope that the celebrations were less staid, the Herald's report is followed by the more animated version in the Gazette;

THE COMING OF PEACE.- Although numerous rumours were present throughout Monday morning that the armistice had been signed, it was not until the afternoon that the official news arrived. Mr. H. Wilmot (postmaster) exhibited the message outside the Post Office, and there was much cheering when it was found that the news was really true. Within a very short time many lines of flags were being hung across the principal streets, and there was hardly a house that did not exhibit a flag. There was great rejoicing at the Red Cross Hospital, the staff and patients vying with each other in their manifestation of delight. On Tuesday there was a solemn service of thanksgiving in the Abbey, conducted by the Vicar (Canon C.D.H. McMillan). It was evident that the large congregation, which included parents who had lost two or more sons, was profoundly moved.

HOW THE NEWS WAS RECEIVED IN MALMESBURY.
The first intimation to reach the town that an armistice had been signed was contained in a telegram from Mr. S.N. Dixon, in London, to his wife, and on the strength of this flags were displayed at several houses. It was not until late in the day that the news was confirmed, and the bells were, it is strange to relate, silent until nearly seven o'clock in the evening, when a scratch team of ringers – the majority of experts are absent on active service – made a heroic effort to give a peal, but it ended in a chime. The streets, too, were in total darkness. Thus was the memorable day of November 11th celebrated in Malmesbury; but, of course, great things are to follow to mark the auspicious event in the loyal old borough.
At the monthly meeting of the Ancient Order of Foresters in the Y.M.C.A. Hall, on Monday evening, the following resolution was carried with enthusiasm: "Resolved that the members of Court King Athelstan, of the Ancient and Loyal Order of Foresters, assembled in Court on this never to be forgotten day, the eleventh day of November, 1918, recognises with profound gratitude the guidance of Almighty God in delivering this country, and its Allies, from the cruel hands of its enemies, whose barbarities have shocked the whole of civilisation; and desires to place on record its congratulations to his Majesty the King, and hearty thanks to Marshal Foch, Sir Douglas Haig, and the other Generals and leaders of the Allied Armies; to our Fleet which has so zealously guarded our shores, and to our brave soldiers and airmen whose deeds of valour will be recorded in history for all generations, and for whose heroism will never be forgotten." It was further resolved that a copy of the resolution should be sent to his Majesty the King, Marshal Foch, and Sir Douglas Haig. The signatories to the resolution on behalf of the Court were: George Exton, Chief Ranger, B. Tugwell, Sub-Chief Ranger, E.E. Taylor, Secretary.

WELCOMING THE NEWS.- Since the writing of the brief report of a negative character which appears on our 7th page the town has risen to the occasion and it is now bright with flags and other forms of bunting, the Union Jack rightly predominating. On Tuesday evening a thanksgiving service was held in the Abbey church, and last night similar services were arranged at the Moravian and Westport Congregational churches.

Although hostilities had ceased, fresh grief affected some families. Cecil H. Clark, eldest son of the late Francis Clark of Market Cross died in Aylesbury Military Hospital on 10th November. Mrs. Florence Batt, eldest daughter of Mr. Hillier Neale of Kingswall, heard that her husband Battery Sergeant Major William George Batt had died at a Casualty Clearing Station on 12th November. He had been wounded three times, had won the D.C.M. and had only been married just over a year. Neither of these two men are commemorated in Malmesbury.

Within days of the armistice arrangements were announced for the demobilisation of soldiers, sailors and war workers. Unemployment pay for those thrown out of work would be 24s. per week for men, 20s. for women plus 6s. for the first dependent child under 15 and 3s. for each extra child. Boy workers between 15 and 18 would get 12s. and girls 10s. The benefits would be payable for a maximum of 13 weeks for civilians and 26 weeks for soldiers. Married men would be given preference over single men for employment. Each soldier would receive a personal identity certificate including a character reference, a railway warrant home, a cash payment and an out-of-work donation policy. He would then get 28 days' leave with pay, ration and separation allowances. At the end of those 28 days he would be no longer a soldier.

A scale of gratuities for discharged soldiers was soon announced. Nothing was paid to conscientious objectors but the rates for soldiers depended upon rank, length of service and the nature of the service. For those who served overseas the rates started for a Private, £5 for the first year with 10s. for each additional month and for a Warrant Officer Class 1 £15 plus 10s. per month. For home service the same figure was paid for the first year but only 5s. per month for subsequent service.

Before the end of the year prisoners of war began to return home as the Standard reported on 7th December;

REPATRIATED.- The following Malmesbury men have returned during the last few days from Germany: Private Harry Wilcox, Walter Norris, John Paginton, William Butt, William Paish, and — Gibbs. They all speak of the ill treatment they received while in bondage, and had it not been for parcels of food received from home they must have succumbed for want of common necessaries.

The Ancient Order of Foresters Roll of Honour showing the names of 25 members who served and the five who died. Alfred Clark, Joseph Tugwell and Edgar Woodman all came from the town and their story is told in Part Two. William Dunsby was the eldest son of William and Ann Dunsby of Corston. He died on 31st August 1918 at the age of 30 whilst serving with 12th Battalion Royal Berkshire Regiment and is buried in Calais South Cemetery in grave E 5 8. Lewis Slade was the son of Frank and Bessie Slade of Lea. He was killed in action on 15th April 1918 at the age of 33. Serving with 1st Battalion Royal Warwickshire Regiment he was killed in a counter attack near Robecq. His body was not recovered and he is commemorated on the Ploegsteert Memorial Panel 2 & 3. (Athelstan Museum)

Home Defence 1914-19

The outbreak of war galvanised the people of Malmesbury to action. Activities reported in the Devizes Guardian of 14th August were; Scoutmaster W.G. Perry having brought the Boy Scouts back from Weymouth that Tuesday had organised 38 of them into a Voluntary Assistance Depot to carry messages and assist the military - Mr. Ponting put a room and telephone at their disposal night and day; the Mayor and Mayoress were sparing no pains to make local arrangements for the Prince of Wales' Relief Fund; there was *a distinct slackening of anxiety lest food should reach famine prices* after shopkeepers firmly discouraged customers from purchasing abnormal quantities; at a meeting arranged by the Mayoress, Mrs. H. Farrant, a Women's War Guild was founded – garments such as socks and shirts would be made at home to be sent to troops and a subscription of threepence a week paid.

One curious story was the arrest of a supposed German spy. A man who could speak little English was spotted acting suspiciously at the railway station. It was believed that he was observing military movements. He was arrested by a couple of Territorials and handed over to Police Sergeant Hillier. Crowds of people witnessed his removal to the Police Station. It was found that he had been in town for a few days. However after a careful search of his possessions it turned out that he was a Russian Jew, a pedlar who had been selling hats at the Market and was anxious to return to his home-country to join their forces.

The Ammunition Column returned to Malmesbury at the beginning of October when the rest of the artillery units sailed for India. Accommodation had to be found in private houses for around 100 men as the unit brought with it men from Tetbury and Swindon. This created a certain amount of excitement not least the accident on 21st October to Gunner Warren. He was riding a horse without a saddle past St. Mary's Church, Gloucester Road when the animal bolted at a furious pace down the hill. The horse galloped into a team and wagon, threw its rider and slipped so that the wagon ran over it. Warren had cuts to his face and hands which bled profusely and was knocked unconscious. After first aid at the scene by Dr. Moore he was taken to hospital. The horse had to be put down. Lord Methuen, Chairman of the Wiltshire Territorial Association had inspected the unit the day before when over 200 men paraded for him. The North Wilts Herald included the following in its description of the visit;

The Ammunition Column is comfortably billeted in the town, but nothing is known as to the length of their stay. So far as can be ascertained 112 men have been accepted for active service, and those will, it is believed, be leaving shortly. Much useful work is being done in the way of drill, &c. Reveille is at 6.30, and the men are well occupied until 4 p.m. in various exercises. Lectures are given every other day to those who are to join the Expeditionary Force. An interesting part of the work being done is trench-digging in fields near the town. In fact, the Column is being thoroughly well-trained for war, and may be counted upon to render good service against the enemy. We understand that arrangements are being made for the band to be stationed at Malmesbury.

Rumours of foreign service appeared to be confirmed the following week when soldiers were said to have been excused duty as a result of being vaccinated. E.H. Lockstone, father of Quarter-Master J. Lockstone, provided about 40 acres of fields for exercises including White Lion, Sloper's Field and Daniel's Hill. Gunner Harold Guest, 18, injured his ankle in Cross Hayes. A proposal to shut the pubs each evening at 8 pm was held to be an insult to these troops who had been, on the whole, of exemplary behaviour.

The Ammunition Column suffered a spate of accidents. On 15th January 1915 Driver Arthur Edwards was badly injured when his horse reared and threw him off. He was knocked down by the horse and broke his left arm. On the 24th another accident, this time fatal, occurred to Driver Samuel William Jones, 27, married with two young children from Swindon. Whilst exercising his horse with a companion off the Sherston road, he chased the other horse after it had thrown its rider. He too was thrown off but one of his feet caught in the stirrup so that he was dragged along until the leather broke. Although they collected his wife from home in a car he died in hospital before she arrived. The body was returned by train to Swindon for burial in the Radnor Street cemetery.

The Town Council first discussed air raid precautions in February;

PRECAUTIONS AGAINST AIRCRAFT.

A circular containing instructions from the military authorities for precautionary measures against hostile aircraft came up for consideration.

Mr. J.A. Jones said the Gas Company must be called upon by the Council to shade all street lamps as to make them invisible from above. The lights inside and outside shops, &c., would be under the supervision of the police. Mr. Jones recommended an aeroplane trip for some of the Council to see what was required (laughter).

Mr. Clark said the railway station was very brightly illuminated.

Mr. Thompson did not think there was any cause to fear danger from aircraft in a little town like Malmesbury.

The Town Clerk said he had heard of people in other towns being summoned for not observing the regulations.

The Mayor said the Gas Company would see to the shading of the lamps and the police to the shop lights. Every tradesman would be only too glad to fall in with any suggestions.

A few Boy Scouts took on a more active defence role;

BOY SCOUTS AS COAST WATCHERS.- Three members of the King Athelstan Troop of Boy Scouts leave to-day to take up important duties. They are Patrol-leaders Arthur Cooke, James Hibbard and Daniel Blackford. With other Boy Scouts from Swindon, they will form a patrol, and their duty will be to watch the coast at Polperro, Looe, in the south of Cornwall. There are only a few lads of the required age – between 15 and 17 years – in the troop; otherwise a whole patrol would have been sent. The boys will have been well instructed by Scout-Master W.G. Perry and the assistant Scout-Masters, and will be sure to prove useful.

Meanwhile, following a large public meeting a few days before, a Company of the Volunteer Training Corps was formed on 22nd March, one of nine formed in Wiltshire that month. It was commanded by Mr. F.G.T. Goldstone, manager of the Capital and Counties Bank with a Committee of Management comprising: Colonel C.N. Miles, the Mayor (Albert Adye), Messrs. F.J. Bates, M.H. Chubb, F.J. Compton, B. de Bertodano, Henry Farrant, Aubrey Hopwood, A.A. Macintyre, C.F. Moir, J. Lee Osborne, Sir R.H. Pollen and Frank Worthington. The purpose of the Corps was home defence, they would be trained to use rifles and patrol the area. Members would be drawn from men either under 18 or above recruiting age, at that time 38. Founding members, showing a few examples of occupation and age, were: J.G. Bartlett, F.J. Bates, H.J.S. Beak, George Bowman, Maurice Carlton, F.J. Compton (draper, 74), W.J. Denly, A. Eatwell (teacher, 48), John Edmonds, Henry Farrant (grocer, 61), S. Fisher, John Furber, F. Golding, Alfred Harris, Aubrey Hopwood, John Milliner, Charles F. Moir (solicitor, 54), F.L. Newman (grocer, aged 58), W.G. Perry (ex-soldier, 53), Thomas Pincott (butcher, 68), W.W. Ponting (ironmonger, 43), E.H. Prior, W. Rymell, Thomas H. Sandy, Henry Sheppard, F.W. Teagle, Joseph West (farmer, 45), H. Wilmot and Frank Worthington. Many more were enrolled the following week. By May the total strength was 141, 82 from Malmesbury, 56 Charlton and 3 Great Somerford. To begin with such units were given armlets with 'GR' inscribed on them and they became known as the Gorgeous Wrecks. However the first greenish grey uniforms arrived in July.

Although the Wiltshire Territorials had gone to India other units had not yet 'combed out' those who were prepared to go overseas. One such was the Ammunition Column. First the Mayor took the opportunity of exhorting them to offer themselves for foreign service during the interval at a social function on 30th March. At that time only three out of 70 present had volunteered. Then they were assembled by a bugle call one Sunday afternoon by their commander Major A.L. Forrester. Although many were on leave, 38 of the 60 or so on parade volunteered. It was rumoured that they would form the basis of an Ammunition Column for a Highland Artillery Brigade. Shortly afterwards 36 men who failed to volunteer left for the South Coast, whilst some of imperial service men went to Blackheath at the end of the April to join the 51st Division Ammunition Column and the remainder stayed in Malmesbury.

At the beginning of April the spectre that Hun raiders may have arrived caused fear to one person in town;

MALMESBURY AIR SCARE.
Scene at the Workhouse.

At a special court yesterday – before Col. C. Napier Miles, C.B. – a woman named Maria Dear (64), of no fixed abode, was charged with damaging a window in the tramp ward at Malmesbury Workhouse.

Mr. H.C.E. Hinks (master) said the woman was admitted at 6.30 p.m. on Wednesday. She had the usual bath and given supper before she went to bed, the door of the women's tramp ward being locked when she had retired. At ten minutes past eight witness heard an awful noise of screaming from the women's tramp ward. There were shouts of "Murder!" "Police!" and "Help!" and a crash as of a window being smashed. Witness found that prisoner had smashed a window with an enamel mug and had screamed because she was frightened. The cost of the damage was 2s.

Prisoner told the magistrate that she was truly sorry she had no money to pay for the damage, she was frightened at hearing a dreadful noise – just like aeroplanes flying around.

Col. Miles: How do you know what aeroplanes are like? Have you ever seen any?

Prisoner: Oh, yes, plenty when I was in my own Reading Workhouse where I worked with the landlady. I screamed because I thought they might get in to me. I broke the window and screamed for help.

Supt. Witt said the woman told him she was a native of Reading. She was not of the usual tramping class.

Col. Miles: How old are you?

Prisoner: Sixty-four? – that is all, sir.

Col. Miles: You must not do this sort of thing again. You are discharged and must leave the town.

"Thank you, sir," said the woman. "I will honestly pay you, on my oath as a woman, when I get work."

Another miscreant was Lance Corporal R.T. Sawyer of the 6th Royal Munster Fusiliers. In May he was on leave at his parents' home in Brokenborough. P.C. Drew, stationed at Long Newnton, suspected that he was an absentee and went to the house to question him. Sawyer admitted that he had overstayed his leave, was arrested and brought before the Mayor. He was remanded to await an escort and P.C. Drew was recommended to receive the usual reward of 5s. for the arrest of an absentee.

An interesting addition to recruiting aids was made by the principal local photographer, Mr. E.E. Basevi of Abbey Studios, Gloucester Street. Since the war began he had photographed hundreds of men in uniform and he arranged these in a composite picture entitled "Some of Kaiser Willie's little worries". At the same time Lord Kitchener appealed for 300,000 extra men to keep existing units up to strength. Three of J.A. Jones' motor garage workers joined the Mechanical Transport Section of the Army Service Corps. They were Henry Curtis, William Farmer from Grittleton and Ernest Goodfield. Stanley Hudson who worked for Mr. F. Hinder also volunteered for similar duties, whilst Henry Blackford left W. Woodman's employment to join the A.S.C. as a baker. Not only were the forces short of manpower but vital industries also. War Munitions workers were sought in June and appeals for women to join the workforce followed. As a result of the first Mr. G.H. Tabor who had assisted A.E. Long's grocery business resigned and returned to his former occupation as an electrical engineer in London but now in the production of munitions.

The last remaining members of the Ammunition Column, those who had signed up for service overseas totalling around 60, left Malmesbury by train on 14th July. Their equipment had been sent the previous day. During the loading a large iron boiler fell off a hand trolley which was derailed and although it was damaged the soldiers moving it avoided injury.

The first anniversary of the declaration of war was marked by a meeting in Cross Hayes organised in connection with the Central Council for Patriotic Organisations. A platform was erected close to the Town Hall. Those attending were charged 1s. for a seat with the proceeds going to the Cottage Hospital. The Boy Scouts, Volunteer Training Corps and Red Cross nurses were on parade to hear speeches from the Mayor, George Terrell M.P., Lieut. Gorst (a wounded local officer) and a sermon from Canon McMillan.

The tribulations of Charles Bennett, a Malmesbury lad, were reported in the middle of August. He was on the trawler Honoria of Grimsby which picked up the crew of the Hermione from Hull which had been sunk by a U-boat. Unfortunately the same submarine then attacked the Honoria, giving the men four minutes to abandon the vessel before it too was sunk. Before departing the U-boat captain shouted *tell Sir Edward Grey and Winston Churchill that we have some more big torpedoes – we shall sink all your English armed cruisers.* The men spent 40 hours at sea before they were picked up by a Norwegian barque and taken to Lerwick.

At a meeting of the Borough Council on 14th September it was noted by Mr. Bartlett that the Roll of Honour was very much out of date. *When it was compiled he understood that space would be left on which the names of those who joined His Majesty's Forces after the war commenced might be entered. The name of everyone who offered his services to his country should be entered at once; they should not wait until the men were killed, or until they came home before their names were inscribed.* The Mayor and Mr. F.H. Summers were given the task although there is no surviving evidence to confirm that this happened. Perhaps the introduction of conscription put an end to its updating.

Friday 8th October saw the arrival of 120 men of the 590 Company (M.T.) Army Service Corps together with 48 transport lorries including a travelling workshop and forge that practically took up the whole of Cross Hayes. The men were billeted around the town and the Town Hall was used as an office. Over the following weeks they engaged in several football matches with other A.S.C. units based at Calne and Lacock and took part in a number of entertainments. During their stay food supply must have been causing concern as it was decided to feed the men at the Bristol Road Drill Hall rather than in their lodgings. Their stay also caused some worry as reported in the Wiltshire Gazette;

A NOVEL EXPERIENCE – Residents of the ancient borough are not yet familiar with military discipline, and although a section of the Army Service Corps (M.T.) with its motor trolleys, has been stationed in the Cross Hayes for the past month, the cars being protected by military guard, all civilians were not aware that they must respond to the call of the sentry, "Who goes there?" between the hours of 10 p.m. and 6 a.m. Accordingly on Thursday night, after the whist drive in the Council Chambers, a party comprising half-a-dozen of both sexes, whilst crossing Cross Hayes on their way home, failed to answer the challenge. It was repeated, but still no response, so the sentry, faithful to his trust, marched off the party to the guard room. Here one gentleman gave his name and address and was released, but the others – including, we are told, a married lady whose husband became delirious at her prolonged absence – were detained until the officer in command was brought upon the scene. After satisfactory explanations had been offered, and accepted, the party were allowed to depart, having gained a little insight into military matters. Next time they will doubtless promptly respond to the challenge, "Friend."

At the end of the year more Boy Scouts left to join the coast watchers;

BOY SCOUTS FOR COAST DEFENCE.- Patrol-leader M. Pearce, of the King Athelstan Troop of Boy Scouts, left for Polperro, Cornwall, recently to take up duty in assisting the coastguards at that place with the Swindon and Malmesbury combined patrol. Last week a call came to the North Wilts Boy Scouts' Association to supply a patrol for Porthallow. Two boys were selected from Swindon, one from Chippenham and one from Malmesbury. To represent the last-named place Patrol-leader James Henry Williams was selected. On arrival at the port he was at once appointed to take charge of a patrol of six boys – a compliment to his troop and Scoutmaster Perry. It is of interest that the other patrol at Polperro is in charge of a Malmesbury boy, Patrol-leader James Hibbard, who has had three months' service there coast-watching. He is shortly to take up munition work, and Scoutmaster Perry hopes to have the honour of sending another boy from his troop to relieve him.

At New Year 1916 the gift of a small purse containing some small gold coins was presented by the members of the Malmesbury Volunteer Training Corps to their drill instructor Company Sergeant Major W.G. Perry. The attendance record of members so far was reported;

MALMESBURY VOLUNTEERS
Drill Attendance Record

From April last year, when the Malmesbury Volunteer Training Corps was formed, to the end of December the following attendances at drill of the Headquarters Platoon have been recorded. ("M" signifies "marksman," 1 "first-class shot," and 2 "second-class shot.")

No. 1 Section – Platoon Sergeant H. Cordy, 38; Section Commander F. Weeks (1), 79; Pte. A. Box, 29; Pte. W.B. Carter, 35; Pte. F.J. Compton (1), 50; Pte. J.D. Curtis, 14; Pte. A.J. Denly (1), 45; Pte. A. Eatell (2), 78; Pte. J. Furber, 17; Pte. F. Golding, 47; Pte. A. Harris, 20; Pte. A.C. Mattick, (1), 37; Pte. R. Neale, (1), 30; Pte. W. Oliver, 45; Pte. F.B. Parsons, 39; Pte. F.J. Pearce, 46; Pte. T.H. Sandy (M), 37, Pte. F.W. Teagle, (1), 41; Pte. T. Smith (M), 18.

No. 2 Section – Orderly Room Sergt. H.J.S. Beak, (1), 75; Section Commander J. Box, (1), 63; Pte. E.E. Basevi, (1), 75; Pte. M.S. Carleton, (2), 52, Pte. J. Edmonds, 66; Pte. S. Fisher, (2), 62; Pte. E.D. Fursey, 46; Pte. J. Milliner, (1), 63; Pte. Wheeler, (1), 56; Pte. G. Alexander, 36; Pte. R. Roper, 39; Pte. J. Baldwin, 32; Pte. J. Sawyer, 34; Pte. A. Chester-Master, 25; Pte. R. Bishop, jun, (M), 26; Pte. Isaac Carey (on postal service).

No. 3 Section – Section Commander E.G. Bartlett, (1), 57; Pte. C. Barnes, 65; Pte. R. Bishop, (1), 40; Pte. W. Gladwin, 61; Pte. H. Iles; Pte. A. Lea, (2), 46; Pte. T. Pincott, 39; Pte. J. Pitt, 63; Pte. F. Pitt, 46; Pte. W. Rymell, (2), 71; Pte. H. Wilmot, (1), 60; Pte. J. Clark, (1), 45; Pte. C. Sheppard, 20; Pte. A. Day, (M), 17; Pte. J.A. Jones, 20; Pte. P.T. Gough, (1), 29; Pte. F.H. Smith, (2), 32; Pte. E. Jones, 29; Pte. W. Hale, (1), 13.

No. 4 Section – Quartermaster Sergt. J. Clark, (M), 42; Section Commander W. Jones, (M), 65; Pte. G. Deadman, (1), 63; Pte. P. Gladwin, (1), 53; Pte. C. Glastonbury, 43; Pte. C. Harris, (1), 58; Pte. W. Gale, (1), 34; Pte. Harold Jones, (1), 52; Pte. C.F. Moir, 48; Pte. W.W. Ponting, (M), 61; Pte. A. Watts, (1), 37; Pte. E.J. Pitt, 8; Pte. F.L. Newman, 34; Pte. W.C. Miles, 31.

The Volunteers needed eight Corporals, four each for the Malmesbury and Charlton Platoons. Ten candidates presented themselves at the Old Drill Hall on 16th January to take oral and written tests. The successful candidates were Private T.H. Sandy, 94 per cent, Private G. Deadman, 91, Private Vattell, 90 and Private H. Wilmot, 78.

Armbands to indicate that the wearer was engaged on war work were now being issued as reported in the Wiltshire Gazette on 20th January;

THOSE ARMLETS:- The loyal badge on the arm is a familiar one on the streets now, quantities being distributed during this week. But we feel sorry for the one individual who is continually being worried as to the reason why he is not the proud possessor of this badge of distinction. May we point out the reasons? This gentleman lives with his aunt, who thought the badge rather "plain," the crown was hardly "good" enough for her, so in the evening this enthusiastic lady set herself the self-imposed task of making an ornamentation around it of the rose, shamrock, and thistle in crewel work. The young man cannot wear the badge, and yet he dare not explain the reason why. Poor fellow!

Due to Zeppelin raids occurring throughout the country a special meeting of the Town Council had to be convened on Monday 14th February.

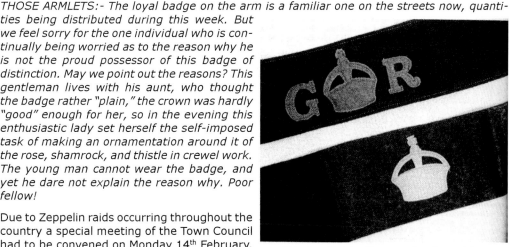

Volunteer Training Corps armband - scarlet on khaki with Derby Scheme below - red on khaki

Before the Ammunition Column finally left town one of the melancholy duties they performed was to take part in military funerals. Here, at a post war funeral, they have just arrived at the Cemetery with the Secondary School gymnasium (later the Cartmell youth centre) in the background. (Athelstan Museum)

The Home Secretary had issued a Lighting Order under the Defence of the Realm Act for the protection and safety of the public. Superintendent F. Witt, the town's police chief addressed the meeting;

Supt. Witt said it was his wish that they would be able to carry out the provisions of the Order without any friction. As a result of an inspection he had made he had prepared a list of street lamps which should be extinguished, leaving only a few lamps to be lighted solely for the safety of the traffic. Those that were to be left lighted must be painted and shaded so as to prevent any light being visible from above, and all other lights were to be shaded. He then read the list.

Mr. J.A. Jones proposed that the list should be approved, and thanked Supt. Witt for the great care he had taken in preparing it so minutely. As a Council they were naturally anxious to assist the police. They were all law-abiding citizens, and however much they regarded the necessity of retaining lights to which they had been accustomed they must recognise after the recent air raid the absolute necessity of something being done for the protection of the town and its inhabitants.

A long discussion followed covering subjects such as the opening hours of shops, the decisions of the Appeals Tribunal and whether to sound an air raid alarm. On the latter issue Mr. Bowman, the Fire Brigade Captain, said when the fire bell was sounded the streets were immediately crowded so that the fire engine was often obstructed. It was decided not to sound any alarm. Mr. M. Thompson was so concerned at this that he asked for the names of those in favour of this should be recorded *so that it could be seen hereafter who were responsible in case of damage.*

The Gazette had an article about the activities of our Scouts in their 30th March edition;

RESULT OF READING "PENNY DREADFULS."- A few weeks ago an exciting tale was published in certain papers, the heroic deeds of a Sea Scout, who was a member of the Malmesbury Boy Scouts, and who, it was stated, after an encounter with German spies on the coast, was subjected to cruel treatment at their hands. Some London papers also took the bait, and it is stated that the photograph of the boy was published in their pages. The authorities, natu-

rally, were elated with the bravery of the lad and soon made efforts to properly reward him for his heroism. He visited Malmesbury shortly afterwards, and – it is rumoured – related his thrilling story on the railway journey with such effect that a party of soldiers, who comprised his audience, entertained him on the way. He was also treated to tea at a certain gentleman's seat at Malmesbury, whilst an effort was on foot at the Technical School to give him a present of a more tangible nature. But "truth will out," and the boy has now admitted that the whole statement was a fabrication, without the slightest foundation in fact, and was only the result of a mild delirium from reading "penny dreadfuls." We hear that Mr. Bird, of Swindon, an official of the Boy Scouts, has had the matter under review, and the boy is now home at Malmesbury – As it has been rumoured that the boy's tale was printed in the Gazette, we take the opportunity of saying that there was no truth in the report. Our Malmesbury representative was informed by the hon. secretary of the Malmesbury Boy Scouts of the receipt by the boy's mother of the details of this "encounter," but that gentleman treated it cum grano salis; and our representative concurring, the readers of the Gazette were spared the trouble of reading the illuminating and imaginary epistle.

The drills of the Volunteer Training Corps were announced weekly in the newspapers. At the end of April it was reported that they had been taken by Army Service Corps lorries one Sunday morning to an undisclosed destination to carry out a railway reconnaissance. The accompanying article could hardly have given the public any confidence in their abilities;

"SOMEWHERE IN ENGLAND."
A Day With the Volunteers.

"Somewhere in England" last Sunday morning there were preparations in many households for the departure on important duty of the local Volunteer Training Corps. "Members must take mid-day rations" was the order and this was variously interpreted according to the gastronomic capacity of each member. From information gleaned here and there it appears that the wives of some of the "G.R." men had a bustling and worrying time in the preparing of the "mid-day rations." How to utilise to advantage the Sunday joint, giving her man a substantial proportion and yet stinting neither herself nor the children was the problem of a man's good wife. Perplexity gives place in some instances to indifference, because the good man, in his excitement of patriotic zeal, could think of nought else but his uniform and especially of the correct twist of his puttees, and could give his wife no aid in suggesting a suitable meal. Result – Bread and butter sandwiches, with the meat to come should he arrive home safely. If he did not arrive, thought the callous wife, so much more meat for her and the children. Then it was "Where's my water-bottle and haversack?" "Who's been using my belt to strap the kid in his chair?" "Gimme my cap out of the wash-house – how the hang can I keep it clean when the ole 'oman wears it on washing days?" "Look sharp, there's the bloomin' bugle gone!" And so on. At last the haggard but proud man sallies forth, a chunk or two of currant cake is added to his bread and butter, a drop of something stimulating in his water-bottle, and a double snack of "finest" in his tobacco-pouch.

In better arranged households there was scarcely less bustle, but the fare for the head of the house, who was going to do his duty for his country, was carefully sorted and packed, "Dad's" best-liked dainties were put in grease-proof paper, stowed neatly away in his haversack, his bottle filled with modest refreshment, and a handy-sized flask with a more potent flavour ticked away somewhere among his baggage. The last and sharpest finishing touches are given to his uniform – a well adjusted hero, a bit of fluff flicked off there by the wifey who bids her hubby "Mind you don't get hurt, dear," and the stately warrior, showing his devotion to the day's demands, dons his Burberry and makes for headquarters to be there punctually "on the dot."

Assembled in the dingy drill hall there are some stragglers to wait for, and meanwhile the prospects of having a fine day are discussed with no little apprehension. Various conjectures are hazarded as to the behaviour of the weather when the wind is in a certain direction or when old X's barometer shows a quick rise or a sudden fall, and the general hope is that rain and wind will keep quiescent for at least 24 hours.

Presently the "fall in" is given, and after some preliminary instructions the "Gorgeous Wrecks" make forth, ready to do or die, to take their place – standing up – in the motor-lorries, stowing their rifles under the imaginary benches. One or two of the most observant members of the Corps wondered how their A.S.C. chauffeurs came so suddenly to develop such superior-like qualities. They, of course, had never known what real duty was, for all they did was ride about in their lorries for all the blessed months the war had been on. And the home defenders proudly extended their patriotic chests and chuckled at the confidence reposed in them by the far-seeing authorities who had been obliged at last to seek their aid in preserving the homeland.

Off through town and country, mile after mile of rural roads being traversed while the gathering clouds, which were evidently of the spoil-sport variety, fetched up all their reinforcements and were clearly coming out to interfere high-and-mighty-like with the nation's work. Smoking and chatting in their chariots, which took fences and brooks with hunter-like leaps, making jerky breaks in the conversation, the closely-packed men in greenish-grey uniforms after a long journey, which to the most eager of them seemed interminable, arrived at their base.

There they found the others of the Company had been allocated to a base of their own miles distant. Disembarking in a wet country and marching across a field or two – or were they ponds? – they were halted on the edge of a precipice. At least, that's what it really was, though a certain cheerful soul who claimed to have had some experience of those things called it an embankment. The party was split up into two; the right wing being told off to guard the western area, and the left the eastern. We go to the west.

First of all, let us have the composition of our western party: "Section Commander, corporal and nine men." That was the make-up. The Section Commander led them down the side of the precipice to a level roadway, on which there were two sets of parallel steel rails. Since picturesque coaches disappeared from our highways these rails have been used by screaming contraptions which convey people and goods from place to place at a break-neck speed. It was necessary to send a fine body of men out on a wet day – to keep people from being run over, presumably. Anyway, down the track – or up, for there are "up" and "down" lines – we marched so gracefully as possible over sharp-edged flints and sleepers set at uncertain distances apart until we reached the base. There we outspanned, first dismissing one of the party to keep watch on a small bridge en route. Who was going to run away with the thing no one knew, but watch it he had to, and good luck to him, rain pouring as it was. He was not the only one, though, as the others were soon to find out, to be left on his lonesome keeping a bridge in its place. At the base bridge another man was posted with strict orders to push along any train that was late and to arrest any men, women, children or other cattle found straying on the land. We bivouacked there for a space. In any case we should have had to halt, for one of the party got entangled in his putties, which his wife had put on too skimpily, evidently thinking his blood would stop circulating if she fixed the spiral abominations on more tightly. All hands took a turn at the wheel – or rather the putty – and soon the caravan was able to resume its journey. Meanwhile the Corporal had taken out another man and lost him. That was on the north side or south, as the case may be. (Take it as you like, we aren't going to tell where it was for any number of wild horses). The remainder foraged around for a place of shelter, for by this time it had got uncomfortably wet, not to mention the leaking water-bottles which had become empty through the contents oozing out of the tops en route. Some tunics and breeches were stained, and although the effect was disconcerting to the wearers of the garments there was a fine aroma reminiscent of a brewery on near approach to them. And beer and porter such a fabulous price, too!

Presently we found what we wanted, a shelter from the stormy blast. (This is not a reference to the sergeant-major's language, but the weather). We commandeered a dug-out – otherwise a hut made of sleepers – with a fireplace (the hut, not the sleepers had a fireplace). To find wood and coal was the work of a moment, for we had with us a prospector with a nose more like a divining-rod for such things. Then we all went down the Str – no, the line – and soon a fire was burning brightly! If the shareholders of that line have to do without dividends next year it is to be hoped that they won't find out that we took the coal.

Whilst the three watchers were on the prowl for lost trains the remnant of us had lunch and smoked. Those who lunched last had smoked lunch. Then it was that we saw the furtive bites at the various "mid-day rations." And how various they were! The conclusion a visitor would come to would be that whatever else was forgotten, if anything, in our equipment, the commissariat lacked nothing.

Time sped along, and a few trains also passed, and then it occurred to the Section Commander to look out of the little wooden hut to see if the other fellows were still holding the bridges and metals down in case of a raid. Lo and behold! All three were signalling frantically for the relief. "Ship ahoy! Send us a lifeboat!" was quickly answered, and the Section Commander and Corporal risked a wetting by taking out the relief men.

Another hour of that, and then the march out to where the chariots were waiting …. Home again to loving hearts and hearths.

To those who have not yet found a job in this war, those who can't go to where the Bosche is active, let us commend the Volunteer Training Corps. Your King and country need you!

However the status of the Volunteer Training Corps was changing at this time which was renamed 1st Wiltshire Volunteer Regiment. New War Office Regulations meant that they would be liable for call-up if invasion was imminent. This had the curious effect of causing some resignations, including that of the Malmesbury Company Commander, F.G.T. Goldstone. He was the manager of the Capital and Counties Bank who stated that they could not allow any of their staff to remain in the V.T.C. Many of their men had joined the forces and they felt their business would be unable to continue if they lost more. Another member F.J. Compton employed by Lloyds Bank also had to resign although he remained the Assistant Treasurer of the Corps. Thus at the end of June 1916 the Herald reported ;

MALMESBURY VOLUNTEERS
"Signing on" Under New Conditions
SOME INTERESTING FACTS

Last evening the Mayor (Ald. A. Adye) again attended at the Drill Hall, Malmesbury, for the purpose of swearing-in Volunteers under the new conditions which have come into force by the application of the Volunteer Act of 1863. Government recognition having been secured at last, the hitherto much slighted and criticised "G.R.'s" now become part of the armed forces of the Crown – "soldiers of the King." Signing-on commenced last week, and the first batch of officers, non-commissioned officers and men numbered 31, all of whom duly subscribed to the oath of allegiance and made verbal declaration thereto in the presence of the chief magistrate of the borough. Last night the total was brought up to nearly 50 of all ranks.

Some interesting facts are connected with this important change which marks the passing away of the Volunteer Training Corps and the inclusion of the Company into the new Wiltshire Volunteer Battalion. When the volunteer movement was started in 1859 Wiltshire was one of the first counties and Malmesbury one of the first towns to enrol patriotic men for home defence. The first name on the roll of the old Malmesbury Volunteers at that time was that of Ensign Beak. Mr. Luce, better known as Col. C.R. Luce V.D. (who is fortunately still living and wonderfully active for all his 87 years) was also one of those who shared the honour of being in the first group of Volunteers in the ancient town. Now there is a clear link with those far-off pioneer days, for No. 1 on the roll of the new Company in Malmesbury is Orderly-Room Sergeant J.S. Beak, son of Ensign Beak, of the "old brigade." Sergt. Beak is the hon. secretary of the Company, and has played an important part by his painstaking and indefatigable work in maintaining the amount of interest shown by a goodly section of the community which has fair reason for terming itself patriotic. The individuals who form that section, whether members or outside supporters of the Volunteers, are sincerely grateful to Sergeant Beak for his praiseworthy efforts, and congratulate him on finding himself in the unique position on the roll occupied by his late esteemed father.

There are in the nucleus of the new company three instances of father and son having joined. Sergt.-Major W.G. Perry, Pte. Edward Jones and Pte. F. Pitt have each a son who signed on with them.

When the establishment is completed there will of necessity be numerous cases of fathers having sons in H.M. forces on active service – "boys" who are in the first line of defence, many of them being already war-scarred veterans, young as they are. In the new roll-book, so far, are the names of half-a-dozen such fathers who have one or more sons in one branch or another of the services; and all of those sons, too, are volunteers. Those proud fathers are: Sergt.-Major W.G. Perry, Corpl. G. Deadman, Ptes. F.W. Teagle, F. Pitt, E. Wheeler and W. Rimell. Of course it is well-known that Sergt.-Major Perry, the popular drill instructor, who has been the mainstay of the present company, is a pensioned Army non-commissioned officer, having a long-service record with the Wilts Regiment. Pte. E. Wheeler is another old "swoddy," with memories of the Egyptian Campaign of 1882. He was a sergeant in the Army. Sergt.-Major Perry has two sons and Pte. Wheeler one in the Army. Corporal Deadman has a son in the Royal Navy and one in the Army. Pte. Teagle's only son is an officer (Lieut. C. Teagle) in the Wilts Regiment (now on his way to a foreign country in charge of a draft of men). Pte. Pitt has a son on H.M.S. "Warspite," and Pte. Rimell a son in the Army, the latter now lying wounded in an Egyptian hospital. The foregoing is not a bad record for the new company, especially when the comparatively small number on the roll is considered. It should certainly stimulate Volunteer recruiting to have such a commendable list to quote before the movement is hardly on its feet. There is at least one instance also, of two brothers having joined - Sergeant W. Jones and Private E. Jones. One other member has had the novel experience of having served in no less than seven different units on sea and land.

Among the early signatories to the altered conditions are quite half-a-dozen farmers who live no short distance from the Drill Hall. They are proving a good example to other men who plead lack of time when invited to do their bit for home defence.

It is to be regretted that so many of those who joined the Volunteer Training Corps in March, 1915, have not been able, through no fault of their own, to re-engage on the conditions of Government recognition. Of the loss of Company Commander R.G.T. Goldstone and Pte. F.J. Compton mention has already been made in the "Herald." Unavoidable circumstances have also conspired to bring about the resignation of Sergeant J.G. Bartlett, Corporal H. Wilmot and Pte. M.S. Carleton. These have the satisfaction of knowing that although they are prevented from fulfilling their desire to help the nation to victory in one direction they will in the official work upon which they are engaged be helping in another not less patriotic way.

Others there are also who may not be able to see their way to taking the path owing to age and health reasons, and these unfortunately must inevitably include some of the keenest of the old members. But their moral support will, we feel sure be forthcoming, and there will undoubtedly tend towards influentially maintaining the principles represented by the existence of the Volunteers.

The following is a list of the first names on the new Volunteer roll up to last night: Company Commander A. Hopwood, Platoon Commander F.J. Bates, Sergt.-Major W.G. Perry, Sergt. F. Weeks, Sergt. W. Jones, Sergt. T.H. Sandy, Corporal A. Eatell, Corporal E.E. Basevi, Corporal G. Deadman, Privates F.W. Teagle, F. Pitt, F.J. Pitt, H. Iles, E. Kitley, E. Wheeler, W. Oliver, C.F. Moir, E. Jones, Harold Jones, T. Shingles, A. Smith, A. Young, H. Tidmarsh, H. Baldwin, J.E. Pitt, P. Gladwin, W.W. Ponting, J. Edmonds, J. Quarrel, W. Rimell, A.J. Denry, J. Riddick, A. Shail, W. Bishop, Robert Bishop, G. Alexander, C.F. Barnes, F. Riddick, C.G.H. Perry, G.C. Woodham and F. Wilkins. It is hoped that the full strength of 150 will be reached.

To try to make up for his disappointment in having to resign from the Corps Mr. Goldstone offered 'substantial' cash prizes to the two members who brought in the most recruits.

The Police quickly began prosecuting occupiers of premises that showed lights at night. The Gazette carried this report on 8th June;

The first case brought by the police in Malmesbury for an offence against the Lighting Order was heard at the Petty Sessions yesterday, the offender being Miss Doris Marion Gladwin, residing with her brother, Mr. William Gladwin, in the parish of the Abbey – Miss Gladwin did not appear, but her father proceeded to go into the dock until Supt. Witt stopped him. – P.S. Harris said that on Monday, May 29th, at 11.15 p.m., he saw a naked light showing from the window of a bedroom in Mr. Gladwin's house. No blind was drawn. He knocked at the door, and on Mr. Gladwin opening it, he asked why he had the light showing. Mr. Gladwin replied, "We were just going to bed, and we cannot go without a light. I shall not, anyhow." Asked who was responsible for the lights in that room, he replied, "My daughter, Doris." Witness saw Miss Gladwin who said she had toothache so bad and forgot the blind. It was 57 minutes after the time for screening the light. The Chairman: Why is not the father summoned? – Supt. Witt: The occupier could be summoned, but as he was down below and the girl upstairs we proceeded against her. – Mr. Gladwin: There is the lamp which was burning, it could not give much light (handing up a small benzoline lamp). – Supt. Witt: I don't object to the lamp being shown, but Mr. Gladwin is not summoned and has no right to make a

statement. – A fine of 10s. was imposed, and Mr. Gladwin said he should appeal.
The Chairman warned the public that future offenders would be dealt with more severely. –
Supt. Witt said several more cases were pending.

Four more cases were heard the next week including Miss Elsie Taylor, an employee of the Post Office, John Furber of the George Hotel and Nahor Riddick, a bootmaker. Also appearing that day was Frederick Newman;

Frederick Newman, grocer, 1, Oxford Street, was summonsed for an offence against the Lighting Order (Defence of the Realm Regulations) and pleaded guilty. – P.S. Harris said that on Sunday, June 4th, at 12.50 a.m. he saw a light in Mr. Newman's bedroom. After watching for five minutes he called out to Mr. Newman, and he then extinguished the light. – Defendant explained that he had been suffering acutely from neuralgia and Mrs. Newman got a light to fetch him a remedy from another part of the house. The light was only burning for about three minutes at the outside. It was quite an oversight that the blind was not drawn. – The Chairman: It may well have been an oversight on your part, but we must be very careful these times in keeping lights obscured. We shall have to fine you 10s. There is nothing for it, you must obey the law. – Mr. Newman: I think it is very harsh. – The Chairman: That is what we have done in the past and I do not think we can go against that.

In August the Town Council received a request from the Superintendent of Police to turn off the street lamps at 9 instead of 10 o'clock. Public houses closed at 9 and it was advisable to put the lamps out as soon as possible after that. The General Purposes Committee considered it was desirable that the lamps should be lit sometime in September rather than 1st October and turned off a little earlier in the spring. There were 32 lamps and the Town Clerk was authorised to negotiate terms with the Gas Company and report back. A contract was subsequently agreed to light the lamps from 17th September to 14th April with the exception of seven nights of each moon, for the sum of £75. They would be lit from one hour after sunset to 9 p.m. Unfortunately the moon did not always co-operate as was reported by the Gazette;

AN UNWELCOME EXPERIENCE. - Sunday was one of those nights when those responsible for the lighting expect the moon to shed her gentle light freely, but last Sunday the moon failed to respond, with the result that much annoyance was caused to pedestrians who were either going to their devotions or else out for a walk. There is a widespread hope that their inconvenience will be obviated in the future.

In August Lieutenant F.J. Bates became the commander of the Malmesbury Volunteer Platoon instead of Charlton's. At the first training session in command he remarked that he was disappointed with the attendance. The percentage of the total number of the Charlton contingent that attended drill was nearly double that in Malmesbury, despite the difficulties that village members had to contend with. This reflected very badly on the town.

In the Spring of 1916 another home defence force, the Royal Defence Corps, had been formed. This was employed in the guarding of railways, vulnerable points and, as a forerunner of the next war's Observer Corps, in providing early warning of Zeppelins and hostile aircraft. Unlike the Volunteers these were employed full time. In September this article appeared in the Herald;

ROYAL DEFENCE CORPS. - Men between the ages of 41 and 60 with experience in Volunteers, Territorials, V.T.C., or other military or Naval Service wishing to join the Royal Defence Corps, stationed at Weymouth, should apply to Mr. E.G. Bartlett, Roundmead, for particulars.

In October Thomas Grubb, 24 and married, from St Johns Street appeared for the second time within a couple of weeks before magistrates charged with desertion. Originally from Highworth, he had moved three months before from Brinkworth. He was serving in the Royal Garrison Artillery and said that he would continue to desert as he did not want to be a soldier. He was remanded to await an escort back to his unit. Just a short while later he appeared again;

DESERTED THREE TIMES.
Highworth Soldier Resists Malmesbury Police.

Thomas Grubb (24), a native of Highworth, and a married man whose wife lives in St. John Street, Malmesbury, was for the third time arrested at Malmesbury on Thursday in last week as a deserter from the Royal Garrison Artillery. He was brought before the Mayor (Mr. A. Adye) on Friday and formally charged.

P.S. Harris stated that on Thursday evening about 9 o'clock, when in St. John Street, with P.C. Ford, he saw Grubb walking towards his house. He had his tunic on his arm and his cap off. Witness accosted him and enquired whether he had a pass. Grubb replied that he had no pass, and witness proceeded to arrest him. Then there was a struggle, for Grubb violently resisted arrest. With the assistance of P.C. Ford, however, witness got him to the Police Station. This was the third time prisoner had deserted within a few weeks.

The Mayor, who remanded prisoner to await an escort, complimented P.S. Harris on his diligence, and said he would recommend him for the reward of 10s.

Grubb, it appears, has been in the Army about six months, but has taken an intense dislike to the life. He was formerly a farm labourer. He arrived at Malmesbury by the last train on Thursday evening, and had not reached his home when he was detected by the police-sergeant. Grubb, who declares he will not remain in the Army, had, he said, broken out of his cell at his barracks. He was escorted back on Saturday.

On 18th October 1918 there was an entry in the Roll of Honour stating that Private Thomas Grubb of Burnivale had been killed on active service by the explosion of a bomb. The Gazette reported; *Mrs. Thomas Grubb, of Burnivale, has had the sad news that her husband, Private Grubb, has been killed by a bomb explosion while on his return from posting a letter to his wife.* He does not appear on any of the town's memorials or at Highworth. The Commonwealth War Graves Commission records that Driver T. Grubb, 202474, 340th Battery, 44th Brigade, Royal Field Artillery was killed on 28th September 1918 and is buried in Peronne Communal Cemetery – was this the same man?

The Volunteer Act 1916 created three sections in Volunteer Regiments;
> A: men over military age,
> B: men of military age not yet called up,
> C: men under military age.

Members were expected to attend 14 one-hour drills a month until passed as efficient. They were then required to attend a minimum number of drills otherwise they would be treated as absent without leave. Later section D was created to cater for those unable to meet this requirement. In December this led to a number of changes in the ranks of our Volunteers as reported in the Herald;

VOLUNTEER CHANGES.- Under the new scheme whereby the Government has taken control of the Volunteers a change has been necessitated in the personnel of the non-commissioned officers. It was found that the Malmesbury detachment had too many n.c.o.'s in proportion to its strength. The explanation of this is that the appointments were made when the company was formed, and it was not then expected that it would become merged with the Chippenham and other detachments as part of a new company. Although in some cases the old rank has been retained, the status of other non-commissioned officers has been reduced. The new appointments, which have been officially announced, are as follows: Company Sergt.-Major W.G. Perry retains his appointment; Quartermaster J. Clark becomes Sergeant (No. 1 section); Sergt. F. Weeks and Sergt. W. Jones retain their appointments, but are transferred to Sections 2 and 3 respectively; Orderly-room Sergt. H.J.S. Beak becomes Senior Corporal, to have command of No. 4 Section, and Sergt. H. Sandy becomes corporal in the same section. Corpls. G. Deadman and A. Eatell retain their appointments and Corpl. E.E. Basevi reverts to the ranks. The net result of the changes, which of course, have taken place according to seniority, will be to consolidate the practical administration of the work of the detachment, and it is hoped that many new members may be forthcoming, and that Malmesbury, with the Charlton platoon, will have a full company of its own. The official announcement having been made that men who have been exempted from regular military service and have joined the Volunteers pending being called up for service with the colours, are not to count on the strength for grants or equipment, it is essential that as many as possible should join in order to achieve the desired end – a full company independent of the exempted men. There are easily to be found a number of eligible men more than sufficient to make up the full roll, and there has been a lamentable indifference to the importance of the movement. The almost criminal neglect of the serious warnings of Lord French must quickly give place to awakened interest, or Malmesbury will lose its hitherto cherished reputation for patriotism.

There was some consternation in the town about the times when street lights were allowed to be illuminated here and elsewhere as illustrated by an exchange at the Borough Council's January 1917 meeting;

TIME FOR OBSCURING LIGHTS
In response to a letter from the Council asking for an extension of the time during which lights may be exposed, Major C.M. De Gwyther, General Staff, Southern Command, wrote that the time for the reduction of lighting in different counties had been fixed by the Home Secretary, and that the competent military authority, Southern Command, had not the power to vary it.
Mr. J.A. Jones said it was strange that in Bath the time for obscuring lights was so much later than in Malmesbury.
Mr. Forrester: Bath is in Somerset.
Mr. Jones said it was the same at Gloucester and Plymouth. He also mentioned Cardiff and Bristol as cities which had brilliantly lighted streets at 6 p.m., whereas little towns like Malmesbury, Chippenham and Devizes, because they were in Wiltshire had to have all lights obscured. Another anomaly was that Larkhill Camp and Shrewton, where there were many thousand Australian soldiers, were also lighted up at 8 o'clock at night.
Mr. Bartlett said there was a system of warning there, and when that warning was given every light had to be put out.
Mr. Forrester: It is put out.
Mr. Jones agreed that there was strict discipline in those places; yet he considered it was strange that Wiltshire towns generally should have to obscure their lights at 5.30. He proposed that a letter should be sent to the Home Secretary asking for an extension of the time before which lights are to be obscured, putting them in the same position as Gloucestershire and Somerset.
Mr. Farrant seconding, it was carried.
Mr. Forrester had small hopes of any such request being granted. "We are only 16 miles from Swindon – that is the answer," he said.

A meeting was held in Malmesbury to raise money to add to contributions from elsewhere in the County to send parcels to prisoners of war who came from Wiltshire. It was expected that the Rural District (24 parishes) would raise £755 per annum and the Borough £95. It had been decided that each county should look after prisoners serving in the local regiment, so Wiltshire would not be responsible for those from the county serving in other regiments. However the Wiltshire Regiment had proportionately more prisoners than other counties and £17,000 per year was needed. A committee was formed to carry out the plan, comprising the Mayor, four Aldermen, the Chairman of each Parish Council in the Malmesbury Union, the Vicar of Malmesbury, Rev. Father T. Morrin (Roman Catholic), Rev. Emlyn H. Davies (Congregational) and Mr. J.A. Jones.

To reflect the enhanced status of the Volunteers a parade was held on Sunday 21st January;

MALMESBURY VOLUNTEER INSPECTION.
Lord Roundway's Good Advice.
NEW COMMAND FOR GEN. CALLEY.
Intensely cold weather did not deter the Malmesbury Detachment of A Company, 1st Battalion Wilts Volunteer Regiment, from turning out in fair numbers for inspection on Sunday, though there certainly might have been fewer absentees. However, allowing for those members who had reasonable excuses for not attending, there was not much fault to find with the muster, which was about 70. At 11 o'clock the detachment, including the Charlton platoon,

paraded in the old Drill Hall under the command of Lieut. Hopwood. It was good to see how well some of the members from the outlying districts turned up, some from Great Somerford, Lea, Hankerton, Brokenborough, &c., besides those from the farther side of Charlton, all having faced no little discomfort in travelling over the ice-bound roads. After roll-call and a preliminary inspection by Lieut. Hopwood the detachment was marched out to the space in front of the Cottage Hospital, and lined up facing the historic Market Cross. It had been arranged for the inspection to take place in the Cross Hayes, but the slippery condition of the frozen road surface forbade this and the idea was abandoned.

About 12 o'clock, the inspecting officer, Lieut.-General H.C. Sclater, G.C.B., Commander-in-Chief, Southern Command, arrived with his staff, accompanied by Lord Roundway, Brig.-Gen. C.P. Calley, C.B., M.V.O. (Commandant, Wilts Volunteers), and Major Allfrey (Commanding Officer, 1st Battalion Wilts Volunteer Regt.). When the party alighted from their motor-cars Lieut. Hopwood was introduced to the General by Brig.-Gen. Calley.

General Sclater made a close inspection of the detachment. Here and there he paused and questioned the n.c.o's and men as to their ages, professions, length of service in the Volunteers, &c., and he left a cheery word with each of those he thus examined. Addressing the detachment after the inspection, General Sclater congratulated all ranks on their appearance; there were so many among them with fine physique. He complimented them on their patriotism in coming forward, an example to their comrades and forming such a fine body. Evidently they were keen and enthusiastic to assist the country in the war. The War Office, he was pleased to tell them, was equally keen to encourage the Volunteers and to facilitate their training in modern fighting methods and trench warfare. He was fortunate in having Brigadier-General Calley, who would be of invaluable assistance. Brigadier-General Calley would have command of the whole of the Volunteers in Southern Command – 35 battalions – and the organisation would be proceeded with without undue delay. He hoped they would all support Brig.-Gen. Calley in the movement, and he wished them every success.

Lord Roundway also made a speech. He endorsed every word of praise that the Commander-in-Chief had spoken. Years ago, when he (Lord Roundway) commanded the old 2nd Wilts Volunteer Battalion, Malmesbury found him a company of men than whom there was no better in the whole county of Wilts, and he was proud of them. The present Volunteers were to be congratulated on coming forward and sustaining the reputation of Malmesbury men. He earnestly appealed to them as true Wiltshiremen to stick to their engagements as Volunteers. Doubtless they would encounter many difficulties, but they should remember that, compared to the hard lot of their comrades at the front, theirs was a "soft job." His lordship congratulated them on their smart turn-out and wished them every success.

The Volunteers obtained helpful instruction in bomb-throwing from Sergeant Middleton of the Cameron Highlanders. He was treated at the hospital for trench foot and during his convalescence found useful employment passing on valuable lessons from the front. He had ten year's service and was particularly skilful as the leader of bombing parties, gaining the Military Medal with two bars. In return for his help he was presented with an engraved silver cigarette case.

A few days later an aeroplane crashed at Charlton Park. It was flying to R.A.F. Rendcombe and apparently got lost. It landed in the park and the pilot Second Lieutenant C.B. Fenton questioned some estate workers to get his bearings. Just after it took off there was a report like the cap in a gun going off, the engine stopped and the machine fell to the earth. Both occupants were taken from the wreckage and Doctor R.M. Moore attended them at the scene. They were both taken to the Cottage Hospital where the Observer, Second Lieutenant B.F. Parsons died from a fracture of the base at the skull. An inquest was held in the Council Chambers, Silver Street where the jury returned a verdict of Accidental Death.

The local committee of the Wilts Prisoner of War Fund met in May 1917. A motion was approved; *That this committee ... desires to draw the attention of the Prime Minister and the member for the Division to the leniency with which enemy prisoners and interned aliens in this country are treated as contrasted with the treatment of our men who are prisoners in enemy countries – particularly Germany. While not advocating reprisals of a similar kind, the committee strongly urges that all prisoners in our hands should be placed on the lowest scale of food and comforts compatible with humanity.*

Further consideration was given to keeping the Roll of Honour up to date. It was said that a little more honour should be offered to the great many men serving at the front, many of whom had been killed in action. The Roll displayed on the wall of the Council Chamber was no longer appropriate. The matter was referred to the Council Chamber's Committee.

The Volunteers continued with a full training programme, with several drills being held every week. Weekend camps were also held and one such took place at the end of July. The Malmesbury detachment, over 40 strong, travelled by the 4.50 p.m. train to Chippenham. There they marched to the camping ground at Englands, joining the local unit and one from Calne. On the Sunday they drilled, practised attacks and fired on the rifle range. They caught the 6.55 p.m. train home. The following weekend Sergeant-Major Perry went on a musketry course to Tidworth, perhaps in anticipation of the Company receiving a Hotchkiss machine-gun. The Gazette reported how the Volunteers were being trained in the latest fighting techniques on 16th August;

VOLUNTEERS AT CHARLTON PARK.- Sunday's drill at Charlton Park was more than usually interesting. The Malmesbury and Charlton platoons assembled soon after eleven a.m. under Lieutenant F.J. Bates commanding the detachment, and Lieut. F. Worthington (Charlton Platoon). The fore-noon's work consisted of drill in artillery formation, a new movement in which, besides riflemen, bombers, rifle-bombers, and machine-gunners were engaged. There was an interval for lunch, after which platoon and squad drill was performed until three o'clock. The Malmesbury platoon during their march home encountered a heavy downpour of rain.

The black-out clearly caused problems and it is ironic that the Gas Works manager came off best in one encounter in the dark;

ACCIDENT TO MR. N. RATCLIFFE.- On Tuesday evening the streets were almost impossible to traverse owing to the darkness. Mr. H. Norman Ratcliffe, chemist, whilst on his way along the High Street about 8 o'clock, collided with Mr. Cookson (gas works manager) with disas- trous results. Mr. Ratcliffe was felled, and, striking his head, was rendered unconscious. He was carried into his house and was attended by Dr. Moore, improving a little later on. Yester- day Mr. Ratcliffe's condition was slightly better. His many friends will wish him a speedy recovery.

The Town Council discussed street lighting in September. Mr. Farrant said that the Saturday night before the meeting had been so dark that nothing could be seen other than the light of a man's pipe, he was never out in such a dark hole in his life. Mr. Adye observed that some lamps were painted too heavily so that the public had to pay for light they never had. In November Superintendent Witt advised that the Council was now required to extinguish all lights when warning was given of approaching hostile aircraft. Should they not do so the lights would need to be obscured more.

In September the Gazette reported the adventures of another Malmesbury man who had sought employment in the Merchant Navy;

THRILLING STORY OF THE SEA.
MALMESBURY LAD IN A TORPEDOED SHIP.
Not many young fellows have had the experience of the world as Charles, the eighteen-year- old son of Mr. and Mrs. Roper, of the Green Dragon Inn, Malmesbury. At the age of 16 he took to a sea-faring life, this was since the outbreak of war, during which the life of the seaman has become a thousand times more hazardous. His employment for the past two years has been with the Union Castle, and the Orient Shipping Companies, and the Atlantic Transport Line. It was whilst in the service of the latter company that he had the awful experience of being shipwrecked through the ship on which he was sailing as steward being torpedoed.
Owing to the rigid censorship we are unable to give details of the experience of this young fellow, but possibly the following facts may be related.

The ship was outward bound and the accident happened at noon when about eight miles from land. It was struck twice by a torpedo, which caused it to sink within the space of four minutes. The vessel was carrying a quantity of valuable bloodstock, including the celebrated race-horse Sunstar II, and the cries of the horses as the ship went down, were pitiable to a degree, the animals seeming to recognise their doom. When the crash came, everybody made for the boats, but there was no panic. The time between the impact and the actual sinking of the vessel was so short that only a few of the boats could be cut away, and of the crew of 150 only about 50 were saved., the majority of those reaching land on wreckage. The noise caused by the bursting of the boilers was deafening, and the spray sent up made a sight not to be forgotten. The ship sank stern first, her bow rising high above the water; the two Marconi operators refused to leave their cabin and went down with her. Meanwhile the crew, despite all their efforts, were unable to make use of the boats, not one of which got away clear of the wreckage. "I jumped off the ship to save myself (I was just getting ready to assist with the dinner), but by this time she was nearly level with the water. I swam for over two and a half hours, hanging on to a raft, before a patrol boat came to our assistance and brought us ashore at ___, which we reached at 8.30 p.m. Provision was made to convey the injured to hospital. We stayed at ___ the night, sleeping four in a bed; we only saved our shirts and trousers, and had to sleep in those, wet as they were, sufficient clothing not being available. In the morning we were fitted out with other apparel, and later on left for home, and I was only too happy to get back to Malmesbury again ... When I had got on the raft I noticed a pet monkey struggling in the sea, and I swam out and rescued it. When we got to ___ the keeper claimed it, so we had a toss up for the animal and I lost the toss – much to my regret ... Although a vigorous watch was kept by the whole of the crew for submarines, none of us saw the U-boat which torpedoed us."

Although passing through this terrible ordeal, Mr. Roper is still in fighting trim, anxious to join another vessel, and do his bit on the ocean wave for the Homeland. Our readers will wish him the best of luck, and Mr. and Mrs. Roper have reason to be proud of their son.

In January 1918 the Prisoner of War committee reported;

WILTS REGIMENT PRISONERS OF WAR FUND, MALMESBURY UNION DISTRICT.- The quota for the District has been collected and paid to the County Fund on November 30th, the end of their financial year. A list of the amounts collected in the different villages is appended, and the Committee wish to thank all who by collecting or subscribing have contributed to the excellent result. The need for funds is unfortunately as great as ever, and it is hoped that the district will again be successful in raising the sum asked for, viz.: £850, in the coming year. Amount received: Malmesbury Borough, *£96 0s. 9d.; Alderton, £25; Brinkworth, £127 17s. 10d.; Brokenborough, *£16 12s. 6d.; Charlton, *£37 2s.; Crudwell, £46; Dauntsey, £28 9s. 6d.; Easton Grey, £11; Foxley, £6 5s.; Garsdon, *£11 1s.; Hankerton, £18; Hullavington, *£60 17s. 7d.; Lea and Cleverton, £21; Luckington, £25; Minety, £44 7s. 10d.; Norton, *£8 7s. 8d.; Oaksey, *£30 3s.; Sherston, £55; Somerford Magna, *£125; Somerford Parva, £18 6s. 2d.; Sopworth, £9; St. Paul's Without, *£105 12s. 9d. - £831 3s. 7d.; sundries, £11 13s. 9d.; paid direct to County Fund, £25 6s. – grand total, £868 7s. 4d. Expenses, £3 14s. 8d. Paid to County Fund, £850 5s. balance in hand November 30th, £14 7s. 6d. Those marked * exceeded the amount asked for. Miss J. Luce, hon. secretary, The Knoll, Malmesbury

The large increase of prisoners of war following the German offensives after 21st March created difficulties for the Prisoners of War Fund. At the end of May their committee heard that the money raised to support their activities was encouraging but more was needed – there had been 1,100 new prisoners, so that 1,700 were solely dependent on the fund for food. The Malmesbury district had raised £279 13s. 6d. in around 6 months. The Hon. Mrs. Neeld had undertaken to pack parcels for 100 men at Malmesbury and she was already packing for 900 imprisoned sailors of the merchant service.

Following the great German attacks in France, the War Office reversed its decision to discharge Section D members of the Volunteer Training Corps. The men in Class D were those who were unable to sign the undertaking given by those in Classes A and B – to do a specified number of drills in each month and to remain in the force until the end of the war.

Many of them were considered useful soldiers who would give a good account of themselves in an emergency. It was estimated that there were around 100,000 D men across the country.

At the beginning of March the Chippenham Company of the Volunteers, including the Malmesbury and Charlton Platoons, paraded at Charlton Park. After a drill session rehearsing for a Battalion parade on Easter Monday the Malmesbury officer commanding, Lieutenant F.J. Bates announced his resignation. His doctor had advised him that he was working at too high pressure and that unless he slowed down his health would be seriously affected. Lieutenant F. Worthington, the Charlton Platoon commander now also took charge of Malmesbury's. The Volunteers' training sessions continued on a regular basis but little more of note was reported for a few months.

In the August of 1918 preparations for the darker nights required yet more consideration of street lighting;

STREET LIGHTING.
The committee appointed to enquire into the conditions of street lighting for the coming winter recommended that the lighting should be reduced to a minimum – 16 lamps instead of 41.
A letter from the Home Office stating that nothing could be done towards a relaxation of the restrictions, was read. The necessity for economy, quite apart from the danger from hostile aircraft, was urged as a reason.
The Mayor proposed that the report be adopted and that the committee be empowered to arrange the terms of the contract with the Gas Company.
Mr. Pinegar seconding, it was carried.
Mr. E. Jones revived the question as to whether the gas should be wasted as before in each lamp or the material painted on the glass removed and only half the gas removed.
The answer was that the police had the sole say in the matter.

Following this the Gazette reported;

TOWN LIGHTING.- The question of public lighting for the coming winter was discussed by the Council on Tuesday and referred for decision at the next meeting. The Town Clerk stated that the prospect of Malmesbury being bombed was more remote than ever, and some members stated that there might just as well be no lights at all as the inadequate provision made last winter. We agree.

The Town Council held a special meeting in September to consider the matter. Mr. Forrester proposed a motion that there should be no public street lamps, seconded by Mr. Bartlett, supported by Messrs. H. Matthews and F. Weeks, opposed by Messrs. E. Jones and F.T. Gough. Messrs. Adye, Farrant and J.A. Jones did not vote due to their interest in the Gas Company. *The resolution for "no lights" was passed so that the prospects for the immediate future are somewhat dark.* This did not end the matter, the press had frequent critical articles and a petition started by Rev. P.A. Smith the Moravian Minister signed by 300 residents led to reconsideration by another special meeting on 19th October. The petition called for street lighting *as the absence of light was a positive danger, especially to the older members of the community, it interfered with the holding of meetings, and it was undesirable that young people engaged in business should have to go to the dark streets for exercise.* The Mayor observed that not all the signatories were ratepayers – Mr. E. Jones stated that only two were not. The Police Inspector had also written drawing attention to the danger of dark streets and the inducement it gave to crime. The Town Clerk said that the issue could be re-examined if the Council ruled that it was an emergency. A quarter of an hour was spent discussing procedure until the Mayor remarked: *We don't want to sit down here and quibble all night.* He proposed that it was an emergency and Mr. Bartlett seconded, the motion being carried. Mr. Bartlett, despite having seconded the original motion that there should be no lighting, now declared that resolution must be got rid of. There was a long discussion on aspects ranging from the method for painting the lamp glass to the number of lamps to be lit. Eventually it was decided to light 16 lamps, the same as the original decision!

Just before the war's end a seaman from Malmesbury was released from internment by the Germans who praised the efforts to send parcels to prisoners of war as reported by the Gazette on 9th November;

The Hon. Mrs. Neeld, of Twatley House, and the numerous subscribers to the excellent philanthropic institution in connection with the Merchant Service, must be very pleased at the statements of Mr. Frank Feebrey, who is in Malmesbury, feeling fairly fit after a long internment in Germany, where he was sustained by the parcels sent with unfailing regularity through the agency of the lady mentioned and her willing staff at Twatley House.

Mr. Feebrey gave a very lucid and detailed account of the treatment meted out by the Germans to the 5,000 odd civilians who have spent nearly four dreary years in exile in Ruhleben Camp. He arrived at Hamburg on July 24th 1914 in a British steamer with a cargo from the River Plate, and some repairs being needed, the ship's journey home was delayed for this to be done. Unfortunately, owing to the engineers' strike, this could not be done with the usual celerity, and the ship had to be put into dry dock. Whilst thus detained, the war broke out, and after a period of detention, Mr. Feebrey was sent with others to Ruhleben, where he spent three years and six months on the racecourse for trotting, the stabling accommodation being supplemented by wooden huts for the reception of the 5,000 interned civilians of English birth. During the first nine months' internment the Germans treated these civilians in the most ruthless manner, the war all going in Germany's favour, and the designation of our fellow countrymen in this pitiable plight was that of "English swine." But the changing fortunes of the war brought little more humane treatment of the interred, and with the punctual arrival of the necessities of life in the Hon. Mrs. Neeld's parcels, things were better, "We looked forward to dinner-time to have a bit of English food."

Food in Germany, even in Ruhleben, must be very scarce, for Mr. Feebrey says the German soldiers were glad to eat odd remnants from the civilians' camp. He describes in detail the horrible treatment of British prisoners of war, and those who may still have the fatal weakness of thinking we should be "not too harsh on Germany" should have a short chat with the gentleman named. They would speedily be convinced that no treatment can be too severe to inflict on these miscreants, who have violated every law of civilisation.

We are sure our readers will wish Mr. Feebrey many years of happy life to compensate him in some degree for his four years' unhappy experience of association with the unspeakable Hun.

The 'peace dividend' was not long in arriving after the armistice, as the Herald of 22nd November 1918 reported;

THE VOLUNTEERS.
Enrolment Suspended.

The Secretary of the War Office announces that, in view of the altered military situation, it has been decided to suspend for the present the appointment of candidate for commissions in the Volunteer Force and the enrolment of men into the various corps. This will involve the suspension of all actions for the enrolment of men exempted by tribunals with the liability to join the Volunteer Force under Section 4 (6) of the Military Service (No. 2) Act, 1918. It has further been decided, with a view to relieving all ranks of the Force, whose time is in many cases fully occupied with their civil duties and responsibilities, of the drill and training obligations to which they are now subject as members of the Volunteer Force and to relax for the present the provisions of the various drills and training agreements into which they have severally entered. For the present, therefore, although training facilities will be continued, attendance at drill will be purely voluntary, and all action of a disciplinary character under the provisions of the Volunteer Act, 1863, will be suspended.

At the end of the year the Volunteers stood down from their high state of readiness;

MALMESBURY VOLUNTEER DETACHMENT.- Members are requested to return their rifles and bayonets to headquarters on Monday or Tuesday next, between 6 and 7.30 p.m. A smoking concert will take place on Thursday, January 2nd, at the Council Chambers, commencing at 7 o'clock. Dress, uniform.

Around 100 members of the Volunteers and their friends attended this event where presentations were made to two of the hard-working non commissioned officers – a silver tea pot to Company Sergeant W.G. Perry and a set of silver tongs and an entrée dish for Orderly-room Sergeant H.J.S. Beak. These mementoes were bought by their colleagues.

The Volunteers heard more about their future at the end of February 1919;

VOLUNTEERS NOT TO DISBAND.
A Period of Suspense.

The Army Council have addressed the following communication to the Lords Lieutenant regarding the position of the Volunteer Force:

"The original purposes for which the Volunteer Force was raised were to provide additional protection to the country from outside attack, and to replace full-time troops in the performance of certain temporary services. Owing to the altered military situation, these purposes have lost some of their urgency. Nevertheless, the general situation cannot be said to be clear, nor can our problems be at an end while the terms of peace remain unratified. A period of suspense is therefore imposed, during which the Council have no intention of breaking up an organisation which, by hard work and keen public spirit, has achieved a considerable degree of military efficiency.

"Although obligatory training and further enrolments have been temporarily suspended, it is intended to keep the Force in being pending the final decision as to its disposal, which must await the trend of events. The Council, therefore, appeal to all ranks to maintain their cohesion as an organisation in every way possible under the altered conditions. Whether the Force shall be ultimately disbanded or invited to form part of the home defence organisation of the future is a matter which cannot be decided at the moment. Meanwhile, as an immediate mark of appreciation of their services the Army Council had decided, under conditions to be laid down, that after the ratification of the terms of peace, volunteer officers shall be allowed to retain honorary rank on retirement, and the right to wear uniform on special occasions, and that other ranks of the Force shall be permitted to retain their uniform (i.e., service dress, cap, puttees, and regimental badges). The question of any further recognition of the valuable services rendered by the Force will remain for later commendation.

"The Council feel that it is due to the Volunteers that, as far as possible, they should be relieved of any anxiety arising out of present uncertainty of their position, and you are therefore requested to take the necessary steps forthwith to circulate the information to all units in your county."

The end of the Volunteers took place in a low key way without ceremony nine months later;

VOLUNTEER DISBANDMENT. – The formal disbandment of the 1st Volunteer Battalion (Duke of Edinburgh's) Wilts Regt., will take place on October 28th, when the Adjutant (Capt. Whiting) and probably the Commanding Officer (Col. Brown) will attend to distribute certificates and receive the equipment.

The Town's Hospitals 1914-19

Ten days after the start of the war the Devizes Guardian reported training of the Malmesbury Men's Detachment of the Red Cross Society. Members of the Women's Detachments of Malmesbury, Charlton and Crudwell had been detailed for duty at Swindon and Charlton House. The Countess of Suffolk, having just returned from Germany, had placed Charlton House with 30 beds at the disposal of the Red Cross with Miss O'Brien the local organising secretary busily engaged in securing hospital equipment.

However the hospital at Charlton Park closed only a year later and an article in the North Wilts Herald of Friday 15th October 1915 fully reports its achievements;

CLOSING OF CHARLTON PARK HOSPITAL.
A Year's Good Work.
Countess of Suffolk's Generosity

At the end of the present month the Countess of Suffolk's Hospital at Charlton House, near Malmesbury, is to be closed after having served a most useful purpose for exactly a year in the treatment and care of sick and wounded soldiers. The definite decision of Lady Suffolk to close Charlton House altogether for an indefinite period, owing to her ladyship having arranged to sail for India next month, has necessitated the change in the original plans with regard to the hospital. The Earl of Suffolk, it will be remembered, is serving in India as major in command of the Wilts Battery, 3rd Wessex Brigade, R.F.A. (Territorials).

By kind permission of the Countess and by courtesy of Mr. Aubrey Hopwood (private secretary), and Miss O'Brien (matron) we are able to publish some interesting details of the noble work done in the hospital during the year it has been open as an auxiliary to the 2nd Southern General Hospital, Bristol. When the war broke out the Earl and Countess of Suffolk were amongst the first of our English nobility to offer their residence as a temporary hospital. Miss O'Brien who had been superintendent of the London University College hospital was at that time in charge of the Red Cross Voluntary Aid Detachments in the Malmesbury district, and her services were at once requisitioned by the Countess as matron of the new hospital. The preparations made were on a lavish scale, for her Ladyship considered that nothing that could be done for our brave soldiers could be too well done as a token of gratitude for their noble sacrifice. Accordingly the magnificent picture gallery at Charlton House was stripped of its art treasures, many of these being priceless art paintings, and the capacious room, the ceiling of which was designed by Inigo Jones, was fitted up as a hospital ward. The ward, when completed, contained 30 beds, all conveniently placed to allow of free access to the patient, so that every needed attention could be given one without disturbing the others. The hospital as a whole was not, of course, confined to the picture gallery, but consisted of a self-contained block, cut off from the rest of the house, and comprising an operating theatre, nurses' quarters, lavatories, baths, etc. Everything that was provided was absolutely new, the equipment being the very best procurable, and no expense being spared in this direction. If we were permitted to name the sum expended, even approximately, it would stagger the general public who have little idea of the enormous expense connected with such a venture. Everything was in order to receive patients for some time, but the first patients did not arrive until October 27th. Later an electrical department was added, this enabling the staff to give the patients radiant heat baths and high frequency treatment. This proved a huge boon for by means of radiant heat and massage certain patients got well in half the time necessary without this modern process.

In the course of the year the whole of the accommodation has at times been utilised, but often there have been beds to spare. Altogether there have been 148 patients and most of these have been surgical cases, shrapnel and similar wounds, the remainder about 30 being medical cases. There were several cases of frost-bite in the early months of this year, and it is gratifying to know that the treatment of these was particularly successful, no amputations being necessary. Indeed the whole record of the hospital has been remarkable in having not a single death, and some of the cases on arrival were serious enough to all appearances.

Miss O'Brien assisted by four fully-trained nurses was responsible for the principal work of the hospital. Eleanor, Countess of Suffolk has been commandant, her Ladyship being indispensable in carrying out what ever duties were possible to her, and those were many, for she had previously become well-trained in home nursing and first-aid, as well as general hospital work in her capacity as Commandant of the Charlton V.A.D. To Lady Agnes Howard fell the task of caring for the men's clothes of which she has had the entire charge. From the time the patients arrived Lady Agnes looked after their clothes and saw that the soldiers' comfort was assured by having their clothes well-aired.

Miss O'Brien herself has been an ideal matron. Our representative was assured of this by many of the soldiers who had been privileged to be cared for at Charlton House. They were loud in their praises of the beautiful hospital and park, which they appreciated to the full. They had had cricket, bowls, and other outdoor games during the fine days of the summer and these largely helped them to regain their health and strength once they became convalescent. With all these advantages however, without Miss O'Brien's admirable skill and constant vigilance in the interests of her patients, they would not have progressed anything like so well and they were one and all deeply indebted to her. The discipline has been excellent. Of course the Matron has been strict, but that policy is always an essential to success in a military hospital.

As to the help rendered by the local members of the Voluntary Aid Detachment, Miss O'Brien paid them a high tribute of praise. "They all worked most loyally and well," said Miss O'Brien "and quite qualified their existence. They have been of the greatest possible use." These Red Cross members have worked in batches each one doing a half-day's work per week, and all having regular days. The Crudwell members have been mainly responsible for the night duty. The following are the list of the members who have helped.

Malmesbury Detachment; Miss Luce (commandant), Mrs. Ramsey (quartermaster), Miss Alexander, Miss G. Alexander, Mrs. Basevi, Miss Bower, Miss Brown, Mrs. Hugh Barker, Mrs. M. Chubb, Miss E. Chubb, Miss P. Chubb, Miss L. Clark, Miss Daniels, Mrs. Edwards, Miss Fisher, Miss R. Farrant, Mrs. Grant, Miss Gay, Miss Hanks, Mrs. F. Jones, Mrs. W. Jones, Miss Jones, Miss Jenkins, Mrs. King, Miss Milner, Miss M. Moore, Miss Pollen, Mrs. Pearce, Miss Smith, Mrs. Tabor, Miss Wilkins, and Miss L Wilkins, with Mrs. Weaver, Mrs. Teagle and Mrs. Gawthropp (attached for temporary duty).

Charlton Detachment; Eleanor, Countess of Suffolk (commandant), Miss Whiting, Mrs. Gwinnett, Miss Lea, Mrs. Pendall, Miss Sisum, Mrs. Davis, Miss Stratton, Miss D Law, Mrs. Shellam, Mrs. Law, Mrs. Cove, Mrs. Finch, Mrs. Porter, Miss Tait, Mademoiselle Eberlin, Mrs.

The picture gallery at Charlton Park with the ward full of wounded soldiers. (John Bowen)

Some of the modern medical equipment in an alcove off the picture gallery at Charlton Park (John Bowen)

Woodhouse, Miss Wilson, Mrs. Coldwell, and Mrs. Chester-Master.
Crudwell Detachment; Mrs. Whitcombe (commandant), Miss Clara Ody, Miss Pattie Chamberlain, Miss Alice Hislop, Miss Elsie Cuss, Miss Blanche White, Miss Esme Whitcombe, Miss Linda Godwin, Miss Ethel Roseblade, Miss Daisy Large, Miss Amy Redfern, Mrs. Sole, Mrs. R. Large and Mrs. Parker.
Mr. Hopwood told our representative that there is no question of the hospital being transferred to Malmesbury or anywhere else. When Lady Suffolk closes Charlton House her Ladyship's connection with the hospital ceases, of course, and whatever might be done to continue the work of an auxiliary hospital elsewhere in the neighbourhood would be quite independent of her effort. This explanation was due said Mr Hopwood, on account of a rumour which appeared to be prevalent in the town that what was going to take place was merely a transfer to another house in Malmesbury or the district.
To the generous benefactress many hearts are sincerely grateful for her noble work, and all will wish her Ladyship, when she leaves for the East, "bon voyage" and a safe return, once to resume in Charlton House, accompanied by the Earl and the family, her position as the Lady Bountiful of the neighbourhood.

The Countess had already visited her husband in India, returning at the end of April. She had only received 3s. per patient per week since June to defray expenses. A proposal by Miss Gertrude Luce to open a Red Cross Hospital in the Manor House at Burton Hill was not taken up. Colonel Miles offered the property rent free and Miss Luce made efforts to ensure that the rates and water charges would be minimal. However it was decided that the necessity for such a facility did not justify the expense of converting the house. It was decided to ask the committee of the Cottage Hospital at the Market Cross if they would consent to be placed on the Red Cross list as an emergency hospital should the need arise.

The decision by the Cottage Hospital to register as a Red Cross emergency hospital led to them being called upon when the large number of casualties started arriving in Britain at the beginning of the Somme battles in July 1916. The Hospital came under the control of the Red Cross on 26th July. At the beginning of July due to the shortage of ministers the Wesleyan Chapel in Oxford Street had closed. The Trustees allowed the ground floor to be adapted as a recreation room with a billiard table provided by the Y.M.C.A. as reported in the Wilts & Gloucester Standard of 19th August;

WESLEYAN SCHOOL AS RED CROSS HOSPITAL.- It is possible that the schoolroom and vestry of the Wesleyan Chapel – recently closed by the shortage of ministers – will shortly be utilised as a Red Cross Hospital. This will not interfere with any service which may be arranged in the chapel, as the schoolroom and vestry are on the ground floor, and admission is gained by a separate door – in Oxford-street. The arrangement, if made, will be temporary only, as it is believed that the chapel will again be fully utilised soon after Christmas.

That autumn more war casualties arrived for hospital treatment, more than 20 having been transferred from Bristol. Colonel Charles Luce gave permission in November for another ward for 10 patients to be opened in the Y.M.C.A. at Cranmore House (now Abbeyfield), to be used by the less seriously wounded. Eleanor, the dowager Countess of Suffolk, continued to act as a nurse in the hospital. Mrs. Alexander of Abbey Brewery House put her lawn and garden at its disposal. Soon the first floor of the Wesleyan Chapel had beds installed in it and it was never used again as a chapel, as the Standard reported after the 1st November opening;

NEW RED CROSS HOSPITAL AT MALMESBURY.
OPENING CEREMONY.

The need for greater hospital accommodation for our brave wounded has been increasingly felt for some time past in Malmesbury, and this need has now been met by the patriotic spirit of the Wesleyan Trustees, whose kindness made it possible for the Wesleyan Chapel in Oxford-street to be converted into a fully equipped Red Cross Hospital. Previously all the seats had been removed and stored by the Stroud Brewery Co., and all that remains of the furnish and fixtures of the interior are the organ, pulpit, platform and heating stove. On the ground floor the large schoolroom now forms the recreation room for the wounded soldiers, the Bible-class room has been transformed into an excellent kitchen and bathroom combined, and is equipped with a large gas cooker and all necessary utensils, a full-sized body bath, lavatory basin, etc. The vestry now forms the sitting-room for the day and night nurse, and has been suitably furnished. The new ward immediately overhead is approached by a broad staircase, and its dimensions are sufficient to accommodate 25 beds, the same number of lockers, besides other hospital equipment. These beds and their accessories were in evidence on Tuesday when the dedicatory opening of the ward took place.

At a large meeting held in the Assembly Room of the Kings Arms Hotel on the last day of February 1917 another expansion was agreed for the Red Cross Hospital. Already this had 60 beds, twenty five each in the Cottage Hospital and the old Wesleyan Chapel with ten in Cranmore House. Another "great push" was expected on the Western Front and, even without that, the number of casualties requiring hospital treatment was increasing due to the large size of the Army. Colonel Miles again offered the Manor House, Burton Hill, free of charge but the cost of converting it to accommodate another 25 patients was significant. Many individuals at the meeting pledged sums ranging from £3 to £10 and the British Farmers' Red Cross Association committed £400 to the project. The new Hospital opened on 6th June. At the opening ceremony Canon McMillan (chairman of the Cottage Hospital and Red Cross Committees) spoke, rather patronisingly;

The accounts of the Red Cross Hospitals were rather intricate, as they had to keep a very strict record of everything. Yet he was pleased to note that of all the accounts sent in from the Malmesbury Red Cross Hospital not one had ever been returned for correction. For that happy state of affairs all praise was due to Miss Luce, the commandant, who had a singularly clear and clever head, and all her abilities were placed absolutely at the disposal of the committee (applause). Mrs. Ramsay (hon. secretary of the hospital and quartermaster of the V.A.D.) was similarly skilled in everything necessary for the welfare of the patients, whilst the Matron (Miss Wellicome), who often held the balance between life and death in her hands, frequently triumphed by her devotion and skill (hear, hear). They might rest assured, therefore, that the hospital would be a success. More voluntary workers in the local Red Cross work which was so sadly needed were being appealed for – more personal help as well as financial – but if both were given they would be doubly grateful (applause).

There was disagreement amongst Councillors over the charge to be made for water used in the new Wesleyan Ward. £2 per quarter was recommended and this was proposed and seconded by Messrs. Forrester and Farrant. Mr. Bartlett considered it mean to charge at all as the War Office only paid 3s. per patient which did not cover expenses and the cost would fall on other contributors. Messrs. Adye and Duck supported this dissenting view. Mr. J.A. Jones said that the charge proposed was the same as that made to the Cottage Hospital and the Y.M.C.A. paid for the Cranmore House hospital extension. Mr. Forrester urged his colleagues to eliminate sentiment and treat the matter as purely business. After the amendment to make no charge was lost by seven votes to four, it was agreed to charge £4 a year.

A fete was held at the Manor House Hospital, Burton Hill, at the end of July 1917 to celebrate the anniversary of the opening of the Malmesbury Red Cross Hospital. The Mayor, Councillor M. Thompson, opened the proceedings and reminded his audience that Charles Luce had founded the town's hospital in 1889 and it was fitting that Miss Gertrude Luce was now commandant. There was a half day of sports activities including a tug-of-war when the nurses beat the wounded soldiers!

The work of the hospital carried on without let-up with frequent evenings of entertainment for the patients. Miss Ursula Luce was a star turn at these events – she sang and took part in comic acts, being able to speak in an excellent Wiltshire dialect. In late October the nurses received a little recognition for their work;

PRAISEWORTHY NURSES.- Posted in the Red Cross Hospital is a worthy tribute of praise to the V.A.D. nurses who have so bravely kept the Red Cross flying in Malmesbury and district throughout the course of the war. It is an order from the Commandant (Miss Luce) and runs as follows: "To the members of the V.A.D., Wilts 22; I congratulate Miss A. Bower and Miss E. Chubb upon being 'mentioned in dispatches.' In the early part of the year I was requested to send up a certain number of names from my detachment of those who had done at least a year's work, the work at Charlton Hospital to be included, the Malmesbury Hospital having only been opened a few months. I replied that where all had worked their best it was impossible to make a selection. The authorities insisted and asked for an immediate reply. I therefore took the names of those who had done night as well as day duty, and of those Miss Bower and Miss Chubb have been chosen. In the honour done to them the whole detachment is honoured. As Commandant my only regret is that I could not recommend every-one."

A couple of weeks later there was a large gathering of the members of the V.A.D. and Red Cross at the Bell Hotel for the presentation of Red Cross badges for those who had completed two years' service. Miss Luce remarked that 16 months before they had started with 15 patients, now they had 75 and she did not know if they would stop at that number. Badges were presented to;

Wilts 28th Detachment (Great Somerford), Mrs. Teagle; Wilts 18th (Charlton), Mrs. Scull, Mrs. Finch, Miss Stratton and Miss Cove; Wilts 20 (Crudwell), Mrs. Sole, Mrs. Parker, Miss Godwin and Miss Chamberlain; Wilts 22 (Malmesbury), Miss Alexander, Miss Bower, Miss Emily Chubb, Mrs. Chubb, Mrs. Edwards, Miss Fisher, Miss Gay, Miss Hanks, Mrs. Dorothy Jones, Mrs. Evelyn Jones, Mrs. King, Mrs. May, Miss Milner, Mrs. Pearce, Miss Pollen, Miss Smith and Miss Vous; Wilts 9 (Men's), Malmesbury, Commandant C.F. Moir, Dr. Moore, Quartermaster Perry, Section-leader F.E. Ponting, Bearers W.T. Clark, A. Clark, A.M.J. Duck, E.F.E. Edwards, E.D. Fursey, A. Greenfield, C. Harris, W.H. Lockstone, F.J. Pearce, H. Sealy, W. Sollis and E. Trevatt; Working Party, Mrs. Angell, Mrs. Beak, Miss Chubb, Mrs. Durston, Miss Pike, Miss Pitt.

The Red Cross made a profit of 400 guineas from a rather unusual source as reported in the Standard in December 1917;

ROMANCE OF A PIG.
Tirpitz, a pig with a history, is to be sold for the benefit of the Red Cross. Formerly he belonged to the German cruiser Dresden.

During the Falkland Islands battle the Germans escaped to the shore after causing an explosion, which sank the Dresden. Tirpitz was left to his fate, but on finding himself in the water he struck out boldly, and an hour later was seen swimming near the Glasgow. Two sailors dived into the sea and brought him aboard. The ship's company of the Glasgow awarded Tirpitz the "Iron Cross" for sticking to his ship after his shipmates had left, and he became a great pet on board.

It was decided to send Tirpitz home, but the regulations against swine fever caused difficulties over a landing, but a certificate from the captain of the Glasgow induced the authorities to pass a special Order in Council making the port at which he landed a place within the meaning of the Act, and Tirpitz was received at the gunnery establishment on Whale Island. Now it has been decided that as he is not earning his keep in producing bacon his sty should be available for more remunerative young pigs. On the instructions of Commodore Luce (late captain of the Glasgow) he will be offered for sale for the benefit of the British Red Cross at Grosvenor Hotel, Chester, by Messrs. Knight, Frank and Rutley, on December 11th.

In January 1918 the past year's performance was reviewed;

MALMESBURY HOSPITAL.
Annual Meeting.

Canon C.D.H. McMillan presided at the annual meeting of the Malmesbury Cottage Hospital yesterday afternoon at the King's Arms Hotel.

Mrs. Ramsay presented the 28th annual report of the committee and it was received with much satisfaction. The work accomplished by the hospital in 1917 had exceeded all previous records, the number of patients admitted being greater than in any former year. There had been 137 patients, whose days in hospital amounted to 4,905 – an average for each patient of 36 days. The out-patients numbered 104, and those paid 1,014 visits. There were 160 operations performed. The work of the district nurse was also felt to be satisfactorily fulfilling the requirements of the town and neighbourhood. Special attention was given to the important work of infant welfare, the rationing of the hospital had been strictly adhered to, exceptions being made only in cases of special diet, and in spite of the ever-increasing cost of food and all hospital requisites the financial position of the hospital would, the committee thought,

The large staff of nurses together with some of their patients in the Market
Cross with the Cottage Hospital to the left and the YMCA ward behind them.

be considered satisfactory. By the death of Lord Suffolk, killed in action in Mesopotamia, on the 21st of April, "the committee record with deep sorrow the loss to the Cottage Hospital of one of the eight remaining trustees and one whose name will ever be associated with all that made for the truest welfare of the hospital and the happiness of the inmates." Lady Agnes Howard having intimated that she would not put forward her name for re-election owing to her approaching marriage, Mrs. McMillan kindly consented to being nominated for the vacancy and was unanimously elected a member of the Committee of Management. The exigencies of war had once more caused changes in the medical staff. Mr. R.C. Pitt left Malmesbury in June on receiving a temporary commission in the R.A.M.C., and, the services of Mr. R.M. Moore and Dr. Aylward, who remain in charge of the hospital, were gratefully acknowledged. Congratulations were accorded to Capt. Heaton on attaining the rank of Major and his further promotion to the rank of Lieut.-Colonel while in charge of a convalescent depot in France. The work of the Red Cross being so closely associated with that of the Cottage Hospital, the committee included in the report reference to the large increase in the number of beds. At the close of 1916 there were 50, but these were now increased to 90. By the kindness of Col. and Mrs. Napier Miles, the Manor House had been placed at the disposal of the Commandant and Red Cross Committee and was staffed by V.A.D. nurses. There had been an increase of 15 beds, 10 at the Manor House and 5 at the Wesleyan Ward. The Commandant (Miss Luce) had worked unceasingly during the past year, combining with the arduous duties of her post that of Divisional Secretary of the Malmesbury branch of the British Red Cross Society, in that capacity Miss Luce organised the highly successful collection made on "Our Day." She also undertook the secretaryship of the French Flag Day and further arranged a series of first-aid lectures given by Mr. R.M. Moore for the V.A. Detachment working at the hospital, personally conducting the many practices which have had such excellent results. Also acknowledged was the faithful work of the sisters and nurses of the V.A.D. and of the members from Charlton, Crudwell and Somerford, and the transport work of the Men's V.A.D. Mention, too, was made of the night duty performed by the voluntary orderlies, organised by Mr. C.F. Moir (acting commandant of the Men's V.A.D.). a further helpful contribution is the weekly work party at the Wesleyan and Manor House Hospitals and the voluntary laundry work done by 24 women in the town. It was with much pleasure and pride to the committees of the Cottage and Red Cross Hospitals and to the whole detachment that the names of Eleanor, Countess of Suffolk (commandant, Officers' Hospital, Devizes), Miss Emily Chubb and Miss Alice Bower had been found "mentioned in despatches" in the October list of women war-workers.

"The committee desire to place on record once more the sense of their deep indebtedness to their Matron (Miss Wellicome), who combines with her well-known nursing capabilities remarkable powers of organisation, both in the management of the hospital with the present additional work, rationing and regulation of food supplies and her dealing with the many stipulations that arise from her control of three hospitals. Her services to the hospital and to the sick and wounded - civilian and military alike – are incalculable, and to her they are truly a labour of love."

Special mention was made of the resourcefulness of Mrs. Jones (King's Arms Hotel), in collecting funds.

The report concluded with thanks expressed to all subscribers and donors, the clergy of all denominations for thanksgiving offerings, the medical staff (including Mr. Pridham), the Hon. Secretary (Mrs. Ramsay), Mr. A. Chubb (hon. local adviser), Mr. F.J. Compton (hon. treasurer), Mr. F.G.T. Goldstone (hon. auditor), the collectors, Matron and staff.

The report was unanimously adopted.

On 24th May 1918 it was reported that Gunner Harry Hinwood R.G.A. was recovering in a London hospital from the effects of gas which relieved the anxiety of his wife and mother. By the end of the month 68 patients were being treated in Malmesbury, 35 at the Manor House with the remainder split between the Cottage Hospital and Wesleyan Ward. There was a sequel to Harry Hinwood's story – he was sent to Malmesbury Hospital. One of the injuries arising from exposure to gas was temporary blindness. When the bandages were removed from his eyes he recognised a lady who he had served in his father's shop and exclaimed, "Oh, Miss Luce, it's you!" The swift reply was; "Commandant Luce to you, Hinwood." Discipline had to be maintained!

The next month Miss E.G. (Gertrude) Luce, Commandant of the Red Cross Hospital, was made a member of the Order of the British Empire. Miss Luce normally walked from her home, the Knoll, to the Cottage Hospital but on Monday 11th Colonel Charles Luce sent his carriage with a convalescent Regimental Sergeant Major to break the news of the award to her. She was not aware that her name had been put forward and was more surprised when a phalanx of wounded soldiers on bicycles preceded her triumphal entry into the High Street. At the hospital she was met by ranks of nurses and soldiers drawn up around the Market Cross (perhaps the photo on page 55). By this time a crowd of townspeople had joined the celebrations. Mrs. Ramsay, Quartermaster and Secretary of the hospital made a speech in which she expressed her admiration for Miss Luce's hard work since the opening of the Red Cross Hospital on 18th July 1916 through to the present when there were 100 beds.

The Matron of the Cottage Hospital, Miss M.A.M. Wellicome, was awarded the Royal Red Cross in July. The Chairman of Trustees, Canon McMillan, praised her ability to combine efficiency with economy as well as her wonderful foresight in purchasing drugs and other medical necessities in the early days of the war. Her management skills were unparalleled and despite the largest wards being devoted to the Red Cross she had been able to treat more civilian patients in 1917 than ever before. A week later Miss Luce and Mrs Ramsay invited hospital workers, their dependants and wounded soldiers to a garden party at the Knoll. The main event was a children's fancy dress competition.

However when the war ended the work of the hospital did not;

WOUNDED SOLDIERS' DINNER.- Provided by means of whist drives organised by Mrs. W.E. Smith (Norton) a Christmas dinner was given to the wounded soldiers at the Red Cross Hospital. Hearty thanks were accorded Mrs. Smith, on the proposition of Mr. F.J. Compton, seconded by Mr. W. Teagle. After dinner the company, numbering about 150, enjoyed a well-arranged "social," Mr. Ernest Hill being at the piano.

RED CROSS WORK RECOGNISED.- In the Wesleyan Ward of the Red Cross Hospital last week, Miss Luce, O.B.E. (Commandant), made a number of interesting presentations. The first recipients were eight workers whose names were recorded on the roll of honourable service, and they each received a certificate signed by Queen Alexandra. They were: Eleanor, Countess of Suffolk (who was, unfortunately, unable to be present), Miss Wellicome (matron of the Cottage Hospital), Miss Harvey (matron of the Manor House Red Cross Hospital), Mrs. Woodhouse (head of the Charlton Red Cross Work Party), Mrs. Whitcombe (head of the Crudwell Red Cross Work Party), Miss Louisa Hanks (member of the Wilts V.A.D. 221), Mrs. Scull (member of Wilts V.A.D. 18) and Mrs. Stoneham (Charlton). Next an illuminated address was presented to Mrs. Ramsay – a gift from the Commandant and the V.A.D. workers. Afterwards, on behalf of the Red Cross Hospital Committee, Miss Luce presented badges and brooches to all the hospital workers. These included the V.A.D.'s of two years' service, special helpers, work parties, voluntary laundresses, domestic staff and night orderlies. Altogether there were about a hundred presentations. The official certificates were presented by Miss Luce on behalf of the Marchioness of Lansdowne (president for the county). Afterwards there was a concert, arranged by the soldier patients and all those present spent a most enjoyable evening. Sergt. Jordan, on behalf of the patients said the hospital helpers deserved all possible praise. In all his experience – he had been in four, or five hospitals – none was as well "run" as that at Malmesbury.

A further member of the hospital's worthy administrators was honoured;

V.A.D. QUARTERMASTER "MENTIONED."- The name of Mrs. E. Ramsay, Quartermaster of the Malmesbury (Women's) V.A.D. appears in the new list of ladies "mentioned" by the Secretary for War for hospital work during the war. Mrs. Ramsay was recently presented with an illuminated address by her detachment, and in it was described as "the best Quartermaster in the world." Mrs. Ramsay, who is a cousin of the late Earl of Suffolk, has worked indefatigably for the Red Cross hospitals. Her management of the nurses and supplies generally has won high praise from those in authority, besides pleasing the numerous patients who have passed through the hospitals. The whole community is proud of the distinction which has been awarded to Mrs. Ramsay.

In the middle of March 1919 one of Malmesbury's well-known local aristocrats returned home;

ELEANOR, COUNTESS OF SUFFOLK.
War-Time Hospital Report.

Eleanor, Countess of Suffolk, has returned to Charlton Cottage, near Malmesbury, after a long absence, during which her ladyship has been engaged in Red Cross work. She is welcomed back by the whole community, for she is beloved by rich and poor alike. The Dowager Countess's record of war work is a proud one. Continuously since 1914, with the exception of a brief interval, she has given of her best in order to serve sick and wounded soldiers. To the brave boys who came under care she was a true comforter and friend; she poured out all the sympathies of her mother-heart for their sakes. In spite of her own personal bereavement in the loss of her son, the Earl of Suffolk, who was killed in action in Mesopotamia, her ladyship kept on, bravely hiding her load of sorrow with an unselfish and untiring devotion in her noble work. From October, 1914, to October, 1915, her ladyship was Commandant of the Charlton Park Hospital, provided by her daughter-in-law, the Countess of Suffolk, at great cost for wounded soldiers. The Dowager Countess is at her best when she is nursing, and at Charlton Park she was perfectly happy in the great work in which she took so commendable a part. From January 31st, 1916, to April 13th, 1916, her ladyship was a staff nurse at the Military Hospital at Exeter, and from July, 1916, to October, 1916 was in charge of a ward at the Malmesbury Red Cross Hospital. From there she went to the Officers' Red Cross Hospital at Devizes, as Commandant, relinquishing the post on February 22nd. In 1917 she was "mentioned" for her good work. On leaving Devizes her ladyship was presented by the committee and staff with a handsome silver rose bowl, on which was the following inscription: "Presented to Eleanor, Countess of Suffolk and Berkshire by the Committee and staff of the Officers' Hospital, Devizes, in grateful recognition of her splendid work."

"Splendid work," indeed, has been that of her ladyship. By giving up her home and everything in the way of personal comfort for over three years to serve our stricken soldiers, she has been a great example and inspiration to English women generally. It is the warmest wish of every-one in the neighbourhood that her ladyship may be spared for many years and that she may have the joy of seeing her grandson the present Earl, take his place worthily as the successor of his greatly lamented and worthy father, not only at Charlton, but in the wider sphere of national affairs.

The investiture of Miss M.A.M. Wellicome with the Royal Red Cross by the King took place on Saturday 7th June 1919. Afterwards she went to Marlborough House where she was presented to Queen Alexandra, the Queen Mother, President of all the nurses in the British Empire. On her return to Malmesbury she supervised the discharge of the last soldier patients before the closure of the Red Cross Hospital on 14th June.

In January 1920 the annual report of the Cottage Hospital for the preceding year made reference to some benefits resulting from their work in the war. First they received a grant of £1,000 from the Joint War Committee of the Red Cross Society and the Order of St. John to be used to extend the hospital. The committee had agreed to purchase the old Y.M.C.A. premises in Cranmore House from Colonel Luce together with the XXX Inn (St. Michael's House) and two cottages adjoining the hospital from the Stroud Brewery for a total of £1,775. Alterations to these premises and repairs to the existing building delayed by the war would be expensive and it was fortunate that the balance of funds from the Red Cross Hospital amounting to £639 5s. had been transferred to them. They were still treating a number of disabled soldiers for which £142 had been received from the War Pensions Committee.

On the Home Front 1914-18

From the beginning of the war many schemes to raise funds for relief or actually provide comforts for the troops were started in the town. The Mayor and Mayoress supported the Prince of Wales' National Relief Fund and held the first of many meetings to further that cause. The Mayoress help set up the Women's War Guild which worked throughout the war.

A camp for Belgian refugees was established at Charlton Park early in the war. It was reported on 19th September 1914 that they would camp on the cricket ground using 14 tents and various buildings. 60 persons were expected but only 15 had arrived - five children, two women and eight men. The following week it was stated that ten more arrived on Tuesday night with a *destitute and dejected* appearance. One old lady amongst them recounted her story;

She was alone in her small cottage at Aerscot, near Louvain, when the Germans made their appearance. They did not harm her, and on leaving chalked on the outside of her door, "An old woman lives here alone; we can do nothing with her." Not long after another party of Germans proved to be not quite so merciful. They looted the cottage of everything and forced the old woman to run away for her life. Four days later she returned, and then found the house destroyed by fire.

The first week of 1915 brought more anxiety for people in the town when Messrs. Shuttleworth Ltd. gave their employees one week's notice of the termination of their employment at the Silk Mills. The Board of Trade confirmed that food prices had increased in the previous six months. Steep increases of around 15% occurred in August 1914 and then fell so that by the end of September the rise was 10% since July. The rises were slightly less in rural areas but sugar, eggs and fish had higher than average increases. The Government tried to soften the news by stating that price increases in Germany were greater!

The Malmesbury and District Belgian Refugee Committee, chaired by Mr. Aubrey Hopwood had their welfare well in hand by February 1915. Nearly £400 had been accumulated which was sufficient to care for them for another year or eighteen months without any further fund raising. 11 Belgian refugees had been relocated from the temporary camp at Charlton Park and had settled in Malmesbury, using dwellings generously lent them. Messrs. Ratcliffe & Son had vacant rooms at their foundry occupied by one family. Others were living in a house in St. Johns Street, rooms in Dr. Moore's stable and with the Misses Hanks in High Street. Another family was due to arrive soon and there would be no more accommodation available in town although Mrs. Lovell of Cole Park had room for three more. The originally proposed

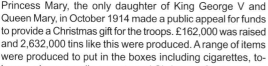

Princess Mary, the only daughter of King George V and Queen Mary, in October 1914 made a public appeal for funds to provide a Christmas gift for the troops. £162,000 was raised and 2,632,000 tins like this were produced. A range of items were produced to put in the boxes including cigarettes, tobacco, pipes, pencils, sweets and Christmas Cards. This example has its original cigarettes and tobacco. Distribution proved difficult with POWs not getting theirs until they were released. (Athelstan Museum)

total of 25 could not be reached because promises respecting four cottages had fallen through, two could not be used due to damp, one landlord objected and one was too far out – at Chedglow. In fact within a couple of weeks the total had risen to 24 with some lodging at King's House and others occupying a house in Holloway. Father Morrin stated that he knew of 102 refugees in the large parish served by our Roman Catholic Church.

The north west of the county suffered an unusually violent storm on Sunday 4th July 1915, with torrents of rain and hail. Many windows were broken but Fraser and Sons glass-houses at the Tetbury Hill Nurseries were devastated. Great stocks of flowers and bedding plants were spoiled and the loss amounted to several hundred pounds. At the same time there was some good news – a company had taken over the Silk Mills from the liquidators of Shuttleworths. Between 20 and 30 hands were employed with the expectation of many more. The factory was used for silk and fancy cotton weaving.

There were various ways in which the community tried to assist the armed services. The Malmesbury and District Vegetable Products Committee for supplying the Navy raised funds for its endeavours in the Town Hall on the 110th anniversary of Trafalgar. The Women's War Guild and others continued to send parcels overseas. A new effort to send comforts to the troops was outlined in a short piece in the Wiltshire Gazette;

TOBACCO FOR OUR SOLDIERS – Mr. Charles Bowman, Borough Surveyor, is engaged on the charitable task of collecting money with which to purchase tobacco to send to men of Malmesbury who are serving at the front, also those who have been so unfortunate as to fall into the hands of the Germans and be interned in their country. Mr. Bowman has at present 28 members on his book, each of whom contributes 6d. weekly, and he will be happy to receive the names of additional members. The tobacco forwarded is the well-known Anstie's brand – the sort men smoked when at home – so that a Wiltshire industry is in part benefited. The tobacco is forwarded by Mr. Heath Lockstone, and up to the present he has sent parcels to Privates J. Bowman (prisoner of war), T. Bowman, Ernest Thornbury, Jack Clark, and Ernest Peters.

A consignment of 650 Anstie's Gold Flake was sent to Private T.H. Bowman who used to be the midday postman for Minety, Crudwell, Charlton and Hankerton. Before Christmas the fund stood at £7 5s. and no further contributions were sought before the New Year.

It would seem that the A.S.C. men who were stationed here in October and November 1915 were not as well behaved as the local men of the Ammunition Column because the Borough Council had to restrict the opening hours of licensed houses. Notices were issued forbidding the proprietors of hotels and public houses to allow members of His Majesty's forces to be on their premises from sunrise to 12 noon and from 2 to 4 p.m.

In spite of the war ordinary civil activities continued;

MOTOR TUITION – There are many places in the vicinity of Malmesbury better suited for budding motor drivers than the streets and sharp curves of the ancient borough. Evidence of this was forthcoming yesterday when a car, being driven by a person under tuition, coming through Dennis Lane into the High Street, lifted a servant in the employment of Mr. Harry Duck, Cross Hayes House, completely off her feet, and landed her on the pavement in front of Mr. Hinwood's shop. Fortunately no serious injury was sustained. Later another car nearly collided with a cyclist at the top of High Street – again being driven for the benefit of a learner. Surely some other place can be selected for this tuition than the principal streets of the town.

Before 590 Company A.S.C. left Malmesbury, Second Lieutenant Frank Turner appeared as a witness in front of the Justices. A man who called himself John McDonall was charged with obtaining £1 by false pretences from 2/Lt. Turner. They had met in the Abbey where McDonall said he was a retired Captain of the 2nd Dragoon Guards whose bag and cheque book had not arrived so could he borrow £1 as one Army man to another? He admitted that he had taken the sovereign but said he intended to repay it. His claim to be an officer proved to be untrue. At the end of the hearing Superintendent Witt indicated that there was another complaint that was not to be prosecuted of obtaining £1 from the Rector of Devonport and 10s. from the Vicar of Corston as well as leaving the George Hotel with part of the bill unpaid. The prisoner asked for leniency as he intended to go to Canada and had a bad record through drink. The magistrates were unimpressed and sentenced him to three months' hard labour. 590 Company moved on from the Town on 24th November. The Council expressed its thanks to the officer commanding for moving out on a Wednesday morning so that the cattle market could be held! However they did damage a water pipe and although they had been granted free use of the water the Council decided to pursue a claim for £3.

The military continued to provide entertainment for the children of the area as the Standard reported in November;

AN AERIAL VISITOR.- An aviator from one of the military flying stations was forced to de-scend in a field off Sherston road on Friday morning owing to engine trouble in his biplane. The machine landed on a slope, and was too badly damaged to permit of another ascent. The pilot sent for assistance, and later in the day a party of men of the Royal Flying Corps arrived with a lorry and removed the disabled biplane. Many people visited the field to see the machine, which had broken stays and propeller.

In December 1915 the Ministry of Munitions introduced new regulations regarding the supply of gas. Mr. J.A. Jones informed the Borough Council that the illuminating power of the gas would be considerably less than in the past. This provoked some hilarity and caustic com-ments about the Gas Company's dividends but it was explained that the supplier would not benefit, in fact it would cost a considerable amount to install the plant to make the change.

On 9th December it was reported that the first lady clerks had been taken on, one each at Lloyds and Capital & Counties Banks. In order to cope with the Christmas mail Malmesbury's Postmaster Mr. H. Wilmot employed three "postwomen" for the first time. He was satisfied that the experiment was fully justified by the manner in which they discharged their duties. Bearing in mind the number of postmen listed as serving on the Roll of Honour it is remark-able that deliveries had continued without interruption before the recruitment of women. Each morning Mr. Wilmot provided coffee, sausage rolls and sandwiches for his workforce. The Standard reported;

LADY "POSTMEN."- Miss Nellie Paginton, of Bristol-street, and Miss Jennie Adye, of High-street, have been initiated into the duties of letter carrying and delivery, and as auxiliary "postmen" are filling their new positions very creditably. Each wears an armlet and carries her own bag of letters, and on these dark mornings and evenings the familiar bulls-eye lantern is an essential that has not been omitted. For the public spirit and enterprise these young girls are exhibiting we wish them good luck.

Two Belgian refugees, F.D. Van Sant and F.H. Wuyta, who had come to the refugee camp at Charlton Park and subsequently found accommodation in Malmesbury and Lea were arrested at Tilbury, Essex in February 1916. They had been working here but were anxious to return to their native land. They failed to get Home Office permission and sought to make their own arrangements. Unfortunately they entered a prohibited area and foolishly were still carrying the Home Office notice refusing permission to leave the country. They were fined £5 each and had to pay 5s. for the interpreter.

On 29th March a meeting was held in the Council Chamber to discuss how to get women to work on the land. In the chair was Colonel Charles Miles supported by the Mayor and Mayor-ess with all classes of the social world represented including a woman with a child in her arms! The Chairman remarked that when he was a boy plenty of women worked on farms but there were very few today. Mrs. Hobbs of Kelmscot spoke at length tackling issues such as were women strong enough - they could bring half-a-dozen children into the world - and arrangements could be made for women with children to work in shifts of three and a half hours. Mr. Rogers, a farmer, remarked that no man must do the work that could be done by a woman and in the Devizes district many women had taken up farm work. He suggested a committee of ladies collect the names of women willing to "deliver the goods."

The annual meeting of the Cirencester Conservative Benefit Society was held in that town. Although based in Cirencester it also had a Malmesbury Lodge. It reported that at the end of December 1915 there were 5,184 members of which around 900 had joined His Majesty's Forces. The total premium collected during the year had been £5,778 15s., whilst a total of £1,616 19s. 7d. had been paid out for sickness and disablement benefits with £477 for maternity benefit. Sick pay was set at three quarters of the normal wage and for serving members would continue for six months after discharge from the Army.

During May it was reported that many gardens in the district remained uncultivated and that it was necessary to make every small space productive as shortages of food were seriously threatened. It was suggested that by friendly co-operation it should be possible to put this right within a week or two before the end of the sowing season.

Further confusion came with the introduction of summer time as a result of the Daylight Saving Act passed in April 1916 reported on 26th May;

DAYLIGHT SAVING – Curious results of the alteration of the time were noticeable on Sunday, particularly in one or two of the places of worship. It is a well-known fact that elderly people, especially those in rural districts, bitterly oppose any innovation likely to interfere with their domestic arrangements or employment. The Summer Time Act does this in quite a revolutionary manner, much to the resentment of the old school. To mention only one instance, the situation last week at the Abbey Row Baptists Church was an example of the perturbing effect on the elderly people of the proposed drastic change in their habits. A meeting was held on Thursday evening, at which the coming alteration was discussed. The feeling of the elderly members was that the services should be held at the old times, but this was strongly resented by the younger generation, the pastor, we understand, taking sides with the "greybeards." No decision was arrived at, however, and when Sunday came the services commenced at the usual times, no notice being taken of the new Act. There were many absentees due to no decision being arrived at beforehand, and at the evening service the pastor from the pulpit referred to the inconvenience arising from the changed times. It is expected, however, that a definite agreement to adhere to one or other of the times will be arrived at, so as to prevent further misunderstanding in the future.

The idea was to increase the daylight hours available for farmers and to save fuel. In July the collection of waste paper was first reported. A consignment sent six weeks before had resulted in a cheque for £6 being received. The proceeds were credited to the Red Cross and Women's War Guild and further collections were planned.

An article in the North Wilts Herald in the same month shows that the reporting and measurement of food price inflation has changed little over the past century;

FOOD PRICES.
1½ Per Cent Increase During June.

According to the "Board of Trade Labour Gazette," retail food prices in the United Kingdom on July 1st were higher than on June 1st by 1½ per cent. Flour and bread were about 5 per cent lower. As compared with July 1st, 1915, retail food prices showed an increase of 22 per cent. Old potatoes were more than double the price of a year ago, and sugar was over 50 per cent higher. The advance recorded in the price of meat ranged from 17 per cent for British ribs of beef to 37 per cent for frozen breast of mutton, averaging about 2½d. per lb. Milk was dearer than a year ago by over 20 per cent, and the average advance in the price of other articles ranged from 10 to 18 per cent, except as regards bread and flour, which showed little change in price.

"Taking the country as a whole," the article proceeds, "and making allowance for the relative household expenditure, the average increase in the retail prices of food since the beginning of the war may be put at 61 per cent, which is reduced to 55 per cent if the increase in the duties on tea and sugar is deducted.

"These figures relate to food only, and in estimating the increased cost of living this percentage must not be applied to the total family expenditure, but only to the proportion which is expended on food. It should be remembered that rents of working-class dwellings are not

appreciably higher than before the war, and although many other items of expenditure have increased, they have not advanced on average so much as food. It may be estimated that the average increase in the cost of living of the working classes, taking food, rent, clothing, fuel and light, and miscellaneous expenditure into consideration, between July, 1914, and the present time, is between 40 and 45 per cent, disregarding increased taxation and assuming the standard of living has not been modified in view of war conditions."

A letter appeared on 1st September under the heading of *Belgian's Quaint Letter* – from a soldier who had stayed as a refugee at Charlton Park in the early days of the war; *Dear Friends, - After been wounded for the third time and to heale, I write you that I am back in the front to do my duty. Dear Friend, I was very pitty that I was in the impossibility to write, because I lose your address and I have got it from ――, which was with me in Charlton Park Hospital. Also dear friends, many thanks for your kindness that you have got for us when we are in the hospital at Malmesbury. With this letter I enclose my photo that I think it will be are very agreeable. I hope that you shall my to recognise; I am that soldier that has written that Flemish letter. My kind regards to ――, and it will be very agreeable to receive also her address to write her. In expectation of a little answer I send you my kind regards and best respects.*

In January 1917 the Council discussed whether there was any vacant land in the Borough for food production which could be seized under new powers. The Mayor stated that there was no recreation ground and no other spare land except perhaps the Water Works field. J.A. Jones suggested it would be a good thing to extend the Borough to include Malmesbury Common. The Mayor: *Malmesbury Common has nothing to do with this Council, nor has the Council anything to do with Malmesbury Common.* To which Mr. Farrant replied: *I hope they never will have anything to do with it; I should like something more lucrative.*

Food prices were continuing to rise and this caused some resentment as outlined in the following letter;

THE PRICE OF TEA AT MALMESBURY
Sir, - Will you kindly allow me to draw attention to the action of certain tradesmen in Malmesbury, who on February 24th put up the price of tea. This was the day after Mr. Lloyd George's speech – sharp practice! The tea, I presume, was in stock, and therefore did not cost them one farthing more. How considerate they are for the well-being of the poor, by putting up the price of goods at every opportunity that presents itself, thus waxing fat by squeezing the life's blood out of those who at the present time have the utmost difficulty in making both ends meet. These are patriotic Englishmen! Such conduct is mean and contemptible in the extreme.
> *Yours faithfully*
> *TEAPOT*

The Malmesbury Gas & Coke Company also announced an increase in the price of gas to 5s. (an increase of 2d.) per 1,000 cubic feet, less 5d. for prompt cash effective from 1st April. Also Adye & Son, grocer, was forced to suspend their delivery service after 40 years because S.A. Adye and their carter had been called up which had left a greatly depleted staff.

Entertainments continued with the Herald of 23rd March reporting; a Soldiers' Whist Drive in the Council Chambers; singing in the Wesleyan Ward of the hospital provided by Misses Ursula Luce & M.E. Alexander, Sister Woolford, Corporals Broadhurst & Rigby and Bombardier Phillips with a humorous sketch performed by Miss Gow, headmistress of Cross Hayes Infants and Miss. J. Box; and Broache Bill's Wild West Exhibition was to erect a mammoth tent capable of seating 5,000 in the Railway Hotel meadow.

The following advertisement appeared on 18th May 1917;

WE, the UNDERSIGNED, through CONTINUED WILFUL DAMAGE done to FENCES, CORN CROPS & MOWING GRASS, in our respective occupations, HEREBY GIVE NOTICE that from this date any person found TRESPASSING, either for bathing or any other purpose, in any Field in our occupation will be Prosecuted.

WILLIAM B. CARTER,
Arches Farm, Malmesbury;
EDWARD H. LOCKSTONE,
Milbourne, Malmesbury;
JOE MOORE,
The Castle House, Malmesbury;
ALBERT J. HISLOP,
Milbourne Farm, Malmesbury.

At the annual meeting of the Old Corporation on 5th June there was much discussion about an expected meeting with the Executive Committee for the Production of Food about cultivation of the Common. The Committee had the power to break up the allotments and cultivate the land as a whole, the cost of which would fall on the commoners. Mr. M.H. Chubb, Deputy High Steward asked if there was any desire that land used for grass should be put to corn. Several commoners told of their experience of planting wheat and barley only for the crops to fail because of wireworm. It was also said that neither the commoners nor the Trustees had sufficient funds to carry out much work. There was reluctance amongst the commoners to commit large amounts because they had no security of tenure on the allotment allocated to them. The general message was 'Hands off the Common!'

The war did not improve profits for businesses as was demonstrated when one of Malmesbury's grocers went bankrupt;

MALMESBURY GROCER'S AFFAIRS.
Trade Lost Through the War.

A meeting of the creditors of Alfred Edward Long, grocer and provision merchant, of High Street, Malmesbury, was held at the offices of the Official Receiver, Swindon, this morning. Debtor's statement of affairs showed the gross liabilities were £2,600 11s. 8d., there being 106 unsecured creditors, and £2,008 11s. 2d. was expected to rank for dividend. The assets were estimated to produce, after deductions for rent, rates, &c. £397 12s. 1d., leaving a deficiency of £1,610 19s. 1d. The book debts were given at £500.

"Expenditure on property, excessive credit resulting in bad debts, and the loss of trade owing to the war" are the main causes of failure attributed by the debtor.

The observations of the Official Receiver (Mr. J.W. Pridham) are: The receiving order and order of adjudication in this case were made on debtor's own petition. He is 45 years of age, and commenced business at his present address 21 years ago. He had no capital of his own, but borrowed the whole from relatives, and this money has never been re-paid. The unsecured liabilities include £1,000 owing to various relatives for moneys advanced to debtor, and there is an overdraft at the bank for £430 which is also guaranteed by a relative of debtor. Debtor purchased a half-share of the premises at Wynward about four years ago for £250, and he states he has spent about £100 on these premises. There is a first, second and third mortgage on his share, and there is not likely to be any equity. Debtor's business was very considerable, his banking account showing a turnover in 1912 of over £5,000. This had, however, dropped to £2,600 in 1916, and debtor stated that this was partly owing to the war. I am keeping the business going pending the meeting of creditors. I ought perhaps to point out that debtor has been unable to lodge a complete statement of affairs, and the figures are provisional only.

The price of the North Wilts Herald increased to 1½d. from 3rd August 1917. The same edition recorded the efforts of the War Savings Committee;

MORE THRIFT NEEDED. – Commenting, in the Parish Magazine, on the quarterly report of the Wilts War Savings Committee, the Vicar (Cannon McMillan) points out that Malmesbury has not come up to expectations in the matter of war savings. At the end of the quarter (March 31st) there were 12,000 members of war savings associations in the county of Wilts. The proportion of the membership was six per 100 inhabitants, and the average savings amounted to £13 for every hundred inhabitants. "The area of Malmesbury," says the Vicar, "is only just half the average of the county, both in respect to the number of associations, namely 3½ per 100 inhabitants, and just short of £7 contributed per 100 inhabitants. We

*need greatly to improve our position; we want more con-
tributors. The possible fighting strength of a country is
usually given as 10 per cent., the possible saving force
of the country should be in excess of the fighting force.
We had done extraordinarily well in this borough in con-
tributing towards the fighting forces of our land – it could
hardly be improved upon – but there is much room for
improvement in mustering the saving forces of the district. The Government needs all the money with which
the people can supply it; war savings associations represent new money." The Vicar added, in effect, that he
hoped those who did not subscribe to the association in
the Parish Room would form an association of their own.*

The Herald also had an exclusive report that potato blight
was rife in this part of the county. An urgent appeal was
issued to spray, as it was claimed that two-thirds of the
crop could be saved. Allotment owners were also advised to be on the look-out for the disease. The Gazette
found fault with the distribution of sugar on 30th August;

A Savings Card (Athelstan Museum)

*FOOD CONTROL.- There is an immense amount of work for the local Food Control Commit-
tees to do, for it would be difficult to name a district in which sugar has been so unfairly
distributed; proof of this was published in the Gazette some weeks ago, illustrations have
been given at the Town Council meeting, and in not a single case have the statements been
challenged. Many grocers have done their duty in distribution loyally and well, be this said to
their honour – but there are others. Numerous applications for sugar for preserving to the
Sugar Control Department, though posted in ample time, have been ignored, the applicants
receiving the typed reply that in so huge a concern it was natural that many applications
should go astray. That may be so, yet it is passing strange that so many went astray from
the Malmesbury district. Not only so, applications for sugar for stone fruit meet with the
same treatment. Half-a-pound of sugar per head weekly we are told is the maximum allowance, but we could cite households of eight, varying to ten and eleven, who are only allowed
two pounds of sugar per week, and this with the full complement of a grocery order for the
week's consumption. Sugar tickets may be a disagreeable innovation to some people, but
there are thousands who will hail them with delight, and possibly in no district will the
principle be welcomed more than in the Malmesbury rural area. We look, then, to the local
Food Control Committee to be energetic in the discharge of their duties, distasteful though
their efforts may be to some of the trading community.*

Local shopkeepers were finding it difficult to keep going when so many men had been called
up and were also concerned to show that they were not profiteering as this advert of 7th
September shows;

EDWARD JONES
JEWELLER, MALMESBURY

*Thanks his numerous customers for the favours of many years. He regrets to inform them of
the following facts: At present he is unable to accept any further Watch Repairs. Watches
sold by him under a guarantee of course will receive his best attention. He can undertake
only a limited number of Clock and Jewellery Repairs. One assistant has decided to leave the
town, and another has been obliged, through illness, to leave the business. The Jeweller's is
a restricted trade. The Controller of National Service will not permit the employment of other
assistants, except under certain conditions, and assistants cannot be found to accept the
conditions.*
*During the course of the war all Goods have been sold at this Establishment at the prices
they were marked when bought, and the greater number were in stock when war broke out.
There is still stock valued at some Hundreds of Pounds to be sold at pre-war prices.*

CUSTOMERS ARE ADVISED TO BUY NOW.

At least one local business had been revived;

FLOURISHING LOCAL INDUSTRY.- it is well to note that the local silk industry is in a flourish-ing condition. The Government have commandeered the whole of certain heavy qualities of silk which is used in the manufacture of aeroplanes and in other important services. Some very fine silk materials are being made locally for dresses as well as for furniture. Difficulties of dyeing have been surmounted, and now the finished goods are equal to the finest pro-duced in France and Italy. It is hoped that the industry will long continue to give employment to the local people, who have been so well taught in the art by skilled weavers from the North.

The concern over price inflation led the Government to introduce price controls and a new local structure was introduced in September 1917;

RURAL FOOD COMMITTEE. – A meeting of the Rural Food Committee was held at the Poor-Law Institution on Tuesday, Mr. F.J. Bates presiding. There were also present Miss Chubb, Messrs. J. Blizzard, A.F. Hiscock, M. Neale, E. Rich, W. Stinchcombe and E.E. Taylor with the Executive Officer (Mr. J.H. Bailey). It was reported that Miss Large (Crudwell) and Mr. G. Mann (Hullavington) had declined to act on the committee. It was therefore decided to ask Mrs. J.C. Ramsay (Hullavington) and Miss Hutt (Crudwell) to accept office. Mr. Bailey stated that he had received a large number of application forms from traders and householders in respect of the sugar scheme, and he had applied for a stock of posters, &c. for the guidance of the public. The committee adopted a scale of prices at which meat is to be sold, and copies of the scale are being sent to the local butchers and those trading in the rural district. The prices will become operative forthwith. It was decided to adopt the scale of jam prices issued by the Food Controller.

The scheme for fixing the price of meat was difficult to put into practice as the Gazette reported on 20th September;

This is the third week of the maximum prices for meat. The fixed retail profit of 2½d. per lb., or of 20 per cent. (whichever is the less), commenced on Monday, but up to the present neither of the local Food Control Committees has justified its existence. The local butchers are in a quandary not knowing how to act; whilst some have exhibited price lists, others have not, and the whole business is another example of the famous "wait and see" policy. One butcher in the rural area sent in a copy of prices he was charging, to the rural Food Control Committee, but at that the matter appears to have terminated, it being the opinion of the Chairman of the Committee that butchers should fix their prices and send them to the Committee for their approval. Such opinion seems totally at variance with the idea of the Food Controller, who lays down that butchers shall keep a record of all purchase, etc., and that the maximum prices retail shall not exceed a 20 per cent. profit, or 2½d. per lb., which ever is the less. So much for meat "control," from enquiries made by us, butchers are perfectly willing to fall into line when they have been given the lead.
As to bread, the majority of bakers are charging 9d. per loaf, delivering, for cash, and in some instances we have heard of credit for a week being given at the same figure. The Cirencester Bakers' Association (which governs the prices of bread in a large area of this district) have decided that no charge shall be made for delivery, but in some instances we have heard of this decision being ignored.
Obviously there is plenty of work for the Food Control Committees to do even now – and their duties will increase rapidly!

The Food Controller issued a Potato Order for the 1917 main crop towards the end of Sep-tember. The lowest price was £6 per ton, the highest £6 10s. for amounts of not less than 1 cwt. The next month the Ministry of Food issued two orders relating to the brewing and sale of beer. National production was fixed at 10 million barrels instead of 26 million. Beer with a gravity of less than 1.036 deg. could not be sold in a public bar for more than 4d. per pint. Beer with a gravity between 1.036 and 1.042 deg. could be described as Government ale and beer and not sold for more than 5d. a pint. All barrels leaving the brewery had to be marked 4d. or 5d.

The Food Control Committees sought to simplify the administration of control by fixing maximum prices as shown by the Rural Committee's advertisement issued at the beginning of November;

For the convenience of the public, the Rural Food Control Committee have caused to be reissued the following MAXIMUM PRICES of MEAT chargeable by Butchers resident in, or retailing Meat within the confines of the Rural area of the Union District of Malmesbury:

BEEF

Steaks	1/8 per lb.	Rump	1/2 per lb.
Sirloin	1/7 "	Chuck	1/3 "
Ribs	1/3½ "	Gravy beef	1/ - "
Top side	1/6 "	Brisket	11d. "
Silver side	1/5 "	Suet	1/ - "
Flank	1/ - "		

MUTTON

Legs	1/6 per lb.	Chops	1/8 per lb.
Loins	1/6 "	Shoulders	1/4 "
Best end of neck		Scrag	11d. "
	1/6 "	Breast	11d. "

VEAL

Oyster	1/5 per lb.	Chump loin	1/4 per lb.
Breasts	1/2 "	Fillet	1/7 "
Best neck	1/4 "	Knuckle	8d. "
Scrag	10d. "	Cutlets	1/9 "
Kidney loin	1/6 "		

PORK

Head	7d. per lb.	Hands	1/3 per lb.
Legs	1/6 "	Flare	1/ - "
Hind loins	1/8 "	Bellies	1/5 "
Fore loins	1/6 "	Chops	1/9 "

(Signed) F.J. BATES
Chairman

Nov 6th., 1917

Later that month efforts were made to introduce rigid economy in the use of food and suggested weekly maximum amounts of staple foods needed were published;

	lb	oz
BREAD		
Men on heavy industrial work or on agricultural work	8	0
Men on ordinary industrial or on agricultural work	7	0
Women on heavy industrial work or on agricultural work	5	0
Men unoccupied or on sedentary work	4	8
Women on ordinary industrial or on agricultural work	4	0
Women unoccupied or on sedentary work	3	8
OTHER FOODS		
Meat	2	0
Cereals (oatmeal, rice, &c.)	0	12
Butter, margarine, lard, oils and fats	0	10
Sugar	0	8

Bread should include all flour which would be substituted at a rate of ¾lb of flour for a pound of bread. Intake of other foods should be the same whatever the occupation.

At the start of 1918 the supply of food was diminishing. The U-boat menace was diminishing but had not been mastered, so greater controls had to be introduced, as recorded in 11th January's Herald;

FOOD CONTROL AT MALMESBURY.
Important Schemes Proposed.
This week has been a busy one for the Malmesbury Borough Food Control Committee and the Rural District Committee. Following a conference with the grocers, the borough committee decided upon a new distribution scheme, whereby tea, sugar and butter are to be rationed. Messrs. H. Farrant, A. Adye and W.H. Lockstone have been appointed as the executive committee by the scheme to act on their behalf, in conjunction with the Executive officer and a joint sub-committee.

Yesterday the butchers of the district conferred with the two committees at the Boardroom of the Workhouse. The butchers were Messrs. T. Rich, W.N. Redman and F. Day (Malmesbury), G. Woodward (Oaksey) and H. Porter (Little Somerford). They expressed their complete willingness to distribute their supplies of meat in accordance with the joint committee's suggestions. Furthermore they stated that they would close their establishments two days in each week, besides the usual half-day on Thursday.

The question of transport presented difficulties, but it was understood that if a working arrangement could be devised it would be carried out by the butchers.

The grocers would probably be able to effect some economy in transport. They have, in fact, been doing something in this direction for some time past.

The Food Control Committee have decided to inform the Divisional Food Commissioner that no need exists for a priority scheme for the provision of milk for children.

Agricultural production in the District was not expanding as quickly as hoped as reported on 25th January;

SPEED THE PLOUGH.
Disappointing Reports from Malmesbury District.
THE CULTIVATION OF THE COMMON.
Col. Turnor presided at a meeting of the Malmesbury Rural War Agricultural Committee at the Workhouse on Saturday. There was a good attendance, those present including Mr. A.L. Forrester (secretary) and Mr. T.W. Ferris.

At a previous meeting it had been arranged that each member of the committee should make investigations in his own parish and report on the prospect of having additional land put under the plough, the extra quota for the district being 1,200 acres.

The Secretary stated that he had received a report from Mr. Read, of Minety, who said he had received no rules or information as to whether or not it was compulsory to plough the acreage required. There was a considerable acreage in Minety of land which had been laid down to grass since 1872 but it was heavy clay land, very difficult to plough in time to produce a crop this year, but if needed for 1919 crops he thought it should be ploughed now. He also thought there should be a system by which every farmer should plough up some of his land. Most of the old plough land was now used for milking purposes. The whole of the Minety Common used to be under the plough or spade, but now it was used for dairy farming.

Reports were also received from Brinkworth, Brokenborough, Dauntsey, Hullavington, Great Somerford, Sherston, Luckington, Little Somerford, Lea, Hankerton and Charlton. In the majority of cases much reluctance was expressed by farmers to plough any more land. Some stated that the land was too heavy and unsuitable for the proposed cropping, whilst others said they had enough to do already. The promises altogether did not amount to 200 acres. Mr. T.W. Ferris said he was sorry to have such poor reports. It was not his wish to go round the farmers, but the position was they had those 1,200 acres to get and if they did not get it done voluntarily it must be done compulsorily. He did not see that he had received any assistance from the reports, looking at them from the voluntary point of view. It would not be anything like enough, because all the land recommended only totalled under 200 acres. The Secretary said it was 173 acres.

Mr. Ferris, continuing, said that they would not get more than about 400 acres, and that being so it was no use going on with the voluntary scheme, and that was a serious matter. They had all seen in the papers Mr. Lloyd George's speech in which the latter said "England must go on or go under." If they had to go under it was all their own fault (hear, hear). He and the others who had gone round the district had never seen land in such a poor state, this *was not only due to the season, but they had been asked to stock their land. The crop next year would have to be from new ground, not only in Malmesbury district, but all over the world. They would have to do what they were asked, there was no shelving it. Those who had gone round scheduling the land had been blackguarded, but they would do their duty. Every farmer was expected to do his share unless he had just cause for not doing what was recommended. He (Mr. Ferris) could say with the rest of them that he did not want to plough the land, but it had to be done.*

Mr. Matthews: The voluntary system is no good.

Mr. Ferris urged the members to each find out in their own parishes what land might be ploughed up.

Mr. Chubb reported on Malmesbury Common. He said he felt there was a very strong feeling that Malmesbury Common ought to provide a large amount of land. Most of them knew that he had been associated with the Common for a great number of years. When the thing was first raised over a year ago he went round and inspected every acre and made notes. He found that there were 150 allotments which had tumbled down during the last 40 years. There was about 200 acres and the owners were principally old widows of Commoners and old Commoners themselves, and he did not suppose that amongst the whole lot they would find a team of horses, probably not a donkey. Not more than half a dozen could afford to pay for the cultivation of their land. Suppose a tractor-plough was sent, they were all poor people and they could not treat Malmesbury Common in the ordinary way: they could not serve land-holders with an order to plough – they had not got the money. What the alternative was he did not know, unless the War Agricultural Committee took the land and farmed it, paying all expenses themselves. He mentioned that in Kent and Surrey the War Agricultural Executive Committees were ploughing up golf courses for the benefit of the nation. Whether such would be done in Wiltshire he did not know.

Mr. Ferris said the Executive Committee had the power to take over any land, but he would not say it meant Malmesbury Common. There had been a discussion about it at Trowbridge and it was considered whether horses could be sent to carry out the work. Another question was whether money could be lent to those people. Personally he thought more good would be done elsewhere where land could be brought in at once.

Mr. Chubb said his opinion of Malmesbury Common was that it was all couch grass. They might have good results on some land by properly treating it, but they might treat Malmesbury Common for 100 years and they would not get rid of the couch. All they could do was plough up and summer fallow it and clean it. It was very wet clay land, very badly drained. The draining process, he suggested, was only possible for a few weeks of the year when it was difficult to get labour. Unless they could do that he thought it was much better left alone. For the good of the country the land should be done, but the commoners could not be expected to do it as they were so poor. "Unless, the War Agricultural Executive Committee," said Mr. Chubb, "can take the land in hand, I don't think they will get very much out of Malmesbury Common."

Eventually it was resolved, on the proposition of Mr. Bates, seconded by Mr. Stinchcomb, that the matter of finding additional land for ploughing be left to the sub-committee with the assistance of the Rural District Council.

At the end of January a joint meeting of the two Food Control Committees was held to discuss preparations for rationing. A scheme had been proposed at a conference held by the Food Commissioner in Swindon but each local committee had to implement it. Tea, margarine and butter were the first commodities to be controlled. A sub-committee was set up to put forward proposals. The full time Executive Officer, J.H. Bailey had resigned and it was resolved to appoint Mr. T.H. Sandy. He would act for both committees and two thirds of his salary of £200 would be paid by the Rural Committee with the balance paid by the Borough. At the same time Adye & Son announced that they were forced to close all day on Thursday due to lack of staff.

Compulsory rationing was introduced in February. It had been found that different standards applied in different parts of the country. A commentator in the Herald remarked; *That compulsory rationing means a loss of individuality can scarcely be denied. It means an accompanying paraphernalia of cards, Inspectors, new laws, and all the necessary evils that are an*

adjunct of the imposing of a new rule in the State. But it also means that seething dissatis-
faction of the poor man against his more wealthy brother disappears. In fact he will, as
generally performing the heaviest labour, be better off, as he will be accorded a bigger
proportion of food. Utopia come to stay is the newest and grandest factor of a terrible war.
The local arrangements for implementation were set out by the sub-committee of the two
Food Control Committees on 20th February and the first advertisement appeared in the Gazette of the 23rd. Application forms would be sent out before 1st March, those to householders
being distributed by the Post Office. The forms would have to be returned by 8th for them to
be registered with retailers by the 18th and the scheme would start on 25th March.

The Borough Food Control Committee received a complimentary letter from Miss Luce, the
Hospital's Commandant; *Will you kindly tell all present how very much I appreciate the*
kindness and generous spirit which all the people in Malmesbury have shown to the hospi-
tals? The trades-people have one and all done everything they can to make our catering as
easy as possible, and though I am afraid this giving of priority to the hospitals, in the matter
of margarine especially, may make it hard for the ordinary population. I feel sure they will
help us here, too, and that we shall none of us mind going without some of the things we
need for the sake of the men who have been in the trenches on our behalf. The committee
was satisfied that the scheme was working so well. The meeting also considered an application from a restaurant operator who asked for increased sugar because of the large number
of teas he provided. This request was refused because the Public Meals Order instructed that
supplies could not be made to caterers who served teas only.

The Local Food Office moved to 45 High Street and issued the following adverts;

MALMESBURY & DISTRICT FOOD CONTROL RATIONING SCHEME
SUGAR FOR JAM
THE DATE for the RETURN of APPLICATIONS for SUGAR for JAM has been EXTENDED to
APRIL 11th. It is hoped that a further supply of forms will be available by Saturday, April
6th.
ASK YOUR DISTRICT COUNCILLOR FOR ONE, or apply to:
T.H. SANDY
Executive Officer
Food Office, Malmesbury

And;

MALMESBURY & DISTRICT FOOD CONTROL RATIONING SCHEME
URGENT NOTICE
Unless all Persons holding RATION CARDS ARE REGISTERED with Butchers, Butter and Mar-
garine Retailers, NO SUPPLIES of Meat, Butter or Margarine CAN BE GUARANTEED to them
NEXT WEEK, when the Rationing Scheme commences.
T.H. SANDY
Executive Officer
Food Office, Malmesbury
April 5th, 1918

The Rural District Council appointed Mr. T.H. Sandy as Executive Officer early in February to
deal with the control of coal supplies. A great deal of trouble was anticipated in regulating
prices and the early appointment was necessary to take action as quickly as possible.

The Gazette drew attention to a particular shortage;

SCARCITY OF BEER.- The oldest inhabitant cannot recall such an Easter as that just passed,
with a total absence of all festivities – and beer. Many licensed houses were closed entirely,
having nothing to sell, neither beer, stout, ale, all spirituous liquors; numerous other licen-
sees had only ale to offer their customers. We are aware of the reasons which cause the
Government to so drastically restrict the output of the breweries, - we trust those are the
only reasons, and that the situation is not being used to forward the cause of Prohibition as
such. But we do protest if rural districts are not receiving their fair share of what beer is
brewed, and there is reason to believe that is the case. The agricultural worker does not

envy his brother engaged in ship building or in the munition factory, but he cannot agree that these classes have a claim superior to his own and should be allowed to have beer ad lib, much of it brewed in the local towns and sent to large centres for consumption, whilst he cannot get a pint for his dinner when following the plough, in the harvest or hay field, or for his supper at home. And who shall say he is wrong? The agricultural worker is in this crisis is as important to the State as the munition worker and the shipwright, his work also is physically exhausting; and he has a claim to equality of treatment in the matter of beer allowance as in the matter of meat rations. Perhaps our Member will ask a question in the House to elicit if the Government realises this.

The heavy loss of life in 1917 was reflected in the annual report of the Cirencester Conservative Benefit Society. During that year 169 members had died, 50% more than 1916 and 121 of them were soldiers. The total death benefit paid was £3,087 16s. 7d. Despite this, membership rose from 6,832 to 6,894 and the largest ever annual surplus was declared, £1,205 12s 11d.

The Willts and Gloucester Standard on 6th April reported another aeroplane incident with an interesting twist at the end;

PLANE DOWN.- A small army biplane came down safely in the Worthys on Tuesday morning, a pilot and observer being aboard. The flier was forced to descend owing to engine defects, and the machine was stationary till the following day, a new engine having to be installed. We understand this was the machine's trial trip. Rumours are current that an aerodrome is to be established in the Worthys – an ideal spot for airmen – but these lack authoritative evidence.

The Malmesbury branch of the National Farmers Union met at the beginning of April. The Chairman expressed regret that the organisation was not called the Agricultural Union with labourers as members. The main business was a discussion about the Education Bill. Its chief proposal was to increase the school leaving age to 16. Whilst anxious that any boy or girl showing mental ability should be given the means of improving his social standing, it was futile to keep every boy at school until he attained the age of 16. They unanimously passed a resolution expressing its empathic protest against the Education Bill on the ground that at this critical juncture of the nation's peril in regard to our food supply every available lad should be given the opportunity of assisting the country's needs in additional culture of the land … When the Act was passed the leaving age increased from 12 to 14.

The struggle to provide finance for the war was given greater impetus by the successful German attacks in France. A War-Bond Week was held in the town during May to try to raise £200,000. Colonel Napier Miles chaired a meeting in the Council Chamber. It was addressed by George Terrell M.P. who recounted his recent experiences in Paris, how the Parisians were in no way panic stricken and they made light of the bombardment by 'Big Bertha.'

Only a few days later on 25th May 1918 Malmesbury lost one of its most prominent citizens;

DEATH OF COL. C. NAPIER MILES.
A Gallant Soldier Mourned.
Impressive Malmesbury Funeral.
A long time will elapse before Malmesbury people, and a good many others besides, will be able to realise that Colonel C. Napier Miles, C.B., M.V.O., is no more. At the age of 64 years he passed away on Saturday morning, after an operation for appendicitis, at Ingelburne Manor, Malmesbury. His end was sudden and quite unexpected, for early last week he was about as usual, apparently in ordinary health.
Colonel Miles was born in April, 1854, the son of the late Colonel Charles William Miles, formerly M.P. for Malmesbury, whose eldest son he was. He joined the Army in 1876 and retired as Colonel of the 1st Life Guards in 1902. His career in the service was eventful and brilliant, culminating in his receiving high honours from his Sovereign. He had passed into the Army from the Militia at the time when commissions were first closed to purchase. He took part in the Egyptian Expedition of 1882, being present at the actions of Magfar and Mahiamah, both actions at Kassasain, the battle of Tel-el-Kebir, and the march to and occu-

pation of Cairo. For that service he received the medal with clasp and bronze star. In the South African War he further distinguished himself. He went out in January, 1900, to take over the command of a composite regiment of Household Cavalry, and was present at the operations in the Transvaal, west of Pretoria, including the action of Eland's River. In the operations in Orange-River Colony he took part in the actions at Bethlehem and Wittebergen, and for his services was mentioned in despatches and received the Queen's Medal with three clasps. The gallant officer was made a C.B. in 1900, and received the M.V.O. (4th class) in the following year. In November, 1901, he returned home and there was great rejoicing at his welcome home to Burton Hill.

The late Colonel Miles married, in 1880, Miss Emily Georgiana Spicer, of Spye Park, Wilts, whose brother, Colonel Spicer, now resides there. Colonel Miles' father died on October 4th, 1892. The latter's father was Mr. Philip John Miles, a wealthy Bristol banker, who left eight sons. Colonel Miles' only surviving brother - there are three sisters, is Mr. Audley Charles Miles, who succeeds. The next heir is Mr. Thomas Gordon Audley Miles, now in the Army holding an important position connected with railway operations in France. Mr. Gordon Miles married Lady Joan Stuart-Wortley, daughter of the Earl of Wharncliffe.

The late Colonel Miles was an ardent follower of the Duke of Beaufort's Hounds, and regularly hunted with the Badminton pack. The Duke and he were inseparable at all the meets. Indeed, apart from the great sport they so much enjoyed together, they were close friends for very many years.

In local public life Colonel Miles was always useful in whatever movement he favoured. For politics he cared but little, we believe, he seemed at times to enjoy watching the game rather than being an active participant. Certainly no-one ever had a keener perception than he of the humorous side of party politics. At the same time he was ever a serious patriot and a loyal up-holder of British traditions, and especially our traditional constitution. His was a personality that typified England, for he loved his King, his Church and his country in the true English way. Ever genial and courteous, kind-hearted and generous, he was beloved by all, and by none more than by his lowliest servant or cottage tenant. His "gentlemanliness" was natural; he was gracious without being patronising, and he had a ready ear for the pleadings of the distressed. Enhancing his extremely charming personality was his striking appearance – his "good looks." It was reputed that he was in his day the handsomest officer in the British army. Colonel Miles maintained his attractiveness to the last, despite the fact that he frequently suffered pain, which many men would have found too intense to bear.

Malmesbury could ill afford to lose Colonel Miles. To every true Malmesburian the Old Corporation is an institution which has no equal in its ancient associations and in its pride of place among the glories of byegone days. Second only to the unique institution itself Malmesbury folk revere the memory of the gentry who had identified themselves with the welfare of the burgesses, the assistant burgesses and the commoners generally, helping them to maintain with worthy dignity all the rights and privileges King Athelstan willed to them for ever. Best esteemed of all that long line of High Stewards of the Old Corporation, Col. Miles will doubtless be spoken of for generations to come. For 25 years he presided at the quaint Court of St. John's and took part in the ceremonies of one of the most exclusive corporations in the country. His presence, to that select body of men, descendants of those who fought the Danes for King Athelstan and received royal reward, was the hall-mark of dignity on their deliberations, of legality on their old-world ritual. Colonel Miles was their ideal High Steward. Only to those who have intimate knowledge of the Malmesbury commoners is it given to truly appreciate the value of their unanimous opinion.

The other public offices held by Colonel Miles were comparatively few. As already indicated, he was faithful to his Church. He formerly held office as Vicar's Warden for several years at St. Mary's, Westport, but following the resignation of the late Sir Richard Pollen – who predeceased him by but a week or two – he became Vicar's Warden at the Abbey Church and was re-elected for the last time at the Easter vestry. He was a faithful Church-warden. The flags at the Abbey Church and St. Mary's, Westport, were flown at half-mast during the week.

As a magistrate sitting for the Malmesbury petty sessional division, Colonel Miles was second in seniority at the time of his death, the venerable Colonel Luce being the senior justice. As Colonel Luce has long since ceased to act, Colonel Miles would have been, had he lived, *chairman of the Bench in succession to the late Sir Richard Pollen.*

Before the present war the National Reserve detachment at Malmesbury was a body of no mean importance. Soon after hostilities commenced many of the men who comprised the detachment volunteered to return to the service of King and country. Their local president was the late Colonel Miles, and no-one was prouder than he that so many of his brave fellow townsmen heeded the call and went – some, alas, soon to make the great sacrifice.

Another organisation which owes its existence directly to the war was greatly helped by Colonel Miles – the local Tribunal. He was its first and only chairman. The Tribunal has now lost two of its members within a few weeks. Colonel Miles himself presided at the last sitting so recently as May 14th.

To every local charitable cause Colonel Miles gave ungrudging support. The Manor House Red Cross Hospital is a memorial to his large-hearted generosity. When the question of increasing the local hospital accommodation was brought forward Colonel Miles not only consented to lend the Manor House, but gave a handsome donation towards its equipment. Many a wounded or sick soldier has cause to be grateful to Colonel Miles, and that gratitude is sincerely shared by the Red Cross and military authorities.

The funeral was a very grand affair. The long procession was headed by convalescent soldiers from the Manor House Hospital commanded by Sergeant Major Harwood D.C.M., accompanied by Miss E.G. Luce, Commandant, Miss Hardy, Matron and two nurses. The coffin was borne on a gun carriage covered with a Union flag with Colonel Miles' plumed helmet and gauntlets on top. Six officers, mainly from the Life Guards, were pall-bearers and 1st Life Guards also provided an escort of six officers and 15 non-commissioned officers. His sisters, nephews and several in-laws formed the chief mourners but his brother Audley (indisposed and died the next year) and nephew Gordon were unable to attend. Civic leaders, members of the Old Corporation including the mace-bearers, aristocracy, tenants, military representatives, tradesmen and many other people from the town attended the service in the Abbey. Afterwards the cortege made its way to Dauntsey where the burial took place.

There had been some restrictions on the use of paper but at the end of May it was announced that the Paper Controller was expected to prohibit the return of unsold newspapers. Readers were strongly advised to order a regular copy from the newsagent to avoid disappointment.

Food supply was still a problem as the Gazette of 13th June reported;

NO BEER.- Complaints are still numerous as to the scarcity of beer, and, with no ale available for the labourers in the harvest field, strong protests from them are frequent, and there are good grounds for their complaints. Sugar is unobtainable for tea or cocoa. The labourer in the harvest field is surely as much entitled to an allowance of beer as the munition worker. Why should a distinction be made?

From 1st July a new Fuel Order came into effect which required the appointment of a Local Fuel Overseer. One of his jobs was to ensure that men essential to the distribution of coal and coke were exempted from call-up. T.H. Sandy was appointed and charged with forming a committee representing coal merchants and the gas company. The Town Council expressed concern at the expense of running committees to control the distribution of food and fuel. However the Town Clerk informed them that there was nothing that could be done but of course local people were benefiting from getting supplies of these commodities and particularly benefiting from cheaper food.

Shortage of coal was causing problems. One scheme put before the Town Council by Councillor H. Farrant was to reduce the hours that water was pumped at the Water Works. For several years the town had benefited from a continuous supply. Years before the water was turned on at 7.30 a.m. until 6 p.m. on weekdays and from 8 to 10 in the morning and 2 to 4 o'clock in the afternoon every Sunday. He proposed that that the water supply should be turned off from at least 7 p.m. to 7 a.m. each night. It was anticipated that there might be complaints about sediment being stirred up but that could be overcome by just letting it run through the pipes, there would be no loss of quality. Mr. Forrester suggested that this major decision required notice for it to be properly considered, so Mr. Farrant formally gave notice of the motion. At the next meeting it was agreed to turn off the pumps from eight o'clock at night to six o'clock in the morning which would save 25% of the coal and 30,000 gallons. Mr. Farrant also drew attention to the inconvenience to the community caused by the suspension of the striking of the steeple clock. Mr. E. Jones explained that it was forbidden for the clock to chime at night and the only way to start it at dawn and stop it at dusk would be for him to manually change the mechanism. Mr. Forrester expressed surprise that clocks striking at night were still prohibited and remarked; "Afraid an aeroplane in Germany might hear it?" It was not until October that the prohibition was removed.

The Mayor, Matthew Thompson, wrote to the Lord Chancellor regarding the appointment of magistrates in the town. He was concerned that following the deaths of Colonel Miles and Sir Richard Pollen a greater burden had fallen on the remaining magistrates including himself and he had been frequently disturbed at home to sign documents. He also suggested that it would be better to appoint magistrates who lived in the town as there had been instances of people trudging many a mile to get a document signed only to be told that it was either the wrong time or to call again. The Mayor commented that the town needed two or three magistrates; *they were living in a democratic age, and in the coming time things would be very different. He instanced the appointment of labour and tradesmen representatives as magistrates. In Tetbury, too, a shopkeeper was recently appointed. He hoped that Malmesbury vacancies would not be filled without the classes he had mentioned being considered.*

In August the Tetbury Poor Law Institute was taken over by the War Office as a hospital for the Australian Flying Corps. Very little notice was given and the Clerk of their Guardians wrote asking that all 24 inmates, seven infirm females, three infirm males, eight young women and three infants be taken into Malmesbury's Workhouse as soon as possible. This was agreed but a charge for their maintenance had to be agreed which had to include a fair share for the services of the staff and upkeep of the establishment.

At a special service the Standards of 1st Life Guards that had been owned by Colonel Napier Miles were presented to the Abbey by Mr. Audley Miles, the Colonel's brother and occupant of Ingleburne Manor (as Col. Miles had re-named Burton Hill House). Most local dignitaries attended but some who lived further away were prevented from joining them by a railway strike. The Vicar, Canon C.D.H. McMillan, accepted them for safekeeping and hoped *that they may ever be an emblem of duty, an incentive to patriotism and an inspiration to service, so that the generations which come after us may faithfully serve their God, their King and their country.* Unfortunately over the years these sentiments were forgotten and Derek Tilney, President of the local Royal British Legion, rescued them around the turn of the Millennium and entrusted them to the care of the Guards Chapel in London.

At the beginning of August 1918 a Gazette article showed the difficulty of making price controls work;

At Malmesbury session yesterday a Bristol dealer named Smith was summoned for buying pigs at prices in excess of the maximum fixed by the Order. The allegation was that he paid "earnest money" to the vendor in addition to the price, and that he told the executive officer that if they did not do so they would be unable to buy at all. The more serious of the two charges was that he paid £1 in this way on a £22 transaction. The case broke down because the prosecution failed to prove to the satisfaction of the bench what were the weights of the pigs, upon which depended whether the total sums paid were or were not excess.

The strict control of the supply and price of food is illustrated by an article that appeared in the Herald during September;

FOOD CONTROL.- Two meetings of the local Food Control Committee were held this week, the first – that for the borough – being presided over by Father Morrin and the second – rural – by Mr. F.J. Bates. It was decided that the price of milk sold by retail should be 8d. per quart during October, November, December and January and 9d. per quart during February, March and April, this price to include delivery; if undelivered, one halfpenny per quart less. The Executive Officer reported that all the sugar for jam had been distributed. There were many more applicants, all of whom had to be told that they were too late.

Amendments to the instructions regarding the rationing of bacon meant that extra coupons could be granted to a wider range of those engaged in heavy work. However price control was not the only problem that had to be dealt with;

THE MILK SUPPLY.- At Wednesday's meeting of the Rural Food Control Committee Mr. F.J. Bates presided. It was resolved to inform the Divisional Commissioner that unless hay was commandeered in less quantities, and unless more artificial feeding stuffs for dairy cattle were released, the supply of milk in the district would be decreased by one-third during the coming winter. At the Borough Food Control Committee meeting (Mr. W. Tinley presiding) it was decided, on the motion of the Mayor (Mr. M. Thompson), to instruct the Executive Officer to write to the Food Controller protesting against the high price paid to farmers for milk. The Mayor said he protested, in the interest of the poor people, who could not afford the excessive cost of an essential food.

The Old Corporation elected a new High Steward at the beginning of October;

The Michaelmas meeting of the Malmesbury Old Corporation was held on Saturday morning in the quaint old hall of St. Johns. Mr. William Clark, retiring Warden, presided, and there were also present Messrs. H. Matthews, J. Matthews, Albert Bailey, Bruce Russell, W. Ponting, C. Box, and J. Boulting (Capital Burgesses). Messrs. T. Tugwell, W. Adye, G. Pike, S. Grey, A. Harris, Jabes Chappell, E. Fry and Luke Exton (Assistant Burgesses) and E. Pike (Sergeant-at-Mace).
The following took the prescribed oath and were duly sworn in to their respective offices: Mr. Charles Box (Warden), Mr. H. Matthews (Deputy Warden), Mr. A.W. Chubb (clerk), and Mr. Epigoney Pike (Sergeant-at-Mace). The Mayor (Mr. M. Thompson) was the only commoner present.

THE NEW HIGH STEWARD

The Warden said that a short time ago he called a meeting to consider the appointment of a High Steward to succeed the late Col. C. Napier Miles, C.B., M.V.O. After due consideration it was unanimously resolved that Mr. Montagu H. Chubb, Deputy High Steward, should be invited to accept the office of High Steward. Mr. Chubb had been connected with the Old Corporation for over 40 years, his father and his grandfather before him. During that time great difficulties had cropped up. Very recently they had much difficulty with regard to Malmesbury Common, and things looked very black indeed for a time. They were told that the Malmesbury Common was going to be taken from the Commoners, letters were flying about, officials poking their noses into their business and meetings held. The Commoners appealed to their Deputy High Steward (Mr. Chubb) and he fought for Malmesbury Common-ers through thick and thin, and no doubt he pulled them through the wood – though perhaps they were not quite yet out of the wood. To show their gratitude they could do no better than elect him the High Steward (hear, hear). Mr. Clark had great pleasure in proposing Mr. Chubb's election, and he hoped every man present would do his duty by supporting the motion.
Mr. T. Tugwell (an Assistant Burgess): I second the proposition with all my heart.
The Mayor: Has one commoner any right to vote or not?
The Clerk replied in the negative.
The Mayor: Well, I do not know what right I have here at all.
The resolution was carried unanimously.

On 27th October it was reported that *a gathering was held at Malmesbury which may be described as marking a new era for agricultural labourers.* The Workers' Union had been canvassing in the district and had a substantial membership. Their Swindon branch brass band led a procession through the town to the Town Hall. The meeting was chaired by a farm worker from Milbourne called Matthews. Mr. H.H. Lawrie, the National Organiser, delivered an impassioned speech deploring the poor conditions of many farm workers. The report ended - *There were several new adherents to the Union as a result of the demonstration.*

The November Borough Council meeting (held just after the armistice came into force) reviewed Food Control;

The Chairman of the Food Control Committee gave a report of the committee's work since August, 1917, and traced the growth of the work through its various stages. The scheme had been carried out with the hearty and loyal co-operation of the traders. Unless such a scheme had been brought about with so little friction the food supplies of the mass of the people would have been very seriously prejudiced.

Mr. Bartlett said the report had been a very interesting and instructive one and brought them to realise the immense amount of work the committee had had to do. He thought it had been stupendous, and it was marvellous, even as far as they could see locally, that it had been done without friction. Thanks were due to the committee for the way they had done their work. He should also like to speak of the very great kindness and the very nice way they had been received at the Food Office by Mr. Sandy (the executive officer). It was wonderful how he could keep an unruffled temper all the while. The report made by Mr. Forrester would be satisfactory to the borough generally.

Mr. Adye, as a food distributor, also expressed thanks. Although the work of the distributors had been very worrying and trying, yet their table had always been spread for them, and they should be thankful.

Mr. Farrant, also a distributor, said the rationing had been a boon alike to the distributor and the public. It was a great thing to be able to tell the grumbler that he had got as much food as the richest man. With regard to the Executive Officer, he had the "patience of Job" more nearly than any man he ever knew.

Mr. Forrester said he thought the food restrictions were likely to last at least twelve months longer.

During December the Ministry of Food issued a statement to emphasise how its activities had benefited the nation. It claimed that Britain had 50% more bread than Germany and supplies per head had increased since the start of the war. We had three times as much meat as our enemy but production had fallen by a third. We were even better off than neutral nations like Holland. The Ministry had built up a world-wide purchasing organisation that had been able to build up supplies from a dangerously low point in the middle of the war. Price control which had been introduced from July 1917 had reduced price inflation. Rationing had reduced queues in the London area from 1.34 million people in the week before its introduction to 15,000 four weeks later.

By the middle of December it was clear that the forces were not being demobilised as quickly as hoped. The general Demobilisation Order had not been issued, only 'pivotal' men were being released. Employers in the building industry were advised to make application to Local Advisory Committees to apply for the release of their pivotal men. At that time the scheme only related to construction.

Old Comrades band together 1919-21

As early as 4th January 1919 the Gazette reported;

DEMOBILISATION is proceeding apace, many local men having returned to their former employment.

Honours were still being awarded for actions during the war;

A GALLANT SOLDIER.- Another Malmesbury soldier has been decorated for gallant conduct in the war. Private (Acting-Sergt.) F. Lovejoy, Military Foot Police, son-in-law of the late Mr. Alfred Player, the Abbey verger, has been awarded the Military Medal. General Sir H. Rawlinson, commanding the Fourth Army, in a letter to the gallant soldier wrote: "I congratulate you on the gallantry and devotion to duty for which you have been awarded the Military Medal." Acting-Sergt. Lovejoy is an old soldier, for he served seven years in the 1st Royal Fusiliers. He has the Tibet (1903-4) Medal with clasp. After leaving the Fusiliers he joined the Metropolitan Police, leaving to re-join the Army when war broke out, though he was not then a Reservist. He has served four years with the Military Foot Police in France. His wife has three brothers in the Army.

A question asked in the House of Commons by one of North Wiltshire's M.P.s Mr. Joynson-Hicks, led to it being disclosed that the fate of 64,000 Empire soldiers was still unknown. The total number missing, including prisoners of war, was approximately 359,800 – 198,000 of whom were estimated to be prisoners, 97,000 presumed dead due to the long period with no indication they were alive, leaving 64,800 whose whereabouts were not known. Strenuous efforts were being made to locate them with strong demands being made on enemy authorities.

More prisoners of war returned home as the Standard reported on 25th January;

Amongst the prisoners of war recently returned to Malmesbury are Private Frank Hinder, formerly postman to Ladyswood, Sherston, etc., and Private Peters, both of the 1st Wilts, who took part in the battle of Mons, being reservists. They were in the "Old Contemptibles," forming part of the first Expeditionary Force.
Private Hinder gave an account of the long years he has been confined in Germany. The treatment was very bad up till the time when the American Army made its appearance on the battlefield, but after that more humane consideration was shown. ... But the "food" was of the vilest type, it hardly kept body and soul together. "We should all have been starved had it not been for the parcels so kindly sent to us by the Wilts Prisoners of War Fund, although many of them were tampered with and part of their contents stolen. I want to thank most heartily – as also does my mate Peters – everyone who kindly subscribed towards the cost of those parcels which alone saved our lives, and also the willing helpers who devoted so much time to the detail work of making up and despatching them." The joy of the exiles at the news of the Armistice may well be imagined – in fact Private Hinder tells of more than one of his mates to whom the joy was too great for their poor physical frames, shattered by the pangs of hunger and brutal treatment, and they died in the camp, whilst others died on the way home. And it is sad indeed to relate that the opportunity of having a good square meal on the boats home also proved fatal to one or more. They were warned by the medical staff to be careful and only to eat the most moderate portions for some time, as their stomachs had become so impaired through privation that to eat a good meal would be to jeopardise their lives. But the temptation was too great for some, and so even good food and plenty of it added to the already heavy toll of the Wiltshires.
Private Hinder and Private Peters both look fairly well now. "I look much better than I feel," said the former. His wife, who is engaged in the scholastic profession, is naturally delighted to have her husband home, a joy which she shares with his mother at Minety, and Private Peters is also welcomed home by his relatives. The same pleasure is also felt by Mrs. W.J. Bowman at the return of her husband, who was also a postman to Sherston, and who was also in the County Regiment and has been interned as a prisoner of war for weary years in Germany. The whole inhabitants of the borough are proud of these heroes – and of others

whose names do not occur as one writes – who have suffered such agonies for civilisation's sake.

The end of March 1919 brought news that must have been of comfort to relatives of the war dead who had been told that the bodies would not be repatriated;

WAR GRAVES IN FRANCE.
Terms of Arrangement With the French Government.

Terms of the treaty arranged between the French and British Governments for the care of British graves in France are announced by the Foreign Office. An explanation of the terms will be of assistance to the relatives of all concerned.

Provisions of the scheme drawn up by Major-General Fabian Ware, Director of War Graves Registration and Inquiries, were embodied in a law under which the French Government purchased the land for these cemeteries and presented it for all time to the British authorities. The French Government do not acknowledge any other authority than the Imperial War Graves Commission. They cannot therefore deal with applications for the purchase of individual graves.

Isolated graves of British soldiers on the sites of old battlefields may be moved with a view to concentrating the bodies in military cemeteries. This work is being carried out by the Army at present in occupation, but nothing in the nature of wholesale exhumation is being done.

The Commission is authorised to put the cemeteries in order in accordance with plans approved by itself, to erect monuments on the graves in them or other buildings, to carry out planting in them, to frame regulations for visiting them, and to choose persons appointed as their guardians.

Demobilisation was well under way by the end of March. All men who enlisted prior to conscription unless vital to demobilisation were being given priority. However civilian clothing was in short supply;

DEMOBILISED MEN.
May Wear Khaki.

The War Office have announced that as sufficient greatcoats have now been returned to establish the necessary reserves for the War Department, and in view of the increasing difficulty which demobilised soldiers are experiencing in obtaining civilian greatcoats, and the hardship to which they are, therefore, liable in having to part with their military greatcoats before obtaining a substitute, the return of the greatcoat will, in future, be optional.

The discharged soldier may either retain it, and forfeit the £1 of his War Gratuity, or he may return it through a railway company, not later than the last day of his demobilisation furlough and obtain £1 in cash.

Should he decide to retain the greatcoat, he must remove shoulder-straps, military buttons and badges of rank. He will not then render himself liable to any legal proceedings. There is no objection to the greatcoat being dyed.

The War Office also announced that owing to the temporary shortage of material, no guarantee can henceforth be given that a suit of plain clothes will be forwarded within 28 days to every soldier who has elected at a Dispersal Station to take a suit of plain clothes in lieu of a money allowance of £2 12s. 6d.

Every effort will be made to deliver the suit within this period, but, when this is impossible, the soldier will be notified by a letter from the Royal Army Clothing Department, and will be given the option of waiting for a suit or of receiving £2 12s. 6d. in lieu.

A soldier who has any complaint as to the non-receipt of his plain clothes 28 days after dispersal, or as to misfit, should write, giving his regimental number, rank, name, and unit, and, in the case of misfit, his correct measurement, to: "The Officer-in Charge, Discharged Soldiers' Clothing Section, Battersea Park, London, S.W.11," who will inquire into the circumstances and communicate with the soldier.

No man is permitted to wear uniform on the expiration of his 28 days' furlough. There is, however, no objection to wearing khaki clothes provided buttons, badges, and shoulder straps have been removed. The field service cap must not be worn.

As a result of demobilisation the Government sought to make service in the Army more attractive. Men were invited to re-enlist for terms of 27, 39 or 51 months and would receive bounties of £20, £40 and £50 respectively. In addition they would be entitled to between two weeks and three months paid leave. Unfortunately demobilisation was not proceeding as quickly as had been hoped and soldiers in the Middle East and India who had been serving since the early days of the war including 1/4th Wiltshires were particularly affected. At the same time proposals were made to re-constitute the Territorial Force. This new organisation was to comprise 14 Divisions, 14 Mounted Brigades and many other miscellaneous units. The county Territorial Force Associations were asked to consider these ideas.

The Regular battalions of the Wiltshire Regiment had by this time been reduced to cadres, just a few men to form the nucleus of the unit . On 9th June they were officially welcomed to Devizes, the home of the Regiment's depot and entertained to lunch. The party representing the 2nd Battalion included just twelve survivors from the men who left for France in 1914.

Yet another award was made in June to one of Malmesbury's premier families;

HIGH HONOURS FOR COL. LUCE'S SON.- Major-General Richard Harman Luce, C.M.G., C.B., M.B., L.R.C.P., R.A.M.C. (T.), was on Tuesday gazetted a K.C.M.G. It was only on Saturday that he received, among the birthday honours, his C.M.G. Sir R.H. Luce is the eldest surviving son of Col. and Mrs. C.H. Luce, of Halcombe, Malmesbury. He served with the Australian Forces as Assistant Director of Medical Supplies in Gallipoli and Egypt. When Gallipoli was evacuated he was with General Birdwood, one of the last officers to leave the peninsular. He was afterwards mentioned in despatches, and eventually received the C.B. for his services. Subsequently came his promotion to Major-General. He has now left the Army, and has resumed his practice as a doctor in Derby. During the war Lady Luce and the family resided for a great part of the time in Malmesbury. Another illustrious son of Col. Luce is Commodore John Luce, C.B., R.N. He commanded H.M.S. "Glasgow" in the memorable Falklands battle, and was instrumental in accounting for some of the enemy ships. It was for this that he was awarded the C.B. Later he received a shore appointment, and afterwards went to the Mediterranean. Recently Capt. J. Luce has not been in good health. Malmesbury share with Col. and Mrs. Luce in the great pride they naturally feel in their distinguished sons.

The progress of the peace talks at Versailles was keenly followed as shown by this rather ironic report published on 4th July 1919 just after the Peace Treaty was signed;

PEACE.- If confirmation of the news that peace was signed on Saturday was sought in Malmesbury the seeker would have been disappointed. A message was displayed in a shop window or two that afternoon, and the announcement was read with about as much interest as would have been shown to a notice of a lost poodle. There were, however, redeeming features. On Monday a squib was discharged in one of the principal streets. This was followed in the evening by two distinct reports, evidence that the news had spread somewhat, and fireworks were "booming." On Tuesday and Wednesday rumours were flying about that something momentous had happened at Versailles, but with a very few exceptions the populace remained outwardly incredulous, notwithstanding that trade in fireworks had extended to a sky-rocket or two. Perhaps Malmesburians are conserving their fervour for the real thing on July 19th, for the Peace Celebration Committee officials have shown signs of feverish activity during the past day or two.

However celebrations of the peace did occurr that weekend;

PEACE THANKSGIVING.
Church and Chapel Services at Malmesbury.
Thanksgiving services were held at Malmesbury on Sunday in the Abbey Church in the morning, and in the Westport Congregational Church in the evening, and both places were crowded to overflowing. The Mayor (Councillor M. Duck) and the Town Council and also members of the Old Corporation, attended both services in state, and they were accompanied by a large company of discharged service men, comprising the Ivy branch of the National Federation of Discharged and Demobilised sailors and soldiers (under Sergt. Kite), Malmesbury Detachment C Company 1st Wilts Volunteers (under Sergt. Sandy), V.A.D. Nurses (Miss Luce, O.B.E.,

Commandant), King Athelstan Troop of Boy Scouts and bugle band (under Scout-master W.G. Perry), members of Court King Athelstan Ancient Order of Foresters in full regalia, Freemasons, Fire Brigade (Mr. C. Bowman, captain). Besides the Mayor the members of the Town Council present were: Councillor M. Thompson (deputy Mayor), Aldermen A.L. Forester, H. Farrant, J.G. Bartlett and A. Adye, Councillors J.A. Jones, E. Jones, F.T. Gough, F.H. Summers, H. Clark, J. Pinegar, F. Weeks, H. Matthews and H. Wilmot, with Mr. A.W. Chubb (deputy town clerk), Mr. F.G.T. Goldstone (borough treasurer), Messrs. J.D. Curtis and F.C. Stepton (borough auditors), Mr. J. Clark (market toll collector), Mr. F. Jefferies (mace-bearer), preceding the Mayor in the procession. The Town Band under the leadership of the Bandmaster, I. Carey, headed the procession. Sergt. H. Cordy in the uniform of the old 2nd Wilts Volunteers, accompanied the Volunteers.

Before entering the Abbey all the public bodies assembled near the Market Cross and formed a square. From a suitable position in front of the Cottage Hospital the Mayor read the King's Proclamation, the Town Band at one stage playing the National Anthem.

The service in the Abbey was deeply impressive. Numerous flags representing the British Empire and Allied countries adorned the walls. An armed sentry (Pte. W. C. Pocock, 1st Wilts Volunteers) and a Scout (Patrol-leader J. Milliner) stood on duty under the pulpit and reading desk respectively, each flanked by flags. An appropriate touch was lent to the occasion by Major R. Clarke, R.A., one of the aldermen, officiating in uniform. Several other officers, naval and military, were in the congregation, but they were not in uniform.

The service was conducted by the Rev. E.G. Munchamp, a chaplain to the Australian Forces, and the lesson was read by the Rev. P.A.H. Smith, Moravian minister. The hymns sung were "O, God, our help in ages past," "All people that on earth do dwell," "Now thank we all our God," and "God Save the King." The choir, led by Mr. W. Brown (organist) sang the anthem, "O sing unto the Lord a new song." The Te Deum was also sung. The offertory, which was a substantial size, was for the St. Dunstan's Hostel for Blinded Soldiers.

The Rev. L. Roadhouse, priest-in-charge, then preached a sermon described by the reporter as both appropriate and acceptable. It was a long rambling text that expressed many un-Christian sentiments about the Germans, stating that they had been preparing their children for over 40 years to hate the British and this had turned them into barbarians. He also ascribed several events including a supposed pause in the Germans' 1914 march on Paris to be acts of God! In the evening the notables marched from Cross Hayes and the King's Proclamation was read in the Triangle. Rev. G.W. Ennos (Westport Congregational minister) took the service, Rev. P.A.H. Smith (Moravian minister) read the lesson, Rev. F.W. Lines (Silver Street Congregational pastor) offered prayers, and Rev. J.H. Hutler (Primitive Methodist minister and President of the Free Church Council) preached another sermon.

The foundation of the Malmesbury branch of the National Federation of Discharged and Demobilised Sailors and Soldiers had taken place a couple of months before the signing of the peace treaty. It was led by ex-Sergeant Kite of the Somerset Light Infantry and H. Iles as secretary who had served with the Royal Naval Division. On 23rd August the members paraded in Cross Hayes and preceded by the Town Band marched to the Primitive Methodist Chapel where they attended a service led by Rev. J.W. Hutler.

The North Wilts Herald in their 25th July edition gave a full report of the celebrations held to mark the ratification of the peace treaty;

PEACE DAY AT MALMESBURY.
Fighters & Workers Honoured.
RAIN SPOILS SPORTS.

Malmesbury residents vied with each other in decorating their houses and places of business with flags and bunting in celebration of Peace Day. Had the weather been fine on Saturday the rejoicing would have been carried out in perfect style. As it was, however, the organisers had to do the best they could in face of the discouraging climatic conditions. Nevertheless it was a brave show, and honour was done to the gallant men who had so nobly served overseas and to the women who had unselfishly borne their share of war work at home.

The hon. secretaries of the Peace Celebrations Committee, Messrs. H.J.S. Beak and H. Wilmot, had for some time been busy with elaborate preparation which, of course, had to be hurried forward owing to the sudden announcement that Peace Day was to be held a month earlier than expected. The committee had divided the town into sections and every household was called upon to contribute to the celebrations fund. The collections amounted to £120. Had the weather been fine on Saturday the sum would have been augmented by revenue from a public tea and also by receipts from visitors to the Abbey who, by permission of the church-wardens, were to have ascended to the roof of the ancient church to view the bonfires on the adjacent hills. An excellent sports programme had been arranged and the Town Band hoped to give pleasure to a considerable number of young people who would dance to the music. There were also to be various side shows reminiscent of the old-time country fair, and Mr. H.W. Abbott, of the White Lion Inn, was to be the refreshment caterer in the grounds of Ingelburne House, where the rejoicings were to take place. But, alas, the weather literally put a damper on all these arrangements and the programme had to be curtailed accordingly. Mr. Audley Miles and Mr. W.B. Carter promised to permit the abandoned sports to be held on Thursday on their grounds.

Despite the unfavourable weather crowds turned out to celebrate the great victory. The company assembled in the Cross Hayes, and immediately in front of the Town Hall, standing in a wagon, was the Mayor, wearing his chain of office. On either side of him stood Mr. H. Adye, Mr. H. Farrant, Mr. A.L. Forrester and the Town Clerk (Mr. M.H. Chubb). Lined up facing the Mayor were a number of V.A.D. nurses in uniform, under their Commandant, Miss Luce, O.B.E., the children from the three schools, about 200 discharged and demobilised sailors and soldiers, and the Boy Scouts (under Scoutmaster W.G. Perry), with their bugle band and banner, whilst at one end of the wagon were the Malmesbury Town Band, and the united choirs of the town, and a large crowd of the general public. The Mayor made a speech praising in particular the women who had run the Red Cross Hospital which had treated 600 soldiers. Then the Band led the procession around the town and on to Burton Hill House garden. As the sports activities were postponed the children were given tea in the Manor House served by V.A.D. nurses. Later the inmates of the Poor Law Institute were treated to a roast beef dinner.

Shortly after these celebrations a father who lost two sons wrote to the Herald;

Sir, - As one who listened to the speech of the Mayor of Malmesbury on Peace Day, I quite agree that the best thanks of us all are due to those who served, or are serving, and to all who worked for peace and by our thanks I mean more than the words, "Thank you." But may I remind the Mayor and Corporation that there are those who have gone forward from the old town and have won distinction upon the battlefields of France, but who will never return. As I write I think of two whose homes are on either side of me, who won such honours. I read that in the great procession in London there was no more impressive moment than when Foch and Haig drew rein to salute our immortal dead. Yet in Malmesbury no mention is made of those who have made the supreme sacrifice. Can it be that they are already forgotten?
    Yours, &c.
            FREDERICK CURTIS   5, Gastons Road

Whilst the Germans had been defeated British forces were still involved in fighting as reported at the end of August;

FROM RUSSIAN BATTLEFIELDS.- Corpl. Dick Bishop (Royal Engineers) of Bristol Street, is home on leave from the North Russian battlefield. He has been on the Murmansk front, where severe fighting is taking place against the Bolshevists. He says the Allies are moving towards Petrograd, but the opposition is formidable and progress necessarily slow. The campaign in that region is fraught with continued hardship for the British soldiers, but they are all cheerfully doing their duty. Treachery abounds among the Russian soldiery, necessitating the strictest vigilance on the part of the British officers. It is difficult to distinguish between friend and foe. The ignorant Russian peasants, having little idea of the true situation, will sometimes fight for either side in turn, as the fancy takes them.

The first anniversary of the end of the war was not marked in any special way. On Sunday 9th November the new Abbey Vicar, Rev. C.R. Paterson, officiated at his first service and the congregation was described as being fairly large. The final item of note reported this year was the demobilisation of the Women's Land Army on 30th November, although no details of their use locally was given.

1920

The year began with the news that the 2nd Battalion Wiltshire Regiment had arrived in Hong Kong for garrison duty. They had travelled on a Portuguese steamer, the Tras Os Montes and the final stage of the voyage from Singapore had taken longer than expected due to a very bad storm. The ship was damaged, many lifeboats were carried away or made unusable. However all 24 officers and 670 men with 24 families came through their ordeal safely.

On 14th January a curious case was heard at the Wiltshire Assizes. Florence Lucy Welch, alias Proctor, aged 30, pleaded not guilty to bigamy. In April 1912 she married Alfred Welch at Finchley and after moving to New Barnet they had two children. When war broke out Welch joined up and was sent to France. He stayed with his wife when on leave in December 1917. However on his next leave in September 1918 he could not find her. She had gone to Malmesbury to work as a charwoman in the Red Cross Hospital. There she met William Proctor, a wounded soldier. In February 1919 they were married, he being a widower and Florence describing herself as a widow. They went to live in Burnley. She said that she thought Welch had been killed. However two facts contradicted this story – she had been drawing separation allowance from the Army and she had written to Welch two months after her second marriage. The jury found her guilty. The Judge said that it was clearly her intention to get a comfortable home for herself and her children. She had taken good care of them and she was sentenced to two days' imprisonment – meaning that she was immediately discharged. Unfortunately the report does not tell us which man she chose to live with!

The local branch of the National Federation of Discharged and Demobilised Sailors and Soldiers enjoyed a smoking concert in the Council Chambers on 16th January. At the start Rev. L. Roundhouse (curate at the Abbey) outlined the proposals for a Red Triangle Club (Y.M.C.A.) in Malmesbury. He said that precious little was being done for the "demobbed" men who had nothing else to do at night but to walk the streets and if they wanted a chat they either stood in the street or went to a pub. They now had the opportunity to purchase the Wesleyan premises for £1,250 and many alterations would be needed. £1,000 had so far been promised but much more was required. It was intended to convert the ground floor to accommodate two billiard tables with a lounge in one corner. There would be a buffet which would charge low prices and be offered to outlying farmers who came to market. They would be appealing for funds from a wide area, but asked for a grant from the Federation. It was hoped to offer low rates for ex-servicemen for at least a year.

A new medal was announced for members of the Territorial Force who were either serving at the outbreak of the war or rejoined then and were prepared to serve overseas. It was aimed particularly at units like the 4th Wiltshires that had been sent to garrison India throughout the war.

The February Town Council meeting heard that a large German artillery gun had been presented to the Borough and was stored in the stone yard. The Surveyor wanted to know what the Council intended to do with it. Mr. Gale suggested that it should be scrapped. The matter was referred to the General Purposes Committee. It was subsequently displayed next to St. John's Bridge, on the site of the present memorial garden (it remained there until May 1940 when the Council resolved to scrap it, Councillor J.A. Jones saying; "we should return it to the Hun in a different form than he handed it to us!"). The same meeting decided to borrow the purchase money for the Town Hall from the Cirencester Conservative Working Men's Association at 6% repayable over 25 years. Also Mrs. E. Jones and Mrs. J.A. Jones were elected to the Profiteering Committee although Mr. Gale protested that it was not right for people in business to investigate those who had made excessive profits.

On 17th February a smoking concert was held in the Scouts' Hall in Charlton to welcome back around 60 discharged and demobilised soldiers. F.J. Bates presided and explained that the meeting had been delayed until all of the parishioners had returned from France, Germany and India. He went on to claim that the village turned out more Volunteers than any other.

There was a national desire, headed by Field Marshal Haig, to try and unite the various ex-servicemen's organisations. A surplus of funds from canteens that had been run in operational areas was used as a lever to speed the unification. On 21st February the Mayor, M. Thompson, held a meeting in the Council Chamber to discuss how Malmesbury's share could be utilised. A Local Welfare Committee was appointed of G. Bradshaw, G. Riddick & G. Weeks (un-attached ex-service men), C. Gale & A.L. Curtis (nominated by the Mayor) R. Pike, A. Phelps, H. Weeks, W. Selby, H. Iles, Tyrell & A. Bailey (all representing the Federation of Discharged and Demobilised Sailors' and Soldiers' Federation). There would be 5s. per ex-service man available from the United Services Fund to be used to assist those in need or dependants of fallen soldiers.

In May the Wiltshire Territorial Army County Association announced the units to form the reconstituted Territorial Army in the county. These were; the Royal Wiltshire Yeomanry; the Wiltshire Battery, 2nd Wessex Brigade, Royal Field Artillery; 2nd (Wiltshire) Heavy Bridging Company, Royal Engineers; 4th Battalion Wiltshire Regiment and Wessex Divisional Train, No. 5 Company, Royal Army Service Corps. The total personnel would be 87 officers and 1,500 men. A number of units in existence prior to the war were abolished including the Ammunition Column, R.F.A. which had been based in Malmesbury.

Another ex-servicemen's group was formed in Malmesbury in June;

COMRADES IN ARMS –
COMRADES IN PEACE.
New Branch at Malmesbury
Address by Major-General Calley.

The initiative for the inauguration of a "post" or branch in Malmesbury of the organisation of officers and ex-service men, known as the Comrades of the Great War, was with that go-ahead member of the Council, Mr. Charles Gale, who saw active service in the great adventure, and who is imbued with the desire to foster the spirit of comradeship which meant so much in the long-drawn-out struggle for the liberty of nations. During the past few weeks he has made a personal canvas of discharged and demobilised sailors and soldiers in Malmesbury and neighbourhood localities, and so many expressed a desire for membership that the establishment of a "post" was a mere matter of form. The applications for membership made at the opening meeting, held in the Council Chambers on Saturday evening, so increased the total that, with the promise of the transfer of a number of members from a near branch, a Malmesbury branch (to form which 100 members are required) is the assured result of Mr. Gale's self-imposed task.

The numerous attendance at the enthusiastic meeting included not only those who had served during the big European War, but several old campaigners and Volunteers. Lieut.-Col. L.E. Morrice, D.S.O., presided, and supporting him were Major-General T.C.F. Calley, C.B., M.V.O. (Burderop Park), Admiral J. Luce (Holcombe), and Major Holland (Lea House). Also present were the Rev. C.E. Paterson (vicar of Malmesbury), Father T. Morrin (Malmesbury), Capt. Stewart Cole, Capt. Truscott and Lieut. A.L. Curtis &c.

The speakers went on to explain that the organisation was non-sectarian and non-political but unlike other ex-service men's organisations allowed officers to join. Major-General Calley had been appointed Commandant for North Wiltshire and explained that an important role was that of welfare, particularly relating to those disabled in the war and war widows. Another principal objective was to perpetuate the memory of those who had died. Lieut.-Col. Morrice was elected branch Commandant, Capt. Truscott (Secondary School headmaster) Secretary, Major Holland Treasurer with Capt. Stuart Cole, Lieut. A.L. Curtis, ex-Sergt.-Major W.G. Perry, ex-Sergt. Duting and Mr. C. Gale appointed to the committee. Sixty nine new members were enrolled and thirty eight local men would transfer from the Cirencester branch.

The Borough Welfare Committee held a public meeting in June

The Comrades' lapel badge
(Mark Sutton)

to report on their deliberations. It was explained that the United Services Fund had a total of £5,500,000 nationally - £4,000,000 for widows and dependents and £1,500,000 for the social benefit of ex-service men. As the town had about 400 ex-service men they had £100 to allocate. They had considered giving a grant to the cottage hospital but the sum was insufficient to permanently endow one bed, had investigated the purchase of a bowling green and making a grant to the Y.M.C.A. but the final recommendation was the establishment of a club. This was unanimously adopted.

Shortly afterwards the Y.M.C.A. reported the progress made in their new premises. The Wesleyan Chapel had been acquired for £1,250 and was being converted to provide a large recreation room to be used for billiards and other games, facilities for reading and a buffet with a lecture hall upstairs which could be used for concerts and dances. The total cost was estimated to be £2,000 and £1,300 had been raised so far including £500 from Colonel Charles Luce. A garden party and sports day was held at Burton Hill House to augment the funds.

The Federation of Discharged and Demobilised Sailors and Soldiers met on 5th October in the White Lion with Sydney Kite in the chair. It was reported that their total funds amounted to £10 11s. 11d. with a bank balance less than half that figure. Only around 30 members regularly paid their subscriptions but the Federation's Headquarters was slow in asking for their percentage of the subscriptions. There was no official confirmation that the amalgamation of ex-service organisations would take place and the name proposed for the new body was either 'The Imperial Comrades' Federation' or 'The United League of ex-Service Men,' and four million men would be involved. Members were told that the Council of the Y.M.C.A. had invited them to parade at the opening ceremony of their new hall.

The prevalence of guns brought back from the war as souvenirs was one of the reasons for the Firearms Act 1920. Members of the public were encouraged to hand in or sell firearms held without good reason during November and December. Stiff penalties were to be imposed on those possessing or intending to acquire guns or ammunition other than smooth-bore shotguns and air guns.

1921

At the end of February the final list of those who died serving in the county regiments was published;

4,766 NAMES.

"THE WILTSHIRES'" ROLL OF HONOUR.

The official roll of the soldiers of the Duke of Edinburgh's (Wiltshire) Regiment who fell in the war has been published. The whole series of the rolls, which will run to 80 parts, is designed to furnish a reliable and permanent record of the sacrifices made by every regiment in the British Army. There is a separate consolidated list for officers. The roll of the Wiltshire Regiment contains 4,766 names, divided as follows: - 1st Battalion, 1,418; 2nd Battalion, 1,304; 3rd Battalion, 35; 5th Battalion, 706; 6th Battalion, 726; 7th Battalion, 250; 8th Battalion, 8; Depot, 50; No. 1 Works Company, 1; No. 2 Works Company, 3; 1st-4th (T.F.) Battalion, 201; 2nd-4th (T.F.) Battalion, 35; 4th (T.F.) Battalion, 26; Depot (T.F.), 3.

The details are complete. The place of birth, place of enlistment, place of residence (where it is other than the place of enlistment), and manner of death (killed in action, died of wounds, died), are given in each case, with the name of the battle area where death occurred or was caused. Of course the full Christian names are stated. We have not attempted an analysis of the 4,766 names, but one cannot help noticing, and with pride, the very large proportion of natives of the county who are included in this Roll of Honour of the County Regiment.

The list will be valued by those whose relatives' names form the Roll and by the towns where they lived or enlisted (this particularly applies to Devizes, which as the Depot town was the great recruiting centre for the Regiment). It is too late to allow many of the committees engaged in prompting memorials to compare their lists, because so many of the memorials are already erected, but some are still in the making, and it would be well in these cases to refer to the Roll. Its price is 2s. 6d., published by H.M. Stationery Office and to be obtained through any bookseller.

The Royal Wiltshire Yeomanry was reported to be nearly up to strength again and would go to its annual fortnight's camp at Weymouth on 8th May. The Wiltshires were one of only ten Yeomanry Regiments to be re-constituted and were now commanded by Lieut.-Colonel W.F. Fuller, D.S.O., T.D. Many old soldiers had rejoined and looked forward to relearning their skills as mounted soldiers rather than the infantry role they had been forced to adopt in 1917.

Around 20 members of the Malmesbury branch of the Comrades of the Great War met in the parish room, Silver Street at the start of March. It was announced that their smoking concert had raised £3 11s. 9d. and eight new members had joined. The Wiltshire Divisional Grand Council was in severe financial difficulty having spent £200 but only received just over £91 from the branches. It was pleasing to note that Malmesbury's payments had been made in full. Head office informed them that it had been agreed in principle to unite the following ex-service men's organisations: The National Association of Discharged Sailors and Soldiers; the National Federation of Discharged and Demobilised Sailors and Soldiers; the Officers' Association and themselves. The provisional title of the united body was The British Legion. Unemployment was now a major concern and the Provisional Unity Committee had decided that there would be a joint relief fund committee. Local differences had to be set aside so that practical help could be given to ex-service men in distress through funds being made available to the town. A sub-committee was elected to meet with a sub-committee from the Federation to start the process. Messrs. G.H. Bunting, E.F.E. Edwards and A.L. Curtis were the Comrades' representatives. Colonel Luce had written expressing his willingness to allow the Comrades to use the rifle range at the Old Drill Hall provided the arrangements did not clash with those of the Boy Scouts.

Just as the War Memorial at the Triangle was being completed, tragedy struck with the death of a young girl;

THE MOTOR FATALITY.

DRIVER EXONERATED BY THE JURY.

An inquiry was held on Thursday by Mr. A.L. Forrester (Coroner) at the Malmesbury Cottage Hospital annexe into the circumstances attending the death of Beatrice Emma Fry (aged 10), daughter of Mr. and Mrs. Arthur Fry, of 18, West Street, who was knocked down in the Triangle, Malmesbury, on March 8th, and was fatally injured, her death occurring at the hospital two hours later.

After the father's evidence of identification, Frederick Bowman, builder, of Oxford Street, gave evidence as to seeing the motor lorry (owned by Messrs. Adye and Hinwood, Ltd., the bacon factory), moving slowly – at a man's walking pace – by the side of the war memorial in the Triangle, into which it had turned from Bristol Street. There were children playing near the memorial, from which the scaffolding was being removed, and he saw the girl "jump" backwards from the memorial across the road towards Mr. Sealy's house. He then saw the front part of the lorry strike the child, and she fell. The front wheels missed her, and he tried to save the child, but she rolled under the off rear wheel of the vehicle. Witness picked up the girl and with the assistance of other men placed her on a hurdle and took her to the Cottage Hospital.

Dr. Maitland Govan deposed to seeing the child on her admission to the hospital. He was told that a wheel of a lorry had passed over her body, but his examination at that time showed no bones were broken. The girl died at 6.20 p.m. the same day from shock and the injuries sustained. His subsequent examination revealed that the wheel had passed over her neck.

Bertie Clark, motor driver, 93, Gloucester Street, stated that he saw the child running back-wards into the lorry. The lorry stopped within 15 feet after passing the body, and at the time of the accident was going about six miles an hour. The lorry was on the left side of the road.

Ernest Paginton, 48, Foundry Road, Malmesbury, the driver of the lorry, said he had been driving about three weeks. He did not see the children until after he had turned into the Triangle. Just as he got alongside the war memorial he saw the witness Bowman with some-thing in his hand waving to the children. They scattered in all directions, and a little girl ran backwards towards the lorry, put her left hand on the splash board, and then turned and faced the lorry. He switched off the engine immediately, and put on the footbrake and the lever, and stopped the lorry at once. There was no possible chance of averting the accident. Bert Goddard, fitter and turner, and an expert motor driver, who was on the seat with Paginton, deposed that he saw a man driving the children from the memorial. The driver was propelling the vehicle carefully, and pulled up as quickly as he (witness) could have done. It was possible to stop the lorry in its own length. Paginton sounded the horn the whole of the way up Bristol Street, and after he had made the corner.

The Coroner directed the jury that what they had to decide was whether Paginton drove the lorry in a negligent manner, and whether such negligent driving was the cause of the girls' death.

The jury returned a verdict that the occurrence was purely accidental, and that no blame was attributable to the driver.

The Coroner expressed sympathy with the parents of the child and the driver of the lorry.

Hardships continued to be endured but this chapter ends with the first Remembrance Day in 1921 as reported by the Wiltshire Gazette;

POPPY DAY.- In response to an appeal by Field Marshal Earl Haig it was arranged to hold a Poppy Day on November 11th, Armistice Day. For the benefit of ex-Service men of all branches, poppies were sold in the streets and by a house to house collection, with the result that the Mayoress (Mrs. F. Weeks) was able to hand over to the British Legion the sum of £25. The collection was carried out in a most able manner by 15 pupils of the Malmesbury Secondary School. The flowers were made by women and children in the devastated areas of France, by which these sorely stricken people will benefit and the profits made by the sale will alleviate a large amount of distress amongst our own ex-Service men and their dependants and the widows and orphans of those who died.

Poppies were chosen as a symbol of remembrance because they had provided a dramatic splash of colour to the devasted battlefields. They had been immortalised in Lt. Col. John McCrae's 1915 poem *In Flanders Field*.

DAY OF REMEMBRANCE.- The Abbey was crowded to excess on Sunday afternoon when a

An Armistice service in the 1920s. Note that there are no poppy wreaths. (John Bowen)

special service was held to commemorate Armistice Day. In a large procession, headed by the Town Band, were upwards of 100 ex-Service men (under Major R. Clarke), the local troop of Boy Scouts (under Scoutmaster, the Rev. N.S. Willis), and a great crowd of people who attended the service. The band accompanied the singing of hymns, and a powerful address was delivered by the Bishop's chaplain, the Rev. F. Welch (at one time curate of Malmesbury). The Mayor read the lesson. After the service the procession visited the War Memorial where a wreath was handed by Mr. Charles Bailey to Major Clarke, who placed it on the memorial. The inscription was "From those who served with you." The proceedings were most impressive and imposing.

Two other wreaths were laid as remembered more than sixty years later by Eileen Cunningham (nee Butler);

I well remember the Armistice Service held in Malmesbury in 1921, eight months after the Memorial Cross had been erected in the Triangle. I was about six and a half years old at the time. A large parade had turned out for a special service at the Abbey which was packed with all the local organisations plus a large number of ex-servicemen who had recently returned from the war. There was quite a crowd of people standing at the back of the Abbey under the organ and choir stalls which at that time were on the west wall.
I was there at the back with my mother and sisters, we were unable to get seats and I remember being lifted to get a glimpse of my father, Captain Butler, who was on parade. The service over, the congregation followed the parade to the new War Memorial and I was amongst many who laid wreathes and flowers. I had been specially chosen to lay a wreath in 'Honour of the Living' as my father, although wounded twice, had returned safely, and a boy whose father had been killed in the war laid flowers in 'Honour of the Dead.'
I recall that my mother had made me a new dress in pale blue 'Malmesbury' silk trimmed with white swansdown. I felt very proud my mother removed my coat and I stepped forward to lay my chaplet which I didn't know at the time but I had placed upside down.

The little boy who laid the flowers in honour of the dead was Dick Exton whose father Corporal Richard Exton had been killed in Gallipoli. The same pair returned in 1991 to repeat their part in the ceremony.

Peace but hardship continues 1919-21

After the armistice the town slowly returned to normal;

FROM WAR TO PEACE.- Lieut.-Col. L.E. Morrice, D.S.O., Royal Warwick Regt., and Mrs. Morrice have resumed residence at The Priory, Burton Hill. Lieut.-Col. Morrice was engaged at the War Office during the war. He was recently made a justice of the peace for Wiltshire.

A KHAKI CHRISTMAS.- Scores of soldiers are spending their Christmas leave at home. These include several who have been prisoners of war in Germany. Lots of local men have already received their discharge and are returning to their former employment.

At the end of January 1919 the Malmesbury branch of the National Farmers' Union held their annual meeting and re-elected Mr. T.W. Ferris as chairman. The main business was the price of milk;

The Chairman, in the course of a discussion on next summer's milk prices, said he was wholly in favour of the agricultural worker receiving wages as high as the price of produce would make possible, but beyond that they could not go. The old laws of political economy must prevail. No man could fix the prices of those commodities in agriculture six months ahead – to do so would be tantamount to defying the laws of the Creator, for no-one else could say what sort of weather we were going to have – agriculture was absolutely in the hands of the Creator. Farming could not be carried on by the clock, but this was what the Food Controller thought could be done. The farmers had been thoroughly loyal all through the war, but now the war was practically over, if every-one else was going to combine they must combine also. Else where would they be? No-one could deny that farmers had been patriotic, but if their workmen had to work only 6½ hours a day where was there a farmer who could carry on? When he was a lad they had to milk cows at a period of 13 hours and 11, but now the suggested hours were 17 and 7, and it could not be done. The old-fashioned sensible farmers were agreed that the plan was not possible. One of the old type of agricultural labourer, who knew his work, even at the age of 80, was preferable for the work of agriculture to a lad of 18 destitute of knowledge in farming work. The fancy proposal of putting a soldier on the land with a small acreage was altogether unworkable, because one bad season would kill him. He could not compete with the farmer equipped with modern implements.

The following resolution was unanimously carried: "That this meeting strongly protests against the present restrictions with regard to the hours of labour. Whilst agreeing that agricultural labourers should receive an adequate wage based on the value of produce, they urge that the present short hours make it most difficult to carry on, and they suggest that the half-holiday would make farming, where milking is concerned, almost impossible. This affects consumers as well as producers, because cows cannot produce their quota of milk if milked at irregular hours."

Mr. Carter impressed upon the meeting that it was no use protesting after the prices of milk had been fixed; they must be up and doing soon. Last May and June every grazing farmer had lost money on his milk. There were only two months left to recoup themselves, and had it not been for the energetic action of the Farmers' Union they would have lost more. They wished to be just to every-one, but they must set their faces against these multifarious restrictions. Mr. Lloyd George promised the people big wages, short hours and cheap food, but could any-one tell how it could be done? It was impossible (hear, hear).

Mr. Saunders suggested that the authorities should be informed that only a small proportion of the farm employees could get the weekly half-holiday, because it would only be given to day-men and not to any-one having charge of his stock.

Mr. Snow commented on the huge cost of The Unemployment Fund, and on the disinclination of those in receipt of out-of-work pay to seek work in agriculture.

Milk producers around Malmesbury had cause to celebrate when the new milk factory in Park Road was opened by the Mayor, Councillor M. Duck on Saturday 1st February. It was a co-operative venture run by Wiltshire Farmers Limited and cost around £7,000. The Directors of the company and many dignitaries from the town and county attended. As well as reporting the long speeches the North Wilts Herald described the plant;

The depot, which can economically deal with 5,000 gallons of milk per day, is probably one of the most up-to-date, both in construction and equipment that can be found throughout the length and breadth of the country. Originally a builder's premises, it is extraordinary how well they have adapted themselves to the purposes of a milk depot. On arrival the milk is weighed on a specially-designed milk weighing machine. The farmers have the option should they wish to sell their milk by the imperial gallon, but payment by weight is much more satisfactory from the farmers' point of view, and in this case be given credit for all that he delivers. From the weighing machine the milk passes to two large receiving tanks, from which it is lifted by means of specially-designed pumps either to the cheese-making room or a large tank on the pasteurising platform, from which tank it falls by gravitation to the centrifugal cleaner, where every particle of foreign substance is extracted. From the cleaner the milk passes into the pasteuriser and from this to the cooler, at which it arrives at a temperature of 150-170 degrees F, eventually finding its way to the railway churns at a temperature very little above freezing point. Churns are filled and despatched either direct to the consuming centres or placed in the cold store, which has a capacity for 2,000 gallons. Power is supplied by a Hornsby oil engine of 35 b.hp. The cold storage is provided by a Stearns condenser of 10 tons capacity. The cheese-making room is provided with four vats, each with a capacity of 500 gallons, and ample cheese room storage is provided in the rooms over. The depot is complete with every modern device for sterilising and cleaning milk cans and churns. The pumps and machinery were supplied and installed by the Agricultural Whole-sale Society, of Mark Lane, London, E.C., and the necessary alterations and extensions to the building were entrusted to Messrs. Downing & Rudman, of Chippenham, who are heartily to be congratulated for the way in which the buildings have been adapted and the efficient workmanship. Mr. Woodbridge, the Manager of the Milk Department of Wiltshire Farmers Limited who was responsible for the whole lay-out of the plant is also to be warmly congratu-lated for the part he has taken in bringing the enterprise to such a successful conclusion.

There was good news for housewives when the Food Controller announced that it would not be necessary to use ration coupons for the purchase of any quantity of margarine from 16th February and after 2nd March they would no longer be restricted to their registered retailer. However butter rationing continued. Later in the month it was announced that controls on the supply of tea would be suspended.

There were still many firearms in the community;

CHILD ACCIDENTALLY SHOT.- A rather serious accident occurred on Sunday evening to a little boy named Monty Mills, aged two years, the only son of Pte. Harold Mills, of Malmesbury. The little fellow, who was staying with his grandfather, Mr. J. Clark, of the Triangle, was accidentally shot by John Clark (17), son of Mr. Clark, who had taken a pistol to shoot a dog which was alleged to be a nuisance to the neighbourhood, but was not afforded the chance of doing so. Whilst he was in the house the weapon went off and the bullet entered the little boy's head at the front of the left ear, passed through the cheek and beneath the upper part of the bone on the outer side of the left eye, missing the eye by a fraction. The child was taken to the Cottage Hospital, where he is progressing favourably.

The Borough Council received a report from its Housing Sub-committee which caused Coun-cillors some concern. They were told that many properties in the town were in poor condition having been neglected for 4½ years. They were responsible under the Housing and Planning Act to condemn houses that were unfit for habitation. If they were condemned families would be thrown out on to the streets unless accommodation could be found for them. The population of the town had been fairly static as ambitious young people tended to leave as the job prospects were not good. Therefore there had been little new building and there was no space in the Borough for extra houses. There was a shortage of labour which was also hampering repairs. Although the Council had the power to build homes outside its area there was discussion as to whether its boundaries should be extended.

There was some good news about food supply reported by the Wiltshire Gazette on 6th March;

THE SUPPLY OF CHEESE.- As a result of protests to the divisional food commissioner (the executive officer reported to the local food committees this week) an extra 336lbs. of cheese per month had been granted to the borough for February and March, and 672lbs extra to the rural district; but supply to the borough was still very short, some retailers having none to sell.

Further information about household bills was announced at the beginning of March 1919;

THE FOOD BILL.
Anticipated Fall in Prices.

The Ministry of Food has issued the following statement: On the basis of family expenditure, assumed in the report of Lord Sumner's Committee (Working Classes Cost of Living Committee), the reduction of prices which have already occurred, or have been announced to occur before the end of March, by the Ministry of Food, should effect a considerable saving ... The total expenditure on food for the standard working-class family (between five and six persons) was put ... at 24s. 11d. in 1914, while that for 1918 was put at 47s. 3d. – that is to say an increase of 90 per cent. Taking, then, the expenditure of the standard working-class family on food ... the reduction ... should work out as follows:

Meat	8¼d.
Butter and Margarine	3d.
Cheese	¾d.
Tea	2½d.
Condensed milk	1d.
Fish and other foods	6½d.
Totalling	1s. 10d.

Among the other foods, included above, are canned salmon, dried fruits, peas and beans, and shredded suet. In addition to the reductions taken into account above, a number of further reductions of prices affecting meat, margarine, milk, eggs, cheese, fish and other cereal products are ... likely to occur in April or May. These should, between them, bring about a further reduction at least as great as that already effected, or announced, and probably somewhat greater. The total should, by the summer, come to the 4s. reduction in weekly working-class expenditure, referred to by the Prime Minister in his speech at the great Industrial Conference, and it is quite possible that even a greater reduction may, in fact, be realised.

On the other hand, there are a number of important foods in respect of which no early reduction can now be anticipated except by direct subsidy. These include bread (which is already subsidised), sugar (which is now being sold below the world price), and potatoes. It is also uncertain whether any early reduction will occur in the price of bacon and lard, which ... will be freed from control almost immediately. These four articles between them account for more than a third of total expenditure calculated by Lord Sumner's Committee.

Further relaxation of rationing was announced;

MEAT CONTROL.
Sept. 30th to be the Final Day.

Assuming that supplies are sufficient, the rationing of meat will cease on June 30th, and the whole of the restrictions on the sale and distribution of live-stock will be removed on September 30th. Prices to the farmers have already been fixed up to that date.

In the event of a rush of cattle to the markets, it may be necessary to place a restriction on the number marketed in any particular district. In any case, during the last month or two before the removal of control, instructions will be given to the Grading Committees in the markets to accept only stock which is fully mature or which is incapable of improvement by further keep.

Throughout the period of live-stock control every effort has been made to put the farmers in Great Britain and Ireland on an equal footing. In any restrictions which may be imposed, this policy will be strictly followed, involving, if necessary, a limitation of the amount of stock accepted from Ireland at each of the ports during the period under consideration.

In April the summer milk prices were announced. These applied to the producers, wholesalers and retailers of milk and cheese. The maximum prices for sale by producer per imperial gallon were;

	May s. d.	June s. d.	July s. d.	Aug s. d.	Sept s. d.
England	1 4	1 3	1 6	1 8	1 10
Scotland	1 6	1 4	1 4	1 7	1 10

As feared by the National Farmers Union, these were lower than farmers needed. These prices applied to cooled milk despatched twice daily, any railway charges between the seller and buyer to be borne by the buyer. Milk delivered once a day was worth ½d. less and milk collected by the buyer 1d. less. Wholesalers were allowed a maximum margin of 3d. per gallon for milk delivered to the buyer's railway station and an average maximum over the five months of 5d. for milk delivered to the buyer's premises. Retail prices were fixed at between 2s. 4d. and 3s. per gallon, but local Food Controllers would adjust them to take into account local distribution costs.

Changes to the method of accounting for rationed products were announced;

FUTURE RATIONING ARRANGEMENTS.
Butter, Sugar and Butcher's Meat.

The coupons in the present ration books run out on May 3rd. The public were warned some time ago to keep carefully their present ration books and these are now to be used after May 3rd for the purchase of uncooked butcher's meat, butter and sugar. The spares on leaves 6 and 6a of the ration book will be used for these purposes – the spaces marked "a" for sugar, those marked "b" for butter, and those marked "c" for meat.

Persons will continue to obtain these articles from the retailers with whom they are at present registered, and their retailers will mark the spaces on the occasion of the purchases. The ration of uncooked butcher's meat per week will be, as at present, twenty-pennyworth per head per week both for adults and children, but retailers may supply amounts in excess of this out of any surplus they may have.

The present ration of 12ozs of sugar per head will be continued but from May 3rd the ration of butter will be 2ozs per head instead of 1oz as at present.

All restrictions on the supply and distribution of jam (except that maximum prices will remain in operation) will be removed from May 4th, and persons may purchase from any supplier any quantity which they may be able to obtain.

There was some local dissent over the fixed price for milk;

Mr. W. Tinley presided at the meeting on Tuesday of the Borough Food Control Committee. Also present were Mrs. Thompson, Messrs. M. Thompson, A. Eatell and F. Weeks, with the executive officer. Notification was received from the Divisional Food Commissioner that the Food Controller had sanctioned the maximum retail prices of milk as follows: June, 1s. 8d. per gallon delivered, 1s. 6d. undelivered; July, 2s. delivered, 1s. 8d. undelivered; August and September, 2s. 4d. delivered, 2s. undelivered. Mrs. Mortimer and Mr. B. Odelands attended as a deputation of milk retailers to protest against the low price ... for milk sold "over the counter." The committee decided, however, that no interference could be made with the prices already fixed, and the retailers were warned that they were bound to carry out the regulations.

The local National Farmers Union branch felt that proposals by the Wages Board to increase wages were a major threat to their livelihoods. It was thought it would hit milk production hard. One member said that obtaining labour was a major problem, he had to pay 8s. and a pint of cider per day. Another suggested that carters ought to work 62 hours a week rather than 50 as they were paid more. Farmers needed a free hand over the cost of production and that cheaper food would enable workers to work harder. The meeting passed a motion calling for the abolition of the Agricultural Wages Board and its substitution with a Board composed of farmers and farm labourers.

Industrial relations were in turmoil and strikes in vital industries were threatened, so local plans were being made to alleviate problems;

MALMESBURY COAL SUPPLY.
Safeguarding Customers.
Mr. F.J. Bates presided at last week's meeting of the Malmesbury Fuel and Lighting Committee.
A communication from the Coal Controller respecting the future of fuel control was considered. The Fuel Overseer was instructed to supply the information requested, which was to the effect that in the opinion of the executive committee control should be maintained with slight modifications.
The Fuel Overseer reported that he had arranged with the principal merchants to hold a large stock of coal, which would only be used in an emergency. Some of the merchants had no storage ground available, so he had interviewed a number of leading residents who had large establishments and had come to an agreement whereby an adequate supply of coal would be available for the whole district so as to tide over a two or three weeks' stoppage of supplies from the collieries should such a contingency unfortunately arise. The Divisional Officer had placed the Local Fuel Overseer's proposal before the Coal Controller, and the latter had expressed his approval of it and desired to thank those who had kindly agreed to purchase a stock of coal for public use if required.
Advice had been received from the Coal Controller that no coal merchant who has not laid down a proper reserve stock as requested by the Local Fuel Overseer will be permitted to deliver stocks of coal to his customers. Merchants who have a proper reserve stock will be permitted, subject to the Local Fuel Overseer's consent, to stock the cellars of their customers up to a year's ration of coal. Until a certain reserve stock is in hand merchants are still prohibited from making deliveries of more than 3cwt. of coal to any customer.

Whilst news of the progress of peace negotiations was cheering, it was not so pleasant to hear that the temporary arrangements made for food rationing after 3rd May 1919 were to continue in place until at least the end of August. Emergency supplies of cheese during July were to be distributed as they had been in June.

In August it was decided to continue control of meat and live-stock until the end of June 1920 and prices were fixed. For cattle sold live the figures were based on 65s.-75s. per cwt. plus an additional sum per cwt. from between 4s. in September to November 1919 to as much as 20s. in May and July 1920. Equivalent prices were paid for dead weight and a similar sliding scale applied to sheep. There were sharp sanctions attached to these regulations as the grocer who ran the Original Store in Brinkworth found out in September. He appeared at Malmesbury Petty Sessions to answer 25 summonses for selling items above the designated maximum prices. The defendant offered to reimburse his customers double the amount that he defrauded them but still had to pay a £30 fine and £11 10s. costs.

In September the railwaymen went on strike for higher wages. The strike was reported by the Herald;

MALMESBURY AND THE STRIKE.- Malmesbury, in common with many other towns in the country, went to bed on Friday night little dreaming of the enforced changed condition of living awaiting it on the morrow, but the awakening was the realisation. The town railway station on Saturday morning resembled Oliver Goldsmith's "deserted village," the engine, kept under steam just outside the shed, conveying the only scene of life, but Malmesbury is living through the storm, and the positive life of the town, necessarily carried on with some difficulty, nevertheless proceeds in a cheerful atmosphere. Thanks to the efficiency and energy of the Executive Officer (Mr. T.H. Sandy) and his staff, an adequate supply of food had been available throughout the district. A plan of campaign, which had been framed by the Ministry of Food beforehand, was quickly put into operation locally, and the retailers loyally responded with all possible speed. These precautions were obviously taken not only to ensure the conservation of stocks, but to prevent any attempts at hoarding. In this connection it is satisfying to know that not a single attempt at this selfish practice has come to light. By the time all instructions had been issued putting the people on strict war ration, the majority had completed their shopping and the surplus goods in the shops constituted Malmesbury's food supply until further arrangements were forthcoming. A food "dump" had been established at Cricklade, and this is the town's chief source of supply, although lorry trips to Bristol, arranged by the Executive Officer, proved quite fruitful. Lack of transport also had the effect of accumulating several thousand gallons of milk at the Milk Factory during Saturday, Sunday and Monday, but the Manager (Mr. Spiers) surmounted the difficulty by converting a large quantity into cheese, and the staff, working with a hearty good will, were turning out one and a half tons of cheese per day. Seeing that the stock was so large the Executive Officer made arrangements for a supply of the June make to the local retailers. On Tuesday the High Street was almost an avenue of transport, whilst overhead passed the Avro aeroplanes. Quite a contingent of R.A.F. motor lorries arrived for the conveyance of over 500 churns of milk to the big central depot in London. The irrepressible drivers, who seemed to see the lighter side of the business, had in almost every case christened the "old bus." For instance we noticed among others the following: "Kittie, the Milkmaid," "The Mobile Dairy Co," "John Bull – Land's End to John o'Groats," "Milk for the Babies, Beer for the Convoy," whilst one lorry in particular, adorned with many names, also had the following inscribed outside the driver's seat: "Please don't throw money at us, as it worries the drivers." Thanks also to the action of the Fuel Overseer, Malmesbury is not without coal. On Saturday morning all coal standing in the railway sidings at Malmesbury, Dauntsey, Great Somerford and Brinkworth, were commandeered by him, and retailers were only allowed to deliver 1 cwt. per week for each household, exceptions being made in special cases such as sickness. The Fuel Overseer has made arrangements for a supply of coal from the Coalpit Heath Colliery. This will be brought by road transport. The public lamps were to have been lit for the first time this year on Wednesday, but this, of course, was stopped, and with economy in the use of gas, Malmesbury's supply at present will last for a fortnight. On Wednesday no small degree of interest was evinced in the passing through the town of a brigade of transport consisting of men of the West Yorks, Durhams, Lancers and R.A.S.C. The lorries and the rest of the paraphernalia were placed in a field at Daniel's Well, while the men were billeted in various parts of the town but chiefly in the Wesleyan Schoolroom. To the relief of the inhabitants the men had brought their own rations, and the next morning they were early risers, continuing their journey to Gloucester. Yesterday afternoon the town's meat supply arrived by road transport, and, judging by the excellent condition after a long journey, there is a hope that this method of meat transport will be continued in the future.

At the Borough Food Control meeting on 1st October there was an extraordinary outburst; Mr. Taylor asked whether they were going to allow the men on strike in Malmesbury and the villages the same rations as they were allowing the patriotic population; whether they were going to safeguard these Bolsheviks who were out to destroy the country and starve them. The Chairman, F.J. Bates and Mr. Stinchcomb both agreed with Mr. Taylor but Mrs. Ramsay was concerned about the strikers' wives and children. However it was resolved to send a strong protest to the Ministry of Food. Farmers would be asked to transport items back to their villages when they had reason to come into town. The Executive Officer was asked to try to get the Malmesbury train running between Swindon and Dauntsey as the driver and fireman on the engine had not joined the strike. The strike did not last long, meanwhile there was a report of a milk lorry stoned on the way from Chippenham and meat supplies were disrupted for a while.

The Wiltshire National Farmers Union expressed annoyance over the Food Controller's decision to de-control the supply of milk from the end of January 1920. Prices had been fixed until the end of April and farmers had purchased heifers and feeding stuffs at a high cost on the understanding of guaranteed selling prices. They complained the Government had broken faith in a most lamentable manner and thrown the whole industry into chaos and confusion. However it was hoped that United Dairies and Wiltshire Farmers would buy at the high prices. The prospects for agriculture did not look good and they felt the 48 Hour Week Bill being discussed by Parliament would reduce production. Further problems resulted from an outbreak of foot and mouth disease at Grittenham before the end of the month which closed 8 markets within a 15 mile radius including Malmesbury's.

It was later confirmed that from 31st January 1920 there would be no control over milk prices and home-produced butter and cream. The Ministry of Food would close at the end of August. The Food Controller expected the price of milk would fall but that home-produced butter would become more expensive than imported butter. Rationing of butter was to continue but the Ministry intended to buy more so that the ration could be increased. The price of imported meat was to be reduced by 2d. per pound and it was hoped that South America would provide ample supplies. The Government expected that some controls would be made permanent after the closure of this Ministry.

At the end of January a national conference of milk producers and sellers met to discuss prices. They decided to lower the price by 4d. per gallon with effect from 1st February. Just after the announcement the Malmesbury Farmers' Union held their annual meeting. It was reported that some farmers had been told that the price they received would be guaranteed until April including such a promise from Wiltshire Farmers. A strong resolution was passed pledging members not to supply those firms that wished to lower the price before April 30th. To add to their worries further outbreaks of foot and mouth were reported in Stratton St. Margaret, Walcot and two cases in Brinkworth.

The Foot and Mouth restrictions were eased at the end of February. No movements were allowed in an area centred around Cricklade but extending as far as the Somerfords and Charlton, although Malmesbury was just outside. Some markets were reopened (it is not clear whether Malmesbury was one of these) but only for cattle going to slaughter.

Food distribution was still causing problems;

FOOD CONTROL.- The Borough Food Control Committee met on Tuesday, the Rev. Father T. Morrin being in the chair. The other members present were Mrs. Jones and Messrs. E. Eatell, W. Tinley, H. Weeks, C. Gale, M. Thompson, and C.C. Barnes. The Executive Officer (Mr. T.H. Sandy) produced a sample of "free" sugar which a retailer had been selling at 1s. per lb. to anyone and in any quantity. He at once stopped it and pointed out that although it was called "free" sugar it was not for distribution among the people. It was privately imported, and was only to be sold to manufacturers. He did not advise a prosecution in this case, as there were so many instances up and down the country where free sugar had been bought under a misapprehension. The Ministry of Food had not been very explicit in their instructions upon the matter. Mr. Gale said he had seen an advertisement in one of the daily papers announcing sugar for sale, but it was not stated that it was for manufacturers only. It was decided to take no action in the matter. Mr. Tinley called attention to the poor quality of the milk. Before the war they got better skimmed milk at a penny a quart than that for which they were now paying such a tremendous price. Mr. Weeks said it was his opinion that the milk was mixed, and all present agreed that the milk was of a poor quality.

Price inflation in 1920 was also a worry;

The Cost of Living.
130 Per Cent Above 1914.

It is estimated by the Ministry of Labour that the increase in the cost of living, as compared with the position at the outbreak of war, amounted at March 1st to 130 per cent. The increase under the principal heads of household expenditure are given in the "Labour Gazette" as follows:

	Per cent		*Per cent*
Food	*133*	*Rent and rates*	*10*
Clothing	*300*	*Fuel and light*	*80 to 85*

In order to arrive at a single figure representing the increase since July, 1914, for all the items taken together, the average increases are combined in accordance with their relative importance, the weights used being as follows: Food, 7½; rent (including rates), 2; clothing, 1½; fuel and light, 1; allowance (corresponding to a weight of ½) also being made for the increase in the prices of soap, soda, domestic ironmongery, brushware and pottery, tobacco, fares and newspapers. The effect of using these weights is to obtain the average percentage increase in the cost of maintaining the pre-war standard of living. The resulting increase of

130 per cent, at March 1st is about the same as at the beginning of February.

During the latter month, owing mainly to the fall in the price of eggs, there was a further slight decline in the general level of retail food prices. Charges for milk also showed a further slight drop, and there was a fall in the price of fish averaging between 5 and 10 per cent. On the other hand the price of Government butter was advanced from 2s. 8d. per lb. to 3s. per lb., while margarine showed an increase rise at March 1st, as compared with Feb. 2nd, of ½d. per lb. In the case of potatoes there was an advance of about 1d. per 7lb. The remaining articles included in the calculation showed no appreciable change in price.

One proposal to deal with the shortage of housing had been under consideration by the Town Council for a while before a discussion was held at the March meeting (unfortunately it was later dropped);

A CHEAP BUILDING SITE

The Town Clerk (Mr. M.H. Chubb) asked the Council to amend the sum of £800 to £820 for the purchase of land at Reed's Farm, Tetbury Hill, for the erection of working-class dwellings.

In reply to Mr. J.A. Jones, the Clerk said the extra £20 was chiefly to purchase two or three extra perches of land.

Mr. Jones said he was discussing with Mr. Stokesbury (their engineer) the expenses of the town generally, and Mr. Stokesbury asked what they were doing about the housing scheme. He (Mr. Jones) said they were paying £100 an acre for the site. Mr. Stokesbury said it had been arranged to build on the outside of Gloucester a little factory and they were asked £1,000 per acre. "Jolly cheap, yours at Malmesbury," added Mr. Stokesbury.

The same meeting also heard about the new heating for the Town Hall. It would comprise a boiler, piping and ten radiators – four for the large hall, two for the large ante-room, one for the small ante-room and one in each of the offices downstairs. The contractor, from Stroud, would install and maintain the system for one year at a cost of £136. This was considered to be a very low figure and the tender was accepted.

Wiltshire Farmers Ltd. reported a loss of £5,581 3s. for 1919, compared to a profit of £2,083 4s. 1d. the year before. The milk department had lost £10,841, but this had included expenses arising from the expansion from one depot to ten, including Malmesbury. Part of the difficulty arose because promised subscriptions from farmers to fund the new depots had not been forthcoming and money had to be borrowed from the bank. In Malmesbury there were continuing complaints that the milk factory was polluting the river.

In June 1920 the Borough Council received notice that the office of local Fuel Overseer should be terminated as soon as possible. State control of coal production and rationing was coming to an end and the officers concerned were praised for the way in which their work had been discharged with tact and a high degree of efficiency. Also at that meeting they considered a proposal to extend the Borough boundaries. It was said that they would have to take into account many additional expenses – extending the water mains & sewage scheme to include the new area and the cost of maintaining district roads including Arches Lane, Foxley Road from Turtle Bridge, Filands road and the Milbourne road as far as the Charlton road. It is interesting to note that only Filands has since been incorporated into the town, Burton Hill and Foxley Road still being outside the town.

Sugar was one of the few foods to remain rationed;

Sugar Supplies.
Welcome Announcement by Food Controller.

It was announced by the Food Controller on Monday that until the second or third week in September there will be included in the sugar ration, as heretofore, a certain proportion of brown moist sugar.

By the middle of September the additional supplies of white sugar which have been arranged for should be in the hands of retailers, who will then be authorised to supply the whole of the present ration of 12 ounces in the form of white sugar.

After September 6th, says the "Daily Chronicle," the public will be free to purchase brown

moist sugar in addition to the weekly ration of 12 ounces.
Purchases of brown moist sugar may be made after September 6th at any shop, and need not be confined to the shop at which the customer is registered.

At the July meeting of the Town Council there was a long discussion about the proposed housing at Reed's Farm. Much concern was expressed about the fact the plan would result in 20 houses outside the borough which would not result in any extra income from rates as the Rural District would benefit. The meeting was also advised that the cost of lighting the town's 46 street lamps would be £117, £26 more than the previous year. Mr. Gale said that 46 lamps were insufficient, there were a number of dangerous places such as by the National Schools and in Burnivale where more light was needed.

Her Highness Princess Helena Victoria visited Malmesbury the following week to open the Y.M.C.A. hall. She was said to be the first member of the Royal Family to visit the town since Charles I. Shops and offices were closed to allow large crowds to line the gaily decorated High Street and adjacent areas.

The North Wilts Herald of 19th November 1920 had an intriguing headline; *A 2000-GALLON COW AT MALMESBURY*. It reported that Lieut.-Col. Morrice of the Priory owned a pedigree British Fresian cow called Wiggington Geraldine (13542) that had produced 2,000 gallons of milk in just 303 days. This was only the tenth cow in the United Kingdom which had achieved this yield and was the first in Wiltshire or the Western Counties to do so. The herd had only been established eighteen months before and its management was in the hands of Mr. H. Foster who had been recruited from Aylesbury. Wiggington Geraldine was the first cow bought for the herd and had calved in January which had doubled her yield.

Although rationing had ended, some matters had yet to be cleared up as the Town Council heard in January 1921;

FOOD CONTROL
The Clerk mentioned that up to a day or so ago £52 was still owing to the Council by the Food Control Ministry; it had been reduced to about £30, but it ought to be paid – it was a scandal. – Mr. Wilmot: I thought food control was over. – Alderman Forrester: They are finishing it up.

At the same meeting Alderman Adye complained that the town's train service was no better than it had been during the war and it was unanimously agreed to write to the Great Western Railway. He explained that the last train from London left at three o'clock arriving at 6.35 p.m. and from Bristol you had to catch the 4.5 p.m. and travel via Bradford-on-Avon. Yet there was a 5.15 p.m. train from London that stopped at Wootton Bassett, but why not at Malmesbury and you could leave Bath at 5.20 p.m. but there was no connection here. Alderman Farrant reminded them that the Government was providing a £25 million subsidy to the railways. Mr. Terrell said that no improvement could be hoped for until Government control ended.

In February a number of public house licences were revoked as reported by the Wiltshire Gazette;

MALMESBURY LICENSES REFERRED.
Supt. Maidment formally objected to the renewal of the licenses of the Green Dragon Inn, the Three Horse Shoes Inn, and the Volunteer Inn, in the parish of St. Paul, Malmesbury Within; also to those of the Barley Mow and the Oddfellows, in the parish of St. Mary, Westport. There were 13 licensed houses in the parish of St. Paul, Malmesbury Within, he said, and 22 licensed houses in the borough. This showed, according to the last census, a license to every 120 persons in Westport, and one to every 83 persons in St. Paul Within. He asked that the licenses of the five houses cited should be referred.
Mr. Roberts offered no opposition on behalf of the owners, but for the licensee of the Barley Mow pointed out that this house accommodated a large number of wayfarers, whom the landlady, who was a war widow with three little children, supplied with food. It was desirable that this class of people should be accommodated, and the house was serving a useful

purpose. *In 1914 the sale was 155 barrels; in 1919, 111 barrels; in 1920, 118 barrels. Mrs. Salter (landlady) bore out Mr Roberts's statement. She admitted that to get to the stable horses would have to come through the house. – The Chairman: I am surprised at the owners allowing such a state of things to exist. – Mr. Roberts: It has gone on for a very long time. – The Chairman: Precisely, and we are now trying to remedy these evils. – Mr. Downing (secretary of the Stroud Brewery Co.): I was not aware that such a thing did exist. – The Chairman: Poor excuse! You should make yourself more conversant with the conditions of your houses (laughter). Mr. Downing: It is very difficult to know everything about them. – The Chairman: The Bench fully recognises this.*
All the houses were referred.

The ending of price control had not brought any comfort to farmers. At a meeting of the local branch of the National Farmers' Union Sherston members proposed a resolution that there should be freedom of contract between employers and employed as farmers were unable to meet the fixed minimum wages due to prices continually falling. Discussions with retailers over milk prices were not concluded and members were exhorted not to make independent contracts. Disquiet was also expressed over the likelihood that the opening of licensed houses between 10 a.m. and 4 p.m. on market days would be ended. The war had ended two years before but the Liquor Control Board still remained and they allowed different closing hours in Gloucestershire and Wiltshire. A lively discussion took place over auctioneers' charges at local markets. It was felt that Malmesbury ought to benefit from the same scale as Chippenham.

At the end of March 1921 there was an indication that wartime privations were no longer acceptable;

LET THERE BE LIGHT!- Many are the complaints made respecting the untidy nature of the hedges in the rural district; farmers have pleaded the exigencies of the war, and hitherto it has been accepted as a successful defence. But the Rural Council now think that the time has come for action in the matter, and those gentlemen who ignore the Surveyor's caution may rely on being brought before the bench for a ruling on the point. At Saturday's meeting of the Rural District Council it was decided to summon Mr. Jesse Wootton, of Thornhill Farm, Malmesbury, for this offence.

Industrial unrest continued and in the middle of April there was the threat of a coal strike. The mines had been handed back to their owners on 31st March and immediately introduced a cut in wages. The public's war-time sense of duty was once again called upon. A meeting with a large attendance was held in the Town Hall chaired by the Mayor, Councillor F. Weeks. A telegram had been received from Mr. Lloyd George asking for volunteers to enrol in special Defence Units. This scheme was based around the Territorial Army units of the Royal Wiltshire Yeomanry and 4th Battalion Wiltshire Regiment. Colonel Morrice said that whatever the rights and wrongs of the dispute it was vital that essential services and food supplies were maintained. The period of service was limited to 90 days but only nine men enrolled. At the same time the Rural District Council was trying to ascertain how much coal there was in the area and so far as they could determine there was a week or ten days' supply. They appointed Mr. Hardwick as overseer to prepare for coal rationing. When the miners returned to work in July their wages were worse than those offered at the beginning of the dispute and this pattern was repeated throughout the economy.

Unemployment is not confined to big industrial centres. There are many in small town and in rural districts who at present find themselves in the ranks of the workless army. Not a small number of men and youths in Malmesbury are unemployed – such was the introduction of a North Wilts Herald report on the September meeting of the Town Council. They considered a letter from the Swindon and District Employment Committee urging that they could carry out improvements to offer extra employment. Schemes discussed were the nasty corner at the bottom of Holloway Hill, the narrow part of the road in the Triangle near the Castle Inn and the narrow road at the foot of Keene's Hill, Bristol Street. However none were agreed as government funding was needed to make these affordable. So much for "a fit country for heroes to live in."

Outline Organisation of the British Army overseas

The main overseas armies were the British Expeditionary Force (France), Mediterranean Expeditionary Force (Gallipoli) and Egyptian Expeditionary Force. Forces in Greece were known as the British Salonika Army and those in Mesopotamia were controlled from India. Other smaller forces operated against German colonies in Africa and Asia.

Army (Up to 5 in the B.E.F.) - contained 2 or more Corps, with extra support troops such as tanks and aircraft.

Corps (Up to 19 British & 4 Empire in the B.E.F., 2 British, 1 Anzac & 1 French in Gallipoli) - contained 2 or more Divisions, with extra logistical units and other support troops such as heavy artillery.

Division, abbreviation Div. (a maximum of 62 simultaneously served in the B.E.F.) - contained 18,000 men with elements of other arms to support the main infantry element, commanded by a Major General.

Brigade, abbreviation Bde. (3 per Division) - contained 4,000 men commanded by a Brigadier General.

Battalion, abbreviations Battn. or Bn. (originally 4 but in 1918 3 per Brigade) - contained 1,000 men commanded by a Lieutenant Colonel.

Company, abbreviation Coy. (4 per Battalion) - contained 200 men commanded by a Captain.

Platoon, abbreviation Pl. (4 per Company) - contained 50 men commanded by a Lieutenant.

Section (4 per Platoon) - contained 10 men commanded by a Corporal.

Equivalent sized units in other arms were;

Infantry	Cavalry	Artillery
Battalion	Regiment	Brigade
Company	Squadron	Battery
Platoon	Troop	Section

Once in action the actual strength quickly fell below establishment and units were often commanded by more junior officers. After the battles of early 1915 it became usual for up to 10% of a Battalion's strength to be kept in reserve so that a nucleus remained to rebuild the unit.

The Wiltshire and Gloucestershire Regiments, like those of most counties, before the war had two Regular battalions (1st & 2nd) and one Special Reserve battalion (3rd) which provided Reservists to bring the Regular units up to war establishment on mobilisation. Wiltshire had just one Territorial Force battalion (4th) but Gloucestershire which included Bristol had three (4th, 5th & 6th).

The wartime expansion of the army added 'Kitchener' or as they were more properly named, Service, battalions. Their numbers thererefore started at the 5th for Wiltshire and 7th for the Gloucesters. Wiltshire only had three (5th, 6th & 7th) with one extra Reserve battalion (8th), whereas Gloucester drawing on the large city populations had seven (7th-10th & 12th-14th) plus three more Reserve battalions (11th, 15th & 16th). Service battalions were technically part of the Regular Army, although their soldiers only signed on for the duration of the war. The Territorial Force also expanded - each battalion split into two active battalions and one Reserve. These were numbered as 1/4th, 2/4th and 3/4th in the case of the Wiltshires.

Part Two
Our Glorious Dead

1914

Once units had been mobilised and brought up to war strength they prepared to embark for France. Most of the fighting troops were taken by train to Southampton and shipped to one of three ports – Le Havre, Rouen or Boulogne. Over five days 1.800 special trains were run in Great Britain and an average of 13 ships sailed each day. A message from the King was given to the men as they left;

You are leaving home to fight for the safety and honour of my Empire.
Belgium, whose country we are pledged to defend, has been attacked, and France is about to be invaded by the same powerful foe.
I have implicit confidence in you, my soldiers. Duty is your watchword, and I know your duty will be nobly done.
I shall follow your every movement with deepest interest and mark with eager satisfaction your daily progress; indeed, your welfare will never be absent from my thoughts.
I pray God will bless you and guard you, and bring you back victorious.

The first infantry battalions arrived on 11th August to a continuous enthusiastic welcome as they marched through the ports. Many soldiers gave away cap badges and buttons in return for quick embraces from pretty girls or food and wine from the not so pretty!

Although the Expeditionary Force was supposed to comprise six Divisions there was a great fear that Britain would be invaded and only four were initially despatched. On 19th August it was decided to send another Division and four battalions intended to guard the Lines of Communication were formed into another Brigade. The troops were taken across France in slow trains composed of wagons marked *Hommes 40, Chevaux en long 8* to the concentration area near Maubeuge in Northern France in a supposedly quiet area on the far left of the French Armies. The concentration was completed by the 20th. The following day the advance to the north began despite the infant Flying Corps reporting a large column of Germans near Louvain. As the day progressed, cavalry moving in front of the main body observed enemy patrols. At dawn on 22nd the first clash took place just north of Mons where C Squadron of 4th Dragoon Guards came off best – killing three and capturing three for no loss.

The B.E.F. were ordered to prepare defensive positions along the canal at Mons. It was here that the German forces were met early on the morning of 23rd August. Although the British gave a good account of themselves that day they were several miles in advance of the French Fifth Army to their right which was retreating. To the west there were some French cavalry and low grade troops so that there was a danger of being outflanked. Therefore the retreat began with the soldiers fatigued from the march to the front and the fighting. Marching was difficult on the cobbled roads and reservists suffered from unyielding stiff boots. Various skirmishes took place over the next few days including the battle of Le Cateau. There was much confusion with many soldiers being separated from their unit. By 5th September the British were south east of Paris having marched at least 200 miles in 13 days. In the process their logistical tail had been disrupted with all the stores in the original ports of disembarkation cleared and moved to the more distant port of St Nazaire for fear of a further advance by the enemy. However a split in the German forces had been detected and General Joffre ordered an advance that became known as the Miracle of the Marne. The B.E.F. turned about, fighting and following the Germans as they moved north. They forced crossings of the River Marne on the 8th and the River Aisne on the 12th before being forced to a halt by defensive positions along the Chemin des Dames. They dug in and the lines of the trenches that would remain in this area for the next three years were established. It was here that British troops had their first experience of being bombarded by 'Black Marias' (8-inch howitzer shells), 'Woolly Bears' (high-explosive shrapnel), 'Jack Johnsons' (named after a negro heavyweight boxing champion) and 'Coalboxes' (15cm German howitzer shells).

The next phase of the war was the 'race to the sea.' Although the Belgians were still holding out at Antwerp and in other parts of their country, there was a large gap between them and the French Sixth Army north east of Compiegne. This 90 miles or so was thinly garrisoned by

North Sea

Holland

Belgium
Brussels
Antwerp
Ghent
Cologne
Aix-la-Chapelle
Liège
Namur
Huy
Charleroi
Mons
Valenciennes
Maubeuge
Givet
Germany

Zeebrugge
Ostend
Dunkirk
R.Yser
JULY 1917
JUNE 1917
Ypres
Passchendaele
Menin
Messines
Bailleul
St.Omer
Hazebrouck
Armentières
Lille
Lillers
MAR. 1915
Neuve Chapelle
Béthune
La Bassée
Loos
SEPT.1915
Lens
St.Pol
APRIL 1917
VIMY
RIDGE
Douai
ARTOIS
Arras
APRIL 1917
Doullens
Cambrai
Bapaume
Le Câteau
JULY 1916
Albert
Amiens
Péronne
R.Somme
JULY 1916
St.Quentin
Guise
PICARDY
Montdidier
Ham
La Fère
Lassigny
Noyon
Compiègne
Soissons
Laon
R.Aisne
APRIL 1917
APRIL 1917
R.Oise
Senlis
R.Ourcq
Chantilly
Reims
APRIL 1917
Paris
Château Thierry
Epernay
R.Marne
APRIL 1917
Châlons
Pt.Morin
Gd.Morin
MARSHES OF ST.GOND
R.Ornain
Bar le Duc
R.Seine
R.Marne

Ardennes
Neufchâteau
Mézières
Sedan
Luxembourg
Virton
Trier
Saarburg
R.Moselle
R.Saar
Longuyon
Thionville
FEB. 1916
Briey
FEB. 1916
Verdun
FOREST OF ARGONNE
Metz
Lorraine
St.Mihiel
Morhange
Toul
Nancy
R.Moselle
R.Meurthe
Charmes
Epinal
Vosges
Belfort
Aisne
Champagne
R.Meuse
R.Scheldt
R.Lys
R.Escaut
R.Sambre
R.Meuse
R.Waal
R.Maas
R.Meuse
R.Rhine

N

From *All the Kaiser's Men*
Sutton Publishing 2003
WESTERN FRONT

▬ ● ▬ ● ▬ Approximate line at end of 1914
⬥⬥⬥⬥⬥⬥ Line at end of Hindenburg Retreat, February 1917
▬▬▬▬▬ Line on 11th Nov. 1918

0   50
Miles

French Territorials with German cavalry roaming around causing alarm and discomfort. General French, commander of the B.E.F., was concerned that he was too far away from the channel ports and the best line of communication with home. He therefore suggested that his forces should be replaced and moved north. They began the move on the night of 1st/2nd October by train, foot and on horseback with the last troops leaving a fortnight later. Remarkably although around 2,000 men had died up to this time, none came from Malmesbury. However some were amongst the 10,000 wounded with National Reservists from our town starting to arrive to fill the gaps in the ranks. Our good fortune was not to last.

Some troops were landed directly to assist the defence of Antwerp. The First Sea Lord, Winston Churchill, had organised supernumerary sailors into two naval brigades which, with a Royal Marine Brigade, were formed into the Royal Naval Division. These raw troops arrived just as the withdrawal from the fortress began and many were interned in Holland when they crossed the border into that neutral country. Another Division, the 7th, was formed from army garrisons returning from the closer parts of the Empire and they were landed at Zeebrugge on the 6th and 7th October. Shortly afterwards the bulk of the B.E.F. began arriving from the south. As the Allies were transferring forces to the north of France and southern Belgium, simultaneously the Germans were concentrating forces there, both with the intention of attacking the other's flank. So the scene was set for an encounter battle with attack and defence in unprepared positions with the front moving one way and the other.

At first the British pushed forward with the object of occupying Lille but were halted by strong counter attacks. Although under great pressure the line held and the focus moved north to the east of Ypres, destined to be an area of extreme hardship for our troops for more than four years. There was optimism that there was still an opportunity to turn the flank and advance to Menin, but these hopes were dashed by clashes with powerful forces of the Fourth and Sixth German Armies. After desperate fighting the front stabilised.

Whilst this fierce fighting had occurred on land, the Royal Navy had some triumphs and a few disasters at sea. The blockade of Germany had been quickly implemented with their merchant fleet interned or largely confined to harbour. This would have a growing effect on their ability to wage war. There had been a number of clashes between surface warships including the Battle of Coronel off South America on 1st November where the British cruisers Good Hope and Monmouth were sunk. Two fast battlecruisers were sent to the area and on 8th December four of the German cruisers were sunk at the Battle of the Falkland Islands. Present at both engagements was H.M.S. Glasgow commanded by Captain John Luce from Malmesbury and he sent reports of the actions that provided some good news for the newspapers.

Unfortunately because two of the three local men killed in 1914 were listed as missing there were no reports in the newspapers so their stories have been compiled from other sources.

Wakefield, William Edgar, Private, 8400, age 24, 2nd Battalion Duke of Edinburgh's (Wiltshire Regiment)

Missing presumed killed, 24th October 1914, commemorated on the Menin Gate Panel 53, Malmesbury Abbey, Congregational Church, Town Hall & Triangle.

The Menin Gate is one of four memorials to the missing in Belgian Flanders which cover the area known as the Ypres Salient. The site of the Menin Gate was chosen because of the hundreds of thousands of men who passed through it on their way to the battlefields. It commemorates those of all Empire nations (except New Zealand) who died in the Salient, in the case of United Kingdom casualties before 16th August 1917. Those and New Zealand servicemen who died after that date are named on the memorial at Tyne Cot, a site which marks the furthest point reached by British forces in Belgium until nearly the end of the war. The Menin Gate memorial, designed by Sir Reginald Blomfield with sculpture by Sir William Reid-Dick, was unveiled by Lord Plumer in July 1927. Councillor S.N. Dixon and his wife from Malmesbury attended the dedication service. Every night the traffic is stopped for the last post to be sounded by buglers of the local Fire Brigade. This ceremony has taken place ever since the opening, only being interrupted during the German occupation in the Second World War.

It is likely that William Edgar Wakefield was a Regular soldier being shown as 'unattached' in the Mayor's Roll of Honour. He was the eldest son of Samuel (a tailor) and Caroline Wakefield, of 30 West Street and had three brothers, Charles, Samuel & Thomas and three sisters, Hilda, Ethel & Anne. He had enlisted originally in Chippenham. The 2nd Battalion Wiltshire Regiment was in Gibraltar at the outbreak of war and arrived at Southampton on 3rd September. As part of the overseas garrison they would have been up to strength but some of their experienced men would have been posted to New Army units as instructors. His unit was part of 7th Division which landed at Zeebrugge on the 7th October. Ordered to advance towards Menin on

19th October they got within two miles of that town. Aerial reconnaissance reported large enemy columns coming in the opposite direction and orders arrived to stop, then to retire. Next day 2nd Wiltshires were part of a force that advanced towards the village of Terhand, but after coming under artillery fire they fell back. By the 22nd the Wiltshires were on the left of 21st Brigade in front of Polygon Wood but there existed a gap between them and the nearest part of 22nd Brigade. Before this could be exploited the 2nd Scots Guards filled in. This junction of the units was heavily bombarded for eight hours and then attacked at 3 p.m. The German infantry advanced over the crest of a ridge and the Official History records; *Struck by gun and machine-gun fire as soon as they came well into sight, the German masses staggered, and, as one British battalion diary states, their dead and wounded literally piled up in heaps, almost before a rifle shot had been fired. Led by their officers, however, some still struggled on: a few got within two hundred yards of the Wiltshire, and others actually penetrated a gap between the Green Howards and the Scots Fusiliers, only to meet their fate at the hands of a reserve company. The 54th Reserve Division, for to this the attackers appear to have be-longed, recoiled; but, after a pause, made one last effort against the flanks of the Wiltshire, again to be driven back decimated by shrapnel and rifle fire.* Throughout the next day the bombardment and attacks continued. Because of particular pressure on the Wiltshires a sec-ond company of Scots Guards had to be sent in support.

The next day brought no let-up in the onslaught. Individuals and small parties of enemy had infiltrated into the wood and these had to be eliminated. On the right of the Wiltshires a company of Royal Scots Fusiliers was forced to withdraw and on the left the Scots Guards were driven back early in the morning. Unfortunately the Wiltshires were not aware of these developments and simultaneous attacks from the front and flanks virtually destroyed the unit. The Battalion war diary records the confused fighting on that day;

Belgium, Near Reutel, Polygon Wood Saturday 24th October 1914

About 5.30 a.m. (just before daybreak) the enemy attacked in a very superior force but were driven back with heavy loss. They attacked again, and after about 2 hours of almost continu-ous fighting in which the enemy lost hundreds in killed and wounded, they broke through the lines having previously contrived to come around on our left through trenches that had been vacated with the exception of about 30 NCOs and men mostly from trenches on right the remainder of Battalion were either killed or captured, a large number being captured. Cpl. Alderton who had escaped from trench on left of BECELARE road together with Privates Dunn Holister and Jones being apparently last to leave the trenches, gathered stragglers together and formed a rear guard to Brigade ambulances by opening out in skirmishing order. On arrival at 7th Divisional HQ he was met by Cpl Bull, and in the evening the Assistant Provost Marshal took party numbering 26 back to Brigade HQ where they met Cpl. Richens and 50 men which included about 12 Lance Corporals. The majority of these men had been driven from their trenches by artillery fire the previous evening. The Quartermaster hearing that Lieut. Macnamara was wounded visited him at the field hospital and afterwards about 4 p.m. collected the 50 men above mentioned taking them to Brigade HQ and was informed that no news of Battalion had been received since early morning.

NOTE: special mention should be made of the gallant worth of Capt. Comyn, the medical officer and stretcher bearers who for the last three days and nights were continuously han-dling wounded or burying dead.

It is estimated that 450 wounded and unwounded men were in the trenches at the start of that day. The first casualty list of 1915 listed Private Wakefield as missing but it was more than a year after his death before confirmation was received by his family. Curiously the Mayor's Roll of Honour did not note that he was missing. The first reference in the newspapers I can find is a short mention in the Wiltshire Gazette of 9th March 1916;

TRIBUTE TO THE FALLEN.- The "Parish Magazine" says: "All honour to Privates William Edgar Wakefield and Arthur Edward Bailey, who have given themselves to their country. We trust their memory and the memory of others who have fallen will be kept before the generations to come, whose freedom has been purchased at the cost of their lives."

William's brother Samuel Walter, another Regular, served with the 1st Wiltshires at Mons but after suffering frostbite was invalided out. Perhaps keen to avenge his brother he rejoined the Gloucesters but on 22nd August 1916 he was seriously wounded in the arms, legs and right eye.

The Menin Gate in 1928, shortly after its completion. (cwgc.org.uk)

Bailey, Arthur Edward, Private, 9703, age 24, 1st Battalion Coldstream Guards
Missing presumed killed, 29th October 1914, commemorated on the Menin Gate Panel 11, Malmesbury Abbey, Town Hall & Triangle.
For a description of the Menin Gate see Private William Wakefield's entry above.
Arthur Bailey was a son of William (a farm labourer) and Annie, Hyam Cottages, Brokenborough and he was born in that village. He had six sisters, Kate, Rose, Bessie, Emily, Ada & Ellen and one brother, Fred. His father worked as a carter for Walter Gorton of Hyam Farm. Sometime later William was drowned after falling in a pool where the school playing field is now. Arthur was another Regular soldier who had enlisted at Devizes in 1912 but transferred to the Guards. When war broke out 1st Battalion of the Coldstreams were on public duties at Windsor. They formed part of the 1st Division, arrived in France on 13th August and took part in the battles of Mons and the Aisne. They were amongst the last units to leave the Chemin des Dames on 15th October. The battalion moved into the front line at Langemarck, to the east of Ypres, on 21st October. They stayed in this position under constant attack for 2 days. On the morning of the 23rd heavy artillery fire was followed by an advance which got within 50 yards of the trenches and forced part of the unit back. That night the division went into reserve. Recalled to reinforce the 2nd Division on the 26th they took part in an attack towards Reutel which made no progress. By the 29th the Coldstreams were the right hand unit of 1st Division dug in north of the Menin Road with the 1st Grenadier Guards of 7th Division south of the road. The Coldstreams were very

Arthur Bailey (www.military-genealogy.co.uk)

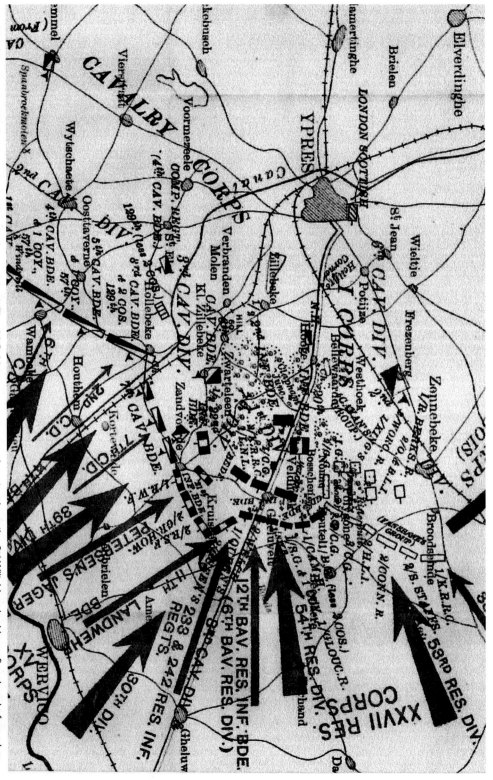

The situation on 29th October when Arthur Bailey perished. The 1st Coldstreams were very close to where the 2nd Wiltshires had been five days before when William Wakefield was lost. Within a fortnight the British had retreated to Hooge where the line remained for nearly three years. (Military Operations 1914)

weak, only 350 strong and unable to hold the front assigned to them, so they were reinforced by companies of 1st Black Watch to their left and right. The trenches were crude with no traverses to prevent shrapnel ripping along the row of defenders and no overhead cover.

In foggy weather at 5.30 a.m. three battalions of Bavarian Infantry attacked just north of the road. Two of the British machine guns jammed and the rifle fire slackened because cartridges were found to be too large. The Germans overran the Black Watch and moved northwards overcoming parties of Coldstreams so that by 6.30 many of them had been killed or captured. Two companies, separated by a considerable gap, formed a defensive flank and continued the fight. However by 10 a.m. they too were overwhelmed. The Coldstreams lost 10 officers and 180 men that day with only the Quartermaster and 80 men answering the roll that night, although later another 60 men found their way back to rejoin their comrades.

Arthur, being an early war casualty from a prestigious unit, had the following biographic entry in the ambitious De Ruvigny's Roll of Honour;

Private, No 9703, 1st Battn. Coldstream Guards, s. of William Bailey, of Hyam Cottages, Malmesbury, Wilts., Farm Labourer, by his wife, Annie, dau. of the late Matthew Clark, of Malmesbury; b. Brokenborough, near Malmesbury, co. Wilts., 2 Aug 1890; educ. Malmesbury National School; enlisted 31 July, 1912, and was killed in the fighting round Ypres. Oct. 1914; unm.

This desperate action took place along the Menin Road, near Gheluvelt.

De Ruvigny intended to provide details of all the men killed in the war but as a result of the fast growing casualty lists had to modify this aim and concentrated on officers, so Arthur is in fine company. More than 25,000 entries were made when finally published, 7,000 of which had photographs, including Arthur's. The only other Malmesbury man to be included was the Revd. E. Davies.

Arthur was posted as missing, it seems that his death was not confirmed until a year later. There was only a short report about him in the North Wilts Herald that appeared in September 1915;

OTHER CASUALTIES.- Yesterday morning Mrs. Bailey, Hyam Cottages, received official notification that her son Private Frederick James Bailey, age 20, of the 6th Leinsters, was missing. He also was in the Dardanelles. Another son, Pte. Arthur E. Bailey, 1st Coldstream Guards, has been missing since October last.

Grey, George, Private, 3/9164, age 34, 1st Battalion Duke of Edinburgh's (Wiltshire Regiment)

Killed in action, 13th November 1914, buried Ypres Reservoir Cemetery IX G 35, commemorated Malmesbury Abbey, Town Hall & Triangle.

Three cemeteries were made near the western gate of Ypres: two between the prison and the reservoir, both now removed into the third on the north side of the prison. The latter was first called the "Cemetery North of the Prison," later Ypres Reservoir North and now Ypres Reservoir. This cemetery was begun in October 1915 and used by fighting units and field ambulances until after the Armistice, when it contained 1,099 graves. It was later enlarged when graves were brought in from smaller cemeteries or from the battlefields of the salient. There are now 2,613 Empire servicemen of the First World War buried or commemorated here. 1,034 of the burials are unidentified. The cemetery was designed by Sir Reginald Blomfield.

George was the youngest son of Robert (a farmer) and Mary Grey, Burnham Road with brothers Henry, Robert & Joseph and sisters Eliza, Mary Jane, Sarah, Annie & Amanda. George was a long standing member of the 3rd Wilts Militia and by 1914 had joined the Special Reserve. His mother had died and George, unmarried, lived with his father. He had been employed by the Borough Council and was recalled to join the 3rd Battalion. He was sent to 1st Battalion in France as a replacement for heavy casualties. The 1st Wiltshires were part of the 3rd Division and landed at Rouen on 14th August 1914, although George was not with them then. He actually arrived in France on the 23rd October and would have been quickly sent to the battalion. They had received seven drafts of reinforcements and he was probably amongst the last group of 40 men arriving on 1st November. The adjutant calculated that since the start of the campaign, having been at Mons, endured the retreat, advanced to the Aisne and then moved up to Ypres, they had suffered 1,000 casualties, the same as the unit's original strength although it then totalled only 530. This was a quiet time on this part of the front but still men were killed or wounded each day. There was more activity the day George died but the war diary entry was still short;

Belgium, Hooge Friday 13th November 1914
In trenches. Enemy shelled steadily, our guns replying. Germans brought up a gun in dead ground to within 100 yards of our trenches. Germans attacked in the afternoon, and S. Lancs were forced back (they were on our immediate right) these trenches were re-taken at dusk. 'A' Coy rejoined from 15th Bde. Gordons relieved firing line about 12 midnight.
3 killed, 6 wounded.

The Wilts & Gloucester Standard of 19th December 1914 reported;

The death of Private George Gray, 3rd Wiltshire Regiment was verified on Thursday morning 17th by War Office officials as having been killed in action 13th November. He was a single man aged 33, the youngest son but one with 4 brothers and 5 sisters of Mr Robert Gray, Burnham Road. When the lad's mother died 9 years ago his father, an old Malmesbury Commoner, in receipt of an old age pension, broke up his home and went to live with his daughter Mrs Mills also in Burnham Road. George lodged with his brother and wife at 4 West Street. Robert has left a wife and young children to go on active service. Another brother Joe is awaiting the call at Tidworth. Deceased has been for some years in the employ of Malmesbury Town Council. During the South African war he was on duty for 13 months at St Helena. Grays of Malmesbury have always been noted for their "fighting blood". He was mobilized with the first unit from Malmesbury but did not arrive in France until October 23. I have been unable to find any record of a younger brother and the Gazette reported that George was the youngest son.

Because his body was buried in an identified grave unlike the first two Malmesbury fatalities, George's was the first death to be confirmed on 10th December although the family unofficially heard of his death from Private Hadrell who was brought back to England fatally wounded. George's body must have been exhumed after the war and reburied in the Ypres Reservoir Cemetery. A memorial service for him was held in the Abbey on 23rd December as the North Wilts Herald reported on 1st January;

HONOURING A HERO.

A memorial service to the late Private George Grey, Wilts Regiment, was held in the Abbey Church last week. There was a large congregation which included the Mayoress (Mrs. A. Adye), Alderman H. Farrant and Alderman J.H. Bartlett, their presence marking the recognition by the Municipality of its deep sense of loss in the death of Pte. Grey, who was the first

Malmesbury soldier to be killed in the war. The Mayoress represented the Mayor, who was attending a funeral at Great Somerford.
There were also present Mr. Robert Grey (father), Messrs. Henry and Joseph Grey (brothers), and also the sisters of the deceased, as well as Mr. Samuel Grey (uncle) and other relatives. Between twenty and thirty soldiers were present.
At the altar steps the Union Jack was draped, and against it was laid a laurel wreath bearing the dead soldier's name. The service was most impressive ... The Vicar, in the course of his address, referred to the fact that Private Grey was the first Malmesbury soldier officially reported killed in the war, and to the sacrifice the young man had made in giving his life in defence of his country. The Vicar hoped that when the war was over Malmesbury would do its duty to its brave sons who had gone forth and laid down their lives on the battlefield. He hoped that the town would erect a memorial here in the Abbey Church and so have a permanent record of the bravery of Malmesbury men.

George Grey's grave in Ypres Reservoir Cemetery.

1915

The attacks on the B.E.F. at Ypres petered out before the end of November 1914 as both sides had suffered huge losses and had no fresh troops to continue. The British had suffered 89,864 casualties on the Western Front – 9,473 killed, 39,361 wounded and 41,030 missing. Most of these losses had been suffered by infantry units, the total strength of the infantry element of the seven divisions forming the B.E.F. was 84,000.

The submarine menace caused some anxiety. The Germans regarded their U-boats as an important striking force whereas we thought submarines were rather 'ungentlemanly' and at first gave them a minor role, mainly in support of the main fleet. Before the end of 1914 five cruisers and a seaplane carrier had been sunk by U-boats with the loss of many lives. Worse was soon to follow.

During the coming year the transfer of Territorial units to the front that had started at the end of 1914 continued. The first of the New Armies also went into action at the battle of Neuve Chapelle in March. This failed with heavy casualties including one Malmesbury man killed. The Germans attacked Ypres the following month using poison gas for the first time and Malmesbury again felt the effects of this fierce fighting. May saw the B.E.F. attack Aubers Ridge. In June it was agreed that the newly formed Third Army would take over 22 miles of the French Front in the Somme area. This enabled our Allies to concentrate forces to co-operate with our First Army in a major attack in September, the battle of Loos. This was the main initiation of Kitchener's New Army troops in a heavy engagement and the unfortunate result was heavy casualties for little gain. This action also saw the British employing poison gas for the first time.

After the heavy fighting on the Western Front the Allies sought new ways to exert pressure on their enemies. One idea was to force the Dardanelles, the strip of water joining the Mediterranean and Black Seas. This was expected to yield two important results – Turkey, which threatened Britain's communication with India,

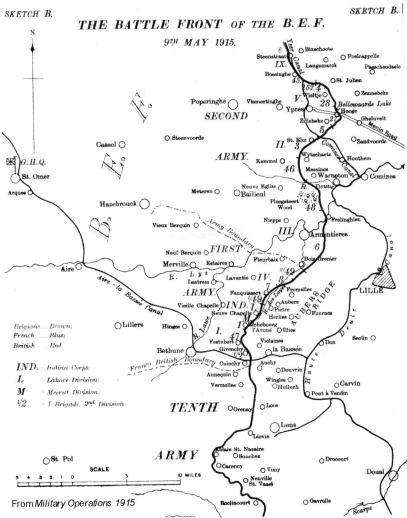

SKETCH B.

SKETCH B.

THE BATTLE FRONT OF THE B.E.F.

9TH MAY 1915.

From *Military Operations 1915*

would be knocked out of the war and strong support could be given to Russia to boost its ability to attack the Eastern Front. The Royal Navy made the first attempt in March. They damaged many of the guns guarding the strait, easily landed parties to cause more damage but mines sunk three battleships and three more were badly damaged. The first landings were made on 25th April by which time the Turks had prepared many defences. Heavy fighting resulted in stalemate. Further reinforcements were sent but no break-through resulted. Therefore in a move reminiscent of the early manoeuvres in France it was decided to make another landing at Suvla Bay in an attempt to out-flank the defences. This brought the 10th (Irish) Division which contained many Malmesbury men to Gallipoli. There was heavy fighting and confusion. Within a few weeks the town had suffered two dead, six wounded and four missing – two of whom were subsequently confirmed as being dead.

The newspapers provided good reports about most of the dead but there are some omissions. By the autumn the North Wilts Herald published an excellent Roll of Honour column. 16 Malmesbury men died during this year, bringing the total to 19.

Morrice, John Walter, Midshipman, age 16, H.M.S. Formidable, Royal Navy
Killed in action, 1st January 1915, commemorated on the Chatham Memorial panel 8, Malmesbury Abbey, Town Hall & Triangle.

After the First World War, an appropriate way had to be found of commemorating those members of the Royal Navy who had no known grave, the majority of deaths having occurred at sea. An Admiralty committee recommended that the three manning ports in Great Britain - Chatham, Plymouth and Portsmouth - should each have an identical memorial of unmistakable naval form, an obelisk, which would serve as a leading mark for shipping. The memorials were designed by Sir Robert Lorimer, who had already carried out a considerable amount of work for the War Graves Commission, with sculpture by Henry Poole. After the Second World War it was decided that the naval memorials should be extended to provide space for commemorating the naval dead without graves of that war, but since the three sites were dissimilar, a different architectural treatment was required for each. The architect for the Second World War extension at Chatham was Sir Edward Maufe (who also designed the Air Forces memorial at Runnymede) and the additional sculpture was by Charles Wheeler and William McMillan. Chatham Naval Memorial commemorates 8,514 sailors of the First World War and 10,098 of the Second World War.

Chatham Naval War Memorial

John was the only son of Major (later Lt. Col.) Lewis Edward Morrice D.S.O. of the Priory, Burton Hill with a younger sister Mary. He joined the Royal Navy's Training Estate in 1911. On the outbreak of war he was rated as a Midshipman and posted to H.M.S. Formidable. This was a pre-Dreadnought Battleship, 15,250 tons, which had been launched in 1898 and first commissioned in 1901.

Whilst on patrol the ship was sunk by two torpedoes from a German submarine 20 miles off Start Point (Cornwall) at 2 a.m., 1st January 1915. The first torpedo hit the number one boiler port side; a second explosion caused the ship to list heavily to starboard. Huge waves thirty feet high lashed the stricken ship, with strong winds, rain and hail, sinking it in less than two hours.

Captain Loxley, his second-in-command, Commander Ballard and the signaller stayed at their posts throughout, sending flares and rockets off at regular intervals. There was no panic, the men waiting calmly for the lifeboats to be lowered. Someone played ragtime on the piano, others sang. The Chaplain, Revd. G Brooke Robinson, went down with the ship by risking his life going below to find cigarettes. Suddenly the ship gave a tremendous lurch, the Captain shouted 'Lads, this is the last, all hands for themselves, and may God bless you and guide you to safety'. He then walked to the forebridge, lit a cigarette and, with his terrier Bruce on duty at his side, waited for the end, in true Royal Naval tradition.

The piano was thrown overboard: many of the boats were smashed as they were lowered into the water, killing all occupants, or else were swamped and sank. 'A piano's better than now't', said one. One pinnace with 70 men on board was picked up by the trawler Provident, 15 miles off Berry Head. The second pinnace took off another 70 men. This boat was soon half-filled with water as the men desperately bailed - with boots, caps, even a blanket, anything that came to hand. One seaman sat over a hole in the boat from the time they started away to the time of rescue. The enormous swell was terrifying, but morale was kept up by any means, humour, singing, even bullying. Petty Officer Bing admitted punching men who wanted to give up. The survivors unanimously agreed they owed their lives to Leading Seaman Carroll, coxswain, who continued to cheer and inspire, not allowing them to sink into despair. Dawn broke out of sight of land; a liner was seen, then eleven other craft, but the pounding seas and huge waves hid the pinnace. Night came, still with relentless gales.

Blackout restrictions were in force, and there are two explanations for the seamen seeing light from the shore. Petty Officer Bing saw a red light seven miles away which could have been the Lyme harbour light. The other explanation from J.H. Taplin, another survivor, was that a sudden bright light shone out three miles off, which may have been from the Assembly Rooms cinema. The machine had broken down and the operator examining it shone the lamp through the window for a second or two.

The pinnace was first seen at Lyme by Miss Gwen Harding and her parents walking home along Marine Parade after dining out with friends. She glimpsed the outline of a boat, her mother confirmed her suspicions and the alarm was raised. So began the rescue. Of the 71 men in the pinnace, 48 were brought ashore alive, six were found to be dead on arrival, 14 died during the 22 hours the men had fought for survival and were buried at sea, and three died after landing.

The Pilot Boat Inn became rescue headquarters. Mrs. Atkins the landlady took in many survivors. Her dog Lassie saved Seaman Cowan, laid on the floor for dead, by licking his face. Many of the townsfolk brought food and blankets. Others took men into their homes to rest and recuperate, while those needing medical aid were sent to hospital. The dead were placed in the entrance to the cinema, a part of the old Assembly Rooms.

In the North Wilts Herald of 8th January it was reported;

MISSING NAVAL OFFICER. - The name of Midshipman J.M. Morrice, son of Major L.E. Morrice, of the Priory, Malmesbury, appears in the list of officers missing from H.M.S. "Formidable." He had only recently joined the ship, and was about 17 years of age.

Ironically the same edition noted the amendment of the Borough Council's Roll of Honour to include his name and amend his father's regiment. His death was not confirmed until April.

H.M.S. Formidable. (firstworldwar.com)

Tugwell, Frank, Private, 8597, age 33, 2nd Battalion Worcestershire Regiment

Died, 25th January 1915, buried in Ste. Marie Cemetery, Le Havre, Div. 14 K 1, commemorated Malmesbury Abbey (his unit is wrongly shown as 4th Battalion), Town Hall & Triangle.

Le Havre was one of the ports at which the British Expeditionary Force disembarked in August 1914. Except for a short interval during the German advance in 1914 it remained No 1 Base throughout the war. By the end of May 1917 it contained three General & two Stationary hospitals and four Convalescent Depots. The first Empire burials took place in Division 14 of Ste. Marie Cemetery in mid August 1914. Burials in Divisions 19, 3, 62 and 64 followed successively. In all 1,689 Empire casualties of the First World War are buried or commemorated in the cemetery. During the Second World War Le Havre was one of the evacuation ports for the British Expeditionary Force in 1940 and towards the end of the war it was used as a supply and reinforcement base. There are 364 Second World War burials (59 of them unidentified). The Empire plots in the cemetery were designed by Sir Reginald Blomfield.

Frank was born Frank Carey as he was the illegitimate son of Annie Carey. She worked at the Silk Factory but when that closed she had to go into the Workhouse where the birth occurred on 5th April 1887. Annie married James Tugwell in 1892 and went on to have two further children James and Maureen. Frank took his step-father's name and became a regular soldier, enlisting on 28th August 1904 at Worcester. He served with the 2nd Worcesters who arrived at Boulogne on 14th August 1914, participating in the battle at Mons, the retreat and the battle of the Marne. However on 22nd September, a quiet day on the Aisne front, Frank suffered a gunshot wound to the shoulder. He was evacuated to England on 13th October and after convalescence returned to France on 28th December. Whilst still at the Base Depot in Le Havre he fell sick. Examined by a doctor early on 25th January he was told to return to his tent, keep warm and not smoke. There was a delay in transferring him to hospital and he died from oedema of the larynx and asphyxia. A Court of Enquiry was held into his death but it was determined that he died by natural causes although the Corporal in charge of the stretcher-bearers was admonished. His name did not appear on the Mayor's Roll of Honour and I have been unable to find any newspaper report of his death.

Lockstone, (Edward) Sharland, Private, 11134, age 25, 2nd Battalion Duke of Edinburgh's (Wiltshire Regiment)

Killed in action, 12th March 1915, commemorated on the Le Touret Memorial Panels 33 and 34, Malmesbury Abbey (& private brass plaque), School, Town Hall & Triangle.

The Memorial in Le Touret Military Cemetery, Richebourg-l'Avoue is one of those erected by the Commonwealth War Graves Commission to record the names of the officers and men who fell in the Great War and whose graves are not known. It serves the area enclosed on the North by the River Lys and a line drawn from Estaires to Fournes, and on the South by the old Southern boundary of the First Army about Grenay. It covers the period from the arrival of the II Corps in Flanders in October 1914 to the eve of the Battle of Loos. It does not include

Sharland Lockstone (North Wilts Herald)

the names of officers and men of Canadian or Indian regiments; they are found on the Memorials at Vimy and Neuve-Chapelle

Sharland was the youngest son of Edward, partner in William & Edward Lockstone grocers, Oxford Street and Elizabeth Lockstone of the Firs, Milbourne, being born on 14th December 1889. His brothers were William & John (known as Heath & Jack), sisters Amy & Mary (known as Mollie). He was educated at Malmesbury Secondary School which he left aged 16 to join the Wilts and Dorset Bank at Bradford-on-Avon. After two years there he moved to Fareham, then Swanage before going to Head Office in Salisbury. He remained with the bank when it amalgamated with Lloyds. At the outbreak of war Sharland was working as Head Clerk in an important branch at Llanelly but immediately enlisted in the Wiltshire Regiment. He also persuaded three other colleagues to join up. After training with the 3rd Battalion at Weymouth he joined the 2nd Battalion at the front on 18th December 1914. His first letter from France said that he had met Privates A. Paginton and A.H. Stevens there. His parents received a letter dated 18th March 1915 from Lance Corporal J. Hossack of 8 Platoon, B Company, 4th Battalion Cameron Highlanders;

Dear Sir, - By this time you will have received intelligence of the noble manner your son fought and fell for the desired end. I just drop you this note to say that two men of my regiment and myself interred his remains respectably. During the occupation we were under shrapnel and rifle fire, so had to leave the spot before I could get a piece of wood to mark the spot; so I took the distance from certain points by observance only. We buried him on Tuesday, March 16th.

In the North Wilts Herald of 26th March his death was noted in the Roll of Honour column;

LOCKSTONE.- March 16th, killed in action, Edward Sharland, beloved youngest son of Mr. and Mrs. E.H. Lockstone, The Firs, Milbourne, Malmesbury.

The Lockstone family wanted more details and their son-in-law wrote to a friend to seek news and this was the reply;

France 7 April 1915

Dear Mr Ponting,

In answer to your letter of the 5th inst., it grieves me very much to have to tell you that the only information I could gather respecting the loss of our respected comrade, Sharland Lockstone, seems only to confirm the statement received by the parents.

I was not with him during the attack at Neuve Chapelle on 12th March, but have seen every man in his section since, and from what I can gather he was lost during the attack on the second line of German trenches, as we went into the first line of German trenches after they were taken, and received orders to take the second line which we succeeded in doing.

The attack was carried out under a very heavy rifle and shell fire, and I am sorry to say Sharland was among the number that did not reach the second trench. Therefore you see he must have fallen between the two trenches, and as the Cameron Highlanders were holding the line, we left. As our regiment did not return, that would explain why the Camerons would bury any of our dead in the vicinity.

It may be a little consolation to know that his end must have without any of the agonies which sometimes accompany a battle of that description, for our stretcher bearers and the R.A.M.C. were at work behind the trenches within an hour after the attack, and their efforts are all concentrated on the wounded, we can but come to the conclusion that Sharland was beyond human aid when they found him. You will probably have heard from the authorities before now, although there is always a delay until everything is satisfactory.

Now, sir, I don't think there is anything more I can tell you at present. I have enclosed a photo taken in the trenches where we spent the winter. I may add that it was taken without the knowledge of any-one in the photo.

Kindly convey my deepest sympathy to Mr. and Mrs. Lockstone and family for the loss of one so dear to them. I can assure them we have lost a comrade who was devoted to his duty, always willing for any task we had to perform, and one who was liked and respected by everyone who knew him.

I am, yours sincerely B. Stevens. Pte 2nd Bn Wilts. Regt.

The war diary provides the following confused description of the action which mentions five other units but not the Camerons;

France, Neuve Chapelle Friday 12th March 1915

Just at the moment the rations were arriving about 5.30 a.m. the Germans carried out a bomb attack along the trench. This attack drove back 'C' Coy and forced part of it into 'A' Coys trench. Unfortunately the end of 'A' Coys trench was uncovered by this attack the consequence of this was that 'A' & part of 'C' Coy were driven (back) into the British trenches. Exactly what happened was not known at this time & it was believed that 'A' Coy had been captured.

The German advance was easily stopped by 'D' Coy. 'C' Coy organized a new attack & made good progress assisted by the bombers of the 2 Yorks. But coming under a heavy machine gun fire they were again driven back. These attacks were most unfortunate as they prevented the issue of water and rations. Still 'B' Coy got theirs & 'D' Coy got a rum issue.

9.30 a.m. - The Borders made an attack which was soon stopped as it was started through some mistake an hour before the artillery bombardment was timed to take place. This attack died away quickly.

10.30 a.m. - The artillery bombardment and about 10.15 a.m. a new bombing attack was started along the German trench. Unfortunately Lt. Morison who led the attack was killed at once and the attack never really started. So the CO organized another with ½ platoon of 'B' Coy and the bombers of the Grenadier Guards. The CO led them out & this time the attack was quite successful.

About 350 persons were captured by a mixed detachment chiefly Wilts. It was just at this time the lost 'A' Coy were discovered in the British trench. So 'A' Coy was pushed forward to assist to hold the captured line. The CO went back to try and collect more men for this purpose so sent forward the remainder of 'B' Coy. The result was that at dusk this line nearly as far as 23-30 was held by a jumbled mass of Wilts, Gordons Warwicks & Scots Guards.

Oram, George, Trooper, 23722, age 31, 18th (Queen Mary's Own) Hussars attached to 2nd Life Guards

Died of wounds, 14th May 1915, commemorated on the Menin Gate Panel 5, Malmesbury Abbey, Town Hall & Triangle. The Commonwealth War Grave Commission list his age as 38 which is wrong.

For a description of the Menin Gate see Private William Wakefield's entry above.

George was the son of George and Rhoda (nee Shingles) Oram, 19 Katifer Lane. His step-brothers (born illegitimately) were Tom Shingles, a mason on the Charlton estate and Harry Shingles (who was killed in January 1918) who had been in South Africa with the Volunteers, then served with the Royal Wilts Yeomanry. His brother was William, a Bombardier in the Territorial Force Ammunition Column. After leaving school George junior worked as a carter for Mrs. M. Ponting builder and decorator, Park Road. At the age of 18 he joined the 10th (Prince of Wales' Own) Royal Hussars. He served in the Boer War gaining the Queen's South Africa Medal 1899-1902 with three bars – Transvaal, Orange Free State and Cape Colony and the King's South Africa Medal 1901-1902. He then served in India and was promoted to Corporal before ending his active service and joining the Reserve in January 1908 for four years. He later joined the Malmesbury Company of the National Reserve but had failed to sign the declaration to serve when called upon prior to the outbreak of war. As a result he did not receive the £10 bounty which the Mayor sought to recover for his mother following his death. He volunteered at the meeting on 8th September. On rejoining George tried to return to 10th Hussars but had to join 18th Hussars. He arrived in France on 3rd December and was attached to the Life Guards. He was wounded in desperate fighting near Verlorenhoek in the Ypres salient.

On 20th May 1915 Mrs. Oram received shocking news of her son in a letter dated 16th May;

Dear Mrs. Oram:- I am taking the liberty, as a great friend of your son George, of writing a

few lines informing you he died of wounds. He was shot through the stomach and died within a few hours of admission to the hospital. I would have let you know before, but I could not find out if he was missing or dead until the following day, so I have lost no time in dropping you a line, which I hope will get to you safely, as I do not suppose you will hear from the War Office for a day or two. I am more than sorry that it has happened, and I sympathise with you greatly for the loss of him, as he was always such a nice fellow. He and I were mates together in Africa, also in India, and we have not parted scarcely a day from one another since we met at Tidworth.

Now, dear Mrs. Oram, if this reaches you safely will you kindly let me know. I am more than sorry that I cannot write to you under different circumstances than this, but I thought it my duty to let you have a line, as I know by what George has told me you are anx-

George Oram (North Wilts Herald)

ious about him. It is no good me trying to explain or describe to you the horrors of the battle we were in; it was awful running about half-a-mile in the open with a shower of shells and bullet fire. Now, dear Mrs. Oram, I will close, trusting this will find you in the best of health as this leaves me at present; but I can thank God only, and so can hundreds more. So hoping you will take this as cool as possible,

I am, yours sincerely,

A.E. Yeates

Only the day before receiving this, Mrs. Oram had a letter from George saying he was in the best of health and 'as fat as ever.' A memorial service was held for him in the Abbey on 10th June;

THE LATE TROOPER ORAM.
Memorial Service at Malmesbury.

There was an impressive service at the Abbey Church, Malmesbury, yesterday, when a memorial service was held for the late Trooper George Oram, attached to the 2nd Life Guards, son of Mrs. Oram, of Katifer Lane, Malmesbury. The church was well filled, the young man, a full account of whose career we have already given in these columns, having been a general favourite in the town.

The Ammunition Column, 3rd Wessex Brigade, R.F.A. (T.F.), under Lieut. J. Pullen, attended, and also a number of senior boys from the National School, Westport, under Mr. W. Tinley (head master) and Mr. W. Clark (assistant master). Trooper Oram, like many another soldier at the front, spent his schooldays in the Westport National School. In the front pew were members of the dead soldier's family – Bombardier William Oram, Wilts Battery (Swindon), 3rd Wessex Brigade, R.F.A. (brother), Mrs. Winch, Kington Langley (sister), Mr. T. Shingles (step-brother) and Mrs. Shingles and Mr. R. Cottle. Trooper Harry Oram, another brother, was unable to attend, as he was with the Royal Wilts Yeomanry in Sussex. Mr. Joe Moore, for whom Trooper Oram formerly worked, was in the congregation, as well as several prominent townsmen, including the Deputy Mayor (Alderman H. Farrant) and Alderman J.G. Bartlett.

Bailey, (Harry) James, Private, 3/8151, age 23, 1st Battalion Bedfordshire Regiment
Died of wounds, 21st June 1915, buried in Boulogne Eastern Cemetery VIII A 87 (family inscription *GOD BE WITH YOU, TILL WE MEET AGAIN DEAR, EVER LOVED, LOVE FROM MAM & DAD*), commemorated Malmesbury Abbey, Town Hall & Triangle.
Boulogne was one of the three base ports most extensively used by the British armies on the Western Front throughout the First World War. It was closed and cleared on the 27th August 1914 when the Allies were forced to fall back ahead of the German advance but was opened again in October and from that month to the end of the war, Boulogne and Wimereux formed one of the chief hospital areas. Until June 1918, the dead from the hospitals at Boulogne itself were buried in the Cimetiere de L'Est, one of the town cemeteries, the Empire graves forming a long, narrow strip along the right hand edge of the cemetery. In the spring of 1918, it was found that space was running short in the Eastern Cemetery in spite of repeated extensions to the south and the site of the new cemetery at Terlincthun was chosen. Boulogne Eastern Cemetery contains 5,577 Empire burials of the First World War and 224 from the Second World War. The British plots were designed by Charles Holden.
James was the fifth son of Charles, a tailor (nicknamed the Colonel due to his dapper appearance) and Susan Bailey, of 80, Triangle. His brothers were Charles, Frederick (who was killed in 1916), William, Francis & Thomas with sisters, Alice (known as Theresa), Eliza (Dora), Annie (Nancy) & Susan (Nellie). James had been a pupil at the Westport Boys' School and during his service corresponded with his old headmaster W. Tinley. On leaving school he first worked for Tom Rich, butcher but was set on becoming a gentleman's servant. He entered service with Colonel C. Napier Miles of Ingleburne Manor before moving on to become footman at the Knoll under Mrs. Luce. He then went to Crookham House, Fleet, Hampshire as Sir Richard Mornton's first footman. His final employment was with Lord Ampthill at Milton Ernest Hall, Bedford. During this time the King's two youngest sons, Princes George and John, convalesced there and Jim took a large part in looking after them. Due to his employer's connection with the local regiment he joined the Special Reserve of the Bedfords. Called up at the start of the war after training he was posted to their 1st Battalion. James was sent to France on 12th May 1915 and wrote the following to his family shortly after his arrival;

My Dear Loving Mother,

I received your loving letter last night and cigarettes, which I was more than pleased to receive; it was good to see a dear old English Woodbine – they are worth £1 cash out here. I am pleased to hear that all are well at home; that is what I was longing to hear and it always pleases me to hear that. I am pleased to say I am grand and quite happy. I feel proud to think I am doing my bit; and proud you must feel, sweetheart, to have your boys serving their King and Country; a great honour to you.

The weather is simply grand out here, the sun is very hot, and it never seems to get cold. I have just got up; it is about four o'clock and the sun is trying to get through. I have made a cup of tea for my pal and me. We are at the back of the firing line at present; those brutal Germans keeping on sending these Jack Johnsons; but we don't take notice of them as they don't do any harm; they make great holes in the ground and knock houses down. They gave us some of their well-known gas the other morning; it's rotten but we have all got pads to put over our faces so it don't hurt us, I think the use of it hurts them most, for after it had blown past our chaps just about went for them, and I think they got more than they bargained for. Near where we are there is a nice lake and yesterday afternoon my brother and me had the advantage of a dip; it was jolly grand and very refreshing although muddy. Of course the German shells were coming over us, but we didn't worry.

The Bedfords have done good work in the war, and have secured a good name. I am pleased that I belong to them.

Well, we shall soon be back to dear England, for the Germans are on their last legs. Don't forget a packet of Woodbines when writing. Goodbye my darling mother.

    Your loving and devoted child
    God be with you til we meet again.
    A day's march nearer home.

James was wounded on 10th June, suffering an injury to the head. One of his comrades, Lance Corporal H. Coxell swiftly wrote to his father; *Jim, whilst attending on an officer, a shell burst near him, inflicting serious injuries to his head. He was removed to hospital, and the extent of his injuries I cannot state. He was my best chum, and I hope he will soon recover.* The Company Sergeant Major G. Hall wrote; *I liked him very much; he has proved himself such a good fellow. The strange part is I only put him officer's servant the other day, and both the officer and your son were wounded by the same shell. I could not refrain from writing as I liked him so much.*

The Bedfords had relieved the 1st Dorsets in trenches at the notorious Hill 60 in the Ypres Salient on 1st June. This was a quiet period ignored by the Official History of the war. Despite that the daily casualties recorded by this one unit are staggering – 3 wounded; 2 killed, 3 wounded; 7 wounded; 1 killed, 7 wounded; none (although *parapets brought down on self & other officers on two occasions*); 11 wounded; 2 killed, 21 wounded; 6 wounded. The entry for 10th June was (unusually James's officer is not named);

Trenches very wet. HdQrs & cutting shelled by howitzers.

Casualties 1 killed, 2 wounded, 1 missing.

James was evacuated to No. 13 General Hospital, Boulogne where he died. After receiving news that he was seriously wounded his father wrote to the hospital for further details and asked for permission for his mother to visit him. In reply the following was received;

I regret to inform you that your son died here at 1.15pm June 21st, he passed away quite peacefully, being unconscious for some time before death.

    Yours faithfully,
    A.J. Luther
    Col. A.M.S., O.C. No. 13 General Hospital

The family received other letters from France and from former employers expressing their sympathy. Lord Ampthill who was the Commander of 3rd Battalion Bedfords wrote to his parents;

I am deeply grieved to hear of the death of your son. Lady Ampthill and I thought very highly of him, and liked him so much, as did all the members of our household. When the first bitterness of your grief has passed you will always be able to reflect with pride that your son fell on the field of battle and died for his country as a gallant British soldier.

The Herald of 2nd July had this report;

Yet another Malmesbury family mourns the loss of a son and brother in the war. This time the sacrifice of a young life has been made by Private James H. Bailey, 1st Bedfords, fifth son of Mr. and Mrs. Charles Bailey, 80, The Triangle. The young soldier was wounded in action on June 10th – the official information was that he received a gunshot wound in the head – and died in No. 13 General Hospital, Boulogne, on June 21st. He was 23 years of age on March 27th last, having been born in 1892.

Bishop, Daniel Percy, Private, 2898, age 20, 6th (Service) Battalion Royal Munster Fusiliers Killed in action, 7th August 1915, commemorated on the Helles Memorial Panel 185 to 190, Malmesbury Abbey, Town Hall & Triangle.

The Helles Memorial serves the dual function of British battle memorial for the whole Gallipoli campaign and place of commemoration for many of those Empire servicemen who died there and have no known grave. The United Kingdom and Indian forces named on the memorial died in operations through-out the peninsula, the Aus-tralians at Helles. There are also panels for those who died or were buried at sea in Gallipoli waters. The memo-rial bears more than 21,000 names. There are four other Memorials to the Missing at Gallipoli. The Lone Pine, Hill 60, and Chunuk Bair Memo-rials commemorate Austral-ian and New Zealanders at Anzac. The Twelve Tree Copse Memorial commemo-rates the New Zealanders at Helles. Naval casualties of the United Kingdom lost or buried at sea are recorded on their respective Memori-als at Portsmouth, Plymouth and Chatham, in the United Kingdom.

Dan's parents, George (an agricultural labourer) and Eliza Bishop lived in Kings Wall before they died with his brothers Charles & William and sisters Maud & Alice. He was small in stature but quick and capable. He had worked as footman to the Misses Luce of the Knoll be-fore spending several years as second horseman to Mr. William Rich. However on the Roll of Honour his employer was noted as Edwards & Son. His brother Charles also served abroad.

He was amongst some 30

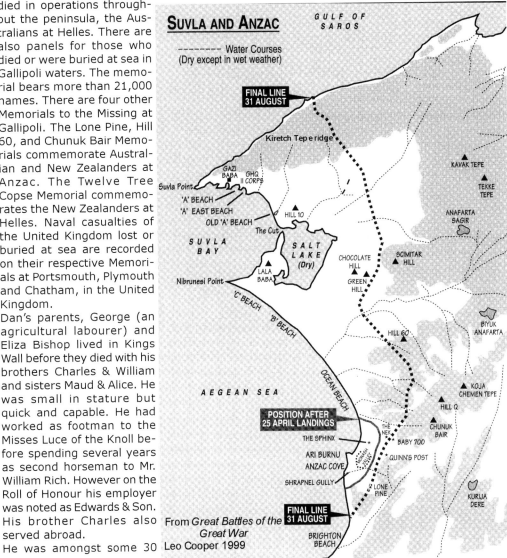

SUVLA AND ANZAC

GULF OF SAROS

- - - - - - Water Courses
(Dry except in wet weather)

FINAL LINE 31 AUGUST

Kiretch Tepe ridge

KAVAK TEPE

GAZI BABA GHQ II CORPS

TEKKE TEPE

Suvla Point

'A' BEACH
'A' EAST BEACH
OLD 'A' BEACH

HILL 10

ANAFARTA SAGIR

The Cut

SUVLA BAY

SALT LAKE (Dry)

CHOCOLATE HILL

SCIMITAR HILL

LALA BABA

Nibrunesi Point

GREEN HILL

'C' BEACH

'B' BEACH

BIYUK ANAFARTA

HILL 60

AEGEAN SEA

OCEAN BEACH

KOJA CHEMEN TEPE

HILL Q

POSITION AFTER 25 APRIL LANDINGS

THE NEK

CHUNUK BAIR

THE SPHINX

BABY 700

ARI BURNU
ANZAC COVE

QUINN'S POST

SHRAPNEL GULLY

LONE PINE

KURIJA DERE

FINAL LINE 31 AUGUST

From *Great Battles of the Great War*
Leo Cooper 1999

BRIGHTON BEACH

men from Malmesbury who, after a recruiting meeting travelled to Devizes to enlist in the Wiltshire Regiment on 12th September. Except among old soldiers and in Belfast, recruiting in Ireland during August 1914 was not as satisfactory as it was in England and in consequence, Lord Kitchener decided early in September to transfer a number of recruits for whom no room could be found in English regiments to fill up the ranks of the 10th (Irish) Division of the First New Army. Within days this Malmesbury group with many other Wiltshire men were transferred to the Curragh, a training ground in Ulster, where they joined Irish regiments. Although allocated the service number 13274 in the Wiltshire Regiment, Dan was posted to 6th Battalion Royal Munster Fusiliers. This unit was raised in Tralee, County Kerry.

The Division moved to the area around Basingstoke in May 1915 before sailing for Gallipoli from Liverpool on 9th July on board the S.S. Mauretania. The 30th Brigade was due to land at Sulva Bay early on 7th August with orders to support the 11th Manchesters who had landed around 11 p.m. the previous night and had advanced 2 miles along the Kiretch Tepe ridge. The 6th Munsters, 25 officers and 749 men, was to be the first unit to disembark. But after getting into lighters they were ordered back on board the fleet minesweepers that had carried them from Mudros on Lemnos Island to await 'special orders'. It was not until 11.30 a.m. that they began to move. Joined by the 7th Munsters they began to climb the ridge about 2.30 p.m. When they were close to the Manchesters' position the unit began to take casualties and Daniel Bishop died on this first day. His death was confirmed at the beginning of September. Unofficial news came in a letter from Private Charles Pinnell who wrote to his father Robert of St. Johns Street at the end of August;

I am sending you a few lines, hoping to find you well. I have not had time to write before, for I have been so busy getting out of the way of bullets and one thing and another.

I am in hospital at Malta with a bullet wound in my left foot; it is nearly right again now, and I am going on fine. I suppose you have heard about poor little Dan Bishop being killed. I was a few yards from him. We were in the sea up to our necks when they started to shell; it was terrible. I got wounded on August 9th.

Selby, William John, Private, 1136, age 21, 6th (Service) Battalion Prince of Wales's Leinster Regiment (Royal Canadians)

Missing presumed killed, 10th August 1915, commemorated on the Helles Memorial Panel 184

The Helles Memorial (cwgc.org.uk)

& 185, Malmesbury Abbey, Town Hall & Triangle. For a description of the Helles Memorial see Private Daniel Bishop above.

William was the eldest son of William (cowman) and Theodora Selby, of 23 Burnivale. He and his brother Sidney were among the men who volunteered at the recruiting meeting on 8th September. At Devizes he was allocated the Regimental Number 13882 in the Wilts. However he and his brother were sent to Ireland where Sidney joined the Munsters and he joined the 6th Leinsters which had been formed in Dublin. This was part of the 29th Brigade which on arrival in Gallipoli was sent to reinforce the Anzacs. After secretly landing on 5th August they were initially held in reserve but were sent to support various Australian positions two days later during a major attack to co-ordinate with the Suvla landings.

Late on 9th August they were ordered to move to a place called the Apex because the forces moving up to a dominating position at Chunuk Bair were exhausted. They were added to a mixed garrison from different brigades who were unfamiliar to each other. The 5th Wiltshires were amongst this group, utterly worn out by four days without sleep. Unfortunately the opposing commander, the charismatic Mustafa Kemal, launched a dawn attack on the 10th. They surprised the sleeping Wiltshires who suffered heavily whilst the Leinsters together with New Zealand machine guns held on to the Apex. That night, apparently warned by a New Zealander who ran down the hill crying "fix your bayonets boys, they're coming!", the Leinsters led by their Commanding Officer charged up the hill without waiting to put on jackets or puttees. The Turks were driven back after hand to hand fighting. No. 9 platoon was sent out in the dark to clear out enemy snipers but was overrun losing half its strength. The positions were held against repeated attacks during the night with the enemy held off by close range fire and bayonet charges. The last attack of the night was met by a counter-charge, the Regimental History recording; *With a ringing yell the line of grey bayonets surged forward against the foe, to prove once again that to attack is not only the best defensive policy but is that best suited to the Irish temperament. The Turks faltered as the charge swept against them, and the Leinsters were at last able to take revenge for the losses of the night. Fatigue and thirst were forgotten and men after much suffering exulted in the taste of victory at last.* D Company is noted as; *they were cut off and never heard of again.* It was 'victory' but at a great cost. In this confusion one of the casualties was Private William Selby. In September the following appeared in the North Wilts Herald;

MORE CASUALTIES.- Mrs. Selby, of 57 Burnivale, has been notified that her son, Pte. William John Selby, of the 6th Leinsters, aged 20, was wounded in action in the Dardanelles on August 10th. Mrs. Selby has, besides the above, her husband, Pte. William Selby, 4th Wilts, and another son, Sergt. Selby, Royal Munster Fusiliers, in the service, the later being in the Dardanelles.

His body was not recovered and he was listed as missing, his death not being confirmed until a year later. Private F.J. Burgess of the same battalion outlined his experience in a letter to his mother written in September and published in the Herald;

Dear mother, we are all so glad to come out of the trenches. We came out of them about a week ago and we are at a rest camp, and I can tell you that we were all so glad when another lot came to relieve us. The Australians came to relieve us, and we were very glad to see them come for it was no joke to be in those trenches for one week to another firing all the time, it makes anybody's shoulder ache. The first morning we went into the trenches we lost very heavy, but the Turks lost a lot heavier; they lost about 10,000. Our company which was about 200 strong came back with about 40, all the others were wounded or else killed, and I think that most of them were wounded and were able to get out of the trenches. But it does not matter; it was all in the fight, and if the _____ do as good as we did they will not do badly, and good luck to them.

The following appeared in the Roll of Honour on 29th September 1916;

SELBY.- Aug. 10th, 1915, killed in action, Pte. William John Selby, Leinster Regiment, eldest son of Mr. William Selby, Burnivale, Malmesbury, aged 21 years.

Exton, Richard, Corporal, 1253, age 34, 6th (Service) Battalion Royal Munster Fusiliers Missing presumed killed, 15th August 1915, commemorated on the Helles Memorial Panels 185 to 190, Malmesbury Abbey, Town Hall & Triangle.

For a description of the Helles Memorial see Private Daniel Bishop above.

Richard, known as Dick, was the only son of George (an agricultural labourer who later became the caretaker of the cemetery) and Catherine Exton with sisters Harriet & Flora. By 1901 Dick was a grocer's assistant in High Wycombe and married Jane Elizabeth Saunders in 1907. He later had his own grocery shop at Wooburn Green, Buckinghamshire next door to a butcher run by Charles Vincent Ing. They had a close relationship with deliveries being made by a bicycle that bore both of their names. Charles married Dick's sister Harriet in 1908. Dick had three children, Richard born in 1908, George 1909, both in Wycombe and Catherine 1913 in Malmesbury. Both Dick and Charles returned to Malmesbury before the war where Charles later had a shop at 123 High Street. Dick volunteered on 8th September and enlisted at Devizes into the Wiltshires with number 13263 on 12th September. Along with other Malmesbury men he was transferred to the Royal Munster Fusiliers on 17th September.

After a week's fighting (described under Daniel Bishop's entry) on the most northerly flank of the British position in Gallipoli, the 6th Munsters received reinforcements who had been left at Mudros on the 14th & !5th August. On the latter date the battalion attacked along the crest of

Flora, Dick and Harriet Exton (Leonard Ing)

the Kiretch Tepe Sirt Ridge. Almost one mile of ground was cleared (this was the biggest opposed advance in the campaign). An enemy counter attack was repulsed at 10 p.m.

Sometime during this fighting Dick was killed and his body was not recovered. He was first reported missing in September but his death was not confirmed for nearly three more years. Years later his eldest son, also called Dick, laid flowers at the first Remembrance Day at the Triangle War Memorial.

Paul, (George) Henry, Sergeant, 3117, age 18, 6th (Service) Battalion Royal Munster Fusiliers

Killed in action, 15th August 1915, commemorated on the Helles Memorial Panels 185 to 190, Malmesbury Abbey, Congregational Church, Town Hall & Triangle.

For a description of the Helles Memorial see Private Daniel Bishop above.

George Henry, who seemed to have been called Henry, was the fifth son of George (an engine driver) and Amelia Paul, of Thornhill Cottage, Foxley Road, with brothers William, Albert, John, Edwin & Thomas and sisters Mary & Kate. He and his brother Edwin volunteered at the 8th September meeting, he being allocated the Wiltshire Regimental number 13279 before being sent to Ireland. Henry must have had good leadership skills to become a senior non-commissioned officer so young. He fell in the same action as Dick Exton. He was reported wounded in letters from comrades, but his death was confirmed before 9th September. His family made a personal memorial for him, they purchased a printed sheet showing the Helles Memorial. In the centre of this form would be pasted the few lines from the entry in the newspaper's death column. However I have not found any reference to Henry's death in newspapers.

Thornbury, (Edward) Ernest, Private, 3224 age 19, 6th (Service) Battalion Royal Munster Fusiliers

Died of wounds, 20th August 1915 (although Commonwealth War Grave Commission says 12th) on a Hospital ship and buried at sea, commemorated on the Helles Memorial Panels 185 to 190, Malmesbury Abbey, Town Hall & Triangle.

For a description of the Helles Memorial see Private Daniel Bishop above.

Registered as Edward Ernest but known as Ernest, he was the eldest son of George (an agricultural labourer) and Sarah Jane Thornbury of Cowbridge. It seems to have been a family tradition to use their second Christian name as his mother was called Jane, elder sister Emily Elizabeth, Elizabeth and younger sister Mabel Catherine, Kate. His cousin William who died a month later was registered Henry William. Ernest had worked for the de Bertodano family at Cowbridge House and then for Mr. W.B. Carter of Arches Farm for whom his father also worked. Ernest was one of the Class 1 National Reservists who left Malmesbury after the big recruiting meeting on 8th September 1914 and sent to Ireland. He was first reported wounded in letters from comrades received in Malmesbury early in September 1915. The final sad news was conveyed to his mother by letter from Red Cross nurses on the hospital ship. The entry in the Herald's Roll of Honour, contradicting the date of recorded death, appeared in September next to that of his cousin Willy Thornbury;

THORNBURY.- Aug. 20, died of wounds received in action in the Dardanelles, Private Ernest Thornbury, 6th Royal Munster Fusiliers, eldest son of Mr. George Thornbury, Cowbridge Road, Malmesbury, aged 19 years.

Price, Richard, Lance Corporal, 14966, age 44, 7th (Service) Battalion Royal Dublin Fusiliers Died of wounds, 10th September 1915 (although Commonwealth War Grave Commission says 22nd August), commemorated on the Helles Memorial Panel 190 to 196, Malmesbury Abbey, Town Hall & Triangle.

For a description of the Helles Memorial see Private Daniel Bishop above.

Dick was the younger son of Henry (labourer) and Caroline Price, originally of Burnivale but later St Johns Street and was unmarried, with one brother, William and three sisters Annie, Rachel & Winnie. Having served in the militia 1889-1903 he volunteered and was enrolled into the Wiltshires (number 619) but was quickly posted to the Dublin Fusiliers.

The 7th Dublins were part of 30th Brigade and landed with the 6th Munsters at Suvla on 7th August. During the first ten days they suffered over 300 casualties and had to be reorganised on the 18th, despite having received 150 reinforcements. They formed the reserve whilst an attack was made on the 21st but came under heavy shell fire. They then moved into the front line where Dick was wounded. The fighting strength of the unit after this episode was 5 officers and 424 other ranks. The following article which contradicts the date of death recorded by the Commonwealth War Graves Commission comes from the North Wilts Herald of 1st October;

THE LATE LCE.-CORPL. R. PRICE.

As briefly intimated in last week's "North Wilts Herald" official news has been received of the death from wounds of L.-Cpl. Richard Price, Royal Dublin Fusiliers. He was wounded in action in the Dardanelles on August 22nd and died on September 10th.

The late L.-Cpl. Price, who was 44 years of age last April and unmarried, was the youngest son of the late Mr. Henry Price and Mrs. Caroline Price, St. John's Street, Malmesbury. He was born in the town and spent his school-days at the Westport National School, under the late Mr. Moyse. At the time he enlisted he was in the employ of Messrs. Martin & Sons, builders, Startley. He was an old soldier, for he had done 14 years' service in the old Wilts Militia. When the South African War broke out he went on active service, becoming attached to the 2nd Wilts. He served throughout the campaign, receiving the Queen's medal with three bars – "Wittebergen," "Transvaal" and "Cape Colony" – and the King's medal with two bars – "South Africa 1901," and "South Africa 1902." When he left the service it was with an exemplary character, and he settled down at home, living with his mother in Burnivale, Malmesbury, who now lives with a daughter in St. John's Street. Three nephews of the deceased are serving in the war – Sergt. W. Price, Pte. Charles Price and Pte. M. Price – sons of Mr. W. Price, Harper's Lane, Malmesbury. L.-Corpl. Price has, besides his widowed mother, a brother, Mr. W. Price, Westport, and a sister, Mrs. W. Paginton, St. John's Street, living in Malmesbury, and another sister, Mrs. Fennell, living at Horfield, Bristol. For all these and especially the aged mother there is felt deep sympathy in their bereavement. It was thought that after having seen active service in South Africa, L.-Cpl. Price would have been considered he had already "done his bit," but, to his infinite credit be it recorded, he could not rest at home when the call came from Lord Kitchener for more men; he was ready as ever he was in his younger days to do the best for his country. He was a true patriot, and it is to such men, who leave their humble homes for the hardships of war, that the British Empire owes a great debt. And his reward? It can be best indicated in the words of L.-Cpl. Price himself. Recalling his South African days, he used to tell how the Chaplain, when preaching to the soldiers before they went into action, made them be of good cheer and not trouble about death, "for," the Chaplain declared "the man who gives his life for his country is sure of heaven." In remembering that incident the soldier now mourned for was indeed quoting his own epitaph and that of thousands who, like him, have "fought a good fight."

His nephews Charles and William Price were to die later in the war.

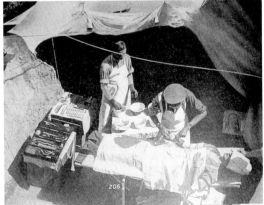
Field surgery in Gallipoli (westernfrontassociation.com)

Thornbury, William Henry, Private, 8894, age 20, 1st Duke of Edinburgh's (Wiltshire Regiment)

Died of wounds, 13th September 1915, buried in Malmesbury Cemetery 592 South (in the same plot as H.R. Weston, with a family inscription *GREATER LOVE, HATH NO MAN THAN THIS*), commemorated Malmesbury Abbey (initials wrongly shown as WS), Town Hall & Triangle.

Malmesbury Cemetery is on Tetbury Hill. Established in 1884 it is jointly run by Malmesbury Town Council and St. Paul Malmesbury Without Parish Council. Plot 592 South is close to the southern path, walk beyond the path leading to the Chapel and it is three rows north and four rows west of the path junction.

William's name was registered at birth as Henry William but this was presumably a mistake as the names were subsequently reversed. He was the only son of Henry (groom) and Louisa Thornbury, 15 St Johns Street. Pre-war he had served in the Ammunition Column before joining the Regular Army. Despite having been a Regular for three years he does not appear on the Mayor's Roll of Honour. He accompanied his battalion to France on 14th August 1914, was wounded in the back at the battle of the Aisne and had some leave at home in October 1914 before rejoining his unit. During that leave he visited his old school, the Westport Boys', where he described how he had been wounded by a piece of German shrapnel and showed the boys the hole in his tunic. He was wounded for the second time in the leg on 7th September 1915. The war diary gave the following details;

Monday 6th September 1915 Belgium, Ypres

Resting on ramparts. Intermittent shelling by enemy most of the day. The whole Battn digging after dark at HOOGE and SANCTUARY WOOD.

2 Casualties.

This suggests that Willy's wound occurred in the early hours of the morning whilst on this working party. He was evacuated to Fairview Red Cross Hospital, Chigwell, Essex. At first he recovered well but on the morning of Sunday 12th a telegram was sent to his mother advising his condition was grave. He died the next day from tetanus. The North Wilts Herald's Roll of Honour entry read;

THORNBURY.- Sept. 13, died of wounds at Fairview Red Cross Hospital, Chigwell, Essex, Private William Thornbury, 1st Wilts Regiment, only son of the late Mr. Henry Thornbury and

Willy Thornbury's funeral cortege coming up the High Street from his home to the Abbey. (Athelstan Museum)

Mrs. Thornbury, 15, St. Johns Street, Malmesbury, aged 20 years.

His body arrived by train on the evening of Wednesday 16th September and the funeral took place the following afternoon. The coffin covered with the Union flag was borne from his home in St Johns Street in a glass sided hearse covered with wreaths. Headed by three buglers, followed by many family members and dignitaries the cortege proceeded to the Abbey for the funeral service. The body was laid to rest in the Cemetery witnessed by hundreds of people. When Mrs Evie Denley, who lost her brother, cousin and uncle, all Malmesbury men, in the Great War, was nearly 100 years old she recalled;

William Thornbury was my brother, we called him Willy. He was the first soldier to be buried in Malmesbury during the war.

That happened in September 1915, I was thirteen.

The whole town turned out to see the gun carriage draped with the Union Jack go along High Street, they had never seen anything like that before. Willy's death broke my Mother's heart. Dad had died when Willy was thirteen and they would not let him leave school until he was fourteen and so he worked in the gardens of Colonel Miles to earn a few pennies. When he joined the army he allowed five shillings a week to be sent home to Mother out of his seven bob a week.

He was wounded in Flanders and brought back to England, but his wounds were infected with tetanus and he died in the Hospital with the 'lockjaw'. Mother saved up to put a simple kerbstone around Willy's grave, but she was told to take it away.

Three years later a local boy, Seaman Weston died and Mother was upset again as they buried him in the same grave as Willy. They were going to exhume the boys and rebury them, but Mother said she did not want any further distress to the families and the boys should be left in peace, and so some years later when the headstones were put up, Willy's was put at the head of their grave and the boy Weston's at the foot.

Woodward, Frank, Private, 3138, age 27, 2/4th Battalion Duke of Edinburgh's (Wiltshire Regiment) Territorial Force

Died, 20th September 1915, commemorated on the Kirkee Memorial Face 7 India, Malmesbury Abbey, Town Hall & Triangle (all Malmesbury memorials show his rank wrongly as Gunner).

Frank was buried in Poona (St Sepulchre's) Cemetery. The Kirkee Memorial commemorates more than 1,800 servicemen who died in India during the First World War. They are buried in around 50 civil and cantonment cemeteries, including Poona, in India and Pakistan where their graves can no longer be properly maintained. The memorial stands within Kirkee War Cemetery which was created to receive Second World War graves from the western and central parts of India where their permanent maintenance could not be assured. The cemetery contains 1,668 Empire burials of the Second World War.

Frank's memorial plaque known as the 'Death Penny', sent to the next of kin of all those who lost their lives. (Dave Ashford)

Frank Woodward in the Ammunition Column's dress uniform. (John Bowen)

Frank was the third son of George (gardener and later estate agent at the Priory) and Elizabeth Woodward of 8 Burnivale. His brothers were William, Albert & James and sisters Carrie, Ethel, Rose & Frances. At the time of his enlistment Frank was working for William R. Phelps esq. at Montacute House, Somerset, having previously been a footman at Badminton House and earlier with Capt. Mackirdy at Abbey House and Major Morrice at the Priory. He went with the Ammunition Column to India but transferred to the infantry. Two brothers, William and Bert, were both Privates in the 4th Wiltshires but were still in England and able to attend his memorial service. His other brother James was still at home and worked alongside his father at the Priory. George received the following letter from Poona dated 21st September;

Dear Sir,

My cable of this morning saying your son was dangerously ill will have broken the sad news of his death. This occurred at the hospital here about 9.55 this morning, the cause being malaria, followed by a severe attack of pneumonia. I find he was feverish for some days, and his friends induced him to go to the hospital on Friday last. It was not known till late last night that he was dangerously ill, and then he became practically unconscious. I went to see him this morning, and Capt. Awdry went at 10.30 last night, but I don't think he knew either of us. The funeral is to be at 5.15 this evening, and the whole of my company will attend. I have found out that many wreaths are being sent by his comrades, and the officers also are sending one. All that could be done for him has been done at the hospital; he had two attendants beside the doctor last night, and they were assiduous in their attentions.

I am sure that all these details will appear to you rather unsympathetic, but I assure you that we all feel most deeply that we have lost a good soldier and comrade in your son, and as his commander I cannot speak too highly of his devotion to duty and steadiness and good conduct at all times.

This letter is written in haste to catch the special mail steamer. I hope to write to you again in a day or two.

    C.W. Maggs Major

In a further letter Major Maggs described the funeral at the soldiers' cemetery about 2 miles from the town. 150 men attended and the service was conducted by the Church of England chaplain. The family's tragedy did not end there as Frank's mother died suddenly on Friday 9th October. It was reported that the unexpected death of one of her sons had preyed upon her mind, producing melancholia that caused her death.

Johnson, Alfred, Lance Corporal, 15334, age 24, 11th (Service) Battalion Welch Regiment Killed in action, 21st September 1915, buried at Assevillers New British Cemetery VI B 2 (with a family inscription HE DIED THAT WE MIGHT LIVE), commemorated Malmesbury Abbey, Cemetery (on his parents' grave, plot 354 North, with the inscription And they sang a new song), Town Hall, Triangle and Tonyrefail, South Wales.

Assevillers was taken by the French in the autumn of 1916, evacuated by the British Fifth Army on the 26th March 1918 and retaken by the 5th Australian Division on the 28th August 1918. Assevillers New British Cemetery was made after the Armistice by the concentration of graves from the battlefields of the Somme and other burial grounds. There are over 800 1914-18 war casualties commemorated in this site. Of these, two-fifths are unidentified and special memorials are erected to 25 soldiers and one airman from the United Kingdom, known or believed to be buried among them. Other special memorials record the names of nine soldiers and two airmen from the United Kingdom, buried in other cemeteries, whose graves were destroyed by shell fire. The cemetery covers an area of 2,655 square metres and is enclosed by a stone rubble wall. One of the burial grounds from which British graves were brought to Assevillers New British Cemetery was Foucaucourt French Military Cemetery, at the South-West corner of the village, where four soldiers from the United Kingdom were buried in 1915 and 1917 (presumably Alfred was one of these).

Alfred was living in Cardiff where he worked on an electric engine at a colliery in Tonyrefail, South Wales. Alfred's father, Isaac, although a native of Malmesbury, spent most of his life in Cardiff where his eldest son, Harry, carried on the business after his parents returned to Malmesbury. They had nine children, eight boys, Harry, George, Edward, Hubert, Oliver, Charles, Alfred & Percy and one girl Hilda. Isaac became a Borough Councillor but his wife Selina died in April 1914. Isaac suffered a serious illness just before his son's death and was forced to resign from the Borough Council due to failing health and eyesight in January 1916 (he lived for another twenty years). Two other sons served in this war – Charles, a gunner on H.M.S. Cumberland and the youngest Percy in the R.A.M.C. attached to the Welch Regiment. Another son, Hubert who emigrated to America, had served with the Yeomanry during the South African War. Alfred enlisted in Cardiff and joined 11th Welch, part of Kitchener's Third Army raised in the city in September 1914. After training in Southern England they landed at Boulogne on 6th September 1915. Amongst the first British troops to move into the Somme area, the unit occupied trenches taken over from the French on the Amiens – St Quentin road on 18th September. Alfred was killed at Cappy. Ironically just over a month later the battalion left the front and a week later sailed from Marseilles to Salonika.

Alfred's was the first death in the Battalion on active service. Second Lieutenant F.C. Phillips wrote to his father;

Alfred's parents' grave in Malmesbury Cemetery.

It is with great sorrow that I have to inform you of the death of your son, Lance-Corpl. Alfred Johnson, who was killed by a shell today. His end was a peaceful and painless one, death being instantaneous. On behalf of his comrades I beg to express to you our great sympathy in the loss you have sustained. Your son was one of the finest men it has been my privilege to meet, and was held in high esteem by myself and the rest of the men under my command. He was one in a thousand.

The Battalion commander, Colonel F. Russell Parkinson and chaplain, Rev. G. Foster also wrote. An extract from Rev. Foster's letter reads;

We all feel it particularly, not only because it was the first death on service of our battalion, but also his company officer tells me that your son was one of his best section commanders. He died instantly from a shell, and I buried him just behind the front line in the presence of the Colonel and a few friends. I am afraid that I cannot at the present time tell you the exact spot but the grave has been carefully registered and a cross will be put up in a day or two so that if you ever feel a desire to visit the spot after the war you will easily find it.

The entry in the North Wilts Herald Roll of Honour was;

JOHNSON.- Sept. 21, killed in action in France, Alfred Johnson, Lance-Corporal, 11th (Service) Battalion, the Welch Regiment, son of Mr. Isaac Johnson, 11, Horsefair, Malmesbury, aged 24 years.

James, Herbert, Private, 3/451, age 38, 6th (Service) Battalion Duke of Edinburgh's (Wiltshire Regiment)

Killed in action, 25th September 1915, commemorated on the Loos Memorial Panel 102, Malmesbury Abbey, Cirencester Benefit Society, Town Hall & Triangle.

The Loos Memorial forms part of Dud Corner Cemetery. This stands almost on the site of a German strong point, the Lens Road Redoubt, captured by the 15th (Scottish) Division on the first day of the battle. The name "Dud Corner" is believed to be due to the large number of unexploded enemy shells found in the neighbourhood after the Armistice. On either side of the cemetery is a wall 15 feet high, to which are fixed tablets on which are carved the names of those commemorated. At the back are four small circular courts, open to the sky, in which the lines of tablets are continued, and between these courts are three semicircular walls or apses, two of which carry tablets, while on the centre apse is erected the Cross of Sacrifice. Herbert was the elder son of Edward (a mason) and Jane James, Lower High Street with one brother, William. Herbert started out as a mason's labourer but then worked as the Workhouse porter for 12 years. He married Ellen Bishop, a niece of his parents' next door neighbour in March 1915 and was admitted as a Commoner in June of that year.

The day after attending the recruiting meeting on 7th August 1914 Herbert applied to the Board of Guardians for leave to join the Army. Permission was granted and the Board undertook to try to keep his position open. As a reservist he waited until recalled. On 4th September accompanied by 18 Class 1 reservists of A Company (Malmesbury) Wiltshire National Reserve he left on the 2.55 train for Devizes. The men had paraded at the Old Drill Hall at 2.15 under the command of Sergt.-Major J. Moore. Included in the party was Trooper George Angell who also was to lose his life. Both Joe Moore and the Mayor Henry Farrant made speeches expressing the pride of the town and that those left behind would *do the best for their wives and children*. Despite these promises his widow experienced many difficulties after Herbert's death. She asked the Guardians for the return of his superannuation contributions. At the outset one of them said they need not hurry as *the woman was able-bodied, quite capable of maintaining herself and not in immediate want*. However this attitude quickly changed and members pressed for her to be treated like those who retired, with a gratuity of two or three years contributions added to the fund. Unfortunately the matter had to be dealt with by the Local Government Board and no reply was received from them until the end of January 1916. They said that the application *had been held up because the general question of allowing gratuities in cases of this kind is under consideration*. Fortunately on 18th February they sanctioned the payment of £12 2s. 9d. which included a gratuity. Even then some Guardians wished to appeal for more.

Herbert died on the first day of the Battle of Loos. His Division was not part of the main attack but the 58th Brigade, which included the 6th Wiltshires, was ordered to give support. At 5.30 a.m. gas was released from cylinders and smoke candles lit in the front line trench. This created a dense pall of smoke over the trenches that did more harm than good. An hour later the 9th Welch Regiment and the 9th Royal Welch Fusiliers attacked. After advancing 80 yards they were stopped by fire. Soon after 7 a.m. the unit on their right asked that the attack be pushed on but only one company of the 6th Wiltshires was sent forward. All of the attackers stalled and soon after noon were ordered back. The North Wilts Herald report had a rather fanciful version of events;

He was a company cook, and as such it was not expected that he would be called upon to take part in operations in the trenches, but when the great advance was ordered on September 24th he, as well as the other cooks, was detailed for duty in the trenches. According to Pte. W. Johnson, who was his "mate", and always with him in the work of cooking, and who is now home on a week's leave, Pte. James, when the order to attack reached the men on that fateful Friday evening, expressed his eagerness to meet the Germans. His dearest wish, he said, was to have a stand-up set-to with the biggest Hun they could find, preferably a Prussian Guard, in good old British style with the bare knuckles. When the dawn of the 25th came

and the troops made their historic dash into the enemy's lines carrying trench after trench, Pte. James was in the thick of it, the next man to him being Pte. Johnson. The two, who were only four yards apart, had climbed out of a trench preparatory to making another dash forward, and Pte. James had placed a sand-bag in position as cover so that he could shoot the better. He then reached out for his rifle, which he had placed on the ground. As he did so an enemy's shell burst near him: he was struck in the head and fell forward, death taking place almost instantly. Capt. Wykes, Lieut. Coleman and Lieut. Moore were struck down in the same attack. After gaining, at heavy cost to the enemy, several lines of trenches, the 6th were obliged to retire a little way, and the bodies of the fallen had to be left between the British and German trenches. "It cost us another twenty lives," declared Pte. Johnson, "in attempts to fetch the dead for decent burial, but the Germans poured on all who ventured out such a merciless fire that our new

Herbert James (North Wilts Herald)   *captain, who took charge by this time, forbade any more* making the attempt. Jack Clark and I volunteered to fetch in poor Bert James' body, but the captain would not hear of it. Lieut. Moore was not killed outright. Two days later he crawled into our trenches, and as he was being borne along to the rear for treatment, he died. Subsequently we got the bodies of the others in, and Bert James was buried in the same grave as Lieut. Coleman."

The battalion's casualties totalled 3 officers and 22 other ranks killed, 2 officers and 65 men wounded and 20 missing. Captain Wykes died of his wounds a couple of weeks later in hospital. In later fighting Herbert's grave was lost, so he is commemorated on the Loos Memorial. The news of his death quickly arrived, not officially but in letters from his comrades Privates George Angell and Arthur Strange (who was wounded in the same action). George Angell wrote again to the widow;

It is with the deepest regret I scribble you these few lines, but as it is the wish of all the Malmesbury boys that I should write and express our deepest sympathy with you in your great loss I feel I could not refuse.

I can assure you poor Bert was liked by all, and there was not a fellow in our company but knew him and had a good word for him. He died like the good soldier he was, and it is a relief to know he suffered no pain. He is buried in the firing line with our platoon leader, Lieut. Coleman. As you know Bert and I were great chums – in fact, like brothers – and I miss him very much. He lived a good life, and I am sure he is gone to a better land, though it is very hard for us to part with our loved ones.

I can see you and him now, coming down Abbey Row when you were going to see him off on his final leave. The last time I saw him was on the Friday afternoon, and he shook hands with me and wished me good luck as I was being sent to the Brigade headquarters for a few days. I shall always remember him from then, looking well and hearty, and in the best of spirits.

I can assure you you have our deepest sympathy, and we trust the One above will give you strength to bear your irreparable loss.

The Battalion war diary entry read less fancifully;

Saturday 25th September 1915 France, Rue de Callioux

At 5.15 a.m. on the 25th an order was received that the attack would commence at 5.50 with asphyciating [sic] gas and smoke candles. The assault signal was given at 6.30 by rockets from Brigade Office. The 58th Brigade's objective was the German lines just in front and rear of Rue d' Auvert. The Welch on our right supported by the Cheshires, the Welsh Fusiliers to our left supported by ourselves made the assault which was carried out by advancing through the saps. Owing to the gas not taking affect the Division on our right were unable to take the "crater" ridge with the result that the enemy on our front were able to bring enfilade fire on our troops. The saps were soon full and the attack was repulsed. 'A' & 'B' did not come into action but 'D' Company on the left went over the parapet and attacked. They were soon held up and suffered heavy casualties. Capt. Wykes and Lt. Wiles were wounded, 2nd Lts. Moore and Coleman were killed and other ranks were 17 killed, 17 missing and 46 wounded. 2nd Lt. Trueman took over charge of the Company and after holding on for a considerable time withdrew the remainder of the Company with considerable judgment to our original firing line under orders from Major Hartley. The enemy remained quiet. The Battalion took over the firing line from the Fusiliers who had suffered heavy losses, Owing to the wet weather considerable difficulty was experienced in bringing back the wounded and clearing up the trenches.

The North Wilts Herald did not have an entry in their Roll of Honour column but a year later this appeared In Memoriam;

JAMES.- In loving memory of my dearly beloved husband, Herbert James, who was killed in France, Sept. 25th, 1915, aged 38 years.

"Greater love hath no man than this – that he lay down his life for his friends."

> *"Gone, but not forgotten."*
> *We think of him in silence,*
> *No eyes can see us weep;*
> *But ever to our aching hearts,*
> *His memory we shall keep,*
> *Not here, but in a better land,*
> *Some day, some day, we'll understand;*

We never thought his time so short,
In this world to remain;
When from our home he went away,
He thought to come again,
          From his sorrowing Wife.

In 1917 another grieving note was inserted;

JAMES.- In ever loving memory of my dear husband, Herbert James, 6th Wilts Regiment, who was killed in action in France, Sept. 25th, 1915.

          "Greater love hath no man than this, that a man lay down his life for his friends."
          From his sorrowing Wife, Malmesbury.

Another entry appeared the following year;

JAMES. –To the loving memory of my dearly-loved husband, Herbert James, who fell in action, Sept. 25th, 1915.

          0, for the touch of a vanished hand,
          And for the voice we loved which is still.
          From his sorrowing Wife, Malmesbury.

Bond, Walter John, Private, 20671, age 26, 6th (Service) Battalion Duke of Edinburgh's (Wiltshire Regiment)

Died of wounds, 10th December 1915, buried in Chocques Military Cemetery I H 41, commemorated Malmesbury Abbey, Town Hall & Triangle.

Chocques was occupied by British forces from the late autumn of 1914 to the end of the war. From January 1915 to April 1918, No. 1 Casualty Clearing Station was posted there. Most of the burials from this period are of casualties who died at the clearing station from wounds received at the Bethune front. After the Armistice, further graves were added to the cemetery from a number of small cemeteries and isolated sites in the area. Chocques Military Cemetery now contains 1,801 Empire burials of the First World War, 134 of them unidentified. There are also 82 German war graves, 47 being unidentified. The cemetery was designed by Sir Edwin Lutyens.

Walter was the second son of Francis (Frank), an agricultural labourer & Sarah Bond, 16 Burnivale (Primrose Bank next to Betty Geezer's Steps) who raised a large family - four boys (Frank, Walter, John & Charles) and four girls (Kate, Mary, Emma & Nellie) survived infancy. Walter married Susan Pearce in Malmesbury in late 1913. The family moved to Corsham where their daughters Phyllis and Iris were born in 1914 and 1915 respectively. Walter arrived in France on 9th September 1915 nearly two months after 6th Wiltshires, so may have been a reinforcement. Susan Bond had a very tough time at the end of 1915. First her daughter Phyllis died shortly before her first birthday, she gave birth to Iris and then she received the news of her husband's death. Private Bond must have been one of the men wounded during his battalion's spell in the trenches between 8th and 10th December as he is buried at the location of Casualty Clearing Station 1. The battalion war diary entry reads;

France, Rue Des Chavatte, near Richebourg Wednesday 8th – 10th December 1915

Battalion held the trenches. Our artillery carried out bombardments to which the enemy replied very little. Casualties were 1 man killed and 2 wounded. Companies relieved every 24 hours. Communication trenches were impassable.

This entry appeared in the Herald's Roll of Honour;

BOND.- December 11th, died of wounds received in action, Pte. Walter Bond, 6th Batt. Wilts Regiment, second son of Mr. Frank Bond, 16, Burnivale, Malmesbury, aged 27 years.

1916

At the very start of the year Gallipoli was evacuated. Some of the units there, including 10th (Irish) Division had been sent to Salonika, whilst others went to Egypt and fought in Palestine. Both of these theatres claimed local men, but the main cause of grief arose on the

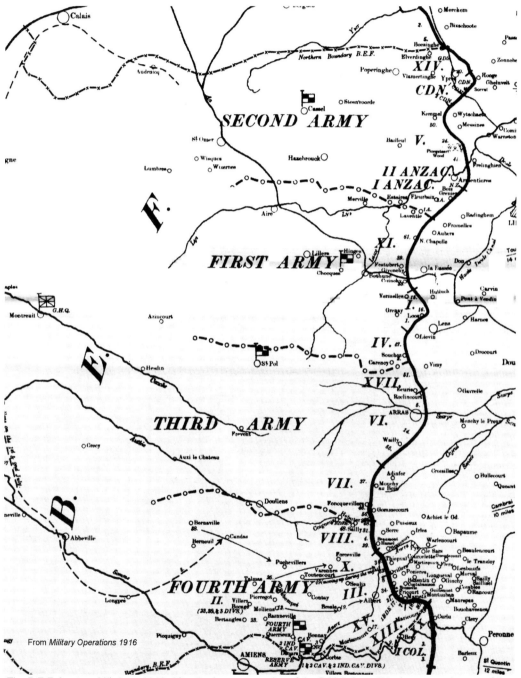

From *Military Operations 1916*

The B.E.F. front on 30th June 1916. After the huge expansion of the British Army it took over much more of the front (see page 107) with the reserves necessary for a big attack. Note the concentration of units in the south.

Western Front – the battle of the Somme that began on 1st July and carried on until November.

After the disappointment of Loos Sir John French was replaced as commander-in-chief by Sir Douglas Haig. He insisted that France & Belgium should be the priority but here the initiative was seized by the enemy. In February the Germans began a series of strong attacks on the fortress town of Verdun. They felt that the French would do their utmost to defend the town and through superior artillery they could be worn down by attrition. Although there were a number of crises General Nivelle's famous order *Ils ne passeront pas* (they shall not pass) was obeyed. However they were severely stretched and urged the British to relieve the pressure. Thus the attack on the Somme was planned.

On 1st July 1916, supported by a French attack to the south, thirteen British Divisions launched an offensive on a line from north of Gommecourt to Maricourt in the south. Despite a preliminary bombardment lasting seven days, the German defences were barely touched and the attack met unexpectedly fierce resistance. Losses were catastrophic and with only small advances on the southern flank, the initial attack was a failure. In the following weeks, huge resources of manpower and equipment were deployed in an attempt to exploit the modest successes of the first day. However, the German Army resisted tenaciously, repeated attacks and counter attacks meant a major battle for every village, copse and farmhouse. At the end of September Thiepval, one of the first day's objectives was finally captured. Attacks north and east continued throughout October and into November in increasingly difficult weather conditions. The Battle of the Somme finally ended on 18th November with the onset of winter. Most of the casualties occurred in units of the New Armies and the losses were particularly felt in communities which had raised 'Pals' battalions. Malmesbury suffered less although there were still nine deaths.

At the end of May the German High Seas Fleet took to sea and encountered the British Grand Fleet at Jutland off the coast of Denmark. Although the Royal Navy suffered slightly greater losses their superiority was confirmed – their next meeting was in November 1918 when the Germans sailed into Scapa Flow after the surrender. The U-boat blockade intensified and Allied shipping losses were 50% higher than in 1915.

During the year the North Wilts Herald Roll of Honour provides excellent coverage and their In Memoriam column begins to be developed. Coverage of the Gloucestershire Regiment is poor but fortunately the Wilts and Gloucester Standard fills that gap well. 18 Malmesbury men were to die this year, bringing to town's total to 37.

Lewis, Alfred John, Private, 14904, age 26, 12th (Service) Battalion Gloucestershire Regiment

Died, 3rd April 1916, buried in Beauval Communal Cemetery A 23, commemorated Malmesbury Abbey, Cirencester Benefit Society, Town Hall & Triangle.

The 4th Casualty Clearing Station was at Beauval from June 1915 to October 1916 and the 47th from October to December 1916. The great majority of the burials were carried out from these hospitals but a few were made as late as March 1918. After the Armistice, graves from Lucheux Military Cemetery were moved to Rows A and G of this cemetery. Beauval Cemetery contains 248 Empire burials of the First World War. The British plot was designed by G H Goldsmith.

Alfred was the sixth son of Edward (a farmer) and Mary Lewis. He came from a large family with six brothers Henry, Arthur, Joseph, Charles, Fred & Walter and three sisters Sarah, Susan & Minnie. The 12th Gloucesters were raised at Bristol by a Citizens' Recruiting Committee on 30th August 1914 and Alfred presumably was in the city at the time. The unit arrived in France on 21st November 1915. The death notice in the Standard noted the date as 2nd April and the North Wilts Herald reported Alfred's death in their 14th April edition;

YOUNG SOLDIER'S DEATH – News has been received of the death in a French hospital of Pte. Alfred John Lewis (26) of the 12th Gloucesters (Bristol's Own Battalion). He was the sixth son of Mr. and Mrs. Edward Lewis, Gastoris, Malmesbury, for whom much sympathy is felt, and the other relatives in their loss. The young man, who died on 3rd April, was in the transport section, and he contracted double pneumonia in the course of his duties. He joined the Army soon after the war broke out, giving up a very good situation at High Wycombe. He was formerly employed by Mr. E.H. Lockstone, of Malmesbury. Another brother, Walter Cecil, is in the Army with the trench mortar guns. Pte. Alfred was well liked by all who knew him.

It is difficult to work out why Alfred is buried in Beauval. The 12th Gloucesters were either serving in the front line north east of Arras or resting at Agnez les Duisans during March and April 1916. One possibility is that he was taken to 42nd Casualty Clearing Station based at Aubigny en Artois just a few miles from Agnez. This unit moved for a short period to Lucheux so Alfred might have gone with them and died there. Alfred's parents received further bad news just a few weeks later as their second son, Arthur Edward, died on 27th April at the age of 32 in Santiago Hospital, Chile.

Pike, Ernest, Able Seaman, J/8992, age 23, H.M.S. Russell, Royal Navy
Killed in action, 27th April 1916, commemorated Portsmouth Naval Memorial panel 13, Malmesbury Abbey (initial wrong, shown as A), Town Hall & Triangle.

The Naval Memorials are described under Midshipman John Morrice's entry above. The architect for the Second World War extension at Portsmouth was Sir Edward Maufe (who also designed the Air Forces memorial at Runnymede) and the additional sculpture was by Charles Wheeler, William McMillan, and Esmond Burton. Portsmouth Naval Memorial commemorates 9,667 sailors of the First World War and 14,918 of the Second World War.

Ernest was the youngest son of Isaac Epigoney (tiler & plasterer) and Ruth Coombs Pike, of 46 Bristol Street, Malmesbury. He had three brothers, Richard, Percy & Francis as well as two sisters, Emily & Ethel. After school he became a grocer's assistant but joined the Navy on his 18th birthday, 29th January 1911, and went as a boy sailor to H.M.S. Ganges, a shore based training establishment at Shotley near Harwich. He served on 7 different ships, being rated an Ordinary Seaman on his 19th birthday and Able Seaman 18 months later. He had served on H.M.S. Irresistible for two years when he wrote home from the Dardanelles in early March 1915:

Of course you will have read where I am long before you read this letter, and I expect you will be worrying about me; but there is no need to, as we take it all as good sport to be able to do a little bit for good old England. Oh, but it is great to see us bombarding. You see a place quite as big as Malmesbury one minute, and in a very short time there is nothing left but a lot of blackened walls and burning buildings. We have been about four miles up to start on some more forts, so I don't expect it will be long before we are paying a visit to the Sultan. We have

H.M.S. Irresistible sinking after it struck a mine whilst bombarding the Turks in the Dardanelles. (firstworldwar.com)

had a pretty warm time of it, but luckily we have not been hit. We have sent parties ashore to finish off the guns, blowing them up; and you should have seen it – a huge explosion, a scattering mass of earth and stones and the guns themselves – and it is all over ... We are having some lovely weather out here; better than at home, I expect. I am going to send Princess Mary's gift by the next mail. I would like you to send me the 'North Wilts Herald' every week, as it would be interesting to read, and will you send me a box of 'Woodbine,' as the canteen is getting short.

A few days later on 18th March 1915 he survived the sinking of the ship when it was mined. Picked up by H.M.S. Queen Elizabeth he wrote again;

You will have read about the loss of our ship before you get this letter, I expect. I lost all the photos I had, all my kit and hammock, in fact, everything but what I had on, which was a great deal. We had plenty of time to get off the ship, and there was no panic, everything was conducted in the most orderly fashion. We struck and listed over to starboard, and very shortly afterwards a torpedo-boat came alongside the port side and nearly everybody got on board, only leaving a few behind to look after the ship. I don't know how long we shall be on board here. This is a very nice ship, and what a ship it is! Any-one could easily lose their way walking around.

The newspaper report ended; *All Malmesbury people share Mr. and Mrs. Pike's hope that their son may come safely through the risks of the great fight in the Turkish Straits.* Although that hope was realised his good fortune only lasted another year. Ernest was posted to H.M.S. Russell, a battleship armed with four 12 inch guns in turrets and twelve 6 inch guns, another ship at Gallipoli. She stayed at Mudros as support alongside H.M.S. Hibernia in November 1915 and eventually took part in the evacuation on 7th January 1916. On her way home, H.M.S. Russell was mined on 27th April 1916 just off the coast of Malta losing 126 of her crew of around 750.

Ernest's death was reported in the North Wilts Herald of 12th May;

YOUNG SAILOR MISSING – Mr. and Mrs. Isaac Pike, Bristol Street, received the sad intimation on Friday that their youngest son, Ernest, an A.B. serving on H.M.S. "Russell," which was mined recently, is missing. He was 23 years of age and had been in the Royal Navy six years. He was on board the "Irresistible" when it was sunk, and after being saved was temporarily on the "Queen Elizabeth." Mr. Pike has two sons in the Army. One of them – Richard – was severely wounded, and is still lying seriously ill in hospital, at Leicester.

Portsmouth Naval Memorial

A fuller report appeared in the Wilts and Gloucester Standard;

H.M.S. RUSSELL.
MALMESBURY LAD DROWNED.

The sympathy of the town is extended to Mr. and Mrs. Isaac Pike, 46, Bristol-street, who have just received official notice that their youngest son, Ernest Pike, A.B. 78993, is amongst the missing of the ill-fated ship Russell. There is every reason to believe the lad has been drowned. Deceased, who was about 23 years of age, was a fine high-spirited lad, and was brought up in the Silver-street Congregational Sunday School, of which the present Mayor is superintendent. His experiences at sea have been varied and tragic. He was on board the battleship Irresistible when she was torpedoed and sunk, and his parents, who feared he had found a watery grave, were shortly afterwards delighted to hear he was among the survivors, though he lost everything but his clothes. Soon afterwards he visited his home and looked the picture of health and fitness. On return to the Navy he was drafted to the Queen Elizabeth, and we understand that for some time since he has been actively engaged on a mine sweeper. Recently he wrote home to his parents stating that he had been transferred to H.M.S. Russell, but he had only been on board about a week when this ship was blown up and either by explosion or by drowning there is little doubt that the lad met his fate. Mr. and Mrs. Pike's elder son Richard has returned seriously wounded from the front and lies in a Leicester hospital in a precarious condition. He has been visited by his wife and children. Another son, Percy, who is married and in the employ of Messrs. Spears, provision merchants in London, has joined up and expects to be called upon directly. To the death of Ernest Pike the Mayor made a feeling reference on Tuesday at the Council meeting.

The Gazette also had a short report;

Ernest Pike, able-seaman, who went down with H.M.S. Russell, was the son of Mr. and Mrs. Isaac Pike, Bristol Street. He was 23 years of age and had been in the Royal Navy six years. Two of his brothers are in the Army. Ernest Pike was a survivor from H.M.S. Irresistible, and later served on the Queen Elizabeth, it was believed that when on the Russell he was on his way home for a well-earned leave, for he had been on active service in the Mediterranean since November, 1914.

At the beginning of June this appeared in the North Wilts Herald Roll of Honour;

PIKE.- Officially reported missing with H.M.S. "Russell," Ernest Pike, A.B., youngest son of Mr. and Mrs. Isaac Pike, Bristol Road, Malmesbury, aged 23 years.

Obviously sadly missed by his parents they placed an entry in the In Memoriam column the following year;

PIKE.- In loving memory of Ernest Pike, youngest son of Isaac and Ruth Pike, Bristol Street, Malmesbury, who lost his life by the sinking of H.M.S. "Russell" in the Mediterranean, April 27th, 1915.

Gone from our sight, but not from our memory or love.
> *We count them "Missing" since beyond our ken,*
> *'Tis but a fog-wreath blots the path we plod.*
> *That Voice speaks clear: "All souls of righteous men*
> *Come life, come death, are in the Hand of God."*
>> *From Mother and Dad.*

The following year another entry was made;

PIKE.- In loving memory of Ernest Pike, who lost his life in the Mediterranean through the sinking of H.M.S. "Russell," April 27th, 1915.
> *We count them missing – we whose eyes are dim,*
> *Whose gaze is bounded by the horizon's bar;*
> *But none are missing in the sight of Him,*
> *Within Whose vision all His creatures are.*
>> *Never forgotten by Mother and Dad.*

The passage of time obviously did not dim the pain as this appeared in 1919;

PIKE.- In loving memory of Ernest Pike, who lost his life by the sinking of H.M.S. "Russell," in the Mediterranean, April 27th, 1915.
> *What will it matter, when war is o'er,*
> *What sea shall contain him or on what shore?*
> *He shall be sleeping far away from his home,*
> *Not there will we look, but to God's great dome.*

> *Where the quiet moon and each shining star*
> *Will tell us that he is not very far,*
> *And so are we comforted, we know, we know,*
> *That youth has come to claim his own again;*
> *That nothing beautiful that God has given*
> *Dies utterly or gives his life in vain.*
>> *Inserted by Mother and Dad, Malmesbury.*

Wood, Charles, Private, 7738, age 30, 1st Battalion Duke of Edinburgh's (Wiltshire Regiment)
Killed in action, 26th May 1916, buried at Ecoivres Military Cemetery, Mont St-Eloi II D 24 (his grave has a family inscription *THY WILL BE DONE*), commemorated at Malmesbury Abbey, Town Hall & Triangle.
This cemetery is really the extension of the communal cemetery, where the French army had

buried over 1,000 men. The 46th (North Midland) Division took over the extension with this part of the line in March 1916, and their graves are in Rows A to F of Plot I. Successive divisions used the French military tramway to bring their dead in from the front line trenches and, from the first row to the last, burials were made almost exactly in the order of date of death. The attack of the 25th Division on Vimy Ridge in May 1916 is recalled in Plots I and II. Ecoivres Military Cemetery contains 1,724 Empire burials of the First World War. There are also 786 French and four German war graves. The cemetery was designed by Sir Reginald Blomfield.

Charles was the third son of Henry (general labourer) and Elizabeth Wood, of Kingswall, with brothers Henry, Colin & Percy (who died later in the war) and sisters Mathilda, Martha, Fanny, Mabel & Emily. After leaving school he became a baker but then joined the Regular Army in 1906. Having served in France from the battle of Mons onwards, he was able to enjoy a week's leave in Malmesbury in July 1915, accompanied by Jim Paginton who had been officially reported wounded several times but had avoided injury. Charles' widowed mother first heard of her son's death through letters sent by Privates P. Boulton and W. Rymell. The Gazette quoted from Boulton's letter;

We have been in the trenches ever since I came back and we have had a very rough time of it in there, too – the worst I ever had, I think; but I am pleased to say I have pulled through it all right so far ... Poor old Charlie Wood got killed up there this time. He was killed instantly – hit through the lung with a piece of shell. I have seen poor old Charlie lots of times since I have been back from leave, carrying wounded fellows through the trenches. He was not in our Company, but I think he was about the finest stretcher-bearer in the regiment. It is a pity he has been knocked out ... I have just been down and seen Charlie Wood's grave before we left.

The North Wilts Herald of 2nd June reported;

KILLED IN ACTION – In a letter from Pte. William Rymell, Wilts Regt., to his wife at Malmesbury, it was stated that Private Charles Wood, of the same regiment, had been killed in action. Pte. Wood was 30 years of age and the youngest son of the late Mr. H. Wood and Mrs. Wood, Kingswall, Malmesbury. He had been 10 years in the Wilts Regiment and had been in the fighting for 18 months continuously. He was the big drummer in the Regimental Band, but since the war started he had, of course, to perform more serious duties. As a stretcher-bearer he saw a lot of the harrowing side of most of the big battles on the British front in Flanders, and his comrades greatly admired his pluck in bringing in the wounded under fire. It was he, by a singular coincidence, who picked up Pte. Tom Paginton, who was badly wounded in a night attack by the Germans. Much sympathy is felt for the widowed mother and the other relatives in the loss they have sustained.

His Company commander wrote to his mother;

Dear Mrs. Wood,

It is with the deepest regret that I am writing to confirm the sad rumour you heard about your son. I was not in command of the Company at the time, and in fact have only just come to it, but he was one of the men in the battalion whom everybody knew. He was universally loved as one of the bravest and best stretcher-bearers in the regiment. Many of his comrades are eternally grateful for the way he has looked after them when they have been wounded. He was hit by a trench mortar in the back and never regained consciousness till he passed away. His loss leaves many hearts here sad. To you it must be cruel grief, but we would like to give you the little consolation of knowing how greatly he was appreciated by us.

The war diary's account reads;

Friday 26th May 1916 France, Pylones

In the trenches. Fire from 2 inch trench mortar in the afternoon drew heavy retaliation from the enemy who replied by firing from a heavy trench mortar once in about every two minutes for one and a quarter hours. Damage was done to the trenches but no casualties were caused. Beyond this the enemy showed little activity: his sniping was far less brisk. Works: wiring during the night of the 25/26th: two flying traverses were erected in Common CT between the outpost line and retrenchment: the outpost line of the centre company was built up in places to give better cover from hostile sniping. On the night of the 26/27th the damage done to Grange CT by trench mortar fire was repaired and further wire put out in front of the centre and left companies.

There were four casualties:- Killed, Bandsman Wood, C., 'D' Company stretcher bearer. Wounded, Pte. Alford, P., 'D' Coy. Ptes. Pike, W.A. and Burt, E. of 'B' Coy. The night passed very quietly. Weather fine.

This entry was made in the Herald's Roll of Honour column;

WOOD.- Killed in action, Bandsman Charles Wood, stretcher bearer, Wilts Regiment, youngest son of the late Mr. H. Wood and Mrs. Wood, Kingswall, Malmesbury, aged 30 years.

A year later the family inserted this in the In Memoriam column;

WOOD.- In affectionate remembrance of Bandsman Charles Wood, stretcher-bearer, Wilts Regiment, who gave his life for his country, May 26th, 1916.

> *"One of the bravest and best."*
>   *The only link which death cannot sever,*
>   *Our fond memories will live for ever.*

Inserted by his Mother, Sisters and Brothers, 9, Kingswall, Malmesbury.

Further entries were made which are recorded under his brother Percy's biography, who died on 27th November 1917.

Wallington, John Henry, Gunner, RMA/13748, age 19, H.M.S. Queen Mary, Royal Marine Artillery

Killed in action, 31st May 1916, commemorated at the Portsmouth Memorial panel 21, Malmesbury Abbey, Town Hall & Triangle.

The Portsmouth Memorial is described under Able Seaman Ernest Pike's entry above.

John was the eldest son of Harry (who worked as a groom for Captain Hamilton, Manor House, Great Somerford) & Emily Wallington, of Pike Cottage, Burton Hill. The family originally came from Didmarton where John had been born. His brothers were Frank & Percy and sisters Elizabeth, Emily & Eva. John joined the Royal Marines in October 1913 and served onshore until being posted to H.M.S. Queen Mary on 28th September 1914. The Queen Mary was a fast but inadequately armoured battle cruiser that was part of the First Battle-cruiser Squadron commanded by Vice Admiral David Beatty. On 31st May 1916 the German High Seas Fleet was reported to be at sea and Beatty's ships were tasked with finding them. This they did and at 3.48 p.m. the battle commenced. Superior German gunnery meant that their guns quickly scored hits but the Queen Mary was the champion gunnery ship of the British fleet and was soon able to effectively reply. However H.M.S. Indefatigable was hit by two salvoes of shells and sank after exploding, taking all but two of her 1,017 crew to the bottom. H.M.S. Lion, the flagship, was badly damaged whilst Queen Mary, after receiving direct hits from the German ships Seydlitz and Derfflinger, blew up with the loss of 1,266 crew with only 9 survivors. Admiral Beatty made the famous comment *There's something wrong with our*

H.M.S. Queen Mary steaming through a calm sea. (firstworldwar.com)

bloody ships today. It was later established that the explosions occurred due to a lack of adequate flash screening between the magazine and handling room meaning that a hit on a turret could ignite the large number of shells stored below.

John was reported missing, his death not being confirmed until July, but in the meantime this appeared in the Herald's Roll of Honour;

WALLINGTON.- Officially reported missing with H.M.S. "Queen Mary," in North Sea battle on May 31st, John Henry Wallington, Royal Marine Artillery, eldest son of Mr. and Mrs. Wallington, Burton Hill, Malmesbury, aged 19 years.

The Gazette also had a short report;

John Henry Wallington, son of Mrs. Wallington, of Burton Hill, was on board the ill-fated Queen Mary in the North Sea battle. He was only 19 years of age and enlisted at Didmarton, where he was born. He had been on the Queen Mary since 1914.

The next year the family put this in the In Memoriam column;

WALLINGTON.- In proud and loving memory of my dear son, Jack (Gunner J.H. Wallington, R.M.A.), who lost his life in the Battle of Jutland on H.M.S. "Queen Mary," May 31st, 1916.

> *Brother, we wish thee joy,*
> *For thee the race is won;*
> *And the sweet word, "Well done,"*
> *Have greeted thee upon the farther shore,*
> *Where sorrow is no more.*
> *We cannot think of thee as in the deep,*
> *Nor yet asleep;*
> *But with thy manly power in full employ,*
> *Brother, we wish thee joy.*

Ever remembered by his Mother, Father, Sisters and Brothers.

Newman, Reginald George, Trooper, 1820, age 24, 1/1st Royal East Kent Yeomanry (the Duke of Connaught's Own, Mounted Rifles) Territorial Force
Died, 15th June 1916, buried in Suez War Memorial Cemetery D 64, commemorated Malmesbury Abbey, School, Town Hall & Triangle (wrong initials RC).

Suez was an important hospital centre during the First World War with two Indian general hospitals, two stationary hospitals and casualty clearing stations based there at various times. Initially, burials took place in a special plot in the Protestant cemetery but the War Memorial Cemetery was established nearby in 1918 and these graves were transferred there, together with some from other burial grounds. There are now 513 Empire casualties of the First World War and 377 from the Second World War buried or commemorated in the cemetery.

Reginald was the middle son of Frederick (a grocer) and Edith L. Newman, of 16 Gloucester Street with brothers Frederick & Victor (who died less than a week later) and sister Edna. His father clearly wished his sons to participate in his business as the name of it became Newman & Son by 1907 and & Sons before 1911. However Reginald was working in Folkestone and enlisted at Broad Oak, Canterbury in a local unit there. The Yeomanry travelled without their horses on the S.S. Olympic from Liverpool on 24th September 1915, arriving in Gallipoli 8th October. They served there until 30th December when they were withdrawn to the Island of Lemnos before going to Egypt in February. Reginald's death was reported in the North Wilts Herald of 30th June;

YOUNG SOLDIER'S DEATH – News has been received of the death in a military hospital of Trooper Reginald George Newman, Royal East Kent Mounted Rifles, second son of Mr. and Mrs. F. Newman (Messrs. Newman & Sons, grocers, High Street and Oxford Street, Malmesbury). Death was due to pneumonia after about ten days illness. When he enlisted in August 1914, soon after war was declared, young Newman was an assistant at Messrs. C.W. Dixon & Co., ironmongers, 69, High Street, Folkestone. The young soldier – he was only 24 years of age last month – had taken part in the Gallipoli enterprise, landing on that ill-fated shore last September. His friends will regret his untimely death. He did his apprenticeship in the ironmongery department of Messrs. J.E. Ponting & Sons, Malmesbury and later had a situation at Bath, before he went to Folkestone. Mr. Newman, senior, to whom and Mrs. Newman and the family much sympathy is felt, is himself an ex-Army man. He served in the Egyptian Campaign of 1882, earning the medal and the Khedive's star. He was a corporal in a cavalry regiment. The two brothers of the deceased are also in the Army – Victor a sergeant in the Gloucesters and Frederick a driver in the R.F.A.

The Wilts and Gloucester Standard had a similar report on 8th July;

MALMESBURY TROOPER'S DEATH AT SUEZ.

Great sympathy has been extended to Mr. and Mrs. F. Newman, of High-street, Malmesbury, on the death of their second son, Reginald George, from pneumonia. Deceased was formerly an apprentice to Messrs. Ponting and Sons, Ironmongers, from whence he removed to Folke-stone and promptly responded to the country's call for young men. He was a trooper in the Royal East Kent Mounted Rifles, and after fighting through the Dardanelles campaign was transferred to Egypt. He died at Suez on June 15th from pneumonia at the age of 24. His father was an old cavalry sergeant who fought through the Egyptian wars. Mr. and Mrs. Newman have two more sons serving their country, Mr. Fred. Newman who is married, an-swering to the call of his group some months ago, and Sergeant Victor Newman, of the Gloucesters.

The Herald's Roll of Honour held the following;

NEWMAN.- June 15th, Trooper Reginald George Newman, Royal East Kent Mounted Rifles, second son of Mr. and Mrs. Fred Newman, High Street, Malmesbury, aged 24 years.

Newman, Victor Garnett, Lance Sergeant, 240948, age 22, 2/5th Battalion Gloucestershire Regiment Territorial Force

Killed in action, 21st June 1916, commemorated on the Loos Memorial Panels 60 to 64, Malmesbury Abbey, School, Town Hall & Triangle.

For a description of the Loos Memorial see Private James Herbert above.

Victor was the younger brother of Reginald who died just one week before him in another theatre of war. Victor was in business in Stroud and enlisted at Gloucester in September 1914, joining the second line battalion of the local Territorial Force unit. After training in England the unit was sent to France, landing at Le Havre on 25th May 1916. On 1st June they received their first experience in the front line. On 15th they took responsibility for the front at Fauquissart near Laventie. During the night of the 20th a raiding party comprising two officers, two N.C.O.s and 22 men went over the top to obtain identification from the German troops opposite them but was held up by wire which had been insufficiently cut. They were exposed to heavy machine-gun fire which compelled them to return to the trenches. Heavy casualties ensued – five other ranks killed, one died of wounds, three officers and 13 other ranks wounded with four missing. One of those missing was Victor. He held the appointment of Lance Ser-geant (a Corporal who was qualified to be a Sergeant but awaiting a vacancy). The Gazette stated that he had been on scouting duty. On the 15th July the Wilts and Gloucester Standard had this report;

MALMESBURY SOLDIER MISSING.

Only last week we had to announce the death of Reginald George Newman, second son of Mr.

The Loos Memorial at the rear of the Dud Corner Cemetery. (Before Endeavours Fade)

and Mrs. Fred Newman, of High-street, Malmesbury, while on active service in Egypt. This week Mr. and Mrs. Newman have been officially informed that their youngest son, Victor Newman, a sergeant in the Gloucesters, is reported missing. In this apparent double loss the town extends to Mr. and Mrs. Newman its deepest sympathy.

The Gazette had this to say;

ANOTHER BLOW. - It was only last week we expressed sympathy with Mr. and Mrs. F. Newman, grocers, etc., of the Market Cross, in the death of their son, Raymond George, in Egypt. Mr. Newman has now had intimation from the War Office that his youngest son, Vic. G. Newman, lance-sergeant in the Gloucester Regiment, is reported missing from the British Expeditionary Force after an engagement on the 21st June. There is little hope that he is alive. The last letter received from him by his parents was dated June 19th. Deceased, whose age was 23, was, prior to entering the Army, in business in Stroud. We understand he was on scouting duty shortly before being missed.

Angell, (Arthur) George, Private, 11416, age 30, 6th (Service) Battalion Duke of Edinburgh's (Wiltshire Regiment)

Killed in action, 2nd July 1916, commemorated on the Thiepval Memorial Pier & Face 13A, Malmesbury Abbey, Cirencester Benefit Society (initial shown as just G), School, Town Hall (initial G) & Triangle (initial G).

THe Thiepval Memorial, the Memorial to the Missing of the Somme, bears the names of more than 72,000 officers and men of the United Kingdom and South African forces who died in the Somme sector before 20th March 1918 and have no known grave. Over 90% of those commemorated died between July and November 1916. The memorial also serves as an Anglo-French Battle Memorial in recognition of the joint nature of the 1916 offensive and a small cemetery containing equal numbers of Empire and French graves lies at its foot. Designed by Sir Edwin Lutyens, the memorial was built between 1928 and 1932. It was unveiled by the Prince of Wales in the presence of the President of France, on 31st July 1932. The dead of other Empire countries who died on the Somme and have no known graves are commemorated on national memorials elsewhere.

George was the third son of Jacob (Borough surveyor who died in 1902) and Bessie Angell (ex Headmistress of the National School) who lived at Avon Terrace, Bristol Street, with older sisters Annie, Jessie & Lottie and four brothers William, James (who both died in childhood), Ernest & Charles. George had previously served in the Royal Wiltshire Yeomanry and then joined the National Reserve. Prior to his recall he spent 14 years working for Tom Rich, butcher, High Street and in 1913 married Rosa Gale at Malmesbury. Before that he had worked for Colonel William Haydon R.E., J.P. of Maidford House, Norton.

As a Class 1 National Reservist George left Malmesbury on Friday 4th September 1914 and was lucky to enrol in the County regiment. Posted to the 6th Battalion he did not go to France until 19th July 1915. In June 1916 he came home on leave to his home at Frapes Villas after which his wife went to Wales where she was when news of his death arrived. The 6th Wiltshires did not take part in the attacks on the first day of the Somme battles (1st July) but just moved forward from Albert. The next afternoon they attacked La Boiselle. The North Wilts Herald reported;

WAR CASUALTIES – In the recent fighting on the Western front several Malmesbury men have fallen. Pte. A.G. Angell, Wilts Regiment, son of Mrs. Angell, of Bristol Street, and of the late Mr. J. Angell, has been killed. He was formerly at Mr. Tom Rich's, High Street, and was a popular young man. He was married, and his wife is on a visit to Wales. Much sympathy is felt for the widow and also for the mother of Pte. Angell. At least five others have been wounded, these including Sergt. F.H. Bailey, son of Mr. C. Bailey, Triangle, Ptes. F. Shaw, W. Rymell, W. Savine and Rufus Bailey. Pte. Rymell was shot in the hand and has lost a finger, and Pte. Rufus Bailey had a shrapnel wound in the shoulder.

The Standard had more detail;

The news of George Angell's death especially brought a feeling of painful regret to many of his old friends in the town and district. Before the war he was foreman to Mr. Tom Rich, butcher, of High-street, and his urbanity and deference to the wishes of the customers made him extremely popular. He found time to give gratuitous services in the interests of the Abbey and Westport Churches, and his work as treasurer of the men's meetings was much valued both by clergy and laity. For some time after joining the army he was company cook. He was

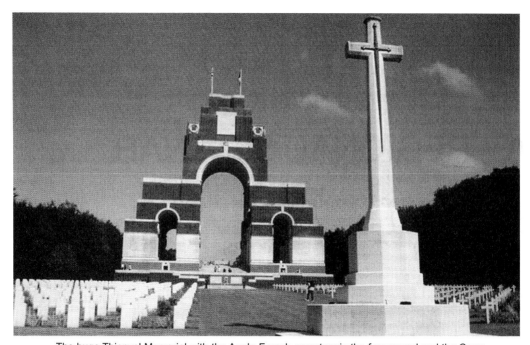
The huge Thiepval Memorial with the Anglo-French cemetery in the foreground and the Cross of Sacrifice found in all Commonwealth War Grave Commission cemeteries. (cwgc.org.uk)

present at the battle of Loos last September, and only a fortnight ago he was shaking hands with his friends on a few days' leave. We understand that at present his wife is paying a visit to friends in Wales. To Mrs. Angell the town extends its deepest sympathy.

The battalion war diary listed the terrible casualties suffered that day;

At 1.30 p.m. orders were received to take up position in front line at 4 p.m. At 4 p.m. Battalion advanced in open order and attacked German front line system of trenches just South of LA BOISSELLE. Two lines of trenches were taken and consolidated. Cheshires were on our right flank and Welch Fusiliers on our left. Our losses were Lt. Hunter, Lts. Allen, King and Biggs killed – Capt. Tanner, Lts. Springette, Reid, Tynan and Capt. Henry (R.A.M.C) wounded. Other ranks were 35 killed, 237 wounded and 35 missing.

The night was spent in consolidating - no counter attacks was made by the enemy.

The attack started well with the enemy distracted by an artillery bombardment of Ovilliers, but quickly became a close quarter struggle with systematic bombing and clearance of dug-outs. Casualties were regarded as 'not excessive'. The Wiltshire Gazette published an article on 7th September that gives a better idea of George's character;

THE LATE PRIVATE A.G. ANGELL.- The Bristol Diocesan Magazine has the following under the head of Malmesbury Men's Service – "It was with genuine sorrow and deep regret that the committee and members of the Men's Service heard that their beloved and respected treasurer, Private Arthur George Angell, of the Wilts Regiment, had been killed in action on Sunday, July 2nd. We felt the blow all the more keenly, because it was exactly a fortnight previously – when home on a well-deserved leave – that he had been present at the monthly service. He had been a most regular attendant at the Men's Service ever since its commencement; and when in due course he was unanimously elected treasurer, he agreed to accept the post, although at the time he was working under great pressure. He had a high sense of duty, and both as treasurer and member of the committee he carried out his duty in a thoroughly efficient manner, and we all feel that by his death upon the battlefield we have lost a true friend and brother – one whom we could ill spare. While in the Army – as we should only expect – he gained the affection and esteem of his officers and comrades. Arthur George Angell was a devoted husband and a loyal son and brother, and we offer our most sincere and heartfelt sympathy to his sorrowing widow, mother, brothers, and sisters. May it be a comfort to them in their great trial to feel that he has heard the words of his Master, "Well done, good

and faithful servant," and has entered into his reward."
The following entry appeared in the Herald's Roll of Honour;
ANGELL.- July 2nd, killed in action, Pte. Arthur George Angell, Wilts Regiment, third son of the late Mr. Jacob Angell and Mrs. Angell, Avon Terrace, Malmesbury, Aged 30 years.

Sharpe, Frank Francis, Private, 6773, age 29, 1st Battalion Duke of Edinburgh's (Wiltshire Regiment)
Died of wounds, 5th July 1916, buried at Puchevillers British Cemetery I C 18, commemorated Malmesbury Abbey (surname spelt Sharp), Town Hall & Triangle (initials TF).
In June 1916, just before the opening of the Battle of the Somme, the 3rd and 44th Casualty Clearing Stations came to Puchevillers. Plots I to V, and almost the whole of Plot VI were made by those hospitals before the end of March 1917. Puchevillers British Cemetery contains 1,763 First World War burials and was designed by Sir Edwin Lutyens.
Frank was the second son of Frederick (general labourer) and Annie Sharpe of Burnivale with three brothers, George, Joseph Harry (who served in the Army Service Corps) & Albert and four sisters, Rose, Elsie, Maud & Nellie. Frank had joined the militia in 1904 and was a railway worker. On the outbreak of war he was called up in the Special Reserve but for some reason was missed off the Roll of Honour. He was mentioned in a letter from Jim Paginton, postman;

February 26th, 1915

Dear Mr. Morse and all the boys at the office. – Just a few lines hoping to find you all well, as it leaves me – "in the pink." We came here for a few days' rest after eight days in the trenches. It has been rather cold lately; quite a coating of snow when we got up this morning, so I shan't forget my birthday in Belgium. I heard J. Sellwood (another Malmesbury postman) was still in England. I wonder if the other three boys are guests of the Kaiser: Have they heard of G. Peters? We have not to put our address on letters now, so, if you write, put "Signallers Headquarters" instead of "Company." I still go to the trenches, but I have a better job on telephone and buzzer. The nearest dug-out we go to the German trenches is only 70 yards. Not far, is it? I may say I have done a little post work in the trenches. Just before Christmas I had two letters handed to me, one from home with three Christmas cards in it, also a bundle for the boys, which I took up the trenches and handed over. We were only 100yards from the German trenches then. I saw my name mentioned in several papers as wounded, but, thank God, it is not correct. I see in the paper that Mr. Cresswell has retired. Just remember me to him. I hope he will live long and enjoy his pension. We get fed very well. I and F. Sharpe are almost always together. We got up this morning and cooked eggs and pig for breakfast. We get a drop of rum at night to keep us in trim. We have a concert to-night, so I can't stay any longer. Remember me to all the boys, and I hope, please God, the luck will continue, so that I may return to you all and my dear ones at home.

> *I remain, Yours truly,*
> *Jim Paginton*

The 1st Wiltshires started the Somme battle in reserve at Varennes, moving into the front line near Authuille during the night of the 2nd July. The North Wilts Herald of 28th July had a brief report;
A SOLDIER HERO – Yet another soldier has been killed in action. News has been received of the death on the battlefield of Private Frank Sharp, of the Wilts Regiment. He was 29 years of age and was the second son of Mr. Frederick Sharp of Burnivale, Malmesbury. He was an old Service man and when war broke out he was called up as a Reservist. He had been through most of the big battles from the very beginning, and it was hoped that, having escaped so far, he would return home safely. Much sympathy is felt for the relatives.
The battalion war diary for the period outlined many casualties;
Sunday 2nd July 1916 France, Varennes
A full kit inspection of all companies in battle order was made by the CO. Church Parade by Rev. L. Dickenson was held at 11.30 a.m. Battn at 1 hours notice. At 3.15 p.m. orders were received to proceed to HEDEAUVILLE. The Battn moved off at 4.10 p.m. and marched to bivouacs outside the village. At 7 p.m. orders were received for Battn to proceed to bivouacs in AVELUY Wood via BOUZINCOURT. At this juncture the 'B' team (those officers, NCOs, and men not taking part in the first assault) left the Battn and joined the Divisional Train at VADENCOURT. 'A' team spent the night in the Assembly Trenches in the wood.
Monday 3rd July 1916 France, Aveluy Wood

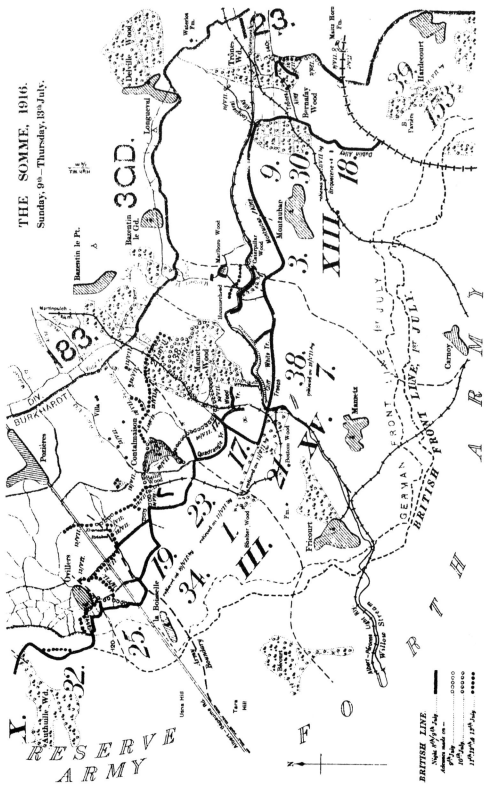

The 6th Wiltshires (George Angell & Frederick Shaw) were part of 19th Division near la Boiselle, 1st Wiltshires (Frank Sharpe) in 25th Division next to them on the northern side of the Albert-Bapaume road and 2nd Wiltshires (John Curtis) in 30th Division east of Montauban in Bernafay Wood. (Military Operations 1916)

The day was spent resting. One stray shell caused 2 casualties in the Battn (16 in all of the other regiments). At 9 p.m. the Battn moved via Black Horse Bridge to the fire line. 'D' & 'C' Coys to our old front line trenches. 'A' Coy to Leipzig Salient 300 yards of trench previously captured from the Germans (on July 1st). 'B' Coy were in support in Tobermory St. and sent up 2 platoons to the help of 'A' Coy. Battn HQ at Campbell post just off Campbell Ave CT. Enemy shelled heavily at midnight for about one and a half hours. Battn relieved in this position 1st Dorsetshire Regt. Highland Light Infantry Manchesters.

Tuesday 4th July 1916 France, Leipzig Salient

Trenches in front of Leipzig Salient.

Battn line was' 'D Coy extending to Thiepval Ave. and relieving the 11th Cheshire Regt. & 8th Borders. 'A' Coy continued to consolidate the Leipzig Salient and extended their line to the right by 150 yards erecting barricades. About 12.30 a.m. a heavy hostile attack was directed against our position in the Leipzig Salient, the enemy were seen to leave their trenches and from information from a prisoner captured it was found that they attacked in waves of 2 platoons. At 12.30 a.m. a very intense bombardment on our front line and continued till 2 a.m of 5th. Casualties:- Wounded 11 Killed 1.

Wednesday 5th July 1916 France, Leipzig Salient

Enemy continued shelling. Shortly after mid-day orders were received that the whole Battn was to move into the old enemy trench in the Leipzig Salient with a view to an attack on the enemy 2nd line, which was very strongly held forming the Leipzig Redoubt. The length of line to be attacked was about 600 yards and necessary operation orders were issued. At 4 p.m. however the length of objective was changed to 300 yards. Operation orders were issued as follows. 'C' & 'D' Coys were selected to do the assault, 'C' Coy on right and 'D' Coy on our left. 'B' Coy half to form carrying parties, half in support. The attack was carried out in following order

Attacking wave of each company, 'C' & 'D', 3 platoons, In support 1 platoon

Two platoons of 'B' Coy were carrying parties, one to each attacking Coy. The remaining half Coy of 'B' were in support holding the line of the Quarry. The time originally appointed for the attack was 6 p.m., this was afterwards changed to 7 p.m. For half min before this, there was an intense artillery bombardment assisted by Stokes Mortars, punctually at 7 p.m. our 1st wave advanced to the attack under heavy rifle and machine gun fire. 'D' Coy on the left under Capt. R.L. Knubley reached their objective without heavy casualties, but 'D' Coy on the left were badly cut up by machine gunfire and though they reached their objective were insufficient in numbers to withstand the heavy German Counter attack which followed immediately, and were compelled to withdraw temporarily. The second wave of each Coy consisting of 1 platoon had followed on the first wave at an interval of about 30-40 yards. 'C' Coy on the right were followed by the carrying party of 1 platoon of 'B' Coy. After the trench had been cleared of Germans, all dugouts were bombed immediately and then took in hand the consolidation of the position gained. Barricades were erected in all the communication trenches leading to the German 3rd line and bombing parties posted. In the case of 1 CT the Germans had erected a strong barricade prior to the attack. Two blocks were also built on the left of the captured trench, the second about thirty yards behind the first as a precautionary measure in case retirement became necessary. The men in this attack were magnificent, all showing the greatest coolness and initiative. Officer casualties in this attack were:-

'D' Coy 2nd Lieut. Starkey, missing. Lieut. Holman, wounded (later died of wounds). 'C' Coy Lieut. G.W. Penruddocke, 2nd Lieut. Troughton.

Very shortly after the attack commenced the enemy began an intense bombardment chiefly directed on their old front line now occupied by our HQ and support company, especially on that portion of it into which the Russian Sap entered, an underground tunnel from the old British front line excavated before first offensive of July 1st 1916.

In this bombardment 1 shell made a direct hit on the trench killing Lieut. Colonel W.S. Brown and wounding RSM Parker and 2nd Lieut. Stockbridge the Battn Signalling Officer. Capt. A.H. Hales acting 2nd in Command who was directing the attack from the line of the Quarries having also been killed, Capt. R.L. Knubley took Command of the Battn until the arrival of Capt. S.S. Ogilvie from the 'B' team. Other officers brought up from the 'B' team were 2nd Lieut. Sharpe, 2nd Lieut. J.R. Tayler. Prisoners taken during this attack 41.

Approx Casualties Killed 20. Missing 22. Wounded 158. Missing believed killed 2

The North Wilts Herald had a short entry in its Roll of Honour;
SHARP.- July 5th, killed in action, Pte. Frank Sharp, second son of Mr. Frederick Sharp, Burnivale, Malmesbury, aged 29 years.

Shaw, Frederick, Private, 22274, age 36, 6th (Service) Battalion Duke of Edinburgh's (Wiltshire Regiment)
Killed in action, 8th July 1916, commemorated on the Thiepval Memorial Pier & Face 13A, Malmesbury Abbey, Town Hall & Triangle.
For a description of Thiepval Memorial see Private George Angell above.
Frederick's parents had an interesting background. His father, John Shaw, was born in the West Indies and became a hawker. After marrying Eliza who came from Tetbury they continued their itinerant lifestyle. Their children were born throughout the south west; Catherine in 1867 at Exeter, for the 1871 census they were in Bristol with William born in 1877 at Bath. Unfortunately John died late in 1880 around the time of Frederick's birth in Malmesbury. By 1881 Eliza had settled in Church Street, Westport but remained a hawker at that time. By 1891 the family was still living in what was now called St. Marys Street but her occupation was charwoman. Catherine had two illegitimate children, William and Lily, before she married John Chivers in 1902. Eliza died in 1911. After her death Frederick gave up working as an agricultural labourer locally to move to South Wales where he was employed in a gas works. He volunteered to join the army shortly after the outbreak of war and enlisted at Tredegar, Monmouthshire but joined our county regiment.
The first report of his death appeared in the Standard of 15th July which casts doubt on the reported date of death (maybe he died of wounds);
Although not yet official, the news has been received by a letter from Private Jones to his wife at Milbourne, and corroborated by a letter from Private Ernest Thornbury to his wife that in the great advance three more Malmesbury lads were killed on July 2nd. They belong to the Wiltshire Regiment, and their names are Privates … Frederick Shaw, whose mother also resides in the parish.
Frederick's death was briefly reported in the North Wilts Herald of 4th August as follows;
News has been received of the death in action of Pte. F. Shaw (36), Wilts Regt., of Malmesbury. His sister, Mrs. Chivers, lives at Burton Hill.
Slightly more was reported the next week;
KILLED IN ACTION.- The late Pte. F Shaw was 38 years of age, and has a sister living at Burton Hill, Malmesbury. Before he joined up he was for three years employed in a gas works in Wales. His sister has received a sympathetic letter from the Chaplain, the Rev. A.A. Davies.
On the 7th the battalion had successfully attacked Bailiff Wood and the war diary entry for the next day was;
Saturday 8th July 1916 France, Albert
Continued consolidating position. The enemy subjected us to heavy artillery fire during the day. Late in the afternoon it was thought enemy were going to attempt a counter attack but nothing came of it, it is thought owing to well directed fire on CONTALMAISON by our heavy artillery, the only result being that enemy retaliated by heavily shelling our position and forming a barrage at HELIGOLAND and SAUSAGE VALLEY.
During the night and early morning of 8/9 Battalion was relieved by Royal Warwicks & Bedfords of 112th Brigade. The Battalion went to billets in Albert. At 9 p.m. the same evening Battalion moved to billets at BAIZZIEUX where a draft of 109 men from the 3rd Battn arrived.
A short entry appeared in the Roll of Honour;
SHAW.- Killed in action, Pte. Frederick Shaw, Wilts Regiment, of Malmesbury, aged 36 years.

Curtis, John, Private, 4887, age 45, 2nd Battalion Duke of Edinburgh's (Wiltshire Regiment)
Killed in action, 8th July 1916, commemorated on the Thiepval Memorial Pier & Face 13A, Malmesbury Abbey & Triangle.
For a description of Thiepval Memorial see Private George Angell above.
John was the son of Samuel (cattleman) and Louisa Jane Curtis of Milbourne with brothers William, Frederick & Walter and sisters Fanny, Mary & Sarah. Samuel died in 1909. John had joined the Militia in 1897 before transferring to the Regular Army a year later. His death was reported in the North Wilts Herald of 11th August;
KILLED IN ACTION – Mrs. Curtis, of Milbourne, has received news that her son, Pte. J. Curtis,

Wilts Regiment, aged 45, has been killed in action. The sad tidings were conveyed in the following letter from Second Lieutenant Vivian H. Clay, dated July 15th: "Dear Mrs. Curtis, - It is my sad duty to tell you that your son, 4887 Pte. J. Curtis was killed in action on July 9th by a shell. His death was instantaneous and quite painless. He was a most reliable man, and always went about his work most cheerfully and he set a fine example. Please accept my deep sympathy in your loss." Private Curtis's father was the late Mr. Samuel Curtis, of Malmesbury, and had been in the Wilts Regiment 18 years last December. He spent most of his service in India. On the return of his battalion to England he was transferred to Gibraltar. On the outbreak of the war he was brought to England for a short period before being sent to France. He took part in the fighting at Neuve Chapelle and was wounded and admitted to Bristol Hospital. On his recovery he again went to France. Previous to joining the Army he was employed by Mr. E. Fry, of the Three Horse Shoes Inn. Deep sympathy is felt for the bereaved mother.

The 2nd Wiltshires were involved in the battle from the start. Although not part of the first attack they supported it by bringing supplies forward. After a brief rest they prepared for the assault on Trones Wood and Maltz Horn Farm. It would seem that John's death must have occurred during the night as the date is variously recorded as the 8th or 9th. The war diary records;

Saturday 8th July 1916 France, Trenches
In the early morning we move , 'B' & 'C' companies to BERNAFAY WOOD, 'A' & 'D' Coys to BRICQUETERIE and assemble for the attack, our part being to follow the Yorks through BERNAFAY and TRONES WOODS and spring from the SE corner of the latter and attack MALTZ HORN TRENCH with two companies and gain connection with the French who are attacking on our right ('A' & 'D') companies remaining at BRICQUETERIE in reserve) On reaching the SE corner of BERNAFAY WOOD however, 'B' & 'C' Coys find the Yorks checked and driven back into the wood. Meanwhile the French attack has succeeded and their left flank is in the air badly needing protection and the French ask for support. The following was therefore ordered and carried out: - 'A' company at once advanced across the open from BRICQUETERIE making for a point S of MALTZ HORN FARM, and succeeded in taking trenches between this farm and the left flank of the French thus protecting the French left.
Meanwhile a re-bombardment of TRONES WOOD followed at 1 p.m. by the assault by 'C' & 'D' companies led by Lt. Col. GILLSON succeeded in taking the southern half of the wood clearing it of Germans, taking many prisoners and establishing a line on the south half of the eastern face of the wood. Col. GILLSON became wounded and handed over command to Lt. SHEP-HERD. During the evening many counter attacks by small parties of Germans are made from the north. These are all beaten off by our very thin line of men holding the ground taken. Reinforcements are called for and troops of the 19th and 18th Manchesters arrive before dark and reinforce. Capt. MACNAMARA who had been in reserve, now came up to TRONES WOOD and assumed command.
About midnight the Germans make a strong counter attack from the north, their only success being to capture a Lewis gun and throw two grenades into our line.

The battalion suffered 235 casualties including John. The Herald's Roll of Honour read;
CURTIS.- July 9th, killed in action, Pte. J. Curtis, Wilts Regiment, son of the late Samuel Curtis, of Malmesbury, and of Mrs. Curtis, Milbourne, aged 45 years.

Garland, (Robert) John, Leading Stoker, 310934, age 35, HM Submarine E41 Royal Navy Killed in action, 15th August 1916, commemorated on the Plymouth Naval Memorial panel 15, Malmesbury Abbey (initials shown as RG) & Triangle (initial just J).
The Plymouth Naval Memorial was made to the same design as those at Chatham and Portsmouth. Plymouth commemorates 7,251 sailors of the First World War and 15,933 of the Second World War.
Always called just John, he was the eldest surviving son of the late William and Sarah Garland (who later married William Carter in 1912 and lived at 11 Gastons Road). His brothers were Richard (who died at the age of 11) & Arthur and sister Gertrude. John joined the Royal Marine Light Infantry at Plymouth before transferring to the Royal Navy in 1906. That same year he married Florence May Bowden in Plymouth and lived at "Peverall," 35 Westeria Terrace, Plymouth. They had a daughter Audrey in 1915. He was based on the submarine depot ship H.M.S. Maidstone and on 15th August was a crewman aboard H.M. Submarine E41.

H.M. Submarine E41 at Harwich in 1918 after it had been salvaged
and converted into a minelayer (seayourhistory.org.uk)

Whilst carrying out anti submarine exercises in the North Sea, H.M.S. E41, acting as a target, had begun a surface passage of 12 knots when H.M.S. E4's periscope appeared 50 yards off her starboard bow, on a collision course. E41 stopped her engines but not before E4 collided forward of the bridge. E41 began to take in water through the forward battery compartment and began to sink by the bow. In less than two minutes the conning tower was under the water. H.M.S. Firdrake, who had been monitoring the exercise, took less than two minutes to reach the scene of the collision to pick up survivors. There were no survivors from E4, 15 were saved from E41, seven of whom escaped as the boat sank but 16 were lost. Both submarines were eventually located, salvaged (E41 in September 1917) and returned to service. The following appeared in the Herald's Roll of Honour;

GARLAND.- Aug. 15th, killed on active service with H.M. ships, Leading-Stoker John Garland (Devonport Division), oldest surviving son of the late William Garland and Mrs. Carter, 11, Gastons Road, Malmesbury, aged 35 years.

It was 1921 before another entry appeared in the North Wilts Herald In Memoriam column;

GARLAND.- In affectionate remembrance of my dear husband, Petty Officer John Garland (of Malmesbury), H.M.S. "Maidstone," who lost his life on Aug. 15th, 1916.

> *One of the dearest, one of the best,*
> *May God grant him eternal rest.*

Inserted by his sorrowing Wife and only Child, Audrey, and Mother.

Price, William Charles, Corporal, 14917, age 23, 10th (Service) Battalion Gloucestershire Regiment
Killed in action, 18th August 1916, commemorated on the Thiepval Memorial Pier & Face 5A 5B, Malmesbury Abbey, Cirencester Benefit Society, Town Hall & Triangle.
For a description of Thiepval Memorial see Private George Angell above.
William was the third son of William (a railway labourer) and Margaret Price, of Burnivale, with brothers Henry, Maurice & Charles (killed in 1918) and sisters Margaret & Ellen. The family had a strong connection with the Great Western Railway as brother Maurice worked for them as a labourer and William was a fireman based at Bristol when he joined up. According to the Mayor's Roll of Honour William joined the 12th Gloucesters. This unit was raised in Bristol by the Citizens' Recruiting Committee at the end of August 1914 but not taken over by the War Office until June 1915. For some reason William transferred to the 10th, another of Bristol's battalions. This unit crossed to France in August 1915 but William did not join them until 1st December. After the start of the Somme offensive they arrived in the battle area on 10th July 1916. They began their spell by burying 400-500 bodies near High Wood. For a month they trained and laboured close to the front. On 15th August they returned to Bazentin-le-Petit relieving 16th Royal Scots in the trenches. On the night of 17th/18th they carried out an unsuccessful attack and the war diary entry was;

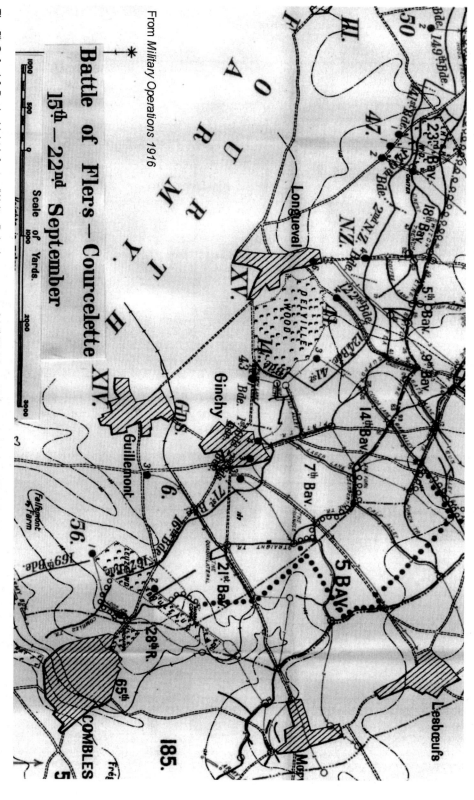

From *Military Operations 1916*

Battle of Flers—Courcelette

15th — 22nd September

Scale of Yards.

The 5th Oxford & Bucks Light Infantry (Walter Baker) were part of 14th Division which moved through Delville Wood and advanced for a considerable distance. 1/7th Middlesex (George Westmacott) in 56th Division fought in Leuze Wood where little progress was made. It was 26th September before Combles was captured.

144

Co-operated by a bombing attack with the 1st Bn. Royal Highlanders who were making an attack on the enemy intermediate line in front of MARTINPUICH. The attack was unsuccessful & in it lost Lieut. C.J.B. De La Bere (missing), Capt. H.St.H. Jeune, Lieut. L.F.C. Chaplin & 2/Lt. A.J.N. Grieves (all wounded). At about the same time a shell blew in a dug-out in the support line killing Lt. L.S.H. Griffin and wounding Capt. J.A. Riddle. Our casualties in other ranks in the action were 10 Killed, 52 Wounded & 4 Missing.

The Wilts and Gloucester Standard had this in their Deaths column;

Aug. 18, killed in action in France, Corporal William Price, Gloucester Regiment, third son of Mr. and Mrs. William Price, Burnivale, Malmesbury, aged 22 years.

William was included in family tributes put in the Herald's In Memoriam columns included under his brother Charles' entry (he was killed on 23rd August 1918).

Jones, Cecil, Private, 19414, age 17, 2nd Battalion Duke of Edinburgh's (Wiltshire Regiment) Died of wounds, 15th September 1916, buried at Bethune Town Cemetery V H 59 (with a family inscription *HE GAVE HIS LIFE, THAT WE MIGHT LIVE, EVER REMEMBERED BY HIS SORROWING MOTHER*), commemorated Malmesbury Town Hall & Triangle.

Bethune Town Cemetery is a large municipal cemetery visited in October 1914 by Mr. Fabian Ware, a former journalist in charge of a British Red Cross Society unit, trying to locate British graves. Here he found a number of British soldiers' graves marked by plain wooden crosses and formulated his idea for permanent memorials. In 1917 he became head of the Imperial War Graves Commission. For much of the First World War, Bethune was comparatively free from bombardment and remained an important railway and hospital centre, as well as a corps and divisional headquarters. The 33rd Casualty Clearing Station stayed in the town until December 1917. Early in 1918, Bethune began to suffer from constant shell fire and in April 1918, German forces reached Locon, five kilometres to the north. The bombardment of 21st May did great damage to the town and it was not till October that pressure from the Germans was relaxed. Bethune Town Cemetery contains 3,004 Empire burials of the First World War. Second World War burials number 19. There are also 122 French and 87 German war graves. The British section of the cemetery was designed by Sir Edwin Lutyens.

Cecil was the youngest son of William (farm carter) and Mary Jones, of 44 Foundry Road. He had brothers George, (William) John, Frederick (who served with the Canadian machine gunners, the second son so named, the first died aged 3), Reginald (Royal Field Artillery) & Bernard (Durham Light Infantry) and sisters Lily, Emma & Margery. Too young for conscription, Cecil must have volunteered when he enlisted at Devizes. The 2nd Wiltshires suffered around 600 casualties in the Somme battles and received a draft of 45 reinforcements (probably including Cecil) on 31st July two days before they left the area. They arrived at Robecq (10 miles north west of Bethune) on 4th August and a week later moved into trenches at Windy Corner, Givenchy. The war diary noted; *Enemy very quiet (Saxons)*. On the 15th August they moved into Brigade support positions which should have been safer but the following day the diary recorded; *'C' company holding three keeps in the ruins of GIVENCHY and 'D' company holding a keep at PONT-FIXE, are shelled in the early morning. Only two casualties. With this exception quiet day.*

One of these casualties was Cecil because over the next month there were no further casualties; this really was a quiet sector. Unfortunately he was transferred to the 33rd Casualty Clearing Station in Bethune which was also being shelled. He was one of only eight patients remaining at the end of August and died before it began accepting new patients again on 19th September. The entry in the Herald's Roll of Honour (note his exaggerated age) was;

JONES.- Sept. 14th, killed in action, youngest son of Mr. William Jones, Westport, Malmesbury, aged 19 years.

An announcement was made in the Herald of 24th November;

ACKNOWLEDGMENT – Mr. and Mrs. William Jones, 44, Foundry Road, wish to thank all those kind friends who sympathised with them in the loss of their son, Cecil, recently killed at the front, the second of their sons to give his life for his country.

I have been unable to trace another son who died either in the South African or Great Wars, however Cecil's loss was keenly felt as an entry In Memoriam in 1917 shows;

JONES. – In ever loving memory of our dear (seventh) son, Pte. Cecil Jones, 2nd Wilts Regiment, killed in action on the Somme, Sept. 15th, 1916.

 I think I see his dear smiling face

As he bade us his last good-bye;
He left his home he loved so dear,
In a foreign land to die,
I loved him then, I love him still,
Forget him? No, I never will.
Lovingly remembered by his Mam and Dad, 44, Foundry Road, Malmesbury.
The following year this appeared;
JONES.- In ever loving memory of our dear boy, Pte. Cecil Jones, 2nd Wilts Regiment, of 44, Foundry Road, Malmesbury, killed in action on the Somme, Sept. 15th, 1916.
He went into the battlefield,
So young and bold and brave,
He took it as his duty,
His country to help save.
Deeply mourned by his sorrowing Mother and Dad.

Baker, Walter, Private, 11072, age 24, 5th (Service) Battalion Oxfordshire and Buckinghamshire Light Infantry
Missing presumed killed, 15th September 1916, commemorated on the Thiepval Memorial Pier & Face 10A 10C, Malmesbury Abbey, Congregational Church, Town Hall & Triangle.
For a description of Thiepval Memorial see Private George Angell above.
Walter was the second son of Frederick (groom) and Sarah A. Baker of 3 Burton Hill, with brothers Frank & Richard and sisters Ethel, Rose & Eleanor. He was born in Maiden Bradley but the family moved to Malmesbury in the mid 1890s. Walter enlisted at Rugby, joining the 5th Oxfordshire & Buckinghamshire Light Infantry. This was the first of four Service battalions of that regiment, being raised in Oxford during August 1914. The unit arrived in France on 21st May 1915. It was involved in an attack on Delville Wood on 14th August 1916 when the battalion suffered 170 casualties. After a brief rest it took part in the battle of Flers/Courcelette starting on 15th September. The Battalion war diary described that day's activity;
4.00 Reveille
5.00 Moved to the south of YORK ALLEY, north of DELVILLE and formed up in artillery formation of platoon files with 5th KSLI in front & 9th KRRC on right. Order 'B' on left 'D' on right 'C' behind 'B', 'A' behind 'D'. Trench mortars & HQ behind 'C'. Vickers & S-Bearers behind 'D'. Lt. Col. Webb wounded in shoulder.
6.20 ZERO moved forward through wood after 41st Bde & finished finally on Bulls Rd.
11.00 when position consolidated
12.30 Lt. Col. Webb again wounded & taken away by stretcher bearers. Major Drury assumed command.
In these operations took 1 French mitrailleuse & 8 field guns. Casualties, Wounded Lt. Col. W.F.R. Webb, Capt. C.W. Maude, Lts. Dearer, Turner, Brooke and Atkins, at duty Capt. Gillespie RAMC & Lt. Rowe. OR killed 14 wounded 119 missing 23.
164 casualties sounds excessive for this brief description. In fact the 41st Brigade led the advance and was supported by three tanks. One of these was knocked out after half an hour, one ditched and the last went off on an adventure of its own. The 42nd Brigade, including 5th OXLI took over the advance around 9 a.m. It was brought to a halt just before it reached Bulls Road (the Flers – Lesboeufs road). The brigade was in front of the flanking units and every movement drew machine-gun fire from right and left. Walter was one of those reported missing. In December the Standard had a short report;
A MISSING SOLDIER.- Official news has been received by Mr. and Mrs. Baker, 3, Burton Hill, that their son, 11072 Private Walter Baker, Oxford and Bucks Light Infantry, has been missing since September 15th last. Pte. Baker, who is 24 years of age, joined at the outbreak of war, and has been at the front 18 months. He was gassed at Loos in September, 1915, and has been wounded. He was also buried after the bursting of a shell, but was rescued. One of his rescuers was Pte. J. Paginton, of the Wilts Regt., a Malmesbury postman. Much sympathy is felt for Mr. and Mrs. Baker in their anxiety, and it is hoped that they may yet have good news of their son.
A year later the following report appeared in the Herald;
Pte. Baker was missed on September 15th, 1916, and now the War Office have notified the parents that they are constrained to presume that he is dead, and at the same time they

conveyed the sympathy of the King and Queen and the War Minister and Army Council.
The following appeared in the Roll of Honour on 14th September 1917;
BAKER.- Sept. 15th, 1916, killed in action, Pte. Walter Baker, Oxford and Bucks Light Infantry, second son of Mr. and Mrs. F. Baker, 3, Burton Hill, Malmesbury.
An In Memoriam entry was made in 1920;
BAKER.- In ever loving memory of our dear son and brother, Pte. Walter Baker, Oxford and Bucks L.I., who was killed in action in France on or since Sept. 15th, 1916, aged 24 years.

> *Do not ask us if we miss him,*
> *There is still his vacant place;*
> *We shall ne'er forget his footsteps*
> *Or his dear young smiling face.*

From his Father, Mother, Sisters and Brothers, 3, Burton Hill, Malmesbury.

Westmacott, George, Private, 5901, age 25, 1/7th Battalion Duke of Cambridge's Own (Middlesex Regiment) Territorial Force
Killed in action, 17th September 1916, buried at Euston Road Colincamps Cemetery I F 34, commemorated Malmesbury Abbey, Town Hall & Triangle (initial C).
Colincamps and "Euston", a road junction a little east of the village, were within the Allied lines before the Somme offensive of July 1916. The cemetery was started as a front line burial ground during and after the unsuccessful attack on Serre on 1 July, but after the German withdrawal to the Hindenburg Line in March 1917 it was scarcely used. It was briefly in German hands towards the end of March 1918, when it marked the limit of the German advance, but the line was held and pushed forward by the New Zealand Division allowing the cemetery to be used again for burials in April and May 1918. The whole of Plot I, except five graves in the last row, represents the original cemetery of 501 graves. After the Armistice, more than 750 graves were brought in from small cemeteries in the neighbouring communes and the battlefields. It now contains 1,293 Empire burials and commemorations of the First World War. 170 of the burials are unidentified but there are special memorials to 32 casualties known or believed to be buried among them, and to two soldiers whose graves in nearby small cemeteries were destroyed in later battles. The cemetery was designed by Sir Reginald Blomfield.
George was a son of Arthur (gasworks stoker) and Caroline Westmacott, Horsefair, with five brothers, William, Frank, Walter, Fred & Ernest and three sisters Elizabeth, Anne & Sarah. Before joining up George lived in Tottenham, London and enlisted at Hornsey. He might have been a pre war Territorial as the 7th Middlesex's headquarters were in Hornsey and one of their Companies was based in Tottenham. The unit was sent to garrison Gibraltar in September 1914 before returning to England in February 1915 and going to France the next month. On 15th September 1916 they took part in an unsuccessful attack on Leuze (known by the troops as Lousy) Wood, suffering heavy casualties – 300 out of 500 of whom 125 were killed. After holding the front line the following day they were withdrawn into Brigade Reserve between Falfemont Farm and Wedge Wood. The War Diary does not note daily casualties and the entry for the 17th is just;
A day of rest and reorganisation.
The headstone of George's grave carries two names as he was buried with a colleague who died at the same time. The other name above George's is Private F.A. Wilkinson, 5817, Middlesex Regiment killed 17th September 1916. It would seem that the bodies must have been removed from another cemetery as Combles is some distance from Colincamps. His death was reported in the North Wilts Herald on 13th October;
KILLED BY A TRENCH MORTAR – Official news has been received by Mr. and Mrs. Arthur Westmacott, of the Horsefair, Malmesbury, of the death of their fifth son, Pte. George Westmacott, Middlesex Regiment. He was 25 years of age, and was killed by a trench mortar. Before joining the Army he was employed at a tobacconist's at Tottenham, and was previously at the India and China Stores, Malmesbury. Mr. and Mrs. Westmacott, who have another son in the Army, have received many expressions of sympathy in their bereavement.

Bond, Cyril Thomas, Private, 14341, age 23, 6th (Service) Battalion Royal Dublin Fusiliers Killed in action, 3rd October 1916, buried at Struma Military Cemetery II G 6, commemorated Malmesbury Abbey, Town Hall & Triangle.

The Struma River flows through Bulgaria southward to the Greek frontier, then south-east into the Aegean Sea. From the Allied base at Salonika, a road ran north-east across the river to Seres and it was this road that the right wing of the Allied army used for the movements of troops and supplies to the Struma front during the Salonika Campaign. In the autumn of 1916, the 40th Casualty Clearing Station was established not far from the road near the 71 Kilometre stone and the cemetery made for it was originally called Kilo 71 Military Cemetery. The original plot, Plot I, was set too close to a ravine and the graves in it were moved after the Armistice to the present plots VIII and IX. The remainder of the cemetery consists almost entirely of graves brought in from the battlefields, from the churchyards at Homondos, Haznatar and Kalendra, and from small front line cemeteries established by field ambulances or fighting units. The most significant of these were Ormanli, Dolab Wood and Big Tree Well. Struma Military Cemetery contains 947 Empire burials of the First World War, 51 of them unidentified. There are also 15 war graves of other nations.

Cyril was another man who originally enlisted at Devizes in the Wiltshire Regiment (number 13000) only to be transferred to Ireland in September 1914. He was the eldest son of Tom (stationary engine driver) and Alice Bond, of 40 Cross Hayes with a sister Alice and brother Walter. The 6th Dublin Fusiliers was formed at Naas in August 1914 as part of Kitchener's First Army. It became part of 30th Brigade, 10th (Irish) Division. They moved to Basingstoke in May 1915 and on 11th July sailed from Devonport, landing at Suvla on 7th August. That October they moved to Macedonia with a strength of 22 officers and 551 men, a higher percentage of their establishment than other battalions. At the end of that month they were amongst the first troops to move north into Serbia in an effort to halt the Bulgarian advance. Unable to do so by 20th December the British army was back in Salonika having suffered many casualties from enemy action and the extreme cold. Despite taking part in further engagements and losing men to illnesses by the beginning of the following October the Dublin's strength stood at 28 officers and 741 men. The war diary for 3rd October 1916 reads;

Bn. moved from KARADMKOJ VILLAGE to attack JENIKOJ [Yenikeui] about 0045, crossing JUNGLE ISLAND BRIDGE about 0230 and took up position for attacks at LONELY JOE 1000 SW of BALK. 6th RDF & 7th RMF Firing line, 7th RDF & 6th RMF Support centre, artillery bombardment of the village commenced at 0520. 'A' & 'D' Coys firing line under Major Lyte 'B' Coy support, 'C' Coy reserve, advanced at 0530, capturing JENIKOJ Village by 0620 with practically no opposition till Coys commenced to consolidate on N Edge, when they were heavily fired on by the enemy. At 0900, 1200 & 1300 enemy made desperate efforts to regain lost position by launching strong counter attacks which were dispersed by our fire. Our artillery work was magnificent. At 1800 Bn. less 'B' Coy were ordered to retire from village to LONELY JOE where rations were issued, men rested & reoccupied village at 0500 following morning. Casualties Capts. Clark, Carroll, Lts. Bolots, Mally & Taylor wounded, OR 30 killed 93 wounded 3 missing.

The Struma War Cemetery with a different type of Cross of Sacrifice (cwgc.org.uk)

Unfortunately the military authorities confused two men named Bond in the same regiment and both from Malmesbury so an incorrect entry was made in the Herald's Roll of Honour;

BOND.- killed in action between the 3rd and 4th of October, Pte. John Bond, Royal Dublin Fusiliers, third son of Mr. Francis Bond, Burnivale, Malmesbury, aged 28 years.

This was corrected the next week, although the Standard stated the date as a day later than that recorded by the War Graves Commission which is probably correct;

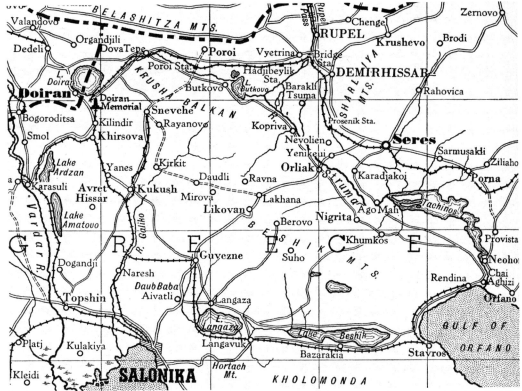

Yenikeui where Cyril Bond was killed is west of Seres. The War Diary's account of its capture fails to reflect the confusion surrounding the action. The morning Bulgar counter attack was repulsed by artillery fire and another early in the afternoon led by an officer on a white charger was also defeated. However the Dublins suffered from heavy shelling, some by the British after a forward observing officer was killed. When another counter attack was made some of the Dublins retired and 6th Royal Irish Rifles had to stop the retreat. At 7.40 p.m. an order to withdraw was given only to be countermanded shortly afterwards. All but one company had by then retired and they held the position overnight. The Bulgars withdrew the following morning. (Twenty Years After, Geo. Newnes)

BOND.- Oct. 4th, killed in action, Pte. Cyril Thomas Bond, Royal Dublin Fusiliers, older son of Mr. and Mrs. Thomas Bond, Cross Hayes, Malmesbury, aged 23 years.

His death was reported on 27th October;

ONE KILLED, ONE WOUNDED – News has been received by Mr. and Mrs. Thomas Bond, of Cross Hayes, that their elder son, Pte. Cyril Thomas Bond, Royal Dublin Fusiliers, was killed in action on October 3rd. Pte. Bond, who was 23 years of age, was employed for some time before his enlistment at Messrs. Jones & Sons' motor garage, Malmesbury. He was a much esteemed young man, and his death is regretted by a host of friends. Much sympathy is felt for the bereaved parents. On the same date Lce-Corpl. Jack Edwards, of the same regiment, formerly undergroom at Col. C.R. Luce's, Holcombe, Malmesbury, was wounded, presumably in the same engagement, though he was in another battalion. Both he and the late Pte. Bond enlisted in the early days of the war at Malmesbury. Lce.-Corpl. Edwards is the son of Mr. and Mrs. Edwards, Badminton.

The Wilts and Gloucester Standard also carried a report;

MALMESBURY SOLDIER KILLED IN ACTION.

The deepest sympathy of the townsfolk is extended to Mr. and Mrs. Tom Bond, of the Cross Hayes, Malmesbury, on receipt of the sad tidings that their eldest boy, Cyril, has been killed in action. Cyril Bond, who was about 23 years of age, joined the colours two years ago, being drafted into one of the Irish regiments, and has seen much active service, his baptism of fire being at Gallipoli. He was a bright, promising lad, had served his apprenticeship to Messrs. Jones and Son, motor proprietors, of Malmesbury, and for some time before joining the army had been one of the firm's most steady and reliable chauffeurs.

Bailey, Frederick Henry, Sergeant, 6990, age 29, 1st Battalion Duke of Edinburgh's (Wiltshire Regiment)

Killed in action, France, 4th October 1916, buried at Regina Trench Cemetery, Grandcourt IX C 12, commemorated Malmesbury Abbey, Town Hall & Triangle.

On 1st July 1916, the first day of the Battle of the Somme, Grandcourt village was reached by part of the 36th (Ulster) Division but it was not until the German withdrawal to the Hindenburg Line, early in February 1917, that it was occupied by patrols of the Howe Battalion, Royal Naval Division. To the south-east of it is Courcelette, taken by the 2nd Canadian Division on 15th September 1916. Regina Trench was a German earthwork, captured for a time by the 5th Canadian Brigade on 1 October 1916, attacked again by the 1st and 3rd Canadian Divisions on 8 October, taken in part by the 18th and 4th Canadian Divisions on 21st October and finally cleared by the 4th Canadian Division on 11th November 1916. The original part of the cemetery (now Plot II, Rows A to D) was made in the winter of 1916-1917. The cemetery was completed after the Armistice when graves were brought in from the battlefields of Courcelette, Grandcourt and Miraumont; most date from October 1916 to February 1917. Many of these graves contain more than one burial and where two names are shown on the one headstone, it is necessary to count the individual names in order to find the correct grave location. Regina Trench Cemetery now contains 2,279 burials and commemorations of the First World War. 1,077 of the burials are unidentified but there are special memorials to 14 casualties believed to be buried among them. The cemetery was designed by Sir Herbert Baker.

Frederick Henry, known as Dick, was a son of Charles (tailor) and Susan Bailey of 80 the Triangle whose family details are on page 113. Dick had been a bugler in the Malmesbury Rifle Volunteers and then joined the Wiltshire Regiment as a drummer, serving with the Colours for seven years. In 1910 he played the side-drum in Malmesbury on King George V's coronation day. He became an attendant at Cirencester Workhouse before moving to Ipswich Poor Law Institution, being responsible for the boys there. He finally moved to Enfield where he was a chargemaster at Chase Farm School. At the outbreak of war he was at home but being a Reservist was required to replace early casualties and arrived in France on 28th August 1914. During his service Dick was wounded at least five times, being reported as being in an English hospital as early as December 1914. His brother James died of wounds in June 1915. On 1st October 1915 the following appeared in the North Wilts Herald;

Corporal F.H. Bailey, more familiarly known as "Dick," is one of the five soldier sons of Mr. C. Bailey, of the Triangle, Malmesbury. He was wounded earlier in the war, and returned to the fighting-line as soon as he had sufficiently recovered. Mr. Bailey has lost one son, who died of wounds, and another has also been wounded. No details have been received of Corporal Bailey's injuries.

He wrote to his parents from hospital in Scotland in July 1916;

... I have never felt better; perhaps that is because the nurse gave me a hot bath last night, and being the first wash for a month it has livened me up immensely.

Well, you have by now noticed that place in the fighting called Montauban. That is where our lads have been through physical drill with bayonets fixed. We were not over the top with the opening offensive; our work was carrying ammunition, bombs, barbed wire, water, etc. All day long and all night we were busy, and at 4.30 on the 2nd inst. we had the order to reinforce the front line ... This was in the village of Montauban. When going through this village we had to cross a couple of snipers watching this road, so we had to dive through like hell. However, I got clear except my right hand; the devil had missed my body, and as my hand was on the swing he caught it. The bullet went through the seat of my trousers, through the sleeve of my coat, and then through the lower part of my hand, but the swine did not catch the bone, only the fleshy part, and I am pleased to tell you that it is healing up fine

I shall probably be in hospital about a week or so in fact, a week in hospital is quite sufficient for this kid. I only want a little rest and a good feed and 'off we go again.' ... We all know that it is an awful word, but nevertheless it has got to be done, and we shall win easily enough if we can only drive them out of France and Belgium, but not before. Anyhow they are still on, battering away, and I hope that before long the time will come when every German on the face of the earth will be under the earth and not show their sickly faces to us any more.

Please let all the boys know that I am in the best of health and spirits, and my best luck to them all. When the war is over we will go down to the 'Slappy' on the Common and drink their 'home-brewed.' I expect to get a leave when I leave here, so cheer-o! God be with us till we meet again. So long! God bless you all!

  Fred

After many traumatic experiences it is quite remarkable that he was so keen to return to the front. William, one of his brothers, was also wounded in July and wrote to his parents;

We were in the trenches three days and nights with hardly any food or water. We went over the top to take a trench, which we took all right, but what loss of life! Our Colonel was quickly killed, and about 500 of our men out in front were soon waiting for stretchers or other assistance ... On the night of the 2nd we camped in some large woods. Of course in these woods there were plenty of trenches, and these were our resting places for the night. During the next day we had two wounded; we were quite close to the firing line – Albert.

Next night we went up and took over trenches after a lot of trouble, as it was so dark. This was a reserve trench, so there was not much doing. Next day we were on fatigue carrying water, ammunition, bombs, &c. – and we had just got back from this when a party of us had to leave our company line and go as covering party to another company some way up the line. As we were getting our objective the Germans opened heavy shell fire on us. We were ordered back to our trenches for the time, but had not been back long – tired, of course – as the Huns were attacking. But we need not have gone out, as the attack soon finished, our bombers did not half put some bombs over! We had to stay there, so we took over a bomb-ing-post, and here had a little rest; but still wet through, cold, and no rations – that was the worst of it – no food. We stood to for a long time, when our officer came up, telling us to get as much rest during the day as we could, as we were making an attack at night. He could see that we were all done up, but he said we had to do it, so we told our sentries off and went into the dug-out. That was about midday and we slept until about four but it did not seem above five minutes. When we came out the sentry reported that a Johnny had gone down and given himself up. I cursed my luck there.

It was now about seven o'clock, and time for our final attack. The guns would give us the time, as they were going to bombard for half a minute, quite long enough, as it was only a small section of front which we had to take, about 50 yards across and 200 yards long. We were all forming up in a crater, getting ready to go over the fighting area called La Boisselle. The guns opened out and the boys went over, we had not to go over until last, as we were barbed wire carriers, but we found we did not want the barbed wire, so our section had to go with bombs. We went like hares and jumped into a communication trench leading to our captured trench. In going across I was hit twice on my 'tin hat' otherwise it would have meant two nice wounds in the head. We handed the bombs in and started to come back again when the cap of a shell hit me on the elbow, that only numbed it for a bit, but all at once a rifle grenade burst close by me, and from that I got three hits in the little finger, nothing much, but a small wound on the back of my hand. All small wounds except the top of the little finger hanging off. Well, I got back to where we started from and took an important message to headquarters for the officers. I delivered the message all right but coming back I got buried by a shell and that didn't half shake me up. I don't know how long I was there, it could not have been very long; any way I found myself in the dressing station. From there we went to a place called Etaps for three days, and you can guess where I came to then, and I was pleased. I hope to be out of hospital in a week or so, and then a joy ride.

The Germans are good fighters but not so at close quarters; their machine guns give our chaps hell, and their snipers are very tricky ... Our bombardments are terrible now, we have guns everywhere, and in the right places too.

The Somme battle continued and both Bailey brothers rejoined the fighting. The 1st Wiltshires moved into trenches between Ovillers and Thiepval (positions familiar to troops who took part in the first assault three months before) on 1st October and moved into Stuff Redoubt on the day Fred died. The war diary for that day reads;

The weather was very wet and trenches in a worse state than the previous day. Enemy's guns were active throughout the day, particularly on HESSIAN trench and ZOLLERN trench. Our guns bombarded the enemy lines at 1 p.m. Rations were delayed and did not arrive that day.

The Wilts and Gloucester Standard had a short report;

MALMESBURY SERGEANT KILLED.

Of the five sons of Mr. and Mrs. Charles Bailey, of the Triangle, serving their country, one has already been killed, and now it is our duty to record that Sergeant F.H. Bailey, of the Wilts Regiment, who had previously been wounded four times, was killed instantaneously on the 4th inst. Popularly known as Dick, Sergeant Bailey was a favourite with his comrades, and only returned from his trip to Malmesbury from convalescence on the 9th September. Two of Mr. Bailey's sons have also been wounded, and Private Dick Pike, writing from No. 3 Ward, Uppingham, to Mr. and Mrs. Bailey says: "I offer you my heartfelt sympathy, as Dick was a general favourite with all his chums. ... He would share his last bit with anyone." Much sympathy is felt for the parents and family in their double sorrow.

The Herald's Roll of Honour had this;

BAILEY.- Oct. 4th, killed in action, Sergt. Frederick Henry Bailey, Wilts Regiment, second son of Mr. and Mrs. Charles Bailey, Triangle, Malmesbury, aged 28 years.

The parents' anguish did not end as the three surviving brothers continued to serve and William was wounded for a fifth time in August 1917. This appeared in the In Memoriam column on the anniversary of Dick's death;

BAILEY. In ever loving and affectionate remembrance of our dear son, Sergt. F.H. Bailey, 1st Wilts Regiment, son of Mr. and Mrs. Charles Bailey, 80, Triangle, Malmesbury, who fell for the King and country, Oct. 4th, 1916.

> I think I see his dear smiling face,
> As he bade us his last good-bye,
> And left his home and those he loved so dear,
> In a foreign land to die.
> "Somewhere abroad," but we know not where,
> our dear Fred sleeps - a hero gone to rest.
> From his ever loving Dad and Mother.

In October 1918 this appeared;

BAILEY.- In ever loving and affectionate remembrance of our two dear sons, Sergt. F. and Pte. J. Bailey, who died fighting in France two and three years ago.

> Had He asked as well we know,
> We should cry, "O, spare this blow";
> Yea, with streaming tears should pray,
> "Lord, we love them let them stay."
> From Dad and Mam, 80, Triangle, Malmesbury.

Curtis, (Joseph) Bernard, Private, 19208, age 29, 8th (Service) Battalion Prince Albert's Own (Somerset Light Infantry)

Killed in action, 19th November 1916, commemorated on the Thiepval Memorial Pier & Face 2A, Malmesbury Abbey, Town Hall & Triangle.

For a description of Thiepval Memorial see Private George Angell above.

Christened Joseph Bernard it seems that he was known just as Bernard as that is how he is commemorated. He was the son of Charles (a butcher's slaughterman) and Rose Curtis of Gastons Road with four sisters Teresa, Mary, Helen & Winifred. On leaving school Bernard became a pony boy but moved to Stratton-on-fosse, Somerset from where he enlisted at Midsomer Norton. He joined the 8th Somerset Light Infantry which was formed as part of Kitchener's Third Army in Taunton at the end of October 1914. For some reason a number of other men from Malmesbury served with this unit including Sergeant Sydney Kite. He was the Battalion's bombing sergeant who survived the war to become the chairman of the Malmesbury branch of the Federation of Discharged and Demobilised Sailors and Soldiers. The 8th Somersets crossed to France on 10th September 1915 and just a fortnight later took part in the Battle of Loos. On 1st July 1916 they attacked Fricourt on the first day of the Somme battle. After suffering heavy casualties its Brigade was transferred from the 21st Division to the 37th. The Somersets also participated in the very last act of the Somme attacks. On 15th November they moved back into the line near Beaucourt. *The History of the Somerset Light Infantry (Prince Albert's) 1914-1919* records the action that took Bernard's life as follows;

At 1 a.m. on 18th November the Somersets moved off by companies through Beaucourt and completed a line of posts from Bois d'Hollande in a westerly direction across the open to Puisieux Road. 'A' Company was on the right from Ancre Trench to Bois d'Hollande, 'B' Company came next in the centre, and 'C' on the left. 'D' Company, about Ancre Trench, had

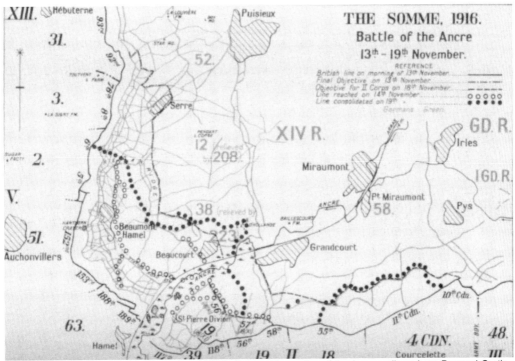

The Somme battles ended in November 1916 in the muddy wastes of the Ancre valley where Bernard Curtis perished. (Military Operation 1916)

orders to reconnoitre Puisieux Trench and establish strong points in that Trench and in Puisieux River Trench if possible. Two Stokes mortars and two machine guns were attached to 'D' Company to assist in the attack on Puisieux Trench. In the worst weather imaginable the Battalion set out on their unenviable and difficult task. Snow was falling, the ground was heavy with filthy, clinging mud and the going was terrible. As the patrols neared Puisieux Trench German patrols were discovered out in front of their line and the Somersets, unable to get near the Trench, took shelter in shell holes.

Coming generations will read of those gallant fellows taking "shelter in shell holes" without a tremor, knowing nothing of the remembrance of agony conjured up in the minds of those who went through the Great War in France and Flanders; of the dull misery of plodding through the seas of vicious mud, weighted down by equipment, pack, rifle and bayonet, ammunition, bombs and rations, clothes soaked through, covered from head to foot in slime, stumbling, slipping, ever expecting death, some even longing for it as a happy release from such untold misery: of the brain atrophied almost by suffering, of the constant expectation of attack and the tremendous nerve tension when moving against a concealed enemy.

By 11 p.m. all companies of the Somersets had been relieved and were located in support trenches and the Quarry just east of Beaucourt.

The day's fighting had cost the Battalion many valuable lives. Four officers had been killed, five officers were wounded and in other ranks the Battalion had lost over one hundred.

Throughout the 19ᵗʰ November, shelled all day, the Battalion remained in support.

Unusually the Official History has a little more detail; *The Somerset L.I. were late in starting and at 11.20 a.m. their commander, Lieut.-Colonel J.W. Scott, went forward to find his men sheltering in shell-holes from the fire of the British artillery. A message was got through to the guns, and, after the assaulting companies had been reorganised, the 4/Middlesex ... was called upon to take part in a combined assault at 1.30 p.m.* I have been unable to find any reports of Bernard's death in local newspapers.

1917

Early in 1917 the German forces in France fell back to their newly prepared defences, the Siegfried-Stellung which we called the Hindenburg Line. As they retired they laid waste to the area and their rear-guards inflicted casualties. Many booby-traps were left, killing one Malmesbury man. The new French commander, General Nivelle had grand plans for the French and British armies to attack in concert, with the French making the main offensive north of the River Aisne. This took place in April, failing dramatically whilst the British attack near Arras had considerable initial success, particularly on the Vimy ridge. The French failure led to a collapse in morale with some units mutinying and few being willing to attack. So for the rest of the year once again the British had to prevent the Germans from exploiting their ally's weakness. On 7th June a very successful attack was made at Messines beginning with the detonation of nineteen huge mines under the German's trenches. Another offensive should have quickly followed to the east of Ypres but there was a gap of six weeks which allowed the Germans to reorganise.

This third Battle of Ypres started on 31st July and was later known as Passchendaele – a name associated with mud and apparently senseless slaughter. However the crisis in the French army was at its height with units refusing to go into the line and Haig felt obliged to continue until 10th November. Just as that battle drew to a close a fresh one was started at Cambrai on 20th November. A concentration of nearly 500 tanks had been concealed close to the front and were expected to punch through the defences. Again success, sufficient for church bells to be rung in England, was followed by German counter attacks that drove the British back.

From *Military Operations 1917*

GERMAN RETIREMENT
25th Feb.–5th April
1917

SCALE OF MILES

In Italy the Austrians with German support broke through at Caporetto in October and forces had to be sent there from the Western Front. On the Salonika front there was stalemate although disease was taking a heavy toll. In the Middle East Baghdad in Mesopotamia was taken and Gaza in Palestine was captured after three battles between 26th March and 7th November.

In February the Germans had resumed unrestricted U-boat warfare. Whilst this created supply difficulties for Britain it did bring the United States into the war, but it took time for their huge resources to be developed. Meanwhile at the end of the year the Bolsheviks seized power in Russia which brought their part in the war to an end. 18 local men were to die this year, bringing the total to 55.

Curtis, Ernest William, Corporal, 990, age 23, 7th (Service) Battalion Prince of Wales's Leinster Regiment (Royal Canadians)

Killed in action, 10th January 1917, buried in Dranoutre Military Cemetery I H 16 (family inscription *UNTIL WE MEET*), commemorated Malmesbury Abbey, Cirencester Benefit Society, Congregational Church, Town Hall (initials shown as EH) & Triangle.

Dranoutre (now Dranouter) was occupied by the 1st Cavalry Division on 14th October 1914. It was captured by the Germans on 25th April 1918, in spite of the stubborn resistance of the 154th French Division. It was recaptured by the British 30th Division on 30th August 1918. Dranoutre Churchyard was used for British burials from October 1914 to July 1915 when the military cemetery was begun. This was used by fighting units and field ambulances until March 1918 (Plots I and II), many of the burials being carried out by the 72nd Brigade (24th Division) in April-June 1916, and Plot III was added in September and October 1918. Dranoutre Military Cemetery now contains 458 Empire burials of the First World War. There is also one German war grave. The cemetery was designed by Charles Holden.

Ernest was the elder son of Frederick (bacon factory hand) and Sarah Ann Curtis, of 5 Gastons Road, with one brother, Walter (who was to die of wounds in 1918) and two sisters, Lily & Ruth. He was one of the early volunteers to join Kitchener's Army who was enrolled into the Wiltshire Regiment (Service No. 13180) only to be sent to Ireland where he was posted to the 6th Leinsters. His younger brother Walter volunteered in London and tried to join him but the 6th Battalion was full so he was sent to the 7th Battalion. His sister Lily died from a brain haemorrhage on 21st June 1915 while Ernest was home on leave and he attended the Inquest. He took part in the Gallipoli campaign and a short report about him appeared in September 1915;

News has been received by Mr. F. Curtis, The Gastons, that his son, Pte. E. Curtis was wounded.

It seems that this refers to the dysentery that caused him to be evacuated to England. After convalescence Ernest was posted to join his brother in the 7th Battalion on the Western Front. He was probably wounded again as his name appears on the list of casualties from Malmesbury published on 4th August 1916.

A full report of his death appeared in the North Wilts Herald of 19th January;

MALMESBURY SOLDIER'S DEATH.

Corpl. E. W. Curtis Killed.

Much sympathy is felt for Mr. and Mrs. F. Curtis, of 5, Gastons Road, Malmesbury, in the loss they have sustained by the death on active service of their elder son, Corpl. Ernest William Curtis, Leinster Regiment. The young soldier was only 23 years of age. He joined the Army in September 1914, during the great recruiting campaign, and after going to Devizes, where he was for a short period with the Wilts Regiment, was transferred to the Leinster Regiment. At the time of his enlistment he was engaged at the Holloway Coachbuilding Works in the employ of Mr. E.F.E. Edwards, to whom he had been apprenticed, and had finished his apprenticeship about twelve months previously.

After a period of training in Ireland, young Curtis served with his famous regiment in the Dardanelles. Whilst he was there he contracted dysentery, and after a stay of three months in hospital at Mudros was brought home to England, spending two months in a Birmingham hospital. When he recovered he spent ten days' leave at home, and re-joined his regiment in March 1916. Soon afterwards he was sent to the front and saw much hard fighting. He was promoted corporal recently. His brother Walter is a sergeant in the same regiment.

The sad news of Corpl. Curtis' death was conveyed in letters from his captain, lieutenant, chaplain and sergeant, as well as from his brother. Sergt. J. Forsythe wrote: "My dear Mrs. Curtis – It pains me ever so much, and I regret to have to write to inform you that your son Ernest Curtis lost his life to-day (January 16th) through a shell exploding in camp. Poor boy! He did not suffer as he died shortly after being hit. It was a great shock to me to learn of Ernest's death, as it was to many of us who knew him since he joined the regiment. He was well liked by the boys of his company and by every-one who came in contact with him … Please accept my sincere sympathy in your sad loss, but do not worry, as Ernest has gone to a far better position."

The letter sent by Sergt. Walter Curtis was full of poignant grief at his brother's sudden end. "I hardly know how to break the awful news of Ern's death," he wrote, "which occurred at 9 a.m. yesterday. We are in reserve to the Brigade and in huts. We were subjected to a very severe bombardment. Ern was in his hut taking his breakfast when a piece of shrapnel came through the roof, and caught him in the back of the head, killing him instantly. I was only two huts away from him, but he was dead before I reached him…. As it happens, we are near a village, and he was buried in the British cemetery there at 5.30 last evening. The carpenters are making a lovely cross, and I am having our cap badge painted on it. The clergyman is writing to you to-day. The Commanding Officer sent for me yesterday, and I said Ern was with him in the Dardanelles and I have to convey to you his deepest sympathy. I was very glad I was with Ern up to 10 o'clock the previous night. The great respect in which he was held is evidenced by the huge numbers of messages from all ranks expressing their sympathy."

Capt. J.M. Carleton, the deceased's company officer, wrote: "It probably won't help by dwelling on the way your son died, but I should like you to know that as a soldier and a comrade he was regarded very highly by myself and all the officers of the battalion, and also by his brother n.c.o.'s and men. He was one of the sort we can ill afford to lose during the present days, and you have every reason to be proud of him. I quite understand that nothing can compensate you for the loss of your son, but we are all in the hands of God out here and trust Him to do what He thinks best."

Equally commendatory of the late Corpl. Curtis was Second Lieut. E. Garland in his letter. The Rev. F. Cowenlock, chaplain, in the course of a kindly letter, said: "Your son died gloriously for his King and country. He laid down his life that Britain might live. He died for his friends, than which, as the Master tells us, there is no greater love. I pray that God the Holy Ghost, the Comforter, will strengthen and sustain you in your dark hour of bereavement and desolation."

The late Corpl. Curtis attended the Westport Congregational Church and Sunday School. At that church next Sunday week a memorial service is to be held. Mr. and Mrs. F. Curtis have received a large number of messages of sympathy in their bereavement.

The Battalion's war diary entry was;

SPAMBROEK SECTOR, DERRY HUTS

10th January. At 8.45 a.m. the enemy sent over H.E. shrapnel badly wounding 1 man and killing a Cpl. The Bn. then moved into the trenches N. of the Camp. At 9.15 a.m. the enemy began to shell the batteries immediately in rear of Derry Huts and kept it up till 2 a.m. sending over 357 shells in all but without doing any damage.

In January 1918 the following appeared in the Herald's In Memoriam column;

CURTIS.- In ever loving memory of Corpl. E.W. Curtis, killed whilst serving his King and country, Jan. 10th, 1917.

> He proudly answered his country's call
> And nobly did his best,
> When he took his chance in the great advance
> To his everlasting rest.
> > Inserted by his sorrowing Sister Ruth

CURTIS.- In loving memory of our dear son, Corpl. E. W. Curtis, of the 7th Leinster Regiment, killed Jan 10th, 1917, somewhere in France, aged 23 years. Sadly missed by all who knew him.

> Sharp and sudden was the call
> Of one so dearly loved by all,
> His gentle voice, his smiling face –
> None can fill our loved one's place.

From his sorrowing Mother and Father, Brother and Sister, - 5, Gastons Road. Malmesbury, Wilts.

CURTIS.- In loving memory of Corpl. Ernest W. Curtis, Leinster Regiment, of Malmesbury, who was killed in action in Flanders on Jan 10th, 1917, aged 23 years.

> "Greater love hath no man than this."
> Oft will the tear the green and steep,
> And sacred be the hero's sleep,
> Till time shall cease to run;
> And ne'er beside his noble grave
> May Briton pass, and fail to draw

A blessing on the fallen brave.
> *Inserted by his Brother Walter.*

January 1919's entry was;

CURTIS.- In loving memory of Corpl. Ernest W. Curtis, Leinster Regiment, of Malmesbury, killed in action in Flanders on Jan 10th, 1917, aged 23 years.
> *Greater love hath no man than this.*
> *We miss our son, but God alone can tell,*
> *How we missed him when he fell;*
> *Far away from those who loved him best*
> *Comrades laid him down to rest,*
> *A noble hero, true and brave,*
> *He peacefully sleeps in a soldier's grave.*

Inserted by his sorrowing Mother and Father and Sister, 5, Gastons Road. Malmesbury, Wilts.
The next year this was the entry;

CURTIS.- In loving memory of our dear son, Corporal Ernest W. Curtis, 7th Leinster Regiment, who was killed in action in France, Jan. 10th, 1917. – R.I.P.
> *In the prime of his life death claimed him,*
> *In the pride of his manhood days;*
> *None knew him but to love him,*
> *None mentioned his name but with praise.*
> *From his loving Mother, Father and Sister.*

Boulton, George, Gunner, 145, age 31, 129th Heavy Battery Royal Garrison Artillery
Died of wounds, 21st February 1917, buried in Malmesbury Cemetery 138 South (family inscription *ROCK OF AGES, CLEFT FOR ME*), commemorated Brokenborough Church and Cirencester Benefit Society.

Plot 138 South is close to the junction of the eastern path which runs parallel to the road and the path leading to the Chapel. It is three rows west and six rows south of that junction.

George was the third son of Henry (farm carter) and Margaret Boulton who lived at Hyam Cottage, Sherston Road, with four brothers Charles, Herbert, Albert & Maurice and a sister, Sarah. He was born in Long Newnton and married Rosina Elizabeth Witchell in 1912 and had a daughter, Hilda in 1913 and a son, George in 1915. George had been a Constable with the Gloucestershire Police in Bristol for 10 years before joining the army in May 1915. Whilst serving in France with 129th Heavy Battery using 60 pounder guns he was kicked by a horse on 4th February 1917. Evacuated to England he died at Frensham Hill Military Hospital, Farnham with the causes listed as (1) Fractured Tibia & Fibula (right) 17 days and (2) Pneumonia 14 days. His name appears on a wooden plaque in the Brokenborough village church.

George's death was fully reported in the Herald of 2nd March;
GLOUCESTERSHIRE CONSTABLE'S DEATH
Funeral at Malmesbury

As a result of an accident the death occurred at Frensham Hill Hospital, near Farnham, on Wednesday of last week of Driver George Boulton, Royal Garrison Artillery, who was before he joined the Army a constable in the Gloucestershire Force. He was the third son of Mr. and Mrs. Henry Boulton, Hyam Cottages, Sherston Road, Malmesbury, and was 32 years of age. It was in May, 1915, that he left the Gloucestershire Constabulary, in which he was a "first-class" constable, for the R.G.A. He was then stationed at Kingswood, Bristol, in the Staple Hill Division. On March 27th last year he went to France, and was there with his battery for 11 months. Then he met with a serious accident, a horse kicking him so violently that his right leg was fractured. On the journey to England he, it is believed, caught a chill, and whilst in hospital pneumonia set in, from which he failed to recover.

The King and Queen sent a message of sympathy, signed by Lord Derby, to the widow, who is left with two small children, and messages of condolence were also received by her from Superintendent Edward Cooke, Staple Hill, Bristol, and Inspector and Mrs. A. Cooke, Kingswood. Supt. Cooke wrote: "I was extremely sorry to hear of the death of your dear husband and our greatly-esteemed colleague. On behalf of myself and the whole of the men of the division I tender you our deepest sympathy in your sad bereavement."

Inspector A. Cooke's letter was: Mrs. Cooke and I were very grieved to hear of the death of your dear husband. I assure you that you and the family have our deepest sympathy in your great trouble. Personally I feel his loss very much, for he was a most trustworthy and honourable man, and I pray that God in His great mercy will bear you up.

The funeral took place on Monday, the burial-place being Malmesbury Cemetery. The Rev. F.W. Nicklin (curate) performed the sad last rites.

The following appeared in the Roll of Honour;

BOULTON.- Feb. 21st, at Frensham Hill Hospital, near Farnham, Driver George Boulton, R.G.A., third son of Mr. and Mrs. H. Boulton, Hyam Cottages, Malmesbury, aged 32 years.

A year later his parents placed the following in the In Memoriam column;

BOULTON,- In loving memory of George Boulton, the beloved son of Henry and Margaret Boulton, of Sherston Road, Malmesbury, who departed this life Feb. 21st 1917.

> One year has passed, our hearts still sore,
> As time flies on we miss him more;
> His welcome smile, his loving face,
> No-one can fill his vacant place.
> We loved him then, we love him still,
> Forget him, no, we never will;
> God's will be done, we'll meet again,
> And then we'll part no more.

Inserted by his loving Father, Mother, Brothers and Widow

In 1919 this appeared;

BOULTON.- In loving memory of George Boulton, son of Mr. and Mrs. Boulton, Hyam Cottages, Malmesbury, who passed away on February 21st, 1917.

> Two years have passed since that sad day
> When he we loved was called away,
> Forget him? No, we never shall
> We loved him then, we love him still.

Inserted by his loving mother, father brothers and sister.

The next year another entry was made;

BOULTON.- In loving memory of George Boulton, the beloved son of Mr. and Mrs. Boulton, of Sherston Road, Malmesbury, who died Feb. 21st, 1917.

> Just three years since that sad day,
> When our dear son was called away;
> We loved him then, we love him still,
> Forget him, no, we never will.
> No daylight dawns, no night begins,
> But that we think of him.

Inserted by his loving Mother, Sister and Brothers.

In 1921 this appeared;

BOULTON.- In ever loving memory of our dear son and brother, George, the beloved son of Mr. and Mrs. Boulton, Sherston Road, near Malmesbury, who passed away Feb. 21st, 1917.

> We do not forget him, nor do we intend,
> We think of him daily and will to the end;
> Gone and forgotten by some he may be,
> But dear to our memory for ever he'll be.

Inserted by his loving Mother, Father, Sister and Brothers.

Newman, Henry John, Sapper, 71478, age 30, 4th Railway Telegraph Signals Royal Engineers

Died of wounds, 26th March 1917, buried at Cayeux Military Cemetery I A 3, commemorated Malmesbury Triangle only.

Cayeux village, which had been in the hands of British forces for just over a year, was lost on 27th March 1918 during the great German advance but recaptured by the Canadian Corps on the following 8th August. The cemetery was begun by French troops. It was used in March, April and May 1917 by the 36th Casualty Clearing Station and again for a few burials in March and August 1918. It was enlarged after the Armistice when graves were brought in mainly from the battlefields to the north. The cemetery now contains 216 Empire burials of the First

World War, 114 of which are unidentified. French and German graves have been removed to other cemeteries. It was designed by W H Cowlishaw.

Henry, sometimes called John, was the third son of William (a bus driver) and Mary Newman of the Star Inn, Bathford, Somerset. He had four brothers and started work as a paper cutter in a mill there. Sometime before the war he moved to Malmesbury. He was employed by the General Post Office as a linesman but is not listed amongst the local volunteers. Early in 1915 he married Edith Bishop and later that year their daughter Dorothy was born. Edith was the daughter of Collin (a stonemason) and Fanny (laundress) of Kingswall who had three other daughters older than Edith – Bessie, Nellie & Maggie. Whilst in France Henry was injured moving heavy reels of wire and returned to a hospital in Blackpool for treatment. He was home for 10 days but overstayed his leave as reported in the Wilts and Gloucester Standard of 27th January 1917;

CHARGED AS A DESERTER.- On Saturday, before Mr. T.L. Hinwood, Sapper John Newman, married, age 29, of 13, High-street, Malmesbury, was brought up charged with being a deserter from the Signal Depot, Royal Engineers Station, Hitchin. P.S. Harris said that on Thursday he went to the prisoner's house and saw him, and asked him if he was not a soldier. He said he was. On being questioned he could not produce a pass, and when the officer told him he would be arrested as a deserter he admitted having been absent since 24th December. Superintendent Witt asked that the prisoner might be remanded to await a military escort, which was on the way, and this was done. – P.S. Harris was recommended for the award of 5s.

Unfortunately Henry had not been back at the front long before he was killed. The Herald's report read;

A SOLDIER'S DEATH – News has been received by Mrs. Newman, Kingswall, of the death of her husband, Sapper Henry John Newman, R.E. It appears that he entered a dug-out in France, when a bomb previously placed there exploded, injuring him mortally. Sapper Newman, who was only 28 years of age, was the son of Mrs. Newman, Bathford. He married Miss Bishop, of High Street, Malmesbury. He leaves a widow and one child, for whom the utmost sympathy is felt.

The Standard had a little more information;

The news has been confirmed of the death of Sapper J. Newman, Royal Engineers, of Malmesbury, which occurred by the explosion of an enemy bomb while deceased was working in a trench at the front. The deceased soldier has been on active service, practically since the outbreak of the war but has on one or two occasions been home on leave. He leaves a young widow and one child who reside in King's Wall, Malmesbury, and to these our warmest sympathy is extended.

The following was in the Roll of Honour;

NEWMAN.- March 26th, killed on active service, Sapper Henry John Newman, Royal Engineers, formerly of High Street, Malmesbury, aged 28 years.

Hibbard, Edmund John, 2nd Lieutenant, 571643, age 27, 1/12th Battalion (County of London) London Regiment (The Rangers)

Killed in action, 9th April 1917, buried at London Cemetery, Neuville-Vitasse I A 4, commemorated Malmesbury Abbey, Town Hall & Triangle.

Neuville-Vitasse was attacked by the 56th (London) Division on 7th April 1917 and captured by them on 9th April. The village was almost entirely lost at the end of March 1918 but regained by the end of the following August. The London Cemetery was made by the 56th Division in April 1917 and greatly extended after the Armistice when graves were brought in from other burial grounds and from the battlefields between Arras, Vis-en-Artois and Croisilles. London Cemetery contains 747 burials and commemorations of the First World War. 318 of the burials are unidentified and on a screen wall are panels bearing the names of casualties buried in four cemeteries in the neighbourhood, whose graves were destroyed by shell fire. The cemetery was designed by Sir Edwin Lutyens.

Edmund was the eldest son of Edmund Thomas and Florence Selina (nee Maundrell) Hibbard who had lived at Paradise Farm, Christian Malford and Ivy House, Burton Hill before coming to Malmesbury at 1 Kingswall. His brother (Ernest) James was killed in action in 1918. After her husband's death his mother moved to 96 High Street. Edmund undertook a three year ap-

ARRAS

ATTACK OF VII CORPS
9ᵗʰ –12ᵗʰ April, 1917.

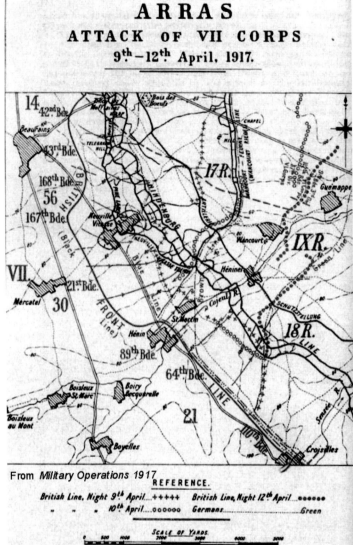

From *Military Operations 1917*

REFERENCE.

British Line, Night 9ᵗʰ April..+++++   British Line, Night 12ᵗʰ April..●●●●●●

- - - - 10ᵗʰ April...oooooo   Germans.............................Green

SCALE OF YARDS.

prenticeship with H. Burnett, grocer of Chippenham from 1907. When war broke out he enlisted in the Rifle Brigade at Aldershot on 2ⁿᵈ September 1914. After training he was posted to the 3ʳᵈ Battalion, serving as a Rifleman and arrived in France on 11ᵗʰ January 1915. He suffered a gun shot wound to the left shoulder on 26ᵗʰ August 1915 and was evacuated to the V.A.D. hospital at Strood, Kent. After convalescence he applied for a commission and following three months' training with No. 6 Officer Training Company he was posted to the 1/12ᵗʰ Londons in October 1916. Returning to France he took part in the battle of Arras and was killed on the first day. That day the Rangers had two officers and 63 other ranks killed, five officers and 125 men wounded and four missing. Edmund's death was fully reported in two Herald articles, the first published 20ᵗʰ April and the other the following week;

MALMESBURY OFFICER KILLED.

Former Resident of Chippenham.

The utmost sympathy is felt for Mr. and Mrs. E.T. Hibbard, No. 1 Kingswall, Malmesbury, in the sad bereavement they have sustained in the death of their eldest son, Second-Lieutenant E.J. Hibbard, London Regiment. On Saturday evening Mr. Hibbard received a telegram from the Record Office conveying the sorrowful information that his son had been killed in action on Easter Monday.

The late Second-Lieutenant Hibbard, who was 27 years of age, was born at Dauntsey. He was educated at the Chippenham Secondary School and subsequently served five years in the employ of Mr. H. Burnett, grocer of Chippenham. He joined the colours in Essex in August, 1914, selecting a Rifle Brigade in which to serve. He was drafted to France in January, 1915, and was in some of the fiercest fighting of that year, being wounded on August 25ᵗʰ. After his recovery and a period of leave he was given a commission in the London Regiment, dating from October 24ᵗʰ, 1916, and went to France a second time last January. Lieutenant Hibbard was a promising young officer, his superior officers esteeming him very highly. Mr. and Mrs. Hibbard have another son in the Army – Private James Hibbard, Training Reserve.

MALMESBURY OFFICER'S DEATH.
"Although Wounded He Pressed On."
OBJECTIVE WON BY HIS HEROISM.

The splendid story of the heroic death of Lieutenant E.T. Hibbard, London Regiment, son of Mr. and Mrs. E.J. Hibbard, of Kingswall, Malmesbury, is told in letters received by the parents from the Commanding Officer and the Chaplain of the Rangers. The following telegram was received by Mr. Hibbard from Buckingham Palace: "The King and Queen deeply regret the loss you and the Army have sustained by the death of your son in the service of his country. Their Majesties truly sympathise with you in your sorrow."

The Colonel's letter was as follows:- "Dear Madam, - I am writing to express to you and yours very sincere sympathy with you in the loss of your gallant son, who fell in action on the 9th of this month. Although twice wounded during the advance he continued to lead and encourage his men. After he had been hit a third time he still continued to encourage and direct their efforts until the end came. You have every right to be proud of his memory, although I fear that will be a small comfort to you in your bereavement. We were fortunately able to recover his body afterwards, and a burial service was conducted by the Regimental Chaplain. The grave is near where he fell, and we have erected a cross over it with his name and the date and the crest of the regiment on it. If there is anything else I can do or any other information you would like, please do not hesitate to write to me. – with sincerest sympathy, yours faithfully, A.D. Bayliffe, Lieutenant-Colonel commanding the Rangers."

The Chaplain wrote:- "Dear Madam, - The Colonel of the –th London Regiment, has asked me to answer your letter of April 23rd to him, as he has himself written to you about your son's death. I was anyhow going to write to tell you how splendidly your son did. He led his men with magnificent courage and complete success against a difficult part of the German trench. Although wounded once, he pressed on and enabled us to secure all our objectives. I was searching the battlefield shortly after things had become a little quieter, and I found your son's body. He was lying quite peacefully on his back in a shell-hole in which his servant had dragged him after he had been hit the second time to try and bandage him up. But this was to no purpose, as he had been killed by a machine-gun bullet. The servant's name is Sidwell (Rifleman A.E.). He was with him at the time of death, but unfortunately he was himself severely wounded a few days later. I do not know to which hospital this man has been taken, but his home address is, I believe, 150, Bowring Road, Manor Park, Essex. You should be able to get in touch with him sooner or later. I was able to take all the personal effects from your boy's body, and these will be sent to you, in due course, through the ordinary official channels. His own men bore his body reverently to the Military Cemetery not far from the spot where he fell, and there we laid him to rest side by side with men whom he had led so bravely and who died in the same engagement. A white cross has been placed over your son's grave with full details painted on it, such as name, regiment and date of death. The cemetery is close to the road near Arras, so that all who pass by can see who lies there. The grave is registered with the Graves Registration Unit, and the whole cemetery has been bought by the British Government to be kept for all time as a sacred spot. Although we had only known him for such a short time, your son had already become very popular. All his men, I know, felt they were led by a good soldier, who wouldn't fail them at a critical moment. Nor indeed did he, as his courage and his example were the means of our gaining our objective with such complete success. He could not have done better or died more nobly. We are more proud of him than we can say. I do not want to offer you any hollow words of comfort, I feel that sorrow of this kind is too sacred for any-one outside to intrude upon it. But I do want you to know that we all feel very much for you in your loss.- Yours very truly, K. Julian F. Richardson, C.F."

Bishop, Arthur Edward, Private, 51038, age 28, 8th (Service) Battalion Welch Regiment (Pioneers)

Died, 3rd May 1917, commemorated on the Basra Panel 24, Malmesbury Abbey, Town Hall & Triangle.

The Basra Memorial commemorates more than 40,500 members of the Empire forces who died in the operations in Mesopotamia from the Autumn of 1914 to the end of August 1921 and whose graves are not known. It consists of a roofed colonnade of white Indian stone, 80 metres long with an obelisk 16 metres high in the centre. Originally sited within the Basra War Cemetery, in 1997 President Saddam Hussein had it moved and re-erected in the middle of a major battleground from the 1991 Gulf War.

Arthur Edward was the eldest son of Walter (a domestic gardener) and Jane Bishop, of 33A Burnivale with two brothers Charles Montague & Cecil Henry (who was killed in September 1918) and three sisters, Jane, Minnie & Lizzie. Walter joined the Wilts National Reserve for home defence whilst Charles had been in the Royal Marines Light Infantry since 1913 and had taken part in the Battle of Jutland. Arthur enlisted at Swindon having been called up in April 1916. He trained with the 22nd (Reserve) Battalion Welch Regiment at Kinmel on the north coast of Wales before being posted to their 8th Battalion in Mesopotamia. Because his body was not found he was transferred to the Training Reserve (as the 22nd Welch had been renamed the 66th Training Reserve Battalion) after he was reported missing – such are the curious ways of the Army. Nonetheless his death was reported as follows;

A SOLDIER DROWNED, - An official intimation, with no detail given, has been received by Mrs. Walter Bishop, of Burnivale, to the effect that her eldest son, Private Arthur Edward Bishop, Welsh Regiment, has been drowned. It is surmised that he was on a torpedoed transport. Mrs. Bishop's husband is serving in the 4th Wilts, he having joined up from the National Reserve. Two other sons are also on active service – one in the Wilts Regiment and the other in the Royal Marine Light Infantry on H.M.S. "Lion." Much sympathy is felt for the bereaved parents. The late Private Bishop was 28 years of age, and had served since April, 1916.

The Standard had more details, although they gave him the wrong name and regiment;

We learn that Private Ernest Bishop, Wilts Regiment, eldest son of Mr. and Mrs. Walter Bishop, of Malmesbury, was among the drowned on board the ill-fated Transylvannia. The townsfolk extend their sympathy to the bereaved parents.

The Times Diary of the War recorded this loss;

British s.s. Transylvannia (14,315 tons) sunk by U-Boat off Cape Vado, Gulf of Genoa; 12 lost. Japanese Mediterranean T.B.D.s assisted in saving the 4,000 soldiers and nurses on board.

The family's remembrances published in subsequent years raise doubt as to whether the drowning took place in the Mediterranean or in Mesopotamia. If the account above is true it is ironic that had his body been found his memorial would have been in Europe rather than the Middle East. The following was in the Herald's Roll of Honour;

BISHOP.- May 3rd, drowned at sea, Pte. Arthur Edward Bishop, Welch Regiment, eldest son of Mr. and Mrs. Walter Bishop, Burnivale, Malmesbury, aged 28 years.

Two years later an entry appeared in the Herald's In Memoriam column;

BISHOP.- In ever loving memory of our dear son, Pte. Arthur Edward Bishop, who was drowned in Mesopotamia, May 3rd, 1917, aged 28 years.

> *An Angel took my flower away,*
> *It caused me to repine;*
> *But Jesus in His bosom wears*
> *The flower that once was mine.*

Inserted by his sorrowing Mother, Father, Brother and Sisters.

The Herald had the following in 1920;

BISHOP.- In ever loving memory of our dear son, Pte. Arthur Edward Bishop, who was drowned in Mesopotamia, May 3rd, 1917, aged 28 years, eldest son of Mr. and Mrs. W. Bishop, 31, Burnivale, Malmesbury, Wilts.

> *Peaceful be your rest, dear Arthur,*
> *'Tis sweet to breathe your name,*
> *In life we loved you dearly,*
> *In death we do the same.*

Inserted by his loving Mother, Father, Sisters and Brother.

In 1921 the following was inserted;

BISHOP.- In ever loving memory of our dear son, Pte. Arthur Edward Bishop, who was drowned in Mesopotamia, May 3rd, 1917, aged 28 years.

> *Where is our soldier boy to-day?*
> *Laid in a soldier's grave;*
> *Far, far away in a foreign land,*
> *He died like a soldier brave.*

Inserted by his sorrowing Mother, Father, Sisters and Brother.

Reeves, Henry Thomas, Private, 30682, age 35, 8th (Service) Battalion Devonshire Regiment

Killed in action, 9th May 1917, commemorated on the Arras Memorial Bay 4, Malmesbury Abbey, Town Hall & Triangle.

The Arras Memorial commemorates almost 35,000 servicemen from the United Kingdom, South Africa and New Zealand who died in the Arras sector between the spring of 1916 and 7th August 1918, the eve of the Advance to Victory, and have no known grave. The most conspicuous events of this period were the Arras offensive of April-May 1917 and the German attack in the spring of 1918. Canadian and Australian servicemen killed in these operations are commemorated by memorials at Vimy and Villers-Bretonneux. A separate memorial remembers those killed in the Battle of Cambrai in 1917. Both cemetery and memorial were designed by Sir Edwin Lutyens with sculpture by Sir William Reid Dick.

Henry was the younger son of Thomas (boot & shoe maker) and Eliza Anne Reeves, of 61 Gloucester Road with a brother George and two sisters Mary & Ellen. Henry continued his father's shoemaking business in the family home. He appealed against conscription in June 1916;

William Jones (40), of 6, West Street, fireman and carter employed by the Town Council, and Henry Thomas Reeves (33), of 61, Gloucester Road, assistant engineer of the Malmesbury Fire Brigade, were appealed for by Mr. B. Bowman (borough surveyor). Both men were considered necessary for the working of the Fire Brigade should a fire occur. Reeves has also appealed on personal grounds. Mr. Bowman said the Brigade had already lost six men who had joined the Army, and the Town Council had passed a resolution to the effect that he should appeal for the men. He produced a letter from the National Fire Brigade Union urging the necessity for exempting a proportion of fire brigade men. Both were exempted until October conditional upon their joining the Volunteer Corps.

In August the military appealed against Henry's exemption and the evidence was heard in private. On the readmission of the public it was announced that the appeal was successful and his exemption ended. On his call up he enlisted at Malmesbury in the Wiltshire Regiment with Service No. 26459. After undertaking training he was sent to France. Whilst at the Infantry Base Depot he was transferred to 8th

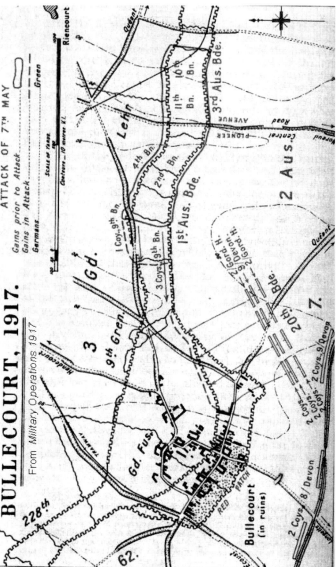

The Arras Memorial

Battalion of the Devons. This unit was involved in the Battle of Arras in April and May 1917. On 3rd May the battalion moved into the trenches near Bullecourt, 39 officers and 740 men strong. From the next day they started sustaining casualties and three officers & fifteen other ranks joined on 7th although they had not been heavily engaged. However on the morning of the 8th they attacked a strong position called the Red Patch on the southern edge of Bullecourt. Whilst good progress was initially made the attackers were driven back through trenches full of sticky mud. The following day another effort was made by two companies that had not taken part the day before. Unfortunately the result was the same and Harry fell during this attempt. An extract from the war diary of this day's fighting reads;

The enemy clearly expected our attack.

As soon as the barrage lifted, the Strong Point was strongly manned with bombers, and supports were seen moving up in three distinct bombing parties which worked up the trench and on the left and right. Simultaneously a most effective shrapnel barrage was put down in the valley immediately East of the Ecoust-Bullecourt Road.

The assaulting troops were compelled to retire some hundred yards and the only two Officers remaining in the Company became casualties.

The Acting Company Sergeant Major then took charge and organised a second attack at about 12.30 p.m. which was again driven back by enemy bombers, and the enemy counterattacked, advanced up Blue Line. The remains of "C" Company being either passed over or driven back in some confusion.

The Standard carried a report of his death;

Although unofficial, credible information has just been received by the relatives of Private Henry Reeves, Devon Regiment, of Malmesbury, that he was killed in action by a piece of a German shell. The sad news was sent by the deceased's Corporal, with expressions of deepest sympathy with the soldier's relatives. Private Harry Reeves, 35 years of age, was the youngest son of the late Mr. Thomas Reeves, bootmaker, of Gloucester-road, Malmesbury, and has only been in France seven weeks, having been transferred to the Devons since his arrival there. He was a steady, industrious young fellow, and carried on his late father's trade until he joined up. For several years he was the capable goalkeeper for the Malmesbury Football Club, and also took an active interest in the Cricket Club before it was disbanded for the lack of playing members. His elder brother George has a boot and shoe business in Lower High-street.

The Herald had an item resulting from a Council meeting;

THE LATE FIREMAN REEVES.

The Mayor referred in sympathetic terms to the death in action of Private H. Reeves, Devon Regiment, who had been a member of the Fire Brigade for several years. He was, said the Mayor, assiduous in his duties, always punctual and regular, and took a great interest in his work as second engineer. He was sure they all deeply regretted the young man's death, and yet they could reflect on his heroism in fighting for them and for the Empire. The Council would no doubt desire him to express their sympathy with the aged mother. He had known the family from his boyhood. The late Henry Reeves' father was apprenticed to the speaker's father, and he (the Mayor) also knew his grandfather. The family was much respected, and Harry Reeves had always been a most dutiful son.

This appeared in the Roll of Honour;

REEVES.- May 9th, killed in action, Pte. Harry Reeves, Devon Regiment, son of Mrs. Reeves, Gloucester Road, Malmesbury, aged 34 years.

Sellwood, James, Gunner, 16124, age 34, 336th Brigade, Royal Horse Artillery
Died, 10th May 1917, buried at Swindon Whitworth Road Cemetery M. 497, commemorated Malmesbury Town Hall & Triangle.

James was the son of Isaac (a coal carter) and Prudence Sellwood, of Great Wishford, Salisbury and married Dora Evelyn Andrews in 1906, who later lived at 68 Paynes Hill, Salisbury. He was a Malmesbury postman living at Keene's Hill, Bristol Street when he was recalled as a Reservist on the outbreak of war. He appeared on the Mayor's Roll of Honour and it seems that he did not go abroad. His death was reported in the Herald on 18th May;

SOLDIER'S DEATH.- The death has occurred at the Swindon Isolation Hospital of Gunner James Sellwood, of Bristol Street, Malmesbury. He was 16 years in the Royal Horse Artillery, and, after serving his time in the Army, did duty as postman from Malmesbury to Sherston. On the outbreak of war he was called up, and was with the colours until the time of his death. On April 19th he came to Malmesbury on furlough, was taken ill with cerebral meningitis, was removed to Swindon Isolation Hospital on April 28th, and died on May 10th from that disease. He leaves a widow and one child. His parents live at Wishford, near Salisbury. Deceased was popular in the Army and in the Post Office. Sincere sympathy will be felt for Mrs. Sellwood in her great sorrow. Deceased was 34 years of age. The interment was at Swindon Cemetery on Wednesday.

The Herald's Roll of Honour entry read;

SELWOOD.- May 10th, at Swindon, whilst on active service, Gunner James Selwood, Royal Horse Artillery, of Malmesbury, son of Mr. Selwood, Wishford, near Salisbury, aged 34 years.

Unusually there was an entry in the Gazette's In Memoriam column of 16th May 1918;

SELLWOOD. – In ever loving memory of my dear husband, Gunner J. SELLWOOD, R.H.A. (late of Malmesbury), who died at Swindon Isolation Hospital, May 10th, 1917. – Sadly missed by his wife, child, parents and brothers. "In the midst of life we are in death; to whom can we look for succour but to Thee, O Lord."

Emery, (Stephen) William, Private, 27839, age 19, 8th (Service) Battalion Prince Albert's (Somerset Light Infantry)
Killed in action, 12th July 1917, buried in Messines Ridge British Cemetery II C 12, commemorated Malmesbury Abbey, Town Hall & Triangle.

Messines Ridge British Cemetery which stands on ground that belonged to the Institution Royale, was made after the Armistice when graves were brought in from the battlefield around Messines and from a number of small burial grounds in the area. Those buried here died from October 1914 to October 1918 but the majority died in the fighting of 1917. There are now 1,531 Empire servicemen of the First World War buried or commemorated in the cemetery. 954 of the burials are unidentified but special memorials commemorate a number of casualties known or believed to be buried among them or who were buried in other cemeteries where their graves were destroyed by shell fire. Both cemetery and the New Zealand Memorial within it were designed by Charles Holden.

Stephen, known as William, was the second son of Stephen (a builder's carter) and Ellen Emery, of 41 Bristol Street, with brothers Richard Alexander (known as Alec) & Charles. He enlisted at Malmesbury and, originally posted to the Wiltshire Regiment, was later transferred to the Somersets. The War Diary for 12th July 1917 simply recorded; *2 O.R. killed in action.* The Regimental History outlines what happened;

The 8th Somersets left Scherpenberg on the night of 29th June and relieved a battalion of the York and Lancs Regiment in the right support line of the left sub-sector, i.e. Joye Farm to Rose Wood. Until the last day of July the month was uneventful, the Battalion doing several tours in the front-line trenches, during which a number of casualties were suffered. The enemy's shell fire was at times very heavy. On 12th Lieut.-Colonel M.C.C. Miers (the C.O.), Major J.G. Underwood and 2/Lieut. H.A. de F. Ford were wounded.

The Herald newspaper reported;

YOUNG SOLDIER KILLED. – Pte. Stephen William Emery (20), Somerset Light Infantry, son of Mrs. E. Emery, of Bristol Street, has been killed in action. His father and brother are serving, the latter having been badly wounded. Much sympathy is felt with his parents and family in their bereavement.

The Standard had more;

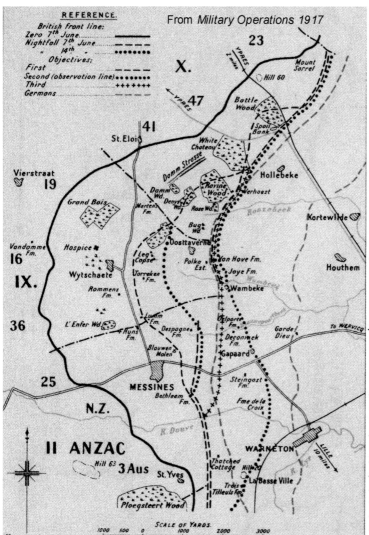

REFERENCE.
British front line:
Zero 7th June..............
Nightfall 7th June..............
" 14th " ....
Objectives:
First..............
Second (observation line)..............
Third..............
Germans..............

From *Military Operations 1917*

With regret we have to record the death of yet another Malmesbury lad, Private William Emery, who in the short space of seven months has begun and finished his "bit" for the sake of King and country. The official notice stated that he was killed in action on July 12, and accompanying was the following signed by Lord Derby: "The King commands me to assure you of the true sympathy of His Majesty and the Queen in your sorrow." The lad would have been 20 years of age next month, and was the second son of Mr. and Mrs. Stephen R. Emery, of Bristol-street. He joined the Wilts Regiment about seven months ago, and on proceeding to active service in France was transferred to the Somerset Light Infantry. He left England last January and has regularly corresponded with his mother, to whom he was a most affectionate and dutiful son. His last field card to her, stating that he was quite well, bore the date of July 12th – unfortunately the date of his death. Needless to say, the heart-broken mother cherishes the little souvenirs her boy had sent home, and among them a very pretty hand-worked sampler was inscribed – "To dear mother, from her affectionate son." "He was a good boy," said the mother tearfully to our representative, "and was to have married his young lady when he came home. There are their portraits, and the poor girl is quite heart-broken and prostrate over the death of her boy. His brother Alec (Wilts) was wounded in action and lost a leg 12 months ago, and has been in Brighton hospital ever since, and now (she added) I suppose they will want my youngest who has passed for general service: Oh! It is hard for a mother!" Our correspondent adds: "True, brave mothers of England, and such commonplaces as one can utter by way of consolation may help to soothe, but can never heal the bitter grief you feel, or lighten the burden you carry, but, be assured, by the deeds of your glorious sons will your homes be free from the invading savage, the honour of your daughter remain inviolate; free nations will be fraternally established, and posterity will thank you for your superb sacrifice and devotion in the hour of your country's peril."

The next week a poem was published in the Roll of Honour;

> No mother on him did attend,
> Nor o'er him did a father bend,

No sister by to shed a tear,
　　　No brother his last words to hear.

Inserted by his loving Mother, Father, Sisters and Brothers, and broken-hearted Sweetheart.
Unfortunately the good relations with William's sweetheart did not last as reported in the Wiltshire Gazette of 9th March 1918;

Miss Edith Reynolds, daughter of Mr. Henry Reynolds, of Rodbourne, sued Mrs. Ellen Emery, 41, Bristol Street, Malmesbury, administrator of the estate of William Emery, for a cow, or £50 estimated as its value. Mr. A.W. Chubb, said the action was brought by the plaintiff, who was a minor, for the delivery of a specific bequest under the will of William Emery, also a minor, and the son of defendant, Mrs. Emery. The testator was killed in action on the 12th July, 1917, being a private in the Somerset Light Infantry, and he made a will which was dated 20th May, 1917, a copy of which he produced, and which read: "To Miss Edith Reynolds I leave one cow, to my eldest brother a pony, to my brother Charles I leave the other cow, and the rest is my mother's who has been so good to me." This will, said Mr. Chubb, was written in a pocket book belonging to the testator, and was picked up on the battlefield by a comrade who saw Miss Reynold's address in the pocket book, and sent it to her, she receiving it on the 17th August, 1917, and after taking advice, her mother handed it to the defendant (his mother) on the 31st August, 1917.

After a legal discussion, His Honour decided to non-suit the plaintiff informing Mr. Chubb that if there was any doubt he could take the opinion of the Divisional Court. But at present there was no valid course of action, and that meant a non-suit.

He was obviously very badly missed by his family as an In Memoriam entry appeared a year later;

EMERY.- In loving memory of my dear son, Pte. W. Emery, who fell in France on July 12th, 1917, aged 19 years and 10 months.

　　　God called him home, it was His will,
　　　But in our hearts he dwelleth still;
　　　His memory is as dear today
　　　As in the hour he passed away.

From his loving Mother, Dad, Brothers and Sisters
41, Bristol Street, Malmesbury.

The following year another notice was published;

EMERY.- In loving memory of our dear son, Pte. W. Emery, of the 8th Somerset Regiment, who fell in France, July 12th, 1917.

　　　Forget him, no, we never will,
　　　We loved him then, we love him still;
　　　His memory is as fresh today
　　　As in the hour he passed away.

From his sorrowing Mother and Dad, Brothers and Sisters, 41, Bristol Street, Malmesbury.

The passage of time obviously did not diminish the family's grief and 1920 saw the following insertion;

EMERY.- In ever loving memory of our darling son, Pte. W. Emery, who fell in France, July 12th, 1917, aged 19 years and 10 months.

　　　Three years have passed – we often think of days gone by,
　　　When we were all together;
　　　A shadow o'er our life is cast,
　　　A beloved son has gone for ever.

Will never be forgotten by his loving Mum, Dad, Brothers and Sisters, 41, Bristol Street, Malmesbury.

Again in 1921 this appeared;

EMERY.- In loving memory of our dear son and brother, Pte. William Emery, who fell in France, July 12th, 1917, aged 19 years and 10 months.

　　　I who loved him, sadly miss him,
　　　As it dawns another year;
　　　In my lonely hours of thinking,
　　　Thoughts of him are always near.

Never forgotten by his loving Mother, Father, Sisters and Brothers.

Weeks, Roland Reginald, Private, 907588 age 38, 5th Battalion (Saskatchewan Regiment) Canadian Infantry
Killed in action, 15th August 1917, commemorated on the Vimy Memorial, Malmesbury Abbey, Town Hall & Triangle.

On the opening day of the Battle of Arras, 9th April 1917 the four divisions of the Canadian Corps, fighting side by side for the first time, scored a huge tactical victory in the capture of the 60 metre high Vimy Ridge. After the war the highest point of the ridge was chosen as the site of the great memorial to all Canadians who served their country in battle during the First World War and particularly to the 60,000 who gave their lives in France. It also bears the names of 11,000 Canadians who have no known grave. The memorial was designed by W S Allward.

Roland was the only son of William (nicknamed Donkey), and Mary Weeks of 2 Burnham Road. William was a domestic gardener before moving to Malmesbury to run the Bath Arms in Horsefair. Roland was born in Farmborough, Somerset, his parents' home before his father moved to Riverhead near Sevenoaks. He had two sisters Frances & Florence. After having served in the Royal Marine Artillery for 12 years Roland emigrated to Canada where he became a farmer. He enlisted in the Canadian Army on 1st April 1916 at Regina, Saskatchewan, joining the 5th Canadian Battalion. In view of his previous experience he was made an Acting Sergeant but anxious to see action reverted to Private. Before he left for France he visited his parents and bought a piece of land for them. He thought that Malmesbury was a growing town and that if he failed to return this would help to provide for them. Unfortunately the land was disposed of long before the White Lion housing estate was built there.

Whilst the Third Battle of Ypres continued in the rain of early August an operation was planned further south to draw away the German reserves. This was to be carried out by the Canadian Corps across ground that would have been familiar to surviving members of the first

CAPTURE OF HILL 70
15th August 1917
From *Military Operations 1917*

British Red
Objectives:
Line reached 15th Aug.
Line reached 16th – 22nd Aug.
Germans Green

The Vimy Memorial which has recently been completely renovated. (westernfrontassociation.com)

Kitchener armies who took part in the Battle of Loos in 1915. The objective was to take the town of Lens but this was not achieved. At 4.25 a.m. on 15th August the Empire artillery barrage crashed on to the defences. It was accompanied by drums of burning oil from which smoke was carried by the breeze over Hill 70, one of the major enemy strongpoints. The 5th and 10th Battalions of the 2nd Canadian Brigade shrouded by the smoke and following the rolling barrage quickly gained the summit of the hill. They consolidated that position and fresh battalions carried the assault onwards. Around 6 a.m. they attempted to move forward to the chalk quarry but the smoke had cleared and they suffered heavily in the attempt. Between 7 a.m. and 9 a.m. the first counter attacks were made but were defeated due to the Canadian preparations, having brought machine guns and artillery observers to the front. Stronger counter attacks, some 18 in all, continued that afternoon but all were repulsed with a terrible slaughter of the Germans. However losses were not one sided, the 5th Battalion had suffered 130 casualties before 6 a.m. and by nightfall there had been many more including Roland Weeks. His death was reported in the Herald thus;

Pte. Rowland Weeks was in the Canadian Expeditionary Force, which he joined in March, 1916. He was an old soldier then, for he had previously served 12 years in the Royal Marines before settling down in Canada. Last November he came to England and held the rank of sergeant. Subsequently, after a few days' leave spent at home, he was appointed an instructor at Folkestone, but he reverted to the ranks at his own request and volunteered for active service. Official intimation was received last week from the War Office that he was killed on August 16th.

The Wiltshire Gazette had slightly different details;

ANOTHER HERO. - We regret to record the death, in action, of Private Rowland Weeks, only son of Mr. and Mrs. William Weeks, of Westport, who for some years kept the "Bath Arms." When a young fellow Private Weeks joined the Royal Marines, in which he saw twelve years' service; he then went to Canada where the call of duty sounded so clearly that he joined the Canadian Forces in March, 1916, coming to England in November with the rank of Sergeant. He came home for a few days, and then was appointed Instructor at Folkestone, but the task did not afford sufficient scope for his energies and enthusiasm so he gave up his stripes, and volunteered for active service as a private. Letters received by his parents were of the most cheery description, and the news of his death, in France (on August 16th) was received by his parents on Thursday in a communication from the War Office.

The Herald's Roll of Honour read;

WEEKS. - Aug 16th, killed in action, Pte. Rowland Weeks, Canadians, only son of Mr. W. Weeks,

Westport, Malmesbury.

On the second anniversary of his death the following appeared In Memoriam;

WEEKS.- In loving memory of Roland Weeks, killed in action in France with the Canadians, Aug. 15th-16th, 1917, the only son of William and Mary Weeks, 43, Foundry Road, Malmesbury.

> A loving son, a brother dear,
> A faithful friend whilst he was here;
> For all of us he did his best
> God, grant to him eternal rest.

Another entry was made in 1920;

WEEKS.- In loving memory of Roland Weeks, our only son, killed in action in France, with the Canadians, August 15th-16th, 1917.

> He stood at his post, like a soldier brave,
> He answered his country's call;
> He sleeps far away in a hero's grave,
> For a country's call he fell.
> Gone, but not forgotten.

William and Mary Weeks, 2, Burnham Road, Malmesbury.

Perry, Archibald James, Private, 41352, age 19, 1/7th Battalion Worcestershire Regiment Territorial Force

Died of wounds, 16th August 1917, buried at Brandhoek New Military No. 3 Cemetery II B 2 (family inscription SAVIOUR, IN THY GRACIOUS KEEPING, LEAVE WE NOW, OUR DEAR BOY SLEEPING), commemorated Malmesbury Abbey, Cemetery (on father's grave, plot 84 South), Town Hall & Triangle.

During the First World War Brandhoek was within the area comparatively safe from shell fire which extended beyond Vlamertinghe Church. Field ambulances were posted there continuously. Until July 1917 burials had been made in the Military Cemetery but the arrival of the 32nd, 3rd Australian and 44th Casualty Clearing Stations, in preparation for the new Allied offensive launched that month, made it necessary to open the New Military Cemetery in August. It continued in use until May 1918 and contains 975 First World War burials. The cemetery was designed by Sir Reginald Blomfield.

Archie was the second son of George and Emily Perry, of High Street, Malmesbury with three brothers, Claude (Alec), Cecil & William and a sister Marie. George was a former Regular soldier who played an important part in the town's military effort in the war. Whilst still serving he was a Colour Sergeant Drill Instructor to A Company of the 2nd Wiltshire Volunteer Battalion here, continuing with the National Reserve and Volunteers after the outbreak of war. He was also the first Scoutmaster. Archie worked in service, first for Mr. G.P. Fuller at Neston Park near Corsham and later as second footman for Sir Henry Farquhar (who had a house in Wiltshire) in Scotland before joining up.

Originally with the Army Ordnance Corps then with the Norfolks, Archie was later posted to 1/7th Worcesters. In July 1917 this unit moved from the Somme as part of the large force concentrated around Ypres for the offensive to follow on after the successful attack at Messines. For the first half of August they trained in preparation for their part in the attack. On the 16th they went forward to the River Steenbeek north of St. Julien. At 11 a.m. they were ordered to cross the Steenbeek and moved off half an hour later. The battalions that had attacked before they arrived had made very little progress. The war diary states:

During the move up shelling was very heavy ... aimed rifle fire from German posts also caused casualties. On the other hand our leading troops found a number of good rifle targets which they dealt with to good effect. The general position was reported to Brigade by message timed 1.45 p.m. At 4.15 orders were received from Brigade to reconnoitre with a view of attacking Mon. du Hibou at dusk.

At 6.20 p.m. orders were received to capture strong point at Triangle Farm, Vancouver and Mon du Hibou without artillery support. ... At Zero 'C' Coy advanced to the attack, they immediately came under heavy machine gun and rifle fire from the German positions on their right and from Mon du Hibou, their leading wave was nearly all wiped out. Capt. Montgomery was shot through the stomach and Lieut. Hazlewood was shot through the knee. 'D' Coy had endeavoured to provide covering fire with Lewis Guns but the rifle and machine gun fire from *the German positions on the right made this very difficult. 2nd Lieut. Gadsby assisted by C.S.M. Mole took over the coy and dug in about 350 yds E of the Steenbeek and facing Mon du Hibou. A telephone message was received from Brigade about 11 p.m. and confirmed by wire received at 1.20 a.m. to renew the attack with Zero at 2.10 a.m. …*

By this time Archie had been wounded and evacuated behind the lines. During two days of fighting the battalion suffered 21 killed, 102 wounded, 16 wounded but remaining in the line and 12 missing other ranks. Clearly Archie did not disappoint his father's high expectations as the Herald's article on his death testifies;

MALMESBURY SOLDIER HERO
Sergt.-Major Perry's Son Killed.

Heartfelt sympathy goes out to Sergt.-Major W.G. Perry and Mrs. Perry of Kingswall, Malmesbury, in the sad loss they have sustained in the death of their second son, Pte. Archibald James Perry, Worcestershire Regiment. On Tuesday a telegram was received conveying the intimation that the young soldier – he was only 19 last March – had been killed in action on August 16th. From the details to hand it appeared that Pte. Perry was wounded and had been borne to an Australian casualty clearing station before he succumbed five hours later.

"Archie" Perry, as he was familiarly called by his friends, was a good son and a smart soldier. As a boy he attended the Westport Boys' School, and now adds another name to the increasing number on the school's roll of honour. He was a skilful Scout, being patrol leader and King's Scout in the King Athelstan Troop, which his father founded 7½ years ago in Malmesbury. He entered the service of Mr. G.P. Fuller, Neston Park, and from there went to the service of Henry Farquhar in Scotland, as second footman. It was from Mauchline, where, by the way, he was Assistant Scoutmaster of the 1st Mauchline (Ayrshire) Troop of Boy Scouts, that he enlisted in the Army Ordnance Corps two years ago. His brother Alec was in the same corps. As soon as he attained the age of 19 Archie was transferred to the Norfolk Regiment. Then came his removal to France, and before going "up the line" he was again transferred – this time to the hard-fighting Worcesters. Only two days before the news of his death arrived a letter was received by his parents telling of his going into battle. After it was over, he said, he hoped to have a long rest. Poor brave lad! He has entered into the rest with a glorious company of British heroes whose memory will never fade.

The following letter, dated August 17th, to Mrs. Perry from Sister Ida O'Dwyer, in charge of a clearing sta-

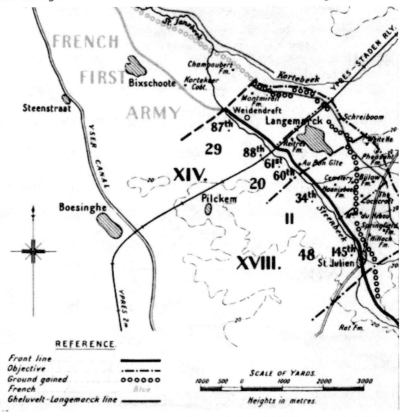

The 1/7th Worcesters followed up the attack of the 145th Brigade, part of 48th Division. (Military Operations 1917)

tion, tells all that there is to tell up to the present time: "I am writing to tell you about your son, Pte. A.J. Perry, 41352. He was brought into this hospital yesterday morning early, about 2 a.m., quite collapsed and very badly wounded in abdomen and right leg. Everything possible was done to revive him, but he did not improve at all, and died at 7 a.m. I told him I would write home and say that he was wounded, and he sent his love and said he would write as soon as he was well enough, as he had no idea that he was dying. I am afraid that it is so little to tell you, but I thought it might be some consolation to you to know that he was in hospital, where he received every possible care and attention, and that he was relieved of all his pain." So died Pte. Archie Perry – brave and unselfish as ever. When he was only 13 he received from General Baden Powell, the Chief Scout, the Merit Medal of the Scouts for saving the life of a boy in the river Avon at Malmesbury.

Many messages of sympathy have reached Sergeant-Major and Mrs. Perry in their sorrow. At the Drill Hall on Tuesday evening Lieut. F.J. Bates, Officer Commanding the detachment, 1st Wilts Volunteer Regiment, addressing the Volunteers on parade, referred feelingly to the sad news that had come that day to their company-sergeant-major. It was a great blow to him and Mrs. Perry, and he (Lieut. Bates) knew that the detachment felt, as he did himself, deep sympathy with them. He would write a letter to that effect on behalf of himself and the whole detachment.

Sergt.-Major Perry, who now holds various public appointments, himself served for 26 years in the Wilts Regiment. He enlisted in 1879, was in South Africa at the time of the first Boer War – 1880-1 – and in 1881 was sent to India, where he was in the two Black Mountain engagements. He took his discharge in 1906, and since that time has accomplished a vast amount of useful work. He greatly assisted the late Earl of Suffolk and Eleanor, Countess of Suffolk, in forming the Voluntary Aid Detachments, and has all the time since been Quartermaster of the Men's V.A.D. He founded the King Athelstan Troop of Boy Scouts, which has a proud record of old boys' service in the war on land and sea. At the outbreak of war the unostentatious pioneer work, which was not in public view, connected with the formation of a Volunteer Training Corps for Malmesbury and district was carried out by him, and when the Government took over the Volunteers he was appointed company-sergeant-major. The sons have followed in their soldier father's footsteps. Lce.-Corpl. C.A. Perry is now in the Essex Regiment, and the late Pte. Archie Perry has proved a worthy son of worthy parents.

The boy rescued from the river was Frank Weeks. He lived until 2000 and always thought of his saviour, who died so young, when he passed the Triangle. The Parish Magazine had another report;

Again we have to place on record the dread toll of war. This time it is a soldier's son, a lad straight and true, who has passed over to rest with the warriors of the past. Archibald James Perry was one of those who responded, with an alacrity which his age hardly warranted, to the call of King and country. With his father's example before him, duty was his uppermost thought. He first joined the Army Ordnance Corps, but eventually was transferred to the Worcestershire Regiment. It was when engaged with his new comrades in the great fight of the past month that he received the wounds which terminated his young life on August 18th.

Brickell, John Percy, Private, 9025, age 26, 1st Battalion Duke of Edinburgh's (Wiltshire Regiment)
Killed in action, 4th September 1917, buried at Menin Road South Military Cemetery II D 16, commemorated Malmesbury Abbey, Town Hall & Triangle.
The Menin Road ran east and a little south from Ypres (now Ieper) to a front line which varied only a few kilometres during the greater part of the war. The position of this cemetery was always within the Allied lines. It was first used in January 1916 by the 8th South Staffords and the 9th East Surreys and it continued to be used by units and Field Ambulances until the summer of 1918. The cemetery was increased after the Armistice when graves were brought in from Menin Road North Military Cemetery and from isolated positions on the battlefields to the east. There are now 1,657 servicemen of the First World War buried or commemorated here. The cemetery was designed by Sir Reginald Blomfield.
John (known as Jack) was the only son of Thomas (a tailor) and Susannah Brickell. He was born in South Wraxall but unfortunately his mother died giving birth. The children were sent to the mother's relatives – the eldest daughter Mary to her widowed Grandmother Lucy, the

younger daughter Lucy to her mother's brother Lot & wife Ellen Mizen and the infant Jack to his mother's sister Elizabeth & husband Edward Porter. The Porters lived initially in South Wraxall but later at Box where Edward was a carter at the mill. Meanwhile Thomas moved to Malmesbury and remarried, living at 80 Lower High Street. Thomas brought his daughters to join him and fathered two more daughters, Dorothy & Gwendolen. Before the war Jack enlisted as a Regular soldier at Devizes and went to France on 14th August 1914 with the 1st Wiltshires. He came home for a short leave during September 1915 staying only a few hours in Malmesbury before spending the rest of the time with his uncle in Box. At that time he was able to report that Charlie Bishop, Fred Bush, Jim Paginton and Frank Sharpe (who was killed in July 1916) all of the same battalion were well.

John was distinctly unlucky as the war diary for the period records;

Tuesday 4th-8th September 1917 Belgium, [Zillebeke Lake]

(4th & 5th) During these two days the Battn remained in Bde Reserve at ZILLEBEKE LAKE. On the morning of the 4th the vicinity of the dugouts was shelled by 8" Hows and there were three casualties, 2 killed and 1 wounded. Subsequently the enemy's artillery was quiet. On the evening of the 5th the Battn was relieved by the 8th L.N. Lancs Regt and went back to VANOUST CAMP near DICKEBUSCH where it remained until the morning of the 8th.

The Herald's report was;

Pte. John Percy Brickell, who was 26 years of age, was in the Wilts Regiment. He was born at South Wraxall and lived most of his life at Box with an uncle who adopted him. Mr. Brickell, the father, has received two letters – one from Second Lieut. White and the other from the Chaplain (the Rev. T.W. Hart).

On 22nd September the Standard had another report;

This week our sympathy is extended to Mr. F. Brickell, of 80, High-street, Malmesbury, whose only son Private J.P. Brickell, Wilts Regiment, had been killed on active service. Mr. and Mrs. Brickell have received the following letter.

September 5, 1917.

Dear Mr. Brickell, - It is with sincere regret and deepest sympathy that I have to inform you that your son, 9025 Private J.P. Brickell, was killed in action on the 4th September, 1917. He suffered no pain as his death was instantaneous and his body has been buried in a cemetery. He was a willing and good soldier and well liked by all the men of his Company. His personal effects will be sent to you as soon as possible. With deepest sympathy in your bereavement.

Yours faithfully, S.H. Warren, Second-Lieutenant,

C Company, Wilts Regiment.

Chaplain's letter

76th Field Ambulance, B.E.F.,
5/9/17.

Dear Mr. Brickell, - It is my sad duty to convey to you the sad news of the death of your son, Private J.P. Brickell, 9025, Wilts Regiment, which occurred yesterday. His regiment was back behind the line at the time but a shell fell quite near him. Death was instantaneous so that he suffered no pain. He was buried in the afternoon and a large number of his comrades followed him to the grave. It was my sad duty to officiate at his funeral. It will be some comfort to you to know that he lies buried in a cemetery where his grave will receive every attention. A cross has already been erected at the head of his grave. I feel that this letter will come as a great shock to you, filling your heart with grief and casting deep shadows across your house. May the God of all consolation be very near to you, nearer than the sorrow that hides in your heart and nearer than the tears that dim your eyes.

I am, Yours in deepest sympathy,

T.W. Hart. (Chaplain)

The following appeared in the Herald's Roll of Honour;

BRICKELL.- Sept. 4th, killed whilst on service, Pte. John Percy Brickell, Wilts Regiment, only son of Mr. Thomas Brickell, Lower High Street, Malmesbury, aged 26 years.

Thompson, Joseph Ewart, Driver, 645260, age 28, 51st Division Ammunition Column Royal Field Artillery

Died of wounds, 8th October 1917, buried at Dozinghem Military Cemetery VIII G 20 (family inscription *I THINK I HAVE DONE MY DUTY, FOR KING AND COUNTRY*), commemorated Malmesbury Abbey, School, Town Hall & Triangle.

In July 1917, in readiness for the forthcoming offensive, groups of casualty clearing stations were placed at three positions called by the troops "Mendinghem, Dozinghem and Bandaghem." The 4th, 47th and 61st Casualty Clearing Stations were posted at Dozinghem and the military cemetery was used by them until early in 1918. There are now 3,174 Empire burials of the First World War in the cemetery and 65 German war graves from this period. It also contains 73 Second World War burials dating from the Allied withdrawal to Dunkirk in May 1940. The cemetery was designed by Sir Reginald Blomfield.

Joseph was born in Malmesbury, the only child of Joseph Thompson but it would seem that his parents died and he was adopted by his uncle Matthew. Joseph joined the Ammunition Column in Malmesbury and went with several others to 51st (Highland) Division in April 1915 only a couple of months after enlistment. The Divisional Ammunition Column's job was to maintain the supply of front line ammunition, mainly for field artillery but also for infantry units. Its B Echelon picked up the ammunition at dumps normally at railheads and took it to the divisional refilling points from where the three sections of A Echelon delivered it to the fighting units. The Division moved into the front line of the Ypres salient north of Keerselare on 20th August 1917. A month later they took part in a large attack towards Poelcappelle in the dreadfully muddy conditions for which this series of battles is remembered. At the end of September the Division was withdrawn to refit but the artillery was left behind to continue giving support. On 4th October Joseph and two others were severely injured and several horses killed by an enemy shell. His death was reported in the North Wilts Herald of 12th October;

KILLED IN ACTION.
Mayor of Malmesbury's Loss.

The Mayor of Malmesbury (Mr. Matthew Thompson) had experienced a sad loss by the death in action of Corpl. Joseph Ewart Thompson, R.F.A. He was a bright young fellow, beloved by all who knew him. When quite a youth he was apprenticed to the coach-building under Mr. Walter Hays, of Malmesbury. At the age of 23 he went to America, to follow his trade. It was there the call of duty came to him under peculiar circumstances, for he had the discomfort of working where only aliens were employed. His employer, who was a German, often used to exasperate him by bringing to his notice temporary German victories in the early stages of the war. Young Thompson could stand it no longer, and one day he took the step so many of his fellow countrymen in the West have taken – he enlisted. Before he did so, however, he had a brief holiday in his native town. He joined the R.F.A. Territorials in February, 1915, and was sent to France in April that year, attached to the ammunition column of a Highland regiment.

When he was home a little time ago he had a very strong presentiment that he was not coming back again, and he put all his affairs in order. He had taken part in seven decisive battles on the Western front and had had several narrow escapes from death. He received mortal wounds on October 6th, the news of his death coming as a tremendous shock to the Mayor and Mrs. Thompson and other relatives.

His captain, writing to the Mayor, said: "It is with deep regret I have to inform you that your son, Driver Thompson, was this morning whilst on duty wounded in the thigh and abdomen. All possible medical assistance was rendered him, almost immediately placed in hospital and receiving the best possible attention. Driver Thompson has always been one of the most diligent drivers, and he will be a sad loss to my unit. I assure you of my sincere sympathy, and trust that before long you will have your dear son at home."

Then followed a letter from Sister May Winter, who wrote: "My dear Mrs. Thompson, - your son, Driver J.E. Thompson, passed away this morning on my ward. The poor boy told me he was your only son, and my heart always goes out to the mothers who are called upon to make the tremendous sacrifice. He was quite happy, and I don't think he had the least idea he was dying, for when I told him I should write to you and asked for a message, he said, "Tell her I shall be at home in a few days, and my wounds are very slight." He was a lovely boy, and we are sad at losing him. I am an Australian sister, and we are very fond of our soldiers and they of us. May God help you to bear this great sorrow. The Church of England minister – Padre Rankin – was with him at the last."

A kind letter was also received from the sister in the hospital, and the Chaplain wrote in the course of a long letter that the deceased's grave had been properly marked and it would be well cared for in future. "My very deep sympathy with you in your sad loss. Your son was a brave, capable and excellent driver, always willing and ready for duty, no matter how dangerous it might be, and by the faithful and fearless discharge of duty won the esteem and respect of his colleagues, who deeply regret his loss, and join with me in a hearty expression of sorrow and sympathy to you and your husband. When I saw him on Saturday evening he was just recovering from an operation, so I was able to speak to him, and he was greatly concerned about two other men who were with him when the fatal injuries were received and were also wounded. I may say one of them is dead, but we have hopes that the other may survive. I didn't think your son was so severely wounded, but everything possible was done for him. My sincere sympathies are with you, and you can console yourself that your son died at his country's call and was 'faithful unto death.'"

The deceased young man was 28 years of age.

The Wilts and Gloucester Standard had another long report;

With extreme regret we record the death from wounds received in action of Private Joseph Thompson, of the H.A.C., and nephew of the Mayor of Malmesbury, Councillor M. Thompson, of Hawarden, Malmesbury. The sad news was conveyed in letters from the deceased's captain and one of the nursing sisters at a hospital in France, and from these it appeared that the young soldier – now about 26 years of age – was wounded in action, being shot through the abdomen a few days ago, and despite the care of the doctors and nurses he succumbed to his injuries two days later. It was, perhaps, the optimism of youth that prevented him from realising that the end was near, for his request to those tending him was: "Write and tell mother and father I am wounded, and I shall soon be back in England again." Only three weeks ago he was home on leave visiting his aunt and uncle, who have been mother and father to the lad and have brought him up from childhood. He had then served over two years in France, and naturally his relatives were overjoyed at the brief re-union. The lad, however, had a presentiment, on returning to the front, that he was bidding his friends a last "good bye," and to them he expressed his belief that he should not see them again. Truly his case is yet another of the tragedies of war. "Joe," as he was familiarly called, was the only child of the late Mr. Joseph Thompson, of High-street, Malmesbury. He was practically orphaned at the age of three years, and was adopted into the family of his uncle, Mr. M. Thompson, the present Mayor of the town. Mr. and Mrs. Thompson brought the boy up as their own, and in return for their kindness he shewed the greatest filial affection, and which the years have failed to lessen. At the age of five years, on the death of an uncle, he became the prospective owner of certain properties, the income derivable being held in trust for the lad until he attained his majority. He was educated at Malmesbury, and was a regular attendant at the Silver-street Congregational Church. On leaving school he was apprenticed by his trustees (in conjunction with the Mayor) to Mr. Walter Hayes, under whom he acquired a practical knowledge of a carpenter and wheelwright's business. Shortly after serving his term of years he felt, like many other lads of a promising and energetic character, that there was no scope for one's activities in a small town, and he responded to the call of the New World and emigrated to the United States. In Cleveland he plied his trade to good effect and his prospects were bright, but another and greater call – that of his country – came to the lad on the outbreak of war, but he at once set sail for England. He joined up very early in the war, and has served his country in France for upwards of two years. Needless to say, the news of his death leaves those whom he has known as "father and mother" well nigh heart broken. Adding to the pathos of the circumstances is the fact that the lad's cousin Nellie, youngest daughter of the Mayor, is on the eve of her marriage, and was one of the last to wish Joe "good bye." While Mr. and Mrs. Thompson are daily receiving messages of sympathy, their daughter's post bears letters of congratulation and good wishes. Truly, joy and sorrow go hand in hand. Our sincere condolences with the stricken family join those they have already received.

The marriage did go ahead, although the usual festivities were dispensed with. The Roll of Honour entry was;

THOMPSON.- Oct 5th, killed in action, Driver Joseph Ewart Thompson, R.F.A., of Malmesbury, aged 28 years.

Deadman, Frank, Rifleman, C/1548, age 24, 16th (Service) Battalion King's Royal Rifle Corps (Church Lads Brigade)
Died of wounds, 25th October 1917, buried at Wimereux Communal Cemetery VI E 26, commemorated Malmesbury Abbey, Town Hall & Triangle.
Wimereux was the headquarters of Queen Mary's Army Auxiliary Corps during the First World War and in 1919 it became the General Headquarters of the British Army. From October 1914 onwards Boulogne and Wimereux formed an important hospital centre. Until June 1918 the medical units at Wimereux used the communal cemetery for burials, the south-eastern half having been set aside for Empire graves although a few burials were also made in the civilian part. By June 1918 this half of the cemetery was filled and subsequent burials from the hospitals were made in the new military cemetery at Terlincthun. Wimereux Communal Cemetery contains 2,847 Empire burials of the First World War, two of them unidentified. Buried among them is Lt.-Col. John McCrae author of the poem "In Flanders Fields." There are also five French and a plot of 170 German war graves. The British section was designed by Charles Holden. Because of the sandy nature of the soil, the headstones lie flat upon the graves.
Frank was the youngest son of George (Head Gardener at Cowbridge House) and Ada Deadman, of Cowbridge Gardens, with one older brother, Frederick and three sisters, Edith, Florence & Doris. Frank was born in Thornton Heath, Surrey but moved with his family to Malmesbury. He was one of the first to join the new Boy Scouts troop in 1905. Following in his father's footsteps he became a gardener. He was employed in Buckinghamshire and enlisted at High Wycombe in September 1915. He was posted to the 16th King's Royal Rifles initially raised at Denham from men who had been in the Church Lads Brigade. On 23rd September 1917 the unit moved to Kruistraathoek just south of Ypres. From there companies were sent to support 1st Queens, 2nd Worcesters, 9th Highland Light Infantry and 222 Field Company R.E. Some of them took part in an attack alongside the Menin Road towards Gheluvelt. By the time the Battalion went out of the line on 28th September four officers had been wounded, 33 other ranks killed, 152 wounded and 31 missing. One of the wounded was Frank which the Herald reported on 12th October 1917;

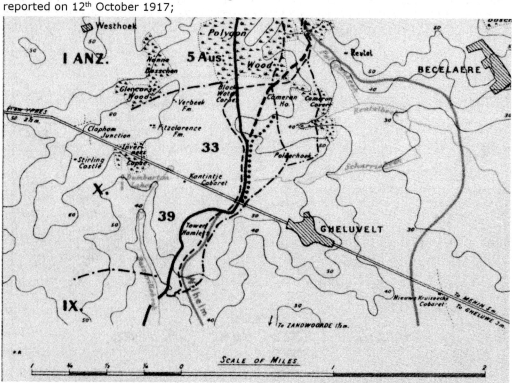

16th KRRC were part of 33rd Division which took part in the Battle of Polygon Wood 25th-28th September when Frank was wounded. (Military Operations 1917)

THIRD TIME DISABLED. - News has been received by Mr. George Deadman, head gardener at Cowbridge House, that his son, Rifleman Frank Deadman, King's Royal Rifles, has been seriously wounded in France, having a compound fracture of the forearm and a wound in the back. This is the third time that Rifleman Deadman has been disabled. On the first occasion he received shrapnel in his side, and all of it has never been extracted. On the second occasion he was sent home with trench foot and was fortunate in being drafted to Malmesbury Red Cross Hospital. It is hoped that the young soldier will soon recover. His parents are anxiously awaiting further news of his condition.

Unfortunately he failed to recover and his death was reported in the 2nd November edition;

DIED OF WOUNDS.

Brave Malmesbury Soldier.

In a previous issue of the "Herald" was published the news that Pte. Frank Deadman, who served in the King's Royal Rifles, had been seriously wounded. Official news has since been received by the parents, Mr. and Mrs. George Deadman, of Cowbridge Cottage, Malmesbury, that the young soldier succumbed to his wounds on October 25th. The utmost sympathy will go out to Mr. and Mrs. Deadman and family in their sad loss.

Rifleman Frank Deadman, who was 23 years of age, was a gardener in the service of Sir Philip Rose, of Penn, Bucks, when he volunteered for the Army in September, 1915. He joined the crack rifle regiment, the King's Royal Rifles, and two months later was in France fighting the fierce battle of Trones Wood. Here he was wounded in the side with shrapnel, which was never removed. He was brought to Brighton Hospital and subsequently to Lewes. On his recovery he went back to France and resumed his hard experiences in the trenches. In January of the present year, when the winter weather was exceptionally severe, he was stricken with "trench feet" and was again sent to England. It was a coincidence that in due course he found himself included in a convoy for Malmesbury Red Cross Hospital, his parents not knowing of his coming until Quartermaster Perry, of the V.A.D., who had superintended the removal of the convoy from the railway station, sent a message announcing their son's arrival. Rifleman Deadman, after about four months' treatment, again re-joined his regiment in France and took part in the recent heavy fighting somewhere in the neighbourhood of Ypres. He was in the front line this last time for four or five months, and early last month received wounds which caused his death – a compound fracture of the right forearm and a wound in the back. Every care was taken of him at the 2nd Australian General Hospital, but when complications ensued his recovery became hopeless.

From the Matron of the hospital Mrs. Deadman received the following kind letter: "It is with much regret that I am writing to let you know the sad news of your son's death. During the last few days we have been very anxious about him, a haemorrhage (internal) causing us much anxiety. I saw him this morning and had a talk with him. He was so very bright and cheerful, and always had a bright smile for us. This evening he became worse, and though everything was done for him that could be done, he quietly passed away at 7.30 p.m. Will you please accept our sincere sympathy in your sadness and feel that the laddie was with his friends. The Chaplain was with him when he passed away, and I am sure he will write to you. With many thoughts and much sympathy. – E. Gray (Matron)."

The Chaplain (the Rev. W.K. Douglas, who was vicar of Port Esperance, Tasmania) wrote: "Just a line of my sincere sympathy with you all over your splendid boy's death. He passed away as easily and gently to-night as possible. We were all so fond of him, and he put up such a plucky fight, but God wanted him, and, though he did not want to go, he was quite ready. I was with him about ten minutes before he died; we expected then that he would live for some hours. All day he had been very weak, but almost to the last we were hoping that he would pull through. His thoughts and prayers have been all along with you at home, and with his aunt at Portsmouth, and with his little girl. He was so very fond of you all and so anxious to get home. Now he waits for you in Paradise. We all pray for you and for him."

Mr. and Mrs. Deadman have another son – their eldest – in the Navy. He was on H.M.S. "Conqueror," but was transferred to a submarine. It is sincerely hoped that he may be spared to return safely from the hazards of the war.

This appeared in the Roll of Honour;

DEADMAN. - Oct. 25th, died of wounds received in action, Rifleman Frank Deadman, King's Royal Rifles, second son of Mr. George Deadman, Cowbridge, Malmesbury, aged 23 years.

Pope, Thomas, Private, M2/055058, age 38, 29th Ammunition Sub Park, Army Service Corps Died, 15th November 1917, buried in Tincourt New British Cemetery II D 12, commemorated Malmesbury Abbey (initial shown as G) & Triangle.

Tincourt was occupied by British troops in March 1917 during the German Retreat to the Hindenburg Line; and from the following May until March 1918 Tincourt became a centre for Casualty Clearing Stations. On the 23rd March 1918 the villages were evacuated and were not recovered until 6th September, in a ruined condition. From that month to December 1918 Casualty Clearing Stations were again posted here. The cemetery was begun in June 1917 and used until September 1919; the few German burials are in Plot VI. After the Armistice it was used for the reburial of soldiers found on the battlefield or buried in small French or German cemeteries. The graves of 136 American soldiers buried here in the autumn of 1918 and one who died in December 1917 and those of two Italian soldiers have been removed to other cemeteries. There are now nearly 2,000 1914-18 war casualties commemorated in this site. Of these over 250 are unidentified and special memorials are erected to seven British soldiers and one Australian, known or believed to be buried among them. Other special memorials record the names of 21 soldiers from the United Kingdom, two from Canada, one from Australia and one from South Africa, buried in other cemeteries, whose graves were destroyed by shell fire. The cemetery covers an area of 6,149 square metres. Burials from 16 other graveyards were concentrated here after the war.

Thomas was born in Hoxton, Middlesex the third son of William (a London policeman) and Anne Pope with brothers Samuel, Charles, William & John and sisters Jane, Isabella, Ann & Alice. In 1909 at Bloomsbury he married Lily Goulding who was the youngest daughter of Henry (ironmonger's labourer) and Sarah Goulding of Malmesbury with a brother, Francis and two sisters Ethel & Ellen. Thomas became chauffeur to Captain Ritchie, the adjutant of the Royal Wiltshire Yeomanry and was in that job at the beginning of the war. I cannot find him in the 1901 census and as he enlisted in London it is possible he was a career soldier serving in South Africa at that time. He may still have been a reservist in 1914. What is known is that he arrived in France on 29th May 1915 and was later posted to the 29th Ammunition Sub Park. This unit was in the Ypres salient during the first part of October 1917. Their lorries were used for a variety of tasks including their main role of moving ammunition. The month was cold with a series of heavy storms from which the vehicles' rudimentary canvas roofs and small windscreens would have given the drivers little protection. A couple of dozen men, including Thomas, were sent with 11 lorries carrying Small Arms Ammunition to 48th Ammunition Sub Park on the Somme on 17th October. The rest of the unit moved south a week later. The detachment rejoined on 7th November but Thomas was not with them. The continuing cold and wet weather must have taken its toll. The Standard reported his death;

MALMESBURY MOTOR DRIVER'S DEATH IN FLANDERS. – Mr. Tom. Pope, formerly chauffeur to Captain Ritchie and son-in-law of Mr. Henry Goulding, of Westport, Malmesbury, has died in Flanders from pneumonia. He joined up as a motor driver and has been many months in active service. He leaves a young widow in delicate health. Lily died in April 1918.

Bishop, Colin George, Private, 201561, age 17, 1/4th Battalion Duke of Edinburgh's (Wiltshire Regiment) Territorial Force Died of wounds, 22nd November 1917, buried in Cairo Military War Memorial Cemetery A 14, commemorated Malmesbury Abbey, Town Hall (initial just C) & Triangle.

At the outbreak of the First World War, Cairo was headquarters to the United Kingdom garrison in Egypt. With Alexandria, it became the main hospital centre for Gallipoli in 1915 and later dealt with the sick and wounded from operations in Egypt and Palestine. Cairo War Memorial Cemetery was formerly part of the New British Protestant Cemetery but plots B, D, F, H, K, M, O, P and Q were ceded to the Commission in 1920. Graves were brought into these plots from elsewhere in the Protestant cemetery and later 85 First World War graves were concentrated from Minia War Cemetery, 200 km south of Cairo, where maintenance could not be assured. One burial of the Second World War was moved from Old Cairo Old Latin Cemetery for the same reason. There are now 2,057 Empire casualties of the First World War and 340 from the Second World War buried or commemorated here.

Colin was the second son of Robert (a carpenter) and Jane Bishop of Lower High Street, with an older brother Harry and sister Lily. He was a sturdy lad and obviously very independent as he had left school before the official leaving age. He then worked for three different employers, including one in Devon before he volunteered at Devizes when he was only 14. He went with a draft of reinforcements to 1/4th Wiltshires on the S.S. Kenilworth Castle to India. In September 1917 they moved to Palestine. Because he was now in a war zone his parents decided to let the authorities know that he was under age. His elder brother Henry, a trooper in the City of London Regiment went to Gaza to get him discharged. Unfortunately he arrived just after Colin had received his mortal wounds. He died nine days later in Gaza Red Cross Hospital. The war diary describes the fierce engagement; *13th November Bn moved to attack enemy, 1st objective EL RUSTINEH, 2nd objective EL MESMIYEH, 1/5th SLI participating in attack on EL MESMIYEH. The attack was carried out 2 Coys in firing line, 2 in reserve, EL RESTINEH found unoccupied. Whilst going through the village and taking up position on the far side, the Bn came under shell fire. At 1100hrs orders were received to attack EL MESMIYEH, Wilts on left, SLI on right. Advance was carried out in artillery formation sections in single file, very few losses sustained during advance of 2 miles under heavy shell fire. Cactus gardens W of EL MESMIYEH were seized by No 1 Coy, No 2 Coy and 1/5th*

Colin Bishop (Derek Tilney)

SLI taking village. 2 Turkish Officers and about 50 OR and personnel of 2 MG Sections were taken together with their MG's in cactus gardens and about 6 Turks killed. Bn then occupied the W and N edge of the garden, and improved communications by cutting roads between cactus fences. These roads proved very useful as the day went on. At about 1530 the Bn. received orders to attack the heights N of EL MESMIYEH. These heights were occupied by the Turks at a distance of about 800 yds from position, numbering roughly 200 and falling S. They had 2 MG's in position, other Turks were facing W and SW of heights still further N. The attack commenced at 1600hrs, with 3 Coys in firing line and 1 Coy in reserve and 1½ Coys SLI in echelon on left rear in support, these were under Capt. TIMMS and gave valuable support. As the Bn. debouched from both sides of Cactus Gardens they came under heavy fire from Artillery, MG's and rifles. The ground was smooth and slope gentle, so that the attack was carried out very quickly and the losses all considered were not heavy. As the Bn. attacked from S, 1/5th Devons attacked from W, as that very few Turks escaped unwounded. 3 MG's were taken and next day some 60 odd Turks buried. On arrival at crest Bn. faced NE and came under very heavy shell fire and dug themselves in. Owing to failing light, and protection men were able to get from their entrenching tools and equipment which they put in front of them, comparatively few losses were sustained. With darkness the shelling ceased. Total casualties:
3 Officers wounded, 10 OR killed, 87 OR wounded.
Signed A Armstrong Lt Col, Commanding 1/4th Wilts Regt 3.12.17
His mother received the following letter describing how her son died;

Gaza Egypt   *December 1917*

Dear Mrs Bishop,
The Sergeant Major of 'D' Company has given me your letter to him about your son, Colin Bishop, who died of wounds last November, and I hope you will allow me to answer it and tell

you how deeply sorry I am that you should have suffered so great a loss.

Your son came to my platoon in India, and I always thought him a good soldier, the more so as he enlisted under age. I was very distressed to hear of his death when I rejoined the Regiment from hospital.

He was wounded in the cactus garden El Meonieze when the Regiment took an important Turkish position, so you will at any rate have the consolation of knowing that he was killed during a very critical engagement and during a great victory for us.

Number 13 platoon was sent up to reinforce the line and he had just turned to speak to his friend Sawyer when a bullet struck him in the neck. Ash (from Holt) and Sawyer carried him back to the Dressing Station and looked after him, and he spoke a little to them; but he was seriously wounded and after he was taken to Hospital in Gaza he died.

I do not believe that he suffered much pain in the end. His great friend in the company was Sergt. Clarke, who was also killed. His father Mr Clarke, 4 Wine Street, Bradford on Avon, would probably give you some information. I sympathise with you in your loss.

      Yours truly

      J. Lockhart Officer Commanding D Company Wiltshire Regiment.

Major Lockhart survived the war and continued to command the Swindon Company of 4th Wiltshires. Colin Bishop was the youngest boy from Malmesbury to lose his life in the Great War. He was 14 years and 10 months old when he sailed with his Battalion for India and just 17 years and 1 month old when he was killed in Gaza. The North Wilts Herald reported his death;

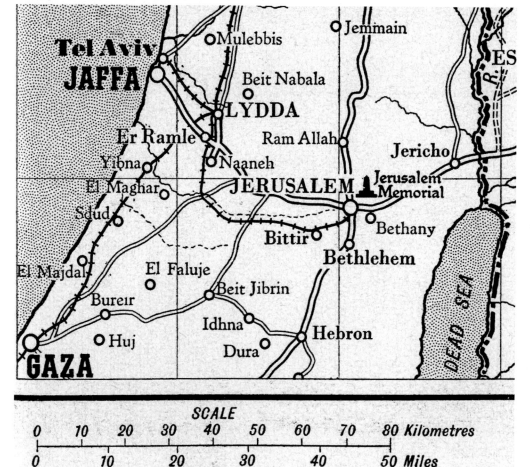

The area of Palestine that was fought so hard over by the 1/4th Wiltshires and the other Empire forces.
(Twenty Years After)

ENLISTED AT FOURTEEN.
Malmesbury Lad's Heroic Death.
At 14 years of age Colin Bishop, second son of Mr. and Mrs. Robert Bishop, Burton Hill, Malmesbury, joined the Wilts Territorial Regiment in April, 1915. He was a fine, well-built lad, and when ultimately he was selected to go with a draft to India it was not suspected by the

No. *2449*

(If replying, please quote above No.)

ARMY FORM B. 104—82.

Infantry _____ Record Office,

EXETER.

26 NOV 1917 191

Sir,

It is my painful duty to inform you that a report has been received from the War Office notifying the death of:—

(No.) *201561* (Rank) *Private*

(Name) *C. Bishop*

(Regiment) *4th WILTS REGT.*

which occurred *with the Egyptian Expeditionary Force*

on the *22nd day of November 1917.*

The report is to the effect that he *died of wounds received in action.*

By His Majesty's command I am to forward the enclosed message of sympathy from Their Gracious Majesties the King and Queen. I am at the same time to express the regret of the Army Council at the soldier's death in his Country's service.

I am to add that any information that may be received as to the soldier's burial will be communicated to you in due course. A separate leaflet dealing more fully with this subject is enclosed.

I am,

Sir,

Your obedient Servant,

Louis Baker Lt-Col

Officer in charge of Records. ~~Colonel,~~

In charge of Records, No. 8 District.

18307. Wt. 15148/M 1365. 175M. 2/17. R. & L., Ltd.

P.T.O.

The notification dreaded by parents and wives of serving soldiers. (Derek Tilney) authorities that he was under military age. From India this plucky boy was coming home with his regiment, and his proud mother and father were looking forward with much joy to seeing him; they counted the days and reckoned that he would be home about November 17th. Alas for their hopes, however! Instead of coming to England the regiment was detailed for service in Palestine, and on November 17th, the day he was expected home, Colin Bishop, a "veteran" at the age of seventeen, received his death wound near Gaza. He died, as brave a lad as ever lived, in Gaza Red Cross Hospital on November 22nd. Pte. Colin Bishop has an older brother, Trooper Harry Bishop, of the Lancers. He is on his way to the Eastern front, and it was his intention to claim his brother, according to custom, from the fighting line. It is pathetic that he should have to receive on his arrival the sad news that his brother had been killed. Mr. Robert Bishop, the father, is an old Volunteer and has a long service medal. He was also a member of the Volunteer Training Corps until recently. The late Pte. Colin Bishop was formerly in the employ of Mrs. Napier Miles, Ingelburne Manor, later at Lady Clifford's in Devonshire, and subsequently at Cowbridge House Farm. The utmost sympathy is felt for Mr. and Mrs. Bishop in their sad loss.

His death was noted in the Roll of Honour column;

BISHOP. – Nov. 22nd at Gaza Red Cross Hospital, of wounds received in action, Pte. Colin Bishop, second son of Mr. Robert Bishop, Burton Hill, Malmesbury, aged 17 years.

In 1919 the following appeared in the Herald;

BISHOP.- In loving memory of our dear son, Colin George Bishop, 4th Wilts Regiment, who died of wounds in Palestine, Nov. 22nd, 1917, aged 17 years.

> Gone, but not forgotten
Could we have raised his dying head and heard his last farewell,
The grief would not have been so hard for those who loved him so well;
Only those who have suffered are able to tell the pain in the heart in not saying farewell,
And the unknown grave is the bitterest blow that an aching heart can ever know.

The following year later this appeared In Memoriam;

BISHOP.- In loving memory of our dear son, Colin George Bishop, 4th Wilts Regiment, who died of wounds in Palestine, Nov. 22nd, 1917, aged 17 years.

> Gone, but not forgotten
> Could we have raised his dying head
> And heard his last farewell,
> The grief would not have been so hard
> Only those who have suffered are able to tell
> The pain in the heart in not saying farewell,
> And the unknown grave is the bitterest blow
> That an aching heart can ever know.

In 1921 this was the entry;

BISHOP.- In loving memory of our dear son, Colin George Bishop, 4th Wilts Regiment, who died of wounds in Palestine, Nov. 22nd, 1917, aged 17 years.

> Could we have raised his dying head
> And heard his last farewell,
> The grief would not have been so hard
> For those who loved him well
> - From his still sorrowing Parents.

Carey, Leslie James, Private, 201645, age 18, 1/4th Battalion Duke of Edinburgh's (Wiltshire Regiment) Territorial Force

Killed in action, 22nd November 1917, buried in Jerusalem War Cemetery Y 54, commemorated Malmesbury Abbey, Town Hall & Triangle.

At the outbreak of the First World War, Palestine (now Israel) was part of the Turkish Empire and was not entered by Allied forces until December 1916. The advance to Jerusalem took a further year, but from 1914 to December 1917, about 250 British Empire prisoners of war were buried in the German and Anglo-German cemeteries of the city. By 21st November 1917, the Egyptian Expeditionary Force had gained a line about five kilometres west of Jerusalem but the city was deliberately spared bombardment and direct attack. Very severe fighting followed, lasting until the evening of 8th December, when the 53rd (Welsh) Division on the south, and the 60ᵗʰ (London) and 74ᵗʰ (Yeomanry) Divisions on the west, had captured all the city's prepared defences. Turkish forces left Jerusalem throughout that night and in the morning of 9ᵗʰ December, the Mayor came to the Allied lines with the Turkish Governor's letter of surrender. Jerusalem was occupied that day and on 11ᵗʰ December General Allenby formally entered the city, followed by representatives of France and Italy. From 26ᵗʰ to 30ᵗʰ December, fierce fighting took place to the north and east of the city but it remained in Allied hands. Jerusalem War Cemetery was begun after the occupation of the city, with 270 burials. It was later enlarged to take graves from the battlefields and smaller cemeteries in the neighbourhood. There are now 2,515 Empire burials of the First World War in the cemetery, 100 of them unidentified. Within it stands the Jerusalem Memorial commemorating 3,300 Empire servicemen who died during the First World War in operations in Egypt or Palestine and who have no known grave.

Leslie was the eldest son of James (general labourer) & Fanny (née Stevens) Carey, of 66 Bristol Street. He came from a large family with brothers Bert, Percival, Reginald, George & Edward and sisters Edith, Daisy, Elsie & Lucy. Although living in a small cottage his mother also took in foster children! Leslie ran away from home at the age of sixteen to join up. His parents traced him to Devizes barracks and after writing to the Commanding Officer went to collect him. He promptly went back to Devizes and they reluctantly accepted the situation, indeed they were proud that he was the youngest volunteer. He was posted to the 1/4ᵗʰ Battalion in Palestine and teamed up with two others, Charlie Emery and Reg Wakefield. Reg recalled; *Three boys from Malmesbury. We were fighting Johnny Turk – when the order came to 'go over the top,' one second Les was there, the next he was gone.* The Battalion war diary entry states;

22ⁿᵈ November Bn. with 1/5 SLI formed an advance guard with objective villages of EL JIB and BIR NEBALA. The Bn. moved as part of the Main Guard. The Advance Guard moved N leaving BIDDU on right. On proceeding about 1 mile came under long range artillery fire from a ridge immediately N. The OC then decided to take the ridge, and keeping to the high ground, attack at 71B from the West. This was attempted but the ridge in question was strongly held by enemy, but owing to formation of ground it was impossible to develop any strength against him, nor could the position be rushed as the ground was too tricky. An attempt was made to ease the situation up a neighbouring spur which converged on to the main ridge. They were able to bring surprise fire on the Turks but with one Lewis gun and 1 platoon, but no great strength could be developed. At night the advance guard fell back on BEIT IZZA leaving 2 Coys on spur 099 R21a where they dug themselves in for the night. Casualties 2 OR killed, 19 OR wounded.

There was no report of Leslie's death in the local paper other than the Roll of Honour entry;

CAREY.- Nov. 22ⁿᵈ, killed in action with the Egyptian Expeditionary Force, Pte. Leslie James Carey, Wilts Regiment, eldest son of Mr. and Mrs. James Carey, of 66, Bristol Road, Malmesbury, aged 18 years.

> *"Sweeping through the gates of new Jerusalem,*
> *Washed in the blood of the Lamb."*

In 1918 his family put the following in the In Memoriam column;

CAREY.- In proud memory of our dear son and brother, Leslie James Carey, who was killed in action in Palestine, Nov. 22ⁿᵈ, 1917, aged 18 years.

> *He died a hero facing the foe,*
> *Defending the country from terror and woe;*
> *God welcomed his spirit, released from the strife,*
> *May He comfort our hearts as we think of his life.*

Inserted by his sorrowing Mother and Father, Sisters and Brothers.

The following year two entries were made;

CAREY.- In loving and sweet remembrance of our dear brother, Pte. Leslie James Carey, killed in action, Nov. 22ⁿᵈ, 1917, aged 18 years.

> *In the heat of battle*
> *He bravely took his part,*
> *He fought and died for Britain*
> *And the honour of his name*
> *A young, good life given for one and all*

Ever remembered by his sorrowing and loving Sister and Brother-in-law, Daisy and Ray Webb, Sunday's Hill Farm, Brinkworth.

CAREY.- *In loving and sweet remembrance of my dear son, Leslie James Carey, who was killed in action in Palestine on Nov. 22nd, 1917.*

> *It is just two years ago today*
> *My dear, poor Leslie passed away*
> *A blow so hard and pain severe*
> *To part with one we loved so dear*

Inserted by his sorrowing Mother, Father, Sisters and Brothers, 66, Bristol Street, Malmesbury.

1920 saw two more insertions;

CAREY.- *In loving memory of our dear brother, Leslie James Carey, who was killed in action in Palestine on Nov. 22nd, 1917.*

> *We often think of days gone by,*
> *When we were all together;*
> *A light from mother's has gone –*
> *Yes, a dear one gone for ever.*

Always remembered by his Sister and Brother, Daisy and Ray Webb

CAREY.- *In loving memory of our dear brother, Leslie James Carey, who was killed in action in Palestine on Nov. 22nd, 1917, aged 18 years.*

> *He sleeps besides his comrades,*
> *In a hallowed grave unknown,*
> *But his name is written in letters of gold*
> *In the hearts he has left at home.*

From his sorrowing Sister Edie and Brother-in-law, Church Road, Hanwell.

The pattern was repeated the next year;

CAREY.- *In loving memory of our dear son and brother, Leslie James Carey, killed in action in Palestine on Nov. 22nd, 1917, aged 18 years.*

> *Sweeping through the gates of the new Jerusalem,*
> *washed in the blood of the Lamb.*

-Ever remembered by his sorrowing Mother and Father, Sisters and Brothers, and Brothers-in-law, Duncan and Ray.

CAREY.- *In ever loving memory of our dear brother, who was killed in action, Nov. 22nd, 1917.*

> *It was on the field of battle, with his comrades by his side,*
> *That a brave lad of England for his country died;*
> *At his post, for his loved ones, he did his best,*
> *God bless our dear one now laid to rest,*
> *Brave and kind-hearted, like a true soldier he fell,*
> *All those who knew him can speak of him well.*

-From his sorrowing Sister Daisy and Brother-in-law, Ray.

Jones, Harold Edward, Second Lieutenant, age 18, 41 Squadron, Royal Flying Corps
Killed in flying accident, 22nd November 1917, buried at Doullens Communal Extension No. 1 Cemetery IV A 7 (family inscription *BY RICH AND POOR ALIKE, BELOVED AT MALMESBURY*), commemorated Malmesbury Abbey, Town Hall & Triangle.

Doullens was Marshal Foch's headquarters early in the War and the scene of the conference in March 1918, after which he assumed command of the Allied armies on the Western Front. From the summer of 1915 to March 1916, Doullens was a junction between the French Tenth Army on the Arras front and the British Third Army on the Somme. The citadelle, overlooking the town from the south, was a French military hospital and the railhead was used by both armies. In March 1916, Empire forces succeeded the French on the Arras front and the 19th Casualty Clearing Station came to Doullens, followed by the 41st, the 35th and the 11th. By the end of 1916, these had given way to the 3rd Canadian Stationary Hospital (which stayed until June 1918) and the 2/1st Northumbrian Casualty Clearing Station. From February 1916 to April 1918 these medical units continued to bury in the French extension (No. 1) of the communal cemetery. In March and April 1918 the German advance and the desperate fighting on this front threw a severe strain on the Canadian Stationary Hospital. The extension was filled, and a second extension begun on the opposite side of the communal cemetery.

Extension No. 1 contains 1,335 Empire burials of the First World War and also seven French and 13 German war graves. The Communal Cemetery Extension No 2 contains 374 Empire burials of the First World War, and 87 German war graves. The extensions were designed by Charles Holden.

Harold was the elder son of Edward (jeweller) and Eveline Travis Jones, of 1 Euclid Villas, Abbey Row. His father's jewellery shop was at 3 High Street. Harold was a popular young man, an excellent pianist who was much sought after to play church organs in the district. A report of Harold's activities appeared on 12th October 1917;

FIRST FLYING OFFICER. – Malmesbury's first flying officer, Second-Lieutenant Harold Jones, son of Mr. and Mrs. Edward Jones, High Street, although only 18½ years of age, is already at work flying in France. His uncle, Captain E.S.T. Cole, M.C., R.F.C., has many meritorious deeds to his credit and is now Squadron Commander in a home station. Sergt. Walter Jones, of the Malmesbury Volunteers, uncle of Second-Lieutenant H. Jones, leaves next week to join the Inns of Court Officers' Training Corps. Another relative, Mr. Monty Jones, is also in the Royal Flying Corps.

Harold was posted to 41 Squadron based at Lealvillers. They had been equipped with the short-lived De Havilland DH5 scout aeroplanes in July 1917. But in October they began to re-equip with the more satisfactory SE5a with a top speed of 138 mph compared to the DH5's 102 mph. Harold was flying an SE5a fighter when it crashed and he was killed. His death was fully reported in the Herald on 30th November;

MALMESBURY FLYING OFFICER KILLED.
Second-Lieut. Harold Jones

The news that Second-Lieutenant Harold Edward Jones, Royal Flying Corps, had been killed in France came as a profound shock to Malmesbury on Monday. He was the elder of the two sons of Mr. and Mrs. Edward Jones, High Street, Malmesbury, and was only 18 years of age. The sad intelligence was conveyed in a War Office telegram to the parents, and later in the week it was confirmed by letters from the Commanding Officer and Chaplain.

Second-Lieut. H.E. Jones had the making of a smart officer, and great hopes were entertained when he joined the Royal Flying Corps that he would emulate his uncle, Capt. E. Stuart Cole, M.C., R.F.C., who has already made a name for himself as a daring "strafer" of German aircraft. Harold Jones was a winsome lad. He received his education at Fulneck Moravian School, near Leeds. When the Malmesbury Volunteer Training Corps was formed he was one of the first to join with his father and two uncles, and he made rapid progress, early being efficient in drill and marksmanship. He did well at an examination for privates wishing to become non-commissioned officers, and was warmly praised by Mr. F.G.T. Goldstone, who was the Commandant of the Corps. It was his earnest wish when he reached the age of 18 to join the Royal Flying Corps, and that wish was gratified. He was not long qualifying as a pilot, and by September he was flying on the French front. His letters home were always cheerful, and he manifested extraordinary keenness for his hazardous duties. We believe we are right in saying that he never had an accident with any machine he had piloted.

Had he remained in civil life Second-Lieut. Jones would surely have made his mark as a musician. On the piano and organ he was a brilliant executant. He frequently played the

Is this the only reference to Malmesbury in any foreign cemetery?

organ in the Malmesbury Moravian Church, where his uncle, Mr. J.A. Jones, is organist and choirmaster, and he had also been honorary organist at Crudwell Church. He often used to cheer the wounded soldiers at the Red Cross Hospital by playing to them in the Wesleyan recreation room. To lose such a promising son is a terrible blow to Mr. and Mrs. Jones. They have received a shoal of sympathetic letters and countless expressions of condolence have been conveyed verbally by friends.

The Chaplain, the Rev. R.W. Duplain (who was a curate at Rugby) wrote: "You will by now have received the news that your son, Second-Lieut. H.E. Jones, R.F.C., was killed while flying on November 22nd. They were just going off in a thick mist to take part in this last battle when the accident happened. Death was instantaneous. We buried his body with those of two brother officers killed at the same time. The major in command of the squadron and several of their brother officers were present and the "last post" was sounded at the end of the service. A cross will be put up in his memory, and the grave will be well kept. I cannot tell you how deeply we all sympathise with you in your loss. These boys do wonderful work and we must thank God for their courage and devotion and for the manner of their death too. But it is hard for those who are left behind – the hardest thing in the world perhaps. May God give you all His strength and comfort now."

The Commanding Officer, in his letter, told how the accident occurred, the machine – which was flying very low in thick mist – crashing against a tree. The writer expressed the sympathy of the deceased's brother officers.

A memorial service to the late Second-Lieut. Jones will probably be held in the Moravian Church on Sunday morning.

That same week's Standard had a report peppered with anti-German sentiment;

MALMESBURY AIRMAN KILLED.

The whole-hearted sympathy of the town of Malmesbury and district is accorded to Councillor and Mrs. Edward Jones, of High-street, who have received confirmation that their eldest son, Harold, R.F.C., age 19, has been killed while flying in Flanders. We understand that Mr. Jones on receiving the tidings telegraphed to France, doubtless hoping that, as on a previous occasion, the report was unfounded, but unfortunately official confirmation came by a reply wire from deceased's Captain. The sad news has come as a great shock to the family and to a large circle of deceased's friends. Harold Jones, only 19, a fresh coloured, well set-up lad, full of life and spirit, an expert motor cyclist, a keen musician, of brilliant promise for the future, has been cut down on the very threshold of manhood. War, the most bloody octopus of all, with its insatiable maw, has put forth yet another tentacle and claimed its own. Were we the offspring of the Apostles of Kultur who ruthlessly throw forward their best as "cannon fodder," we should feel these things less keenly, but civilised beings possessed of human hearts, dwellers in the fair homes of England, can but mourn over the terrible toll being exacted from our best young manhood, yet sustained by the belief that the sacrifice is not in vain. For the great principles of righteousness, honour, justice, and liberty, for the peace – the enduring peace among men – no sacrifice can be in vain. Harold Jones was a most popular lad, exceptionally quick and intelligent. A great music lover, he had acted as pianist at many a local function, and was fast becoming proficient as an organist. At home learning his father's trade – that of a jeweller – the call to arms found him quickly responsive as soon as his age justified the step. He joined the R.F.C. and soon made rapid strides in the art of flying, and having passed his tests he was given the commission of second-lieutenant. Recently (after six or seven months' training) he flew his machine over to France and was engaged on active service at the front when he made the supreme sacrifice. Second-Lieutenant Harold Jones was flying on patrol duty on November 22nd in a high wind when his plane collided with a tree and was wrecked, the young officer killed instantly by the fall. He was buried on Saturday at Doullens.

The Herald's Roll of Honour entry;

JONES.- Nov. 22nd, killed whilst flying in France, Second-Lieut. Harold Edward Jones, Royal Flying Corps, elder son of Mr. Edward Jones, High Street, Malmesbury, aged 18 years.

Wood, Percy, Private, 16453, age 29, 2nd Battalion Scots Guards
Died of wounds, 27th November 1917, buried at Rocquigny-Equancourt Road British Cemetery, Manancourt III E 4, commemorated Malmesbury Abbey (name shown as Woods), Town Hall & Triangle.

Etricourt-Manancourt was occupied by Empire troops at the beginning of April 1917 during the German withdrawal to the Hindenburg Line. It was lost on the 23rd March 1918 when the Germans advanced, but regained at the beginning of September. The cemetery was begun in 1917 and used until March 1918, mainly by the 21st and 48th Casualty Clearing Stations posted at Ytres, and to a small extent by the Germans. Burials were resumed by Empire troops in September 1918 and the 3rd Canadian and 18th Casualty Clearing Stations used it in October and November 1918. The cemetery contains 1,838 Empire burials and commemorations of the First World War. 21 of the burials are unidentified and nine Empire graves made by the Germans which cannot now be found are represented by special memorials. The cemetery also contains 198 German war burials and the graves of ten French civilians. The cemetery was designed by Sir Reginald Blomfield.

Percy was the youngest son of Henry and Elizabeth Wood, of Kingswall whose family details are shown on page 132, his brother Charles having been killed on 26th May 1916. The only attestation form that has survived shows that Percy enlisted in Whitehall using the name William Ward on 18th January 1917, apparently working as a footman in Baker Street, London. Sent to the Guards Depot at Caterham for training, his false name was detected as he was put in the Guard Room on 13th March. Nine days later he was court-martialled, the charges being that he lost his kit in Dublin a week before his Whitehall enlistment and fraudulent enlistment. It would seem that he had previously enlisted in Dublin where con-

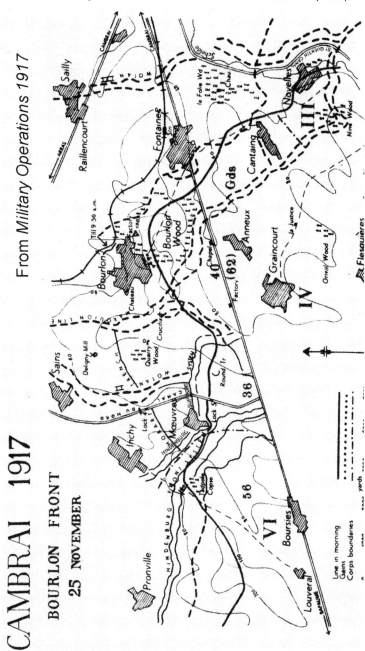

From Military Operations 1917

CAMBRAI 1917
BOURLON FRONT
25 NOVEMBER

scription did not operate and had disposed of his kit when he went absent. He was convicted and sentenced to 56 days detention and stoppages of £1 11s. 3d. Half of the sentence was remitted with another four days for good conduct so he was released on 15th April. On completion of his training he was posted to the 1st Battalion and shipped via Southampton and Le Havre to Harfleur on 24th October. A week later he was transferred to the 2nd Battalion as an officer's servant, joining them in the field on 3rd November. On the 23rd the unit moved forward to take part in the Battle of Cambrai. The following day they moved into Bourlon Wood described as *a nightmare sort of place – pitch dark and no one knew its tortuous ways or quite where the Germans were.* The Guards suffered severe casualties and failed to clear the wood. After such an experience they hoped to get a rest but after being in support for a day were called forward to attack the village of Fontaine. Although only in support, it was during this operation that Percy received a gun shot wound to the back on the 26th. He was evacuated to 48th Casualty Clearing Station where he died the next day.

The Gazette reported his death on 6th December;

WIDOW'S TWO SONS KILLED.- Private Percy Wood, of a Guards' regiment, son of Mrs. Wood, Kingswall, has died of wounds received in action. He was about 28 years of age and a smart soldier. When he first joined up he was employed at the Vice-regal Lodge, Dublin. He joined an Irish regiment but subsequently transferred to the Guards. News that he was severely wounded was received last week and on Monday came a letter announcing his death. Mrs. Wood, who is heartbroken at the loss of her two sons – the other was Bandsman Charles Wood, Wiltshire Regiment – has the sympathy of the whole community.

The Standard of 8th December carried another report of his death;

This week Mrs. Henry Wood, of King's Wall, has been notified of the death of another of her sons, Private Percy Wood, aged 28, who was transferred from an Irish regiment in Dublin to the Scots Guards division. He had only been on the Western front about three weeks when he was killed.

The Herald had this entry in the Roll of Honour;

WOOD.- Died of wounds received in action, Pte. Percy Woods, Scots Guards, fourth son of the late Mr. H. Wood and Mrs. Wood, Kingswall, Malmesbury, aged 30 years.

He and his brother were remembered on the anniversary of Percy's death In Memoriam;

WOOD.- A tribute of love to the memory of Pte. Percy Woods, Scots Guards, who died from wounds received in action, Nov. 27th, 1917; and Charlie, 1st Wilts Regiment, who fell nobly doing his duty as stretcher bearer, May 26th, 1916.

> *Honour to those in battle slain*
> *Who died that we might freedom gain:*
> *To their brave memory homage give –*
> *On history's page their deeds shall live.*

Sadly missed and always in the thoughts of Mother, Sisters and Brothers, 9, Kingswall, Malmesbury.

On 26th November 1920 this appeared;

WOOD.- In loving remembrance of Pte. Charley Wood, who was killed in action May 26th, 1916; also Percy, his brother, who died of wounds in France, Nov. 27th, 1917.

> *Deep in our hearts you are fondly remembered,*
> *Many happy memories embrace around your names;*
> *True Hearts that loved you with deepest affection,*
> *Always will love you in death just the same*

Fondly remembered by Mother, Sisters and Brothers, 9, Kingswall, Malmesbury.

1918

Although victory was achieved towards the end of the year many difficulties had to be over-come and large numbers of Empire troops were killed, wounded or taken prisoner before that. The politicians at home mistrusted Haig's leadership and tried to prevent a repeat of the losses incurred during the previous two years. They retained many trained soldiers in England, creating a manpower crisis at the front. Divisions had to be reorganised to reduce their strength from twelve infantry battalions to nine and many units were disbanded or reduced to cadres. At the same time the French, still suffering from morale problems, pressed for the British to take over more of the front. During January an additional 42 miles was taken over making the British responsible from north of Ypres to south of the River Oise.

The Germans, freed from fighting in Russia, brought large reinforcements to the Western Front. They realised that they had to act before the huge American Army could be introduced into the fighting. They felt they had one last oppor-tunity to win the war by eliminating the British. Therefore on 21st March they attacked the weak-est part of the British line near St. Quentin, only recently taken over, with the object of driving a wedge between the two allies and forcing the British to retreat to the Channel coast. The first week was a stunning success, the British Fifth Army under General Gough were driven back nearly 30 miles towards Amiens. However the at-tack lost momentum, General Foch was ap-pointed commander of all allied land forces and the tide was stemmed. On 9th April another attack was made further north across the River Lys. Again this initially was successful but within ten days the line had stabi-lised. On 26th May yet another attack was made but with a different ob-jective, Paris. The Ger-mans struck the French front along the Chemin des Dames – an area that had been quiet for a year and had been cho-sen as a back-water

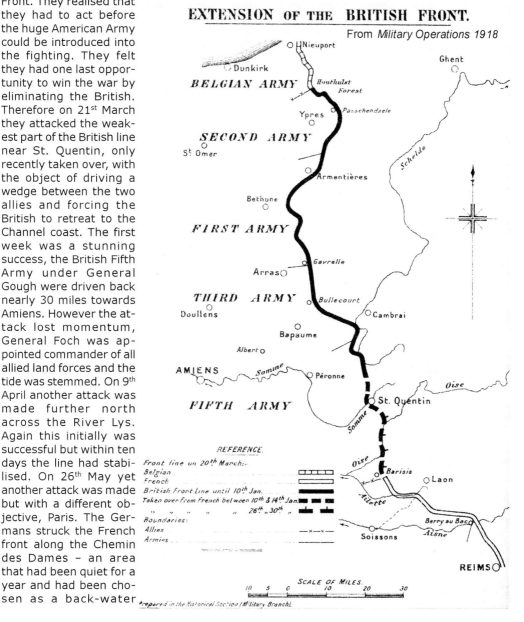

EXTENSION OF THE BRITISH FRONT.

From *Military Operations 1918*

where British units hard hit in the earlier offensives could recuperate. The impetus was again quickly lost but the fighting in this area continued after General Foch launched a counter-attack with American and British support on 18th July.

The main Allied attack began on 8th August when British, Australian, Canadian and French troops drove the Germans more than five miles back on a 15 mile front to the east of Amiens and continued until the Armistice, later known as the Hundred Days. Ludendorff called the first day "the Black Day of the German Army." The Armies of the British Empire became the main allied striking force from this moment for the remainder of the war. Although many enemy soldiers surrendered during this period, others continued to exact a heavy toll. In addition the Spanish Influenza epidemic inflicted misery throughout the world. The British Army with a large proportion of conscripts had become a very effective force which resolutely pushed the Germans back to the very last. Unfortunately this relentlessness came at a price – 294,843 Empire casualties during the Hundred Days.

Although British units had been withdrawn from other fronts to help stabilise the Western Front, the stalemate broke during the autumn. Advances were made in Italy, Macedonia, Palestine and Mesopotamia. In Africa the German Empire had been slowly overcome through-out the war – Togoland in 1914, South-West Africa in 1915, Cameroon in 1916 with only forces in German East Africa still unvanquished in November 1918.

The end of the war came suddenly, Turkey signed an armistice on 30th October followed by Austria-Hungary on 4th November and finally Germany on the 11th. The Armistice was initially only effective for 36 days but its terms made it impossible for Germany to restart hostilities. The combination of circumstances led to greater loss amongst local service personnel this year than any other, 22 men and one woman, to make a total of 78.

Ratcliffe, Herbert John, Private, M/351179, age 39, No. 1 Reserve Depot, Army Service Corps

Died, 5th January 1918, buried in Malmesbury Cemetery 651 North (private family head-stone), commemorated Malmesbury Cirencester Benefit Society only (initials wrongly shown as HI).

Plot 651 North is north east of the Chapel, seven rows south of the northern path and five rows west of the eastern path. Herbert is buried with his uncle George and sister Edith Mary. Herbert was the elder son of Edwin (who died on 14th June 1916) and Ellen Ratcliffe, Westport Ironworks, Foundry Road with one brother, Edwin and two sisters, Mabel & Edith. His father was the founder of the Ironworks which he opened in 1870, the name of which became Ratcliffe & Son in 1903 and & Sons in 1916. Herbert was educated at a Grammar School in Wallingford. He married Ethel Mary Gould in 1906 at Stroud. They had three children, Eileen in 1908, Phyllis 1910 and Kenneth 1914. Herbert's younger brother Edwin volunteered early in the war. Herbert appealed against conscription in July 1916;

A FIRE BRIGADE ENGINEER

Herbert J. Ratcliffe (38), of the firm of Messrs. Ratcliffe & Sons, Westport Engineering Works, was granted conditional exemption, his business being considered to be in the national inter-est. He is the chief engineer of the Malmesbury Fire Brigade, and his brother, a partner in the firm, is on war service in France.

An appeal against exemption was made to the Tribunal in June 1917;

Herbert J. Ratcliffe (39), married, 57, Gloucester Road, agricultural engineer, motor me-chanic and iron founder, had been previously conditionally exempted – The military applica-tion was disallowed.

In October another appeal by the military led to him losing his exemption as reported by the Gazette;

The Recruiting Officer asked for a review of the certificate granted to Herbert John Ratcliffe, 39, married (B1), Malmesbury on the ground "that this man should be made available for military service, as he is not engaged in work for which he was exempted." – As Ratcliffe did not appear the appeal was granted.

He must have been called up soon after and joined No. 1 Reserve Depot, Army Service Corps. Herbert's death was reported first in the Gazette of 10th January;

OBITUARY.- Regret is felt for the untimely death of Private Herbert J. Ratcliffe, for some years manager of the old-established business of Ratcliffe and Son, Westport Iron Works. Suffering from a painful disease, the effects of which had caused pained and hushed comment from his

large circle of friends for some time, this once jolly, energetic young townsman had but a fragile body when the military required his services. Service in the Army he saw nothing of, as soon as he enlisted his health broke down still further, and a paralytic seizure drew the curtain, on Saturday, on what was a promising life, at the age of 40, at Chiseldon Military Hospital. Deceased leaves a young wife and three children, for whom much sympathy is felt. He was first engineer in the Fire Brigade. The funeral takes place this (Thursday) afternoon at Malmesbury.

The next day's Herald was able to report the funeral;

THE LATE PTE. H.J. RATCLIFFE.- On Thursday the body of the late Pte. H.J. Ratcliffe, of Gloucester Road, who died in Chiseldon Camp Hospital in his 40th year, arrived by train for interment in the local cemetery. The tolling of the passing bell apprised the people of the sad fact. The elm brass-mounted coffin was borne to the grave by four local bearers, and the vicar (Canon McMillan) performed the last offices. The mourners were Mr. H.N. Ratcliffe (uncle), Mr. Bert Ratcliffe, Bucklebury (cousin), Mr. C. Cole, Rodbourne Rail (brother-in-law), Mr. Goole (father-in-law). The funeral procession included Messrs. M.J. Duck, F.E. Ponting, W.H. Lockstone, J. Walker, W.G. Perry, E.F. Edwards and C. Bowman (the Fire Brigade), Major Clarke, Mr. Brown (Newnton), Mr. K. Holborow (Willesley), Mr. W.E. Phillips (foreman at the Foundry), Supt. Witt, Sergt. H. Young (representing the military), and the undertaker (Mr. H. Matthews). Much sympathy is felt for Mrs. Ratcliffe and her children in their bereavement.

The entry in the Herald's Roll of Honour was;

RATCLIFFE.- Jan. 6th, at Chiseldon, Herbert J. Ratcliffe, Army Service Corps, of Malmesbury, aged 39 years.

Shingles, Harry, Lance Corporal, 204095, age 38, 6th (Service) Battalion Duke of Edinburgh's (Wiltshire Regiment)

Killed in action, 22nd January 1918, buried at Fifteen Ravine British Cemetery, Villers-Plouich Special Memorial B13 (gravestone inscribed *Believed to be buried in this cemetery* at the top with *Their Glory shall not be blotted out* at the base), commemorated Malmesbury Abbey, Town Hall & Triangle.

"Fifteen Ravine" was the name given by the Army to the shallow ravine, once bordered by fifteen trees, which ran at right angles to the railway about 800 metres south of the village of Villers-Plouich, but the cemetery is in fact in "Farm Ravine," on the east side of the railway line, nearer to the village. It was begun by the 17th Welch Regiment in April 1917, a few days after the capture of the ravine by the 12th South Wales Borderers. It continued in use during the Battle of Cambrai (November 1917) and until March 1918, when the ravine formed the boundary between the Third and Fifth Armies. On 22nd March, the second day of the great German offensive, the ground passed into their hands after severe fighting and it was not regained until the end of the following September. In March 1918 the cemetery contained 107 graves (now Plot I) but it was greatly enlarged after the Armistice when graves were brought in from other cemeteries and from the battlefields south-west of Cambrai. Fifteen Ravine Cemetery now contains 1,264 Empire burials and commemorations of the First World War. 740 of the burials are unidentified but there are special memorials to 44 casualties known or believed to be buried among them. The cemetery was designed by Sir Herbert Baker.

Harry was the second illegitimate son of Rhoda Shingles (a domestic servant), his brother Arthur Thomas having been born 18 months before him. Rhoda then married George Oram having two sons by him; George who was killed in 1915 and William. Harry Shingles was a keen part time soldier. He served in the Boer War as a Private in A Company 2nd Volunteer Battalion Wiltshire Regiment. He then joined the Wiltshire Yeomanry. After mobilisation and having served in France for more than a year this unit was disbanded with the men transferred to the 6th Wiltshires in September 1917. The war diary records;

Monday 21st January 1918 France, Hawes Camp

Relieved 10th Worcester Regt in right Subsector. 'B' and 'A' Coys in front Line - 'D' in support, 'C' in Reserve.

Remarks   LA VACQUERIE

Tuesday 22nd January 1918

Enemy artillery active shelling our outpost Line - 5 Other ranks killed - Inter Company relief 'D' relieving 'B' Coy. 'C' Coy relieving 'A' Coy.

The North Wilts Herald had a short report;

SOLDIER REPORTED KILLED.- In a letter from the soldier son of Mr. Charles Bowman (borough surveyor) it was stated that Corpl. Harry Shingles, Wilts Regiment, was killed in action on Jan. 24th. Corpl. Shingles, who was 39 years of age, was a tiler and plasterer before the war. He was in the Wilts Yeomanry and was transferred to the infantry. Only about a fortnight ago he was home on leave, and must have been killed almost as soon as he reached the front. His brother George, of the Life Guards, was killed early in the war, and his mother did not long survive afterwards.

Hibbard, (Ernest) James, Private, 30147, age 19, 2/4th Battalion Dorsetshire Regiment Territorial Force

Killed in action, 15th March 1918, buried at Ramleh Cemetery U 10, commemorated Malmesbury Abbey, Town Hall & Triangle.

Ramleh (now Ramla) was occupied by the 1st Australian Light Horse Brigade on 1st November 1917. Field ambulances and later, casualty clearing stations, were posted at Ramleh and Lydda from December 1917 onwards. The cemetery was begun by the medical units but some graves were brought in later from the battlefields and from Latron, Sarona and Wilhema Military and Indian Cemeteries. During the Second World War, it was used by the Ramla Royal Air Force Station and by various British hospitals posted in turn to the area for varying periods. Ramleh War Cemetery contains 3,300 Empire burials of the First World War, 964 of them unidentified. Second World War burials number 1,168. There are also 891 war graves of other nationalities from both wars, and 525 non-war burials, many from the RAF and garrison stations at Ramleh in the inter war years and until the end of the British Mandate in Palestine in 1948.

James was the youngest son of Edmund and Florence Hibbard, of Kingswall and later of 96 High Street. His elder brother Edmund was killed in April 1917. James's activities as a Boy Scout are described in Part One. When called up after training he was posted to Palestine where he became a motor cycle despatch rider. The battalion war diary for 15th March reads;

0600 Patrol went out to V1 a & b north of Wadi Lehham to view the country and look for traces of the enemy. Enemy were found to be holding the ridge, with supports near Semaneh and patrol came into collision with enemy outpost and exchanged shots at point blank range. Enemy killed – two. Our casualties nil.

1000 Conference of company commanders held as to the defence.

1500 Enemy shelled our area. Casualties one O.R. killed.

1700 Enemy aeroplane flying low dropped bombs of which three exploded in our bivouac area. Casualties nil

James was unfortunate to be in the wrong place on a 'quiet' day. The Commonwealth War Graves Commission has incorrectly recorded his age as 24. The Herald had a short report of his death;

A SECOND SON KILLED.- Mr. and Mrs. E. Hibbard, of Kingswall, have had the inconsolable sorrow of the loss of a second son in action – Pte. James Hibbard, Dorset Regt. The sad news was received on Tuesday, and the sincerest sympathy of the whole community goes out to the bereaved parents. They had previously lost in action their son, Lieut. E. Hibbard, another promising young man. Pte. J. Hibbard was a youth of excellent promise. He bore an unimpeachable character in civil and military life. As a boy he was in the King Athelstan Troop of Boy Scouts and became a King's Scout. When war broke out he served a long period as a coast-watcher with the Sea Scouts. He is mourned by a wide circle of friends.

The Gazette had a similar report on 28th March;

OBITUARY.- Our sympathy is offered to Mr. C.J. Hibbard in the loss of his youngest son, Ernest James, in Palestine. He was a prominent member of the Boy Scouts in Malmesbury, and served a year on the coast of Cornwall as a Sea Scout. Joining up in February 1917, he was attached to the Dorset regiment, and has seen considerable service, but the brave fellow met his end on March 15th in Palestine. Details are not to hand, but our readers' sympathy will be extended to Mr. and Mrs. Hibbard in the loss of this, their second son in the short space of 11 months.

The Roll of Honour entry wrongly identified the country;

HIBBARD.- Killed in action in Mesopotamia, Pte. James Hibbard, Dorset Regiment, youngest son of Mr. E. Hibbard, Kingswall, Malmesbury, aged 19 years.

Davies, the Revd Emlyn Holt, Chaplain, age 42, Young Men's Christian Association
Died, 18th March 1918, buried in Cerisy-Gailly Military Cemetery II B 5 (family inscription *FAITHFUL UNTO DEATH, REV 11.10*), commemorated Malmesbury Congregational Church & Triangle only.

Gailly was the site of the 39th and 13th Casualty Clearing Stations during the early part of 1917 and of the 41st Stationary Hospital from May 1917 to March 1918. The villages were then captured by the Germans but were retaken by the Australian Corps in August 1918. Cerisy-Gailly Military Cemetery was begun in February 1917 and used by medical units until March 1918. it expanded after the Armistice when graves were brought in from the battlefields of the Somme and five other small cemeteries. It now contains 745 Empire burials and commemorations of the First World War, 114 of the burials are unidentified and special memorials commemorate five casualties buried at Maricourt and Ste. Helene whose graves could not be found. The cemetery was designed by Sir Edwin Lutyens.

The Reverend Emlyn Davies was the eldest son of D. Edward and Mary Davies, of Bronwylfa, Aberystwyth. He became Minister of the Congregational Church in St. Marys Street in 1915 and Chaplain to the Red Cross Hospital, working there as a night-time orderly. In 1917 the Y.M.C.A. called for volunteers to go to France and one particular need was men who could work with Indians. Emlyn had been a missionary (but had to give up due to ill-health) and was therefore familiar with their customs and languages. Although he was over 40, married with three young children, he felt he could not ignore the call and was granted four months' leave of absence. He arrived in France on 8th January 1918 and was attached to 59th Burma Labour Corps. Unfortunately he contracted meningitis and died at the 41st Stationary Hospital at Gailly where he was buried. The North Wilts Herald reported his death;

MALMESBURY MINISTER'S SACRIFICE.
Rev. Emlyn H. Davies Dies in France.

To the long roll of heroes who have gone out from Malmesbury and laid down their lives in the Empire's cause must be added the name of the Rev. Emlyn H. Davies, B.A., B.D., pastor of the Westport Congregational Church, Malmesbury. The news that he had died of meningitis in France was received on Wednesday, and the whole community was profoundly shocked. Much sympathy is felt for Mrs. Davies, the bereaved wife, and the three young children. Mr. Davies was in December granted four months' leave of absence by his church to enable him to take up work among the troops on behalf of the Y.M.C.A. Soon after Christmas he left for France, and was posted for duty among Indian troops. For this he was specially qualified, having formerly been a missionary, for the London Missionary Society, in India.

Mr. Davies, who was a native of North Wales, was 42 years of age. He was exceptionally well fitted for his calling, possessing a rare gift of sympathy and a capacity for lightening the sorrows of others. He was a scholar not only by training but also by natural endowment.

Frail of body, sensitive of soul, yet robust in mind and intellect, Mr. Davies was not a man generally looked upon as one likely to offer himself for service in the war amidst horrors and hardships. Yet he volunteered for such work and went out with the zest and keenness of a man entrusted with a divine commission. To those who ex-

pressed doubt that he would be able to withstand the rigours of war he had but one and the same answer, "I feel that I have a call which I cannot but obey; I must go and work among the Indian troops, for there are so few who can do so." He had a great affection for the Indians, and, writing home, spoke hopefully and respectfully of his mission. Latterly he divided his time between the Indian and English troops, being very happy with the latter.

News of Mr. Davies' illness was received on Monday, and in quick succession came messages of increasing gravity, culminating by Wednesday with the sad tidings that he had passed away. To Mrs. Davies and her three young children will go out a large measure of sympathy.

On Wednesday evening, at St. Mary's, Westport, the Vicar (Canon C.D.H. McMillan) made special reference in the prayers to the bereaved widow and family. The Vicar also directed

Rev. Emlyn Davies looking very martial (military-genealogy.com) *the flag on the church should be flown at half-mast.*

A very large service of commemoration was held in the Congregational Church on Tuesday 26th March. Led by Rev. W.H. Dash, Congregational Minister from Tetbury, clergymen from the Abbey, Baptists, Silver Street Congregationalists, Primitive Methodists and Moravians attended. Civic leaders, local authority officers, members of the medical profession, military men and many others packed the church. Mr Cameron as president of the local Y.M.C.A. gave the following eulogy;

We remember eight or nine months ago when an appeal was issued from the Y.M.C.A. head-quarters in London for helpers at the front to work among the soldiers in the huts. That cry was raised by London and it reached Malmesbury, Mr. Davies heard the cry and it must have appealed to him much as the cry from Macedonia appealed to St. Paul when he heard the call, "Come over and help us." Mr. Davies responded, and when he heard the cry for help nothing would stop him or upset his resolve once he decided to go forward. Friends tried to persuade him not to go, but he said: "I feel there is a call for me to go forward." In the words of the Scripture he must have said, "Here am I, send me." The question was asked; Why did he go? I believe he went not for self-gratification, but to play the man. He felt it was his duty to go out to France and he went to render his services, more particularly among the Indian troops. He died making the great sacrifice, trying to cheer and comfort those soldiers who came from India to stand loyal and true by the side of their English friends at the front in defending their King and country. He was a brave and noble heart, with a big fine soul within a very frail, fragile body. Yet he could be a lion when there was something wanting pluck and grit. He would stand up for the right, come what may, and they felt he went out there to do his duty and undertake whatever difficult task was placed before him, and to do his best to fulfil that task. The Y.M.C.A. branch felt more than proud - they felt honoured – that they could send from Malmesbury one of their most gifted members to work among the soldiers. Not only that, but they felt honoured that they could send a member who was capable of rendering some assistance to Indian troops. That was the best of all, and that was why they felt proud in Malmesbury. We all hope that the day is far distant when they would forget to honour the name of their late pastor. An honest man was the noblest gift of God, and they fully believed Mr. Davies was an honest man, and true as steel, an honourable opponent, and never vindictive. By his life amongst them they felt that he had passed beyond and had entered into higher service.

Mrs. Davies returned to Abertillery where she resumed her former work as schoolmistress. The following appeared in the Herald's Roll of Honour;

DAVIES.- Died whilst on duty with the troops in France, the Rev. Emlyn Holt Davies, B.A., B.D., pastor of Westport Congregational Church, Malmesbury, aged 42 years.

Mackirdy, Charles David Scott, Lieutenant, 30188, age 24, 11th (Prince Albert's Own) Hussars

Died of wounds in German hands, 22nd March 1918, commemorated on Pozieres Memorial Panel 4, Malmesbury Abbey, Town Hall & Triangle.

The Pozieres Memorial relates to the period of crisis in March and April 1918 when the British Fifth Army was driven back by overwhelming numbers across the former Somme battlefields and the months that followed before the Advance to Victory which began on 8th August 1918. The Memorial commemorates over 14,000 casualties of the United Kingdom and 300 of the South African Forces who have no known grave and who died on the Somme from 21st March to 7th August 1918. There are now 2,755 Empire servicemen of the First World War buried or commemorated in this cemetery. 1,375 of the burials are unidentified but there are special memorials to 23 casualties known or believed to be buried among them. The cemetery and memorial were designed by W.H. Cowlishaw.

Charles was a son of William Augustus Scott and Lucy Scott Mackirdy (née Bell), of Birkwood, Lanarkshire. His elder brother Elliott Mackirdy Scott Mackirdy moved to Abbey House around 1906 and they had a sister Anna Mary. Before the war Charles and his cousin Leopald Fawcett were frequently in Malmesbury before Charles joined the Army. He enrolled in the Royal Military College, Sandhurst from Exeter College Oxford in August 1914. Students at Sandhurst had to pay £150 per year whilst there. On completion of the course he was commissioned into the 11th Hussars and posted to the Western Front arriving in Rouen on 18th October 1915. He was promoted to Lieutenant on 17th August 1916. His regiment were in France for the whole of the war but after early 1915 were mainly kept in reserve awaiting the elusive breakthrough. In March 1918 they were just behind the lines near Peronne on the Somme.

When the Germans attacked on 21st that afternoon the Hussars took up a position in a wood near the River Omignon between Vermand and Villecholles with the 9th East Surreys. The next morning around 10 a.m. a heavy enemy bombardment took place followed by a strong attack. Troops north of the river fell back and the order to retire was given at 11.40 a.m. It was difficult to contact all of the troops and some were missing when the unit reassembled. One of these was Charles Mackirdy. Enquiries to the Red Cross in Geneva confirmed his death in early July. The North Wilts Herald carried the following report later that month;

The Pozieres Memorial

THE LATE LIEUT. SCOTT MACKIRDY.- Lieut. C.D. Scott Mackirdy, Hussars, who was posted wounded and missing on March 22nd is now unofficially reported to have died of wounds on that date. He was born at Rothesay, Isle of Bute, the old home of the Mackirdy family, on September 25th, 1893, and was educated at Uppingham School and Exeter College, Oxford. He got his commission as a regular officer in November, 1914, from Sandhurst, and he had served continuously with his regiment in France since October, 1915. He was promoted lieutenant on August 17th, 1917. Mr. Mackirdy was the younger brother of Captain Eliot Mackirdy of Birkwood Castle, Lanarkshire, and Abbey House, Malmesbury, Royal Horse Guards, who was invalided home from France in December, 1916, after service with the Household Battalion.

The same paper's Roll of Honour included;

SCOTT MACKIRDY.-Wounded and missing since March 22nd, 1918, now reported died of wounds on that date, Charles David Scott Mackirdy, Lieutenant Hussars, younger son of the late W.A. Scott Mackirdy, J.P., D.L., of Birkwood Castle, Lesmahagow.

GERMAN ADVANCE
27th. March — 5th. April.

From *Military Operations 1918*

Tugwell, Joseph Mark Washington, Signaller, 202658, age 25, 1/4th Battalion Duke of Edinburgh's (Wiltshire Regiment) Territorial Force

Killed in action, 9th April 1918, buried in Ramleh Cemetery S 66, commemorated Malmesbury Abbey (initials showed as JSW), Town Hall, Triangle and in Swindon.

For a description of Ramleh Cemetery see Private Ernest James Hibbard above.

Joseph was the middle son of John (a breeches maker) and Tryphena Tugwell of Cross Hayes, with brothers George & Francis and sisters Elizabeth & Elsie. In 1913 he married Minnie Gertrude Woollacott, had a daughter Doreen in 1915 at Malmesbury and moved to 9 Witney St., Swindon. He was called up on 1st January 1917 and posted to the Wiltshire Regiment. Trained as a signaller he was sent as a reinforcement to 1/4th Battalion in Palestine. Signallers were specialists within an infantry unit with a number of privileges. There were up to 18 in a battalion under a sergeant with their own billet out of the line and were exempt from fatigues. However the disadvantage was that at the front telephone lines were tested every 15 minutes and if there was no response two 'wire-boys' would have to trace the route and repair the break. This was done whatever the weather, often exposed to enemy fire and at any time of the day or night. The war diary reads;

Tuesday 9th April 1918 Palestine, 099 A25 c55

0515. The Battalion moved out to the starting point for its share in the days operations. The general intention was for the 75th Division to advance its line to KH el FAKHAKHIR (098 S 27b) - ridge in S26 c,d - SH SUBIH ridge (084 N 24 d, 098 s19c, d) - ARARA (084 N 29 a,b) - RAFAT (085 V 4,a) - 085 V 7a HILL 839. The part allotted to this battalion was to take part of SH SUBIH ridge from the tomb (exclusive) to the E end.

0630. The Battalion was in preliminary position ready to advance, No 1 and 3 Coys in firing line, and No 2 and 4 in reserve, the LG's of the two reserve Coys being grouped under Lieut H M Thurgar. In the meantime Major C.G. Bennett, with Signallers and spare LG men for filling magazines (Post A) proceeded up the WADI ARAK and took up position at A7c 39 in the N ridge of the wadi.

Owing to the advance being delayed longer than was anticipated the Battalion remained in this position during the greater part of the day. The front line in moving forward a short distance down the S ridge of the WADI ARAK came under sniper and MG fire and there were several casualties. At night the Battalion moved down into the WADI ARAK and took up a position across the head of the wadi (A7a).

The Herald reported his death as follows;

Signaller Joseph Mark Washington Tugwell was killed in action in Egypt on April 9th. He was the son of Mr. J. Tugwell, of Cross Hayes, Malmesbury, and a son-in-law of Mr. W.H. Woollacott, of 9, Witney Street, Swindon. He joined the Army on Jan. 1st, 1917. His intention was to go into the Royal Engineers, but he was drafted into the Wiltshires as a signaller. He went out to

Egypt in November. He was 25 years of age, and had been married for four years. He leaves a widow and one child. The Wilts & Gloucester Standard had this in its Death Column on 11th May;

TUGWELL.- April 9, killed in action in Palestine, Signaller Joseph M.W. Tugwell, Wilts Regt., son of Mr. J. Tugwell, Cross Hayes, Malmesbury, 25 years.

Part of Ramleh Cemetery

Bye, (Albert) William, Private, 37395, age 18, 1/5th Battalion Duke of Cornwall's Light Infantry Territorial Force

Missing presumed killed, 12th April 1918 (although the Commonwealth War Graves Commission say 17th), commemorated on the Loos Memorial Panel 68 and Malmesbury Triangle only. For a description of the Loos Memorial see Private James Herbert above.

Albert Willie (who used William as his Christian name) Bye seems to have had a troubled background. His mother, Topsey Twinn, was apparently born in Chelmsford but by 1891 she had married Obed Bye, a Malmesbury blacksmith. The couple lived with his widowed mother in Gloucester Street. Topsey became a silk weaver and had at least four sons; Napier, James, Alfred & William. William was born on 9th May 1899 in the Workhouse and no father is named on the certificate. At the time of the 1901 census the mother, by now widowed, was still in the workhouse with her four sons. William was again unfortunate in that after his call up men were rushed to France to try to stop the German advance. He was posted to the 1/5th Battalion Duke of Cornwall's Light Infantry (5th DCLI) which was the Pioneer unit of 61st Division.

This division was involved in heavy fighting on the Somme during the period 21st-31st March and was moved north to a quieter area along the River Lys. The Regimental history described them thus; *But the whole of the draft (more than 400 men had just joined the battalion) were youths without any experience of real war and the change, practically from the barrack square to the firing line against a well-trained, war-bitten enemy was a terrible experience.* Unfortunately this was where the Germans attacked on 9th April and The 5th DCLI was drawn into the battle on the 11th under the command of 51st Division. The previous night they were in billets at Thiennes and the next morning they moved into the front line south of Merville. Although subjected to fire from enemy machine guns this position was not attacked until 7.30 a.m. the following day. Units on either side of the DCLI withdrew and since the enemy had worked around both flanks the Cornwalls withdrew to near Calonne sur la Lys. This line was held for 1½ hours despite no formed unit of troops being on ei-

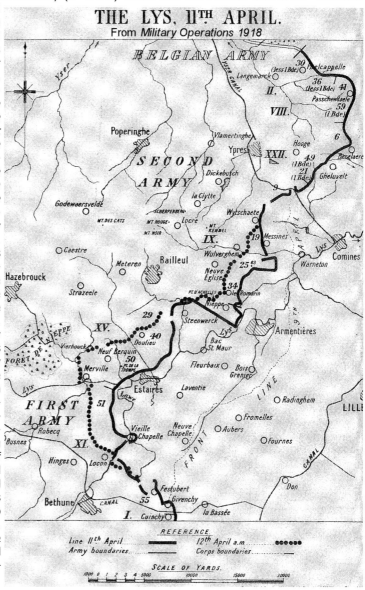

THE LYS, 11TH APRIL.
From *Military Operations 1918*

197

ther side of them. Thus another withdrawal was required which continued slowly during the day as they had little support. Heavy casualties were suffered throughout the day. At midnight they were taken out of the line and the unit went back to its usual function of preparing defensive positions close to the front. No details of casualties are recorded after the 12th when conditions became less chaotic so it is most likely that William died on the 12th. However he was posted as missing so his death was not confirmed until after Mrs. Duck's memorial had been completed.

The Herald's Roll of Honour entry appeared 16 months later on 8th August 1919;

BYE – Pte. William Bye, 1/5th Duke of Cornwall's Light Infantry, fourth son of Mrs. Bye, of Foxley Road, Malmesbury, killed in action in France, between April 11th and 17th, 1918, aged 18 years.

Poole, Henry George, Private, 1308, age 28, 15th Battalion Army Cyclist Corps
Died of wounds, 14th April 1918, buried in Aire Communal Cemetery, II C 8 (family inscription *EVER MOURNED BY, HIS SORROWING MOTHER, BROTHERS AND SISTERS, REST IN PEACE*), commemorated Malmesbury Abbey, Town Hall & Triangle.

From March 1915 to February 1918, Aire was a busy but peaceful centre used by British forces as corps headquarters. The Highland Casualty Clearing Station was based there as was the 39th Stationary Hospital (from May 1917) and other medical units. Plot I contains burials from this period. The burials in plots II, III and IV (rows A to F) relate to the fighting of 1918, when the 54th Casualty Clearing Station came to Aire and the town was, for a while, within 13 kilometres of the German lines. The cemetery now contains 894 Empire burials of the First World War and a few French and German war graves. There are also 21 Second World War burials. The British plots were designed by Sir Herbert Baker.

Henry was a son of Dennis (who worked for Newman's Grocers and died in 1916) and Rosa Poole, of 16 King's Wall. He had two older brothers James & Arthur, two younger brothers William & Frederick and four sisters Minnie, Emily, Eliza & Evelyn. Rosa lived to become the oldest woman in Malmesbury, dying at the age of 97 on Christmas Day 1952. Henry joined the Wiltshire Regiment on 11th August 1908 after having worked as a gardener. He was posted to the 2nd Battalion in Gibraltar which returned to England on the outbreak of war. He served on the Western Front from 6th October 1914. In August 1915 he was reported well;

LOCAL SOLDIERS IN FRANCE.- From "somewhere in France," Corpl. C. Gale, 6th Wilts, has written home to say that there was a football match on Saturday between teams of the 6th and the 2nd Battalion of the Wilts Regiment. The battalions are only five miles apart. The 6th won the match by 2 goals to 1. The Malmesbury men in the 6th met several old friends. Willis Tugwell encountered Dick Pike and Harry Poole at the football match, and a compact was made between them to visit each other as soon as possible.

Harry transferred to the Army Cyclist Corps in January 1915, being posted to A Company of 15th Battalion and came home on leave in February 1916 and July 1917. Although the Cyclist Corps was intended to be used as mobile troops for home defence or scouts similar to cavalry, for the most part they were used on more mundane duties on the lines of communications or as labourers. However during the fast moving battles of the Spring of 1918 they were again used in their original role, being able to move quickly to plug holes in the line. When the Germans launched their Lys offensive on 9th April the main blow fell on the 2nd Portuguese Division which was swept away. XV Corps to their North sought to stabilise the position by moving two brigades led by patrols from 15th Battalion Army Cyclist Corps behind the Portuguese. They quickly became embroiled in battle. For the next three days they supported 5th, 6th and 8th Durham Light Infantry as well as patrolling to check the enemy's progress. By the night of the 12th their casualties were one officer and two men killed, four officers and 38 men wounded and 12 missing (two believed to be prisoners). One of the wounded was Henry Poole who was evacuated to Aire, the base of 39th Stationary Hospital where he died from a fractured skull. The Wilts and Gloucester Standard carried a short report on 27th April;

A wire has reached Mrs. D. Poole of King's Wall, Malmesbury, to the effect that her son, Private Harry Poole, has been killed in action in Flanders. He was a bright and cheerful lad, a regular attendant at Silver-street Church, and much respected. Great sympathy is extended to the bereaved mother and the family which has contributed three soldier sons to the Army.

Savine, Hubert John, Gunner, 133077 age 28, 88th Brigade Royal Field Artillery
Died of wounds, 15th April 1918, buried at Wimereux Communal Cemetery XI A 1 (family inscription *OBEDIENT UNTO DEATH, FOR GOD, KING AND COUNTRY*), commemorated Malmesbury Abbey, Town Hall & Triangle.
For a description of Wimereux Cemetery see Rifleman Frank Deadman above.
Hubert (known as Bertram) was the eldest son of John (a cattle dealer who had previously run the Suffolk Arms) and Eliza Savine, of Filands. Bert had two brothers, Ernest & Stanley and a sister, Elsie. He served in 'A' Battery of the 88th Brigade of the Royal Field Artillery firing 18 pounder guns in support of the 19th Division which included the 6th Wiltshires. Little information about his service can be found and the war diary gives no information about personnel. The Brigade was heavily involved in the major German attack between 21st and 27th March after which it was sent north for a rest. 'A' Battery went into action on 3rd April but another major enemy assault began on the 9th. The following day the unit took part in a gallant stand that resulted in a V.C. for its commander, Capt. E.S. Dougall, as recounted in *The Nineteenth Division 1914-1918*;
This officer maintained his guns in action near Messines on the 10th of April throughout the heavy concentration of hostile shell-fire. When, finding he could not clear the the crest of the ridge, owing to the withdrawal of our line, Capt. Dougall ran his guns on to the top of the ridge to fire over open sights. By this time our infantry had been pressed back in line with the guns. Capt Dougall at once assumed command of the situation, rallied and organised the infantry, supplied them with Lewis-guns and armed as many gunners as he could spare with rifles. With these he formed a line in front of his battery which, during this period, was harassing the advancing Germans with rapid fire. When one gun was turned over by a direct hit and the detachment knocked out, casualties were replaced and the gun brought into action again. Although exposed to both rifle and machine-gun fire, Capt. Dougall fearlessly walked about as though on parade, calmly giving orders and encouraging everyone. His remark to the infantry at this juncture: "So long as you stick to your trenches I will keep my guns here," had a most inspiring effect on all ranks. The line was maintained throughout the day, thereby delaying the enemy's entry into Messines for over twelve hours. In the evening, having expended all their ammunition, the battery received orders to withdraw. This was done by man-handling the guns over a distance of about 800 yards of shell-cratered country, an almost impossible feat considering the ground and intense machine-gun fire.
Perhaps Hubert was wounded during this desperate fight. The Standard on 20th April stated;
It is also variously reported that the eldest son of Mr. and Mrs. John Savine has been killed or seriously wounded.
The North Wilts Herald reported;
Yet another family, that of Mr. J. Savine, Filands, has been bereaved by the death from wounds of Bertram, Mr. and Mrs. Savine's eldest son. He had served in the R.F.A. for two years. As a result of shell wounds he had to undergo amputation of the left leg, with fatal result. Much sympathy is felt for the parents in their sorrow. They have two other sons serving.
The Roll of Honour entry was;
SAVINE.- April 15th, of wounds received in action in France, Hubert John Savine, R.F.A., eldest son of Mr. John Savine, Filands, Malmesbury, aged 28 years.

Willis, Herbert James, Private, 35969, age 18, 6th (Service) Battalion Duke of Edinburgh's (Wiltshire Regiment)
Killed in action, 15th April 1918, commemorated at Tyne Cot Memorial Panel 119 to 120, Malmesbury Abbey, Town Hall & Triangle.
The Tyne Cot Memorial is one of four memorials to the missing in Belgian Flanders which cover the Ypres Salient. Broadly speaking, the Salient stretched from Langemarck in the north to the northern edge in Ploegsteert Wood in the south, but it varied in area and shape throughout the war. The battles of the Ypres Salient claimed many lives on both sides and it quickly became clear that the commemoration of members of the Empire forces with no known grave would have to be divided between several different sites. Those United Kingdom and New Zealand servicemen who died after 16th August 1917 are named on the memorial at Tyne Cot, a site which marks the furthest point reached by British forces in Belgium until nearly the end of the war. The Memorial bears the names of almost 35,000 officers and men

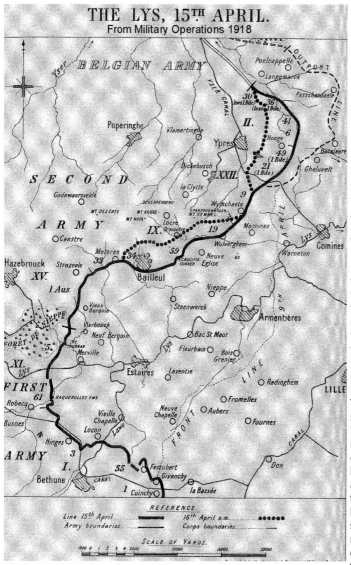

THE LYS, 15TH APRIL.
From Military Operations 1918

REFERENCE.
Line 15th April............ ▪▪▪▪▪ 16th April a.m. ....●●●●●●
Army boundaries............━━━━ Corps boundaries............━━━━

SCALE OF YARDS.

whose graves are not known. Designed by Sir Herbert Baker with sculpture by Joseph Armitage and F. V. Blundstone, it was unveiled by Sir Gilbert Dyett in July 1927. The memorial forms the north-eastern boundary of Tyne Cot Cemetery, which was established around a captured German blockhouse or pill-box used as an advanced dressing station. The original battlefield cemetery of 343 graves was greatly enlarged after the Armistice when remains were brought in from the battlefields of Passchendaele and Langemarck and from a few small burial grounds. It is now the largest Commonwealth war cemetery in the world in terms of burials. At the suggestion of King George V who visited the cemetery in 1922, the Cross of Sacrifice was placed on the original large pill-box. There are three other pill-boxes in the cemetery. There are now 11,952 Empire servicemen of the First World War buried or commemorated in Tyne Cot Cemetery. 8,365 of the burials are unidentified but there are special memorials to more than 80 casualties known or believed to be buried among them. Other special memorials commemorate 20 casualties whose graves were destroyed by shell fire.

Herbert was the eldest son of James and Agnes Willis. James was born in Sherston where he developed a wood working business before moving to Malmesbury in the early years of the 20th Century. He lived at 38 St. John's Street with his children Doris, Gladys, Nellie and Herbert's younger brother Frederick (who later had four sons - still in business known as Willis Brothers and famed for event course construction throughout the world).

Herbert had a police record as reported in the Wiltshire Gazette on 4th January 1917;

Herbert Willis, a youth, was charged with using obscene language in Archer's Lane, Burton Hill, on December 12th, at 8 p.m. in company with other lads. Sergeant Harris stated the facts, which were corroborated by Supt. Witt, and defendant was fined 2s. 6d., being allowed to pay within a week.

He was conscripted shortly after his birthday in late 1917 and sent to Devizes. He was unfortunate because, following the big German offensive of 21st March, it was decided to send 18 year olds to the front. He arrived in France on 2nd April and probably was part of the draft that joined 6th Wiltshires on 12th April as described in the war diary;

On the 12th April the Bn. was withdrawn to ROSSIGNOL CAMP near KEMMEL.

270 Reinforcements were waiting here & the Battn. was re-organised mustering 450 strong - and moved to BABADOS camp via CLYTTE for the night.

At 10.30 a.m. the next day orders were received to stand by ready to move & a quarter of an hour later the Battn. was ordered to march to a position of readiness between LA CLYTTE & KEMMEL east of the main road. At 12 noon C.Os were warned that the Bde. would take over the lines that night from the S. African Bde. Details of the relief could not be given until 4.30 p.m. at the S. Africans Bde. H.Q. & then were very complicated. The Bn. was to take over from 4 units - a portion of the 4th S. African Bn., the whole of the 1st S. African Bn., 2 Coys. of the 10th R. Warwicks R. & 1 Coy. of the S.W.B. The front it was to take over was about 800 yds. & included the extremely important high ground at the SPANBROEK - MOLEN CRATER. The Bn. marched up from its position of readiness and although all companies were in position by 3 a.m., the relief was not reported complete till 6 a.m.

The Bn. was disposed as follows from left to right –

'A' Coy. two platoons front line, one in support east of SPAENBROEK MOLEN CRATER.

'B', 'C' & 'D' Coys each two platoons in front line & one in support from left to right. On the right of 'D' Coy. were the 12th R.I.R. and on the left of 'A' Coy. were the 9th R.W.F.

Bn. H.Q. were 300 yards in rear of the front line just W. of SPANBROEK MOLEN CRATER.

The 14th April was an abnormally quiet day; the enemy Artillery was more or less inactive except on the area round Bn. H.Q. which later moved to REGENT ST. DUG OUTS. N29.c.central.

On the night of the 14th it was decided that the dispositions of the Bn. required adjustment - It was decided to push up the whole of 'A' & 'D' Coys into the front line & withdraw the whole of 'B' & 'C' Coys. into support, 'B' on the left 'C' on the right, covering 'A' & 'D' respectively.

In addition to ensure the security of SPANBROEK MOLEN the G.O.C. placed 1 Coy. of the 9th Welch at the disposal of O.C. 6th Wilts R. The O.C. this Coy. ('B' Coy) was accordingly ordered to send 1 platoon to be in close support to 'A' Coy. just east of the CRATER, and place the remainder of his Company in a position S. West of the CRATER from which it would be ready to launch an immediate counter attack against the high ground should this be lost, or reinforce the front lines.

These alterations in the dispositions of the Battn. were carried out during the night of the 14th/15th.

At dawn on the 15th the enemy opened a heavy H.E. barrage on the whole subsector particularly along support line, and in the area round REGENT ST DUG OUTS.

About 5.45 a.m. the S.O.S. went up on the left Coy. front. The enemy were attacking on the right Coy. front and on the front of the battn. on our right.

The attack failed to reach our front line, but the enemy succeeded in penetrating the front of the 12th R.I.R. who were at the time attempting to carry out a withdrawal, using their left flank as a pivot - The enemy occupied R.E. & SHELL FARMS and made it necessary, first for half of 'C' Coy. to move up & occupy a line, running approximately E. & W. North of SHELL farm and secondly for 'D' Coy. in order to safeguard its right flank, to bend its right back on to the left of the 'C' Coy's front line.

The line therefore was intact, though thinly held; enemy snipers and machine guns were extremely active, & being close, hindered movement & the organisation of our new front on the Southern flank.

On the remainder of the Battn. front enemy movement was vigorously checked by snipers & Lewis guns - In spite of very heavy shelling in the earlier part of the day, casualties on the left half of the front were slight.

As the line was so thinly held on right, it was decided to dribble 1 platoon of 'B' Coy of the 9th Welch up into the front line held by 'C' & 'D' Coys. and to move 1 platoon up into support behind 'D' Coy's left. This was successfully done.

That night orders were received to withdraw from the front line South of the SPANBROEK MOLEN CRATER - this meant that the line occupied by three Coys. 'B', 'C' & 'D' was to be evacuated, while that held by 'A' Coy was to be handed over to the 62nd Bde. att. 9th Division. This Coy. which consisted of about 120 men (including the supporting platoon of 'B' Coy, 9th Welch) handed over the line to 19 men of the 1/7th West Yorks and it was due to this severe weakening of the garrison of such important ground that the crater was lost the next day (16th inst.)

During the night of the 15th/16th the Battn. withdrew without molestation, according to the orders outlined above - At dawn it was taking up positions astride the KEMMEL - WYTSCHAETE road, just E. of PARRAIN FARM where Bn. H.Q. were established. The Battn. was here in support to the 9th Welch who were holding the line from a point just S. of SPANBROEKMOLEN CRATER to SPY FARM.

'B' Coy. was ordered to dig a series of posts in the N.E. corner of N.28.b and 'A', 'C' & 'D' Coys. were distributed in partly dug positions over the area N. & S. of PARRAIN FARM.

The Battn. remained in these positions for two days - during which time SPANBROEKMOLEN was lost.

Appendix

APPROXIMATE CASUALTIES to the 6th Wilts R. between the 10th April & 20th April 1918 –

1. No. going into the line on the night of the 7th/8th April;- 11 Officers, 580 Other ranks.
2. No. coming out of the line 12th April - 5 Officers, 175 Other ranks.
   Reinforcements & attachments 5 Officers, 270 Other ranks.
3. No. going into the line on the night of the 13th April - 10 Officer, 380 Other ranks.
4. No. coming out of the line on the night of the 18th/19th April - 4 Officers, 250 Other Ranks.

The Spanbroekmolen Crater was created by one of the 19 mines exploded at the start of the Messines battle in June 1917. After the war it filled with water, was bought by Toc H and is now called the Pool of Peace.

On 10th May the first newspaper report stated that Herbert was missing;

BELIEVED MISSING.- Pte. Herbert Willis (18½), of 38, St. Johns Street, who is in the Wilts Regiment, is believed to be missing since April 15th.

However the following week his death was confirmed. The Gazette had this report on 16th May;

Harold Willis, who, previously engaged in a fish shop in the town, joined the Wilts Regiment at the age of 18½ years, on the 2nd November, and on 2nd April put foot on French soil. By the 15th April he was killed, and much sympathy is felt with his parents, who live in St. John Street.

On 30th May this appeared in the Deaths column;

WILLIS.- April 15th, killed in action in France, Private Herbert Willis, Wilts Regiment, son of James Willis, St. John Street, Malmesbury, aged 18 years.

A year later the following appeared in the In Memoriam column of the North Wilts Herald;

WILLIS.- In loving memory of our dear boy, Pte. Herbert Willis, 4th Wilts Regiment, killed in action, April 15th, 1918, aged 18½ years.

> He bravely answered his country's call,
> He gave his young life for one and all;
> His heart was good, his spirit brave,
> God bless him in his hero's grave.
>   Rest in Peace

Inserted by his loving Mother and Father, Brother and Sisters, 38, St. John Street, Malmesbury. And in 1921 the entry read;

WILLIS.- In ever loving memory of Pte. Herbert Willis, killed in action on April 15th, 1918, aged 18½ years.

> No morning dawns, no night returns,
> But that we think of him,
> Who gave his life and fought so brave,
> He slumbers now in a hero's grave.

Ever remembered by his sorrowing Mother and Father, Brother and Sisters, 38, St. John Street, Malmesbury.

Barnes, William, Gunner, 144961, age 27, 27th Siege Battery Royal Garrison Artillery
Died of wounds, 17th April 1918, buried in Malmesbury Baptist Cemetery (private grave-stone), commemorated Malmesbury Abbey, Cirencester Benefit Society, Town Hall & Triangle. Malmesbury Baptist Cemetery is in Burnham Road on the north side between Halfway House and No. 15. William's grave is to the left of the path about five metres from the north wall. He is buried in the same grave as his elder brother, Joseph, mother Emily and sister Ellen. William was the eldest son of Joseph (carpenter) & Emily (who died in 1899) Barnes, 56 High Street, with brothers Joseph (who died aged 2) & Edward and sisters Mary, Adelaide, Ellen

(died in 1905) & Margaret. He enlisted in the Militia on 4th Dec 1906 but did not transfer to the Special Reserve when that was formed in 1908. He was a carpenter, the family trade, living with his parents and unmarried when he enlisted under the Derby Scheme 9th December 1915 (the day before the scheme ended). Edward, his younger brother, enlisted on the same day and being only 20 was called up on 29th February 1916. William then appealed against conscription in April 1916. The report in the Gazette was;

Messrs. Barnes & Son, of High Street, Malmesbury, appealed

Victims of mustard gas. (westernfrontassociation.com)

for William Barnes, 25, (who had been put back ten groups), carpenter, joiner and undertaker. Mr. Barnes said if he were called up the business, which had been established for 40 years, would have to be closed, as his father was 70 years of age, and unable to take any active part in the work. His younger brother, who had worked in the trade for seven years had been called up; and as his work consisted chiefly in undertaking it was necessary and important from the national point of view. - The Chairman: We give you up to 1st of July, but we think you might join the Volunteer Training Corps in which to get ready - learn how to use the rifle, etc. Will you do this? - Appellant: Oh, yes, I will. - The Chairman: Very well, the exemption is granted on those conditions.

Another appeal was heard in December 1916 when a final date for exemption of 1st March was given.

William was called up on 14th March 1917 and posted to 385th Siege Battery, Royal Garrison Artillery at Plymouth for training. Sent to France on 17th July 1917 he joined 27th Siege Battery equipped with 6" howitzers. In early 1918 they were based near Vermelles, between Bethune and Lens. Artillery units were frequently shelled with a large proportion of gas being used to impair their efficiency. The Germans first used lethal gas (chlorine) released from cylinders in April 1915. That June they introduced Phosgene (Green Cross, so called because such a mark was painted on shells filled with it) and the more persistent Mustard (Yellow Cross) in July 1917. The latter was actually a liquid which collected on the ground and slowly vaporised over a period of hours or days. If splashed on to flesh it would create blisters. Mustard gas was the preferred agent for artillery positions, exposure to it caused severe pains in the head, throat and eyes as well as vomiting and bronchial irritation. William was gassed on 8th April 1918 and admitted to 35th Field Ambulance. From there he went to 14th General Hospital at Wimereux before being evacuated on the 13th on the Army Transport 'Brighton' to Norwich War Hospital where he died.

The Wilts and Gloucester Standard reported on 20th April;

Mr. Joseph Barnes, of High-street, Malmesbury, this week received the news that his eldest son Private William Barnes, was lying in a hospital at Dover suffering badly from gas in the recent fighting. Besides the pain engendered by that devilish mode of fighting, we understand that the poor lad had been blinded as well.

Mr. Barnes and sister journeyed to Dover to visit the sufferer in hospital, but immediately after their departure a wire was handed in at the home stating that Private Barnes had succumbed. The young fellow was a most steady and respected lad and belonged to the third generation of the Barnes family who carry on the business of carpenters and undertakers. The greatest sympathy is felt for the father and brother and sisters of the deceased.

There is no indication in his Service Record that William was admitted to a Dover Hospital and the 'Morning State of Sick' on his file was issued by the Norfolk War Hospital, Thorpe showing the causes of death as (1) Gas poisoning with Shell Gas (2) Broncho-pneumonia, 12.45 p.m., 17.4.1918. The funeral was held the following week;

Although it is usual to give one who falls for his country on active service full military honours, yet on Tuesday the wishes of Mr. Joseph Barnes and family were respected and the young man of 27, Gunner William Barnes, who succumbed to German gas, was laid to rest, after a quiet and impressive ceremony in the chapel he so long attended at Abbey Row. The passing bell apprised the townspeople of the sad event, while the Abbey and Westport St. Mary's flags stood at half-mast. Many people lined the streets as the cortege passed through to the service at the Baptist Chapel, and every token of respect was paid to the memory of the deceased soldier. Among the earliest attendants were the Vicar (Canon McMillan) and his curate, Rev. F.R. Webb. The coffin was of polished oak with brass furniture and bore a floral cross – the family tribute. The hearse was followed by two mourning coaches, the mourners being Mr. Joseph Barnes (father), his three daughters, and his sister, Miss Barnes …
After the closing hymn the rites of interment were performed by Mr. Farmer in the Baptist Cemetery, Burnham-road. The deceased's younger brother Ted is serving in France.

The Herald's Roll of Honour reads;

BARNES.- April 17th, at Norwich, after gas poisoning whilst on active service, Gunner William Barnes, R.G.A., elder son of Mr. Joseph Barnes, of 56, High Street, Malmesbury, aged 27 years.

Woodman, Edgar, Private, 260214, age 31, 2/5th Battalion Gloucestershire Regiment Territorial Force

Died of wounds, 24th April 1918, buried at St. Venant-Robecq Road British Cemetery, Robecq IV C 15 (family inscription *GREATER LOVE HATH NO MAN, THAT HE GIVETH HIS LIFE, FOR HIS LOVED ONES*), commemorated Malmesbury Abbey, Congregational Church, School, Town Hall & Triangle.

For much of the First World War, the villages of St. Venant and Robecq remained practically undamaged, but in April 1918, in the Battle of the Lys, the German line was established within 2 kilometres of the road that joins them. The cemetery was begun around 12th April and used as a front line cemetery until the end of July. At the Armistice it contained 47 burials, but was then greatly enlarged when graves were brought in from the battlefields south of St. Venant and from other cemeteries in the vicinity. St. Venant-Robecq Road British Cemetery now contains 479 burials and commemorations of the First World War. 85 of the graves are unidentified but there are special memorials to five casualties known or believed to be buried among them. The cemetery was designed by Sir Herbert Baker.

Edgar was the son of John (a carpenter & joiner) and Mary Woodman, with brothers Arthur & Harold and sisters Ada, Carrie & Annie. He married Lillian Ethel Goddard in 1908 and later that year their son William Horace was born. Their second son Leslie, who was to die in the next war, was born in 1915. Edgar joined the Army under the Derby Scheme and was attested in Malmesbury on 25th November 1915. However in December 1916 his employer appealed to the Tribunal;

William Dyer (39), married, 24, Gastons-road, Malmesbury, solicitor's clerk, C3 and Edgar Woodman (29), married, 35, Gastons-road, clerk to the Registrar and High Bailiff of the County Court, were appealed for by Messrs. Forrester, Moir and Co., their employers. Dyer was given conditional exemption, and Woodman till March 13th.

An appeal was made to the County Tribunal in January 1917;

An appeal was made by Messrs. Forrester and Moir, solicitors, of Malmesbury, for Edgar Woodman, a clerk, of Gaston's-road, Malmesbury. The man is 30 years of age, married, and passed for general service. The Tribunal held that some other clerk should be put in Woodman's place, and the decision of the local Tribunal was upheld.

Edgar was clerk to St. Paul Without Parish Council who agreed in February to appoint a temporary clerk during his military service. Mobilised on 16th March 1917 he joined the Wiltshire Territorial Force reserve unit with whom he trained. Shipped to France on 18th June 1917, he was transferred to the Gloucesters on 20th July. He was posted to their 2/5th Battalion as part of a large draft of reinforcements following many casualties in the Spring battles around Arras. That August they took part in the offensive near Ypres before moving back to Arras in September. In both places many men became casualties but these were not nearly as heavy as those suffered in the last ten days of March 1918. The battalion was then in the front line reserve, manning the Battle Zone in Holnon Wood west of St. Quentin, when the German offensive struck. They took part in particularly fierce fighting as they retreated losing 20 officers and 550 men, leaving only 150 men. After only a fortnight they returned to the front near St. Venant, north west of Bethune. On 23rd April the battalion was ordered to straighten out a kink in the line and recover Bacquerolles Farm to the east of Robecq. The attack started at 4.30 a.m. and was completely successful. An extract from the war diary reads;

4.25AM Barrage commenced 4.30AM Advance commenced 4.33AM Barrage magnificent. Objectives gained with slight casualties. Reports received from Coys. 5.15AM C.O. goes up to superintend consolidation. 5.15AM All objectives consolidated.

79 prisoners and 10 to 14 machine-guns (some were later destroyed) were captured. However the enemy began a heavy bombardment at noon which lasted until 5 a.m. the following morning when they counter-attacked. Unfortunately Edgar was one of the casualties which totalled three officers and 28 other ranks killed, 21 missing as well as one officer and 100 men wounded. The North Wilts Herald reported his death;

MALMESBURY SOLDIER KILLED.

The Late Pte. E. Woodman.

One of the most popular young men in Malmesbury was Mr. Edgar Woodman, of Gastons Road, clerk to the office of Messrs. Forrester, Moir and Company. Early in 1916 he joined the Army, and in due course served with his regiment – the Gloucesters – in France. Very severe fighting was experienced by him and he wrote to his wife (who is the daughter of Mr. W. Goddard) and also to Mr. Moir cheery letters. On Friday, however, the news was received that he had been killed on April 24th. The sad message was a grievous blow to his young wife. To her and her two children will be extended the sincere sympathy of a wide circle of friends.

The late Pte. E. Woodman, who was 31 years of age, entered the services of Messrs. Forrester, Moir & Co. in 1902. That was in the late Mr. Forrester's time, and Mr. Moir recalls how Mr. Forrester introduced him to the diminutive boy who, in the years which followed developed into a most capable man and a worthy citizen. Mr. Woodman eventually became chief County Court clerk under the Registrar (Mr. C.F. Moir). The duties of the office were carried out by him in a wonderfully efficient manner; he was careful and painstaking, and a marvel of accuracy in the intricate work. He was also assistant overseer of the parish of St. Paul Without, and good work was done by him as secretary of Court King Athelstan, A.O.F. He was regarded with affectionate esteem by his Forester Brethren, for he had served them loyally. At a meeting on Monday evening the Court unanimously passed a vote of condolence and sympathy with Mrs. Woodman and the family in their bereavement.

In a letter to Mrs. Woodman Corpl. Flowers wrote; "It is after much thought and with much pain that I write these few lines of sympathy. We all hoped to the last that your husband would get over his wounds, we were very sorry that he had succumbed to them. We were undergoing a terrific bombardment at the time when he was hit. I was some little way off, but I immediately rushed to him. All that could be done for him was done for him, but wounds in the head are so difficult to deal with. You have probably heard from the Chaplain and officers of our Platoon who have told you that he had a proper burial. He made but few friends, but I am pleased to say I was one of them. You may think that we with seeing so much death grow callous and cold, such is not true, and we miss him badly. I knew him for what he was, a Christian man with the highest principles. I am pleased to say he was true to the last. I knew his devotion to you and the children and I do pray God's blessing on them and you. I can realise a little of what you must feel. Allow me to offer you my deepest sympathy. I feel for you and my deepest thoughts are with you. May he watch over you in the difficult days that are before you."

The 2/5th Gloucesters were part of 61st Division.

The Gazette had a similar report which additionally said; *a very recent message to his wife stated that he had just come through a tight engagement unhurt, and was now in a rest camp, where an impromptu band helped to make matters bright and comfortable.* Mrs. Woodman received another letter from her husband's platoon commander, who seems to have been lucky enough to survive the war;

British Expeditionary Force France   Saturday 4 May 1918

Dear Mrs Woodman,

I have no doubt ere this, the official news of your husband's death will have reached you. In one way I am glad, for I think it would be too painful for me to be the first to convey the sad news to you.

Your husband was in my platoon and at the time of his receiving his wound, I was in the next post, about 10 yards away. It is very hard to write to you explaining my sorrow when I know yours is so much heavier and deeper. I can, and do commend you in your dark hour to God who comforts us in all our tribulations, that we may be able to comfort them which are in any trouble by the comfort wherewith we ourselves are comforted of God. (2 Cor 1-4).

We in the platoon have lost a friend and a comrade, but you have lost so much more, a husband.

I can only in a little measure enter into your sorrow, but I eternally pray that God give you His grace and consolation. Words are so cold, but God does answer prayer.

Of one thing I am glad, your husband was a Christian and because of that would not have us sorrow as those who have no hope. For we have a clear hope by faith through our Lord Jesus Christ that soon all who trust in God will be happily reunited in His presence.

My warmest sympathy and remembrance in prayer goes out to you and your children at this time. I commend you to Him who has promised to be a husband to the widow and a father to the fatherless.

Your husband's wound was in the head and he was quite unconscious till he passed away.

Believe me
Very sincerely yours
H.G. Mansfield 2 Lieut. 2/5 Gloucestershires

On 23rd May the Gazette told of his memorial service;

THE LATE PRIVATE E. WOODMAN.- A memorial service for the late Private Edgar Woodman, Gloucestershire Regiment killed in action, was held at Westport Congregational Chapel last evening. For several years the deceased was a sincere worshipper there, and he was beloved by his fellow members. This church has a long roll of honour, including the late pastor, the Rev. Emlyn H. Davies. Last night's service was attended by a large and representative congregation, including Foresters in full regalia, Bro. Woodman being the secretary of the local court. Canon McMillan (vicar) took part in the service – an impressive one – and a splendid tribute to deceased's character was given from the pulpit.

In April 1919 this appeared In Memoriam;

WOODMAN.- In loving memory of our dear son and brother, Pte. Edgar Woodman (260214), 2/5th Gloucesters, killed in action, April 24th, 1918.

> *He nobly answered duty's call,*
> *His life he gave for one and all;*
> *A loving son, a brother kind,*
> *A beautiful memory left behind.*

Inserted by Mother, Sister and Brother, Corston

The following year two entries were made;

WOODMAN.- In loving memory of my dear husband, Edgar Woodman, Private, 2/5th Gloucesters, who fell in action in France, April 24th, 1918.

> *Time does not change my thoughts of him,*
> *Love and dear memories linger still;*
> *I have lost, but heaven has gained,*
> *One of the best this world contained.*

From his sorrowing Wife and little Sonnies, Horace and Leslie

WOODMAN.- In loving memory of our dear son and brother, Pte. Edgar Woodman (260214), 2/5th Gloucesters, who fell in action, April 24th, 1918.

> *Death divides, but memory clings.*

Inserted by Mother, Sister and Brother, Corston

Jones, (James) Montague, Air Mechanic 1st Class, 91196, age 25, 89 Squadron, Royal Air Force

Died, 7th August 1918, buried in Malmesbury Moravian Churchyard (Private gravestone), commemorated Malmesbury Abbey, Cirencester Benefit Society, School, Town Hall & Triangle.

Malmesbury Moravian Churchyard is on the north side of Oxford Street. Montague's grave has a flat gravestone just proud of the ground which is to the left of the path close to the side wall, fifth plot from the road.

James, known as Monty, was the eldest son of James Alfred (cycle & musical instrument dealer, Clerk to the Gas Company and Borough Councillor) and Jane Jones of 10 Oxford Street with an older sister Jennie and brothers Alfred & Vivian. In June 1917 Monty married Gertrude Adye, third daughter of Cllr. & Mrs. Adye of Ingram House and they lived at 54 High Street. Their son Albert James was born on 12th October 1917.

In December 1916 Monty appealed against being called-up;

Mr. James Montagu Jones, 23, single, manager of motor and general engineering works, turner and fitter, passed in C1, and part proprietor of Jones & Son, motor works, appealed. Mr. Jones was rejected in December, 1915, as a result of an injury to his knee, which had resulted in "recurring synovitis." Dr. Pitt is always afraid of tuberculosis setting up, and treats him accordingly. – Thirteen men from the firm have joined the Colours. – The father appealed personally and in a lengthy statement setting forth the work done by the firm, mentioned fetching two ladies from Cheltenham at night. – Sir Audley Neeld asked if it was a matter of national importance to carry ladies from Cheltenham at night? – Mr. Jones: They were ladies engaged in Red Cross work, and could not get apartments in Cheltenham for the night. – Sir Audley offered a vigorous opposition, as C1 men were badly wanted in the Army. – Mr. Jones replied with a strong appeal on medical grounds and also on account of the business.- Sir Audley said the military opposed, and only a short exemption should be given, which should be final.- March 1st, when he can appeal again.

A further appeal was made in March 1917;

James Montague Jones (23), single, 17, High Street, Malmesbury, passed for C1, manager of engineering works and motor-car repairing business, was appealed for by his father, Mr. J.A. Jones.

William Huxley (33), married (six children), 17, Coxstalls, Wootton Bassett, also passed for C1, foreman mechanic and engineer, was also appealed for by Mr. Jones.

The military considered one of the men should go.

Mr. Jones said he pleaded the needs of the neighbourhood – that was his only ground for the moment. If they considered the area of the neighbourhood and the number of men able to do essential work they would agree that it was only a small number. There was no engineer in Tetbury, the nearest being at Nailsworth, and there was, besides his own men, only Mr. Ratcliffe in Malmesbury. Mr. Ratcliffe had only one assistant. He (Mr. Jones) was not himself an engineer and he had three assistants in that branch, one of whom was not able-bodied, being frequently subject to illness, and had been medically rejected for the Army. Really, therefore, he had only two men to conduct the business, which was of considerable magnitude. In addition to the motor-car work there were the farmers' cars and goods and tractors in connection with which the engineering work was growing month by month. Motor tractors were becoming more and more general, and those were constantly requiring attention, so there must be more men to see to them. Mr. Jones mentioned other local demands which were of importance. He also referred to his son's health. Fifteen men had left his employ for the Army.

The Tribunal decided to give the son exemption until June 1st and the appeal for Huxley was refused.

Another appeal followed in June;

James Montague Jones (23), single, 17, High Street, Malmesbury, manager of motor garage and general engineering works, passed for C1, was appealed for by his father, Messrs. Jones & Son, motor engineer, &c.

The military considered Mr. J.A. Jones should manage the business himself.

Mr. J.A. Jones said that it was not a question of managing, but of repairing the large number of motor-cars sent to the garage. There was only another competent repairer and he had just

been called up.

The decision, after a lengthy deliberation, was that the young man should be given a further period until August 1st – and that in the meantime Mr. J.A. Jones should endeavour to replace him.

Mr. Jones: That is just my difficulty. I cannot replace him. I dare not attempt to employ another man, as in our trade it is now against the law to do so.

A letter appeared the next week;

A MALMESBURY TRIBUNAL CASE

Sir, According to your report of the County Tribunal case concerning the garage manager for Messrs. Jones & Son of Malmesbury, Mr. Jones, sen., in discussing the repair of motor tractors, made a statement that his son (C1) was the only mechanic he had capable of carrying out such repairs, his other mechanic, R.G. May (C3), being unable to do so.

In common fairness to the C3 man – and just to hint at the strength of Mr. Jones' imagination – the following facts clamour for publication: The owner of the only tractor which figures in the case of Messrs. Jones & Son wrote to Mr. Jones asking him to fit a new big-end bearings in his machine. Mr. Jones replied stating his inability to do so, on the grounds that R.G. May had been called up. Through the influence of the owner of the tractor an extension of leave was granted to R.G. May in order that he might carry out the repairs. The work was duly completed without the assistance of Mr. Jones, who was away at the time. If any further information is needed to disprove the implied incapacity of R.G. May he is able to supply such.

Yours, &c.,

THE MAN WHO DID THE JOB

Monty was enlisted on 30th July 1917 with the rank of Air Mechanic 2nd Class and posted to 89th Squadron at Upper Heyford, Bicester. After 6 months' service he was appointed an Air Mechanic 1st Class. Unfortunately he suffered a dreadful accident first reported in the Gazette on the 8th August;

ACCIDENT TO AN AIRMAN.- It is stated that a serious accident has occurred to Air Mechanic Montagu Jones, eldest son of Mr. J.A. Jones, whilst on service at an aerodrome, at which a fire broke out, and he was badly burnt. He is in hospital where his parents visited him yesterday, and phoned back that he is in a precarious condition.

The North Wilts Herald had a more complete report;

Montague Jones' gravestone.

SOLDIER'S FATAL BURNS.
Impressive Funeral at Malmesbury.

The sad facts concerning the death by burning of First Air Mechanic James Montagu Jones, Royal Air Force, son of Mr. J.A. Jones, of Malmesbury, were told at the inquest held at Oxford on Saturday.

Mr. J.A. Jones gave formal evidence of identification, stating that his son was 25 years and married.

Sergt. Eldred, R.A.F., said that about 9.25 p.m. on Tuesday, August 6th, as he was passing a shed close to a Leyland lorry at an aerodrome, he heard an explosion, and on going to the lorry found it on fire. He saw Air Mechanic Jones rush from the back of the lorry, the clothing of the upper part of his body being in flames. He tripped him up, rolled him on the ground and flung earth over him, extinguishing the flames. Others had come and assisted, and deceased was able to walk into a shed near by, where the medical officer attended to him. He was soaked in linseed oil and afterwards sent on an ambulance to Oxford.

Lieut. R.F. Mallabar, R.A.F., deposed that he was in the office at the aerodrome and heard the report of the explosion. He ran out and assisted, and was present when the ambulance started for the Hospital. It was the deceased's duty to sleep in the lorry because of the valuable kit of tools kept in his care.

Major Mallam, R.A.M.C. (medical officer), said Air-Mechanic Jones arrived at the hospital about 11 p.m. The upper portion of his body was very badly burned. He had made a statement to witness, which was: "I had been cleaning my clothes with petrol just before dusk and afterwards lit a lamp, when everything seemed to burst into flames." He died about 9.10 p.m. on Wednesday from shock, the result of the burns.

The jury's verdict was "Accidental death."

THE FUNERAL

The funeral at Malmesbury on Tuesday was particularly impressive, and was attended by a large number of sympathisers. The body, which arrived by train on Monday afternoon, was borne from the deceased's house, at the corner of Ingram Street and High Street, to the Silver Street Congregational Church. A party of air-mechanics of the R.A.F., under a sergeant, were bearers, and a party of Volunteers belonging to the Malmesbury detachment, 1st Batt. Wilts (Duke of Edinburgh's) Volunteer Regiment attended as pall-bearers.

As the funeral party entered the church Mr. A.H. May (organist) played a funeral march. The congregation filled every part of the building. The service was conducted by the Rev. F.W. Lines (Congregational pastor), and the Rev. A.J. Heath (principal of the Moravian Mission College, Bristol), delivered an address full of comfort and consolation to the bereaved. Appropriate hymns were sung. As the body was carried out the Organist played "O, Rest in the Lord."

Going by way of Silver Street, St Denis Lane, High Street and Oxford Street, the funeral procession reached the Moravian burial-ground, where the interment took place. There were many sadly pathetic thoughts in the minds of many present, for only a few weeks ago was buried Mrs. May, eldest daughter of Mr. and Mrs. J.A. Jones.

The Herald's Roll of Honour entry was;

JONES.- Aug. 7th, at the 3rd Southern Command Military Hospital, Oxford, 1st Air Mechanic, James Montague Jones, Royal Air Force, eldest son of James A. Jones, Malmesbury, aged 25 years.

Price, Charles William, Private, 20988, age 21, 12th (Service) Battalion Gloucestershire Regiment

Killed in action, 23rd (although Commonwealth War Grave Commission says 25th) August 1918, commemorated on the Vis-en-Artois Memorial Panel 6, Malmesbury Abbey & Triangle. The Vis-en-Artois Memorial bears the names of over 9,000 men who fell in the period from 8th August 1918 to the date of the Armistice in the Advance to Victory in Picardy and Artois, between the Somme and Loos and who have no known grave. They belonged to the forces of Great Britain & Ireland and South Africa; the Canadian, Australian and New Zealand forces being commemorated on other memorials. The Memorial consists of a concave screen wall in three parts and carries stone panels on which the names are carved. The middle part is 26 feet high flanked by pylons 70 feet high. The Stone of Remembrance stands exactly between the pylons and behind it, in the middle of the screen, is a group in relief representing St George and the Dragon. Each part forms the back of a roofed colonnade; and at each end is a small building. The cemetery was designed by J.R. Truelove.

Charles William was the fourth son of William (GWR labourer) and Margaret Price, of Burnivale. His brothers were Henry, Maurice & William (killed on 18th August 1916) and sisters Margaret & Ellen. Charles was posted to in the 12th Gloucesters, the same battalion that his brother William had originally enlisted in. It is not clear when he joined them in France but after a spell in Italy they suffered heavy casualties during the April 1918 fighting. Having rested behind the lines around Doullens they moved into the front line on 21st August near Puisieux north of Albert. Early that morning the British began to attack. At first the Gloucesters were in reserve but soon were in the leading wave. Over 100 casualties were suffered that day. The next day they reorganised but had to fight off a counter attack. On 23rd the attack continued as recorded in the war diary;

Orders were received for the capture of the Final Objective.

At 11 a.m. attack commenced, troops moving forward under creeping barrage. Enemy had constructed machine-gun nests along railway and these caused numerous casualties before they were overcome. There was also a considerable amount of M.G. fire from the direction of

Miramont which had not yet been taken by N.Z. Division. Owing to losses 12 Glosters (who had been reinforced by 'B' & 'D' Coys of 1/DCLI) were unable to advance beyond ridge before Irles and reinforcements were asked for. Before these arrived however Lt. Col. H.A. Colt M.C. 12/Gloucestershire Rgt. at the head of the remainder of the 12/Glosters + 2 companies of Cornwalls had succeeded in rushing the village and had consolidated on the final objective. Lt. Col. Colt being wounded, however, whilst superintending consolidation. Casualties were very heavy In addition to Lt. Col. H.A. Colt M.C. the following Officers were wounded Lt. A. Laird M.C., 2/Lt. R.H. Anstey, 2/Lt. G.G.L. Nicks, 2/Lt. J.T.N. Miles, Lt. F.H. LaTrobe M.C., Lt. T.C. Greenhalgh M.C., 2/Lt. T.P. Gunning, 2/Lt. J. Ibbotson and Capt. & Adjt. J.H. Maywood was killed. Losses in OR about 200 on this day.

The Wilts and Gloucester Standard had a report on 14th September;

Private Charles Price, son of Mr. and Mrs. John Price, of Burnivale, has been killed. He was aged 21, and was in the Gloucesters, and had been on active service three times in France and once in Italy. His brother was killed 2 years and 5 days previously by the side of Private S.W. Wakefield, of the Horsefair. The sympathy of the town is extended to the parents.

Two years were to pass before the family placed an item in the In Memoriam column of the North Wilts Herald for both brothers;

PRICE.- In ever loving memory of our dear boys, Cpl. William Price, killed in action, Aug. 8th, 1916, aged 22 years; and Pte. Charles Price, killed in action, Aug. 23rd, aged 21 years. Never forgotten by their loving Father, Mother, Sisters and Brothers, Burnivale, Malmesbury.

> *Our loved ones have departed and we ne'er shall see them more*
> *Till we meet before the pure and crystal sea;*
> *Till we clasp the hands we loved so well upon the golden shore,*
> *What a meeting, what a meeting that will be.*

Bishop, Cecil Henry, Private 235317, age 20, 13th (Service) Battalion Royal Welch Fusiliers Killed in action, 1st September 1918, commemorated on the Vis-en-Artois Memorial Panel 6, Malmesbury Abbey, Town Hall & Triangle.

For a description of the Vis-en-Artois Memorial see Private Charles Price above.

Cecil was the youngest son of Walter and Jane Bishop, of 31 Burnivale, whose brother Arthur had died on 3rd May 1917. Cecil was a warehouseman before being conscripted. He reported to Sergeant H. Young at Chippenham on 8th March 1917 and was sent to the Wiltshire Regimental depot at Devizes where he was enrolled into that Regiment with the Service Number 202837. He undertook his training with the 4th Reserve Wilts Battalion. In June he went to the 5th Infantry Base Depot in France where he was transferred to the Royal Welch Fusiliers. On 24th June he was posted to 13th Battalion, arriving with them on 30th. In December he suffered an injury to his heel and spent a week at 130th Field Ambulance.

Cecil lost his life during an evening attack on Sailly Sailisel (just east of Combles in the Somme Departement). The Official History describes it thus; *The operation was carried out at 7 p.m. under converging creeping barrages, and was entirely successful; by 10 p.m. the eastern outskirts of the village had been occupied.* Cecil paid the price for this small success. The battalion war diary has slightly more detail;

Objective – trenches East of village ... 16th R.W.F. on the right 13th on the left, each 500 yds front.

7 p.m. 113 Bde followed creeping barrage. 13 RWF deployed as follows – 'A' Coy. left, 'C' Coy. centre, 'D' Coy. right, 'B' Coy. in support.

8 p.m. Sailly-Saillisel occupied without opposition, our line established E of village.

Casualties Lt. J.S. Bordage, 2/Lt. H.S. Barlow, 2/Lt. R.H. Ellis wounded. OR Killed 7, Wounded 30, Missing 16.

Cecil must have been amongst the missing as his death was not noted on his service record until 26th September and the Standard of 12th October reported;

Mr. Walter Bishop, of Burnivale, Malmesbury has received official news of his youngest son, Private Cecil Henry Bishop, having been killed in action on September 1st. Private Bishop was reported wounded on that day, but later news was of his being killed. He was 20 years of age. His eldest son, Arthur Edward, was drowned in Mesopotamia in the early months of last year. Mr. Bishop is serving in the Royal Defence Corps.

The entry in the Herald's Roll of Honour did not appear until October;

BISHOP.- Sept. 1st, killed in action, Pte. Cecil Henry Bishop, son of Pte. and Mrs. Walter Bishop, Burnivale, Malmesbury, aged 20 years.

His mother inserted an entry In Memoriam in 1920;

BISHOP.- In ever loving memory of our dear son, Pte. Cecil Henry Bishop, killed in action in France, Sept. 1st, 1918, aged 20 years, youngest son of Mrs. W. Bishop, 31, Burnivale, Malmesbury.

> *When alone in my sorrow the bitter tears flow,*
> *There stealeth a dream of the sweet long ago;*
> *When unknown to the world he stands by my side*
> *And whispers, "Dear mother, death cannot divide."*

From his sorrowing Father, Mother, Sisters and Brothers.

Another appeared the following year;

BISHOP.- In ever loving memory of our dear son, Pte. Cecil Henry Bishop, who was killed in France, Sept. 1st, 1918, aged 20 years.

> *It was on the field of battle, with his comrades by his side,*
> *That a brave lad of England for his country died;*
> *God bless our dear one laid to rest,*
> *At his post for his loved ones he did his best,*
> *Brave and kind-hearted like a soldier he fell,*
> *All those who knew him speak of him well.*

Inserted by his ever loving Mother, Father, Sisters and Brother.

Liddington, Henry (Harry) Charles, Private, 35870, age 21, 1/4th Battalion Duke of Edinburgh's (Wiltshire Regiment) Territorial Force

Killed in action, 19th September 1918, buried at Ramleh Cemetery F 49, commemorated Malmesbury Abbey, Town Hall & Triangle.

For a description of Ramleh Cemetery see Private Ernest James Hibbard above.

Harry was the younger son of Thomas (gardener & cowman) and Emma (who died in 1898) Liddington, 77 Gloucester Road, with a brother Thomas and sister Emily. He enlisted at Devizes into the Royal Army Medical Corps (number 27641) and arrived in Palestine on 31st December 1915. After the 1/4th Wiltshires entered the region in September 1917 he transferred to that battalion. The war diary entry for the time of his death read;

Tuesday 17th September 1918 Palestine, Mullebis

The Bn. left MULLEBIS at 1900hrs on 17th inst and marched to head of BORDER VALLEY where it bivouacked for the night and following day, during the night 17th-18th. No 3 and 4 Companies went out in front of E12 to E15 to cover parties laying jumping off places and marking places for gaps in wire.

On the night 18th/19th the Bn. marched to point of assembly C9 b55 FEJJA C3 Map. Arriving there at 2230hrs and bivouacking. At 0200 all ranks had water served out and at 0315 the Bn. moved off to jumping off place in front of E12 to E14, on arrival the Bn. formed up in two ranks, with 2/3 Gurkhas on Left and 72nd Punjabis in support. At ZERO -5 MINUTES the Bn. advanced and the enemy's work F26 was taken by 2 platoons. Continuing to advance the Bn. rapidly took the other objectives with very slight opposition until reaching MISKEH about 1½ miles SW of ET TIRE, where the enemy were strongly entrenched. The Bn. advanced in same formation with 2/3 Gurkhas on left and became heavily engaged, No 1 and 2 Companies reinforced No 3 and 4 companies and under cover of S.A.F.A advanced and forced the enemy to evacuate the positions in front of ET TIRE. It was during the taking of this line of defence the Bn had the majority of the casualties, Col. Armstrong, Capt. Knight and 2Lt. Doddrell were killed and 6 other officers wounded, 13 OR killed and 55 OR wounded. The enemy took up a position through T23 A B to T24 B behind cactus gardens but were driven out by Lewis Guns supported by Artillery.

The Bn. advanced and captured the Enemy's Army Corps HQ at T17a an outpost line was then put out running E and W from T23b 38 to T24a 38. No 1 and 2 in piquet line No 3 and 4 in supports (time 1300). At 1800hrs the Bn. was relieved by 3rd Kashmir Rifles and withdrew to T29a 83 and bivouacked.

There was a short entry in the newspaper's Roll of Honour;

LIDDINGTON.- Sept. 19th, killed in action in Egypt, Pte. Harry Liddington, Wilts Regiment,

second son of Mr. Thomas Liddington, Gloucester Road, Malmesbury, aged 22 years.
There was a fuller entry the following week;
YOUNG SOLDIER KILLED.- Mr. Thomas Liddington, of Gloucester Road, has received official intimation that his second son, Pte. Harry Liddington, of the Wilts Regt., was killed in action in Egypt on September 19th. Pte. Liddington was for 3½ years in the R.A.M.C., but for the last six months, had been with the Wilts Regiment. He was only 22 years of age. The utmost sympathy is felt for the bereaved relatives.

Weston, Harry Redvers, Ordinary Seaman, BZ/2635, age 18, Royal Navy Volunteer Reserve
Died, 5th October 1918, buried in Malmesbury Cemetery 592 South (family inscription *PEACE PERFECT PEACE*), commemorated Malmesbury Abbey, Town Hall & Triangle.
Plot 592 South is close to the southern path, walk beyond the path leading to the Chapel and it is three rows north and four rows west of the path junction.
Harry was the second son of Michael John (who had been Police Constable but after retirement became a meat salesman) and Mary Jane Weston, 34 West Street, with a brother Thomas and sisters Lucy, Nellie & Muriel (who died three months after Harry aged 12). Harry volunteered at Bristol on 16th July 1918 before he turned 18 and would be called up, having previously worked as a stableman. He was posted to H.M.S. Victory VI, the training establishment for sailors destined for the Royal Naval Division on the Western Front. This was based in wooden huts on the lower terrace at Crystal Palace, Sydenham. Complications arose after Harry was inoculated and he was admitted to Norwood Cottage Hospital, Croydon where he died.
The Standard had the following report;
The death took place on Saturday, 10th instant at Norwood Cottage Hospital, London, S.E., of Private Harry Redvers Weston, second son of Mr. and Mrs. John Weston, 23, Gastons-road, Malmesbury, at the age of 18 years and 2 months, the cause of death being influenza followed by pneumonia. The young soldier joined the Royal Navy Volunteer Reserve only a few short weeks ago, and was in training. The funeral took place on Thursday, at Malmesbury Cemetery. The Vicar, Rev. C.H.D. McMillan, officiated. The mourners were Mr. and Mrs. John Weston (father and mother), Mr. Thomas Weston (brother), Miss Nellie Weston (sister), Mr. Frederick Bailey (uncle), and Mr. Brinkworth (former employer). The bearers were from the parents, sisters and brothers, Mr. and Mrs. Brinkworth, E. Paginton and Bert Wilkins, and one from his old school-chums. Buglers Tom Bailey and Harry Prior sounded the "Last Post." The utmost sympathy goes out to the bereaved parents.
In the same paper was another report that added an extra detail but confirmed that the death had taken place on the 5th;
YOUNG SAILOR'S DEATH.- After only a short service in the Navy, Harry, son of Mr. and Mrs. Michael J. Weston, of the Gastons-lane, Malmesbury, died on Friday in a London Military Hospital from the result of an accident following inoculation. He was only 18 years of age and volunteered for service. The funeral took place on Thursday.
The Herald's Roll of Honour had;
WESTON.- Oct. 5th, at Norwood Cottage Hospital, London, Harry Redvers Weston, R.N.V.R., second son of Mr. John Weston, of 23, Gaston's Road, Malmesbury, aged 18 years.

Curtis, Walter George, Corporal, 1934, age 24, 7th (Service) Battalion the Prince of Wales's Leinster Regiment (Royal Canadians)
Died of wounds, 10th October 1918, buried in Malmesbury Cemetery 717 North (family inscription, *THE LORD IS MY SHEPHERD*), commemorated Malmesbury Abbey (initials shown as WS), Cirencester Benefit Society, Congregational Church, Town Hall & Triangle.
Plot 717 North is north west of the Chapel, three rows south of the northern path and five rows east of the western path.
Walter was the second son of Frederick and Sarah Ann Curtis, 5 Gastons Road, with two younger sisters Lily & Ruth. Walter left his job as a Provision Porter in London and volunteered for service in October 1914. He must have asked to join his brother Ernest (killed in January 1917) and was sent to Birr, Ireland where he was enrolled into the 7th Leinster Regiment. This was not the same battalion as his brother who went off to Gallipoli. After contracting dysentery there Ernest was evacuated to England and on recovery was posted to 7th Battalion.

Walter was promoted to Corporal on 16th March 1915 and Lance Sergeant 7th June. Unfortunately following a misdemeanour he was demoted to Private on 25th February 1916. His unit was in France from December 1915 from where he wrote to the Herald nine months later;

A LETTER FROM THE TRENCHES

Sir, - A copy of your issue of August 11th has just reached me, and in reading the report of the proceedings of the Malmesbury Tribunal on August 9th I as a Malmesburian was astonished to see the most remarkable statement, elicited by Mr. Matthew Thompson from the Recruiting Officer concerning the latter's prerogative to exempt "certain young men" from service without them even appealing to the Local Tribunal. Could not some local patriot effect an arrangement whereby this chosen band could be made recipients of some souvenir in recognition of their devotion to many in "keeping the home fires burning" whilst the rest of us are "doing their bit" for King and country, so many of our townsmen having already made the "great sacrifice?" – Yours faithfully,

W.G. Curtis

Leinster Regiment, B.E.F., France

He wrote another published letter in October which demonstrated his good education and intense patriotism;

Future historians will unquestionably note, as one of the most outstanding and marvellous facts of this terrible war, that, as if touched by a magician's wand, the gossamer threads which held the Overseas Dominions of Great Britain to the Motherland tightened, at the tocsin of battle, to steel. What might have been, what the Teutonic organisers of the war hoped would be, did not occur. What did happen was that the world witnessed the most wonderful exhibition of Imperial patriotism and loyalty that it has ever known. There was no compulsion: the rally of Britain's sons from both at home and overseas was entirely spontaneous and voluntary. Those magnificent Canadian soldiers who, on the never-to-be-forgotten day when the line of the great Allied troops was nearly broken, stood in the gap and saved the situation were all volunteers. So were the Australian heroes, who, despite the withering hail of lead poured into their ranks by a strong enemy, leapt boldly ashore in that portion of the "Near East" made classic by Homer, and who, with the New Zealanders together with that renowned division of Englishmen and Irishmen, earned imperishable renown, and outvied the deeds of Trojans and Greeks of old. How gallantly those fine troops, now known as the "Anzacs," ably supported by battalions of the British Army hung on by the skin of their teeth to the Gallipoli Peninsula, notwithstanding the desperate attempts made by the enemy to dislodge them! Then we have the spirit of India, the same as that of the Colonies, as is evidenced by the unshakeable loyalty and intense enthusiasm with which the native races are fighting for the Empire in the various parts of the three continents of Europe, Asia and Africa. The martial spirit – or is it the glamour of a great and noble enthusiasm? – seems to endow with life even the inanimate objects it touches, and to make them companionable with man. The lilt of a tune, the chorus of a song, the colours of a regiment, how they seem to be part and parcel, not alone of the pageantry of war, but that transcendental spirit and soul of it, which is itself sublime.

"The martial airs of England
Encircle still the earth,
And roll back to their cradle
Around a planet's girth."

Daniel Webster has given us a fine apostrophe, and in even grander language, when he speaks of our country as "a power which has dotted over the surface of the whole globe with her possessions and her military posts, whose morning drum-beat, following the sun and keeping company with the hour, circles the earth with one continuous and unbroken strain of the martial airs of England." Those martial airs have kept alive in all portions of His Majesty's dominions that magnificent spirit that has brought forth from every part of them what the Empire still needs – namely, men to fight her battles, and turn aside the blows with which her enemies are attempting to destroy her, or, in a word, to win this war, which at present seems to be a forlorn hope, thanks to the fine men of Great Britain and her Colonial forces.

Walter's Service Record illustrates the casualty evacuation system. On 7th April 1917 he was wounded, incidentally close to where his brother had been killed three months earlier. The following day he was admitted to 113th Field Ambulance, where his wound was diagnosed as a gunshot wound to the posterior of the chest. The same day he was transferred to 53rd Casualty Clearing Station at Mont des Cats. On 13th April he moved to 13th General Hospital, Boulogne from where he was evacuated to England by Hospital Ship five days later. Unfortunately this spinal injury turned him into a paraplegic and after a spell in Halifax, then at the 2nd Southern General Hospital he was moved to Malmesbury Red Cross Hospital. Curiously when taken off the strength of 7th Battalion on posting to the Depot he was reinstated as a Corporal. In June 1917 there was a short report in the Wilts and Gloucester Standard;

Mr. and Mrs. Fred Curtis, of Westport, Malmesbury, have received information from the matron of the hospital at Halifax that no hope is entertained of the recovery of their son, Sergeant Walter Curtis (Leinsters), who is 23 years of age, and was wounded at Easter in the big push on Arras.

He succumbed to his injuries 18 months later in Malmesbury Hospital. The Standard had a full report;

Once again we have to record the death of a gallant young soldier, Sergeant Walter George Curtis, second and youngest son of Mr. and Mrs. Frederick Curtis of 5, Gastons-road, Malmesbury, he having died in the Red Cross Hospital, Malmesbury, on October 10th, from wounds received in action just 1 year and 6 months ago. Sergeant Curtis joined up in the first month of the war and was in the Leinsters. During the greater part of last year he was in Halifax Military Hospital, afterwards being transferred to Bristol, and for the last few weeks he has been a patient of the Malmesbury Hospital. His case was hopeless from the first, the lower part of his body being paralysed. His brother, Corporal Ernest, was killed in action on January 10th, 1917, so that his parents have been bereaved of both sons in the war. The greatest sympathy is extended to them.

The Standard also reported the funeral;

MEMORIAL SERVICE. – A memorial service for the late Sergeant Curtis, particulars of whose death we have previously recorded, was held in the Westport Congregational Church on Sunday evening, and numerously attended. The minister, the Rev. Mr. Enos, delivered a suitable address based on the words, "Naked came I out of my mother's womb, and naked shall I return; the Lord gave and the Lord hath taken away, blessed be the name of the Lord."

The Herald's Roll of Honour column recorded;

CURTIS.- Oct. 10th, at Malmesbury Red Cross Hospital, the result of wounds received in action, Corpl. Walter George Curtis, Leinsters, second son of Mr. Frederick Curtis, of 5, Gastons Road, Malmesbury, aged 23 years.

The following year this entry was made In Memoriam;

CURTIS.- In loving memory of Walter George Curtis, who died of wounds, Oct. 10th, 1918, at Malmesbury Cottage Hospital.

> *Your birthday! Just twelve months ago it ended,*
> *Your bright young life and all our hopes in you;*
> *But then began for you the vision splendid –*
> *New life, new work, new powers, all things made new.*

Inserted by his loving Father, Mother and Sister Ruth, 5, Gastons Road, Malmesbury.

Clark, Alfred, Private, 241826, age 24, 1/8th Battalion Worcestershire Regiment Territorial Force

Killed in action, 4th November 1918, buried at Landrecies British Cemetery B 34, commemorated Malmesbury Abbey (surname spelt Clarke), Town Hall & Triangle.

Landrecies was the scene of rear-guard fighting on 25 August 1914, after the Battle of Mons, and from that date it remained in German hands until it was captured by the 25th Division on 4th November 1918. Landrecies British Cemetery was made by the 25th Division in November 1918 and all burials date from the period October 1918 to January 1919. The Cemetery contains 165 Empire burials of the First World War, 14 of which are unidentified.

Alfred was born in Sherston, the eldest son of Alfred and Mary Clark (both natives of Malmesbury), with brothers Napier & Mark. Unfortunately nothing is known of Alfred's military career except that he was serving in the Worcesters prior to 1917. The battalion war diary has this to say about the operation in which he died;

At 0615 the Battalion advanced to the attack on Landrecies behind the 1/5 Glouc. Regt. and the 1/8 Rl. Wark. Regt. Roles were as follows; the Gloucesters and Warwicks were to make good the crossing of the Sambre Canal and the 1/8 Worc. Regt. were to go through them, cross the Canal capture Landrecies, occupy the Red line and push out outposts to the Dotted Red line. 'D' Coy. on the right advanced rapidly, crossed the Canal on enemy bridge, captured a battery in action and were established on this line by 1115. 'A' Coy (centre) overcoming the resistance of a m.g. nest with the aid of a Tank crossed the canal at the lock over R.E. right bridge at 1245, and reached their objective shortly afterwards. 'C' Coy (left) advanced to the canal overcoming heavy resistance by enemy machine guns, crossed the Canal on rafts under the heavy fire of guns of all sizes and every description and reached their objective. Flank units 96th Bde., 16th Lancs Fus (right) and 149th Bde., 3rd R.F. (left).

The Battalion captured 13 officers and 235 men, 14 guns, 37 machine guns and 28 horses but suffered four officers wounded, four other ranks killed and 61 wounded.

Only a brief report appeared in the Standard on 7th December;

Mr. Alfred Clark, of St. John's-street, Malmesbury, has received news that his eldest son Alfred, was killed in action on November 4th. Before joining up the young soldier was an employee of the Malmesbury Rural District Council.

On 14th December they published another short article, now able to mention the unit concerned;

The sympathy of Malmesbury is extended to Mr. and Mrs. Alfred Clarke, of St. John-street, in the death of their son, Private Alfred Clarke, of the 1/8 Worcestershire Regiment, who was killed in action on the 4th ult., thus being debarred after an arduous campaign, from sharing in the fruits of victory. He was only 23 years of age.

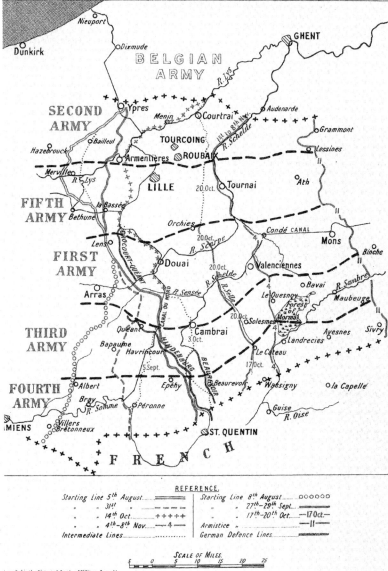

THE BRITISH ADVANCE TO VICTORY
8th Aug.—11th Nov. 1918.

Armer, Alice Ruth, Member, 22699, age 25, Women's Royal Air Force
Died, 12th November 1918, General Hospital Cheltenham, buried in Malmesbury Cemetery 392 South (private gravestone), but not commemorated in Malmesbury.

Plot 392 South is alongside the path leading from the southern part towards the Chapel and twelve rows north of the southern path (about half way).

Alice was the only daughter of William (a coachman) and Alice Crockley, born in Paddington with two brothers William & Arthur and two sisters Elsie & Annie. She married Arthur Armer, son of John and Sarah Jane Armer, of 11 Fairbank, Kirkby Lonsdale, Westmorland in 1909. Arthur served with the 1/4th Battalion Border Regiment before returning to England and joining their 1st Battalion in June 1916. Selected for officer training he was posted to the 11th Battalion Border Regiment as a Second Lieutenant and was killed in action on 5th September 1917. An extract from the regimental history of the Border Regiment reads; *After taking part in operations about Nieuport in July 1917 the 11th Battalion spent some time in the neighbourhood of Coxyde, and then in the latter part of August and beginning of September was at Oost Dunkerque, where the camp was heavily shelled by a long range high velocity gun, the transport lines being hit and four officers' chargers killed. After this the enemy shelling became more regular and hardly a day passed without casualties. 1 officer (2nd Lt. A. Armer) and 8 other ranks being killed. 2nd Lt. D. Walker and 18 men being wounded.*

On 14th October 1918 Alice enlisted in the Women's Royal Air Force at Bristol, giving her home address as Cowbridge House, Malmesbury. The WRAF was a short-lived service being formed on 1st April 1918 and rapidly run down at the war's end until final disbandment in 1921. Their strength was a maximum of only 24,400. Alice volunteered to be a 'mobile' member – in other words available for service at home and abroad. She became a Storekeeper living at Rendcombe Manor north of Cirencester and serving at RAF Rendcombe 1½ miles north east

of North Cerney on the road to Calmsden. This was a flying training station for the Royal Flying Corps opened in early 1916. By the middle of 1918 it was the 45th Training Depot Station with an assortment of aircraft. The Station was closed in 1919 but the airfield, although not marked on Ordnance Survey maps, is still used by an aerobatic team. Although Alice had passed as fit on enlistment she unfortunately became a victim of the influenza epidemic. The causes of her death were (1) Influenza and (2) Pneumonia. Her mother who was living at Cowbridge House brought her body back to Malmesbury for burial in the cemetery. The large headstone looks as though she intended to be buried in the same plot but when her employer Baldermero de Bertodano died she left Malmesbury. The Wilts and Gloucester Standard had the following in their Deaths column on 30th November;

ARMER. – Nov. 12, at Cheltenham Hospital, Alice Ruth, widow of the late Mr. Armer, and eldest daughter of Mr. and Mrs. W. Crockley, of Cowbridge, Malmesbury, aged 25 years.

Alice's gravestone with space for other names.

Salter, Frederick Joseph, Private, 35640, age 38, 2nd Battalion Hampshire Regiment
Died, 23rd November 1918, buried at Malmesbury Cemetery 773 North (family inscription *IN THE SHADOW OF HIS WING, THERE IS REST*), commemorated Malmesbury Congregational Church, Town Hall & Triangle.
Plot 773 North is north of the Chapel, two rows south of the northern path and just west of a line north from the Chapel.
Frederick was the eldest son of Richard and Lucy Salter. Richard was a Police Constable in the Wiltshire Constabulary and his children were born in various places around the county, Fred's birth place being Westbury. Richard retired to Malmesbury and became a meat salesman. Fred had two brothers, Percy & Dennis and three sisters Nellie, Annie & Lilian. After being a bricklayer's labourer he became the licensee of the Barley Mow beershop in the Horsefair (actually St Marys Street). In 1903 he married Minnie Carter who had been a waitress in the Kings Arms and presumably had the idea to take over the Barley Mow as she continued to run it after his death. They had three children Frederick, Eveline and Lewin.
Fred was called up on 31st May 1916 and sent to the Hampshire Regiment. After training he was posted to their 2nd Battalion. Shipped to France on 11th March 1917 he fell sick on 22nd before he had left the Base Depot. The 2nd Canadian Stationary Hospital invalided him to England. He was transferred to 744th Labour Company and then the 442nd Agricultural Company, Labour Corps. The Labour Corps was formed in January 1917 to concentrate units raised for different purposes to ensure that labour was used with economy. By the end of the war it provided 10% of the total Army strength but comprised men of lower medical grades, ex-convalescent or older men. Frederick was sent to Ireland and on 29th March 1918 the following was reported at the Malmesbury Tribunal;
The Tribunal unanimously agreed to support the appeal by Mr. Ferris for the return of Pte. F. Salter of Malmesbury, who is in a low category, and stationed in Ireland, and who has four allotments and a garden on which, it was thought, he would be doing far more useful service than he is performing in the Army.
He was medically re-examined at Newtownards on 1st April 1918 and reclassified B3, meaning that he was fit for service abroad on sedentary work as a clerk or storeman, but not general service. He returned to Malmesbury and unfortunately fell victim to the influenza epidemic. He was admitted to the Bath War Hospital and took with him £50, a huge sum, to buy a very special shotgun. After he died the money was not returned to his home with the body. His widow continued to run the Barley Mow until its licence was lost. She bought it from the Stroud Brewery and it remained her home until she died in 1950. The Standard's Deaths column included;
SALTER.- Nov. 23, at Bath War Hospital, Frederick Salter, of the Barley Mow, Malmesbury, aged 38 years.

Lewis, Samuel Edward, Private, 3179, age 26, 6th (Service) Battalion Royal Munster Fusiliers
Died, 6th December 1918, buried in Kirechkoi-Hortakoi Military Cemetery 551, commemorated Malmesbury Abbey & Triangle.
XVI Corps Headquarters were at Kirechkoi from January 1916, soon after the opening of the Salonika campaign, until the advance to the Struma in September 1916. The cemetery was begun in March 1916 but it remained very small until September 1917, when the 60th, 65th and 66th General Hospitals came to the neighbourhood. In June, July and September 1918 other hospitals were brought to the high and healthy country beside the Salonika-Hortakoi road. Then in September 1918 the influenza epidemic began which raged for three months and filled three-quarters of the cemetery. The last burial took place in January 1919 but in 1937 12 graves were brought into the cemetery from Salonika Protestant Cemetery where their permanent maintenance could not be assured. The cemetery now contains 588 Empire burials of the First World War and 58 Bulgarian war graves. There are also 17 burials from the Second World War.
Samuel was the fourth son of George (a painter & plumber) and Charlotte Lewis of 1 Silver Street with brothers John, Francis & Frederick. He was one of the 51 men who volunteered to join the Army from the town in September 1914. Posted to the 6th Munsters he went with them to Gallipoli, landing on 9th July 1915 where he was wounded the next month. He seems

Kirechkoi-Hortakoi Military Cemetery (cwgc.org.uk)

to have been wounded again in July 1916 and was transferred to 960th Company, Labour Corps who remained in Macedonia after the Munsters left in September 1917. The lines of communication could only be kept open with considerable effort. Much of this work relied upon the units of the Labour Corps, most of whom were of lower medical grades. Many fatalities occurred when the influenza epidemic arrived in the autumn of 1918 and as Samuel was already suffering from malaria he paid the ultimate price.

The entry in the Roll of Honour read;

LEWIS.- Dec. 6th, at Salonika, of pneumonia and malaria, Pte. Samuel E. Lewis, Labour Corps, son of Mr. Lewis, 1, Silver Street, Malmesbury, aged 25 years.

A year after his death an entry was made In Memoriam

LEWIS.- In loving memory of Samuel Edward, youngest son of Mr. and Mrs. George Lewis, No. 1, Silver Street, Malmesbury, who died in Salonika, Dec. 6th, 1918.

> *Nobly he did his duty, bravely he fought and fell,*
> *But the sorrow of those that mourn him only aching hearts can tell;*
> *It may be a soldier's honour for his country's cause to fall,*
> *But we cannot think of the glory for the sorrow it has caused us all.*

Never forgotten by his loving Mother, Dad and Brothers.

Reed, Sydney George Herbert, Lieutenant, 154995, age 25, 104th Battalion Machine Gun Corps (Infantry)

Died, 24th December 1918, buried at Kortrijk (St Jan) Communal Cemetery B 5, commemorated Malmesbury Cirencester Benefit Society only and Swindon.

Courtrai (now Kortrijk) was in German hands for most of the First World War. In April 1915, its railway junction was severely damaged by Allied airmen and on 16 October 1918, the town was entered by the 12th Royal Irish Rifles. St.-Jan Cemetery was largely used and extended by the Germans, who erected a screen bearing the names of the dead by nationalities. (The German Extension is in the commune of Heule.) In November 1918, No. 44 Casualty Clearing Station was posted at Kortrijk for a week, and it was followed for a period of eight months by No. 62. These two hospitals made a new plot in the south-west part of the cemetery, in which Empire soldiers were buried. This plot was enlarged after the Armistice when graves were brought in from the German plots, the German extension and La Madeleine Cemetery. There are now 221 Empire servicemen of the First World War buried or commemorated in this cemetery. 11 of the burials are unidentified and there are special memorials to more than 30 casualties who died in 1914-15 and were buried in the German plot but whose graves could not be found.

Sydney was the eldest child of Thomas and Kate Reed, and was born at 32 Cross Hayes. At that time his father was in partnership with Esau Duck, running the brewery behind the house in Silver Street. When Esau died in 1908 Thomas took his family back to Swindon and became a brewer there. The North Wilts Herald had the following in the Roll of Honour column on 3rd January 1919;

REED.- Dec. 24th at No. 62 Casualty Clearing Station, Courtrai, France (from pneumonia), Lieut. Sydney George Herbert Reed, 104th Batt. Machine Gun Corps (attached Westminster Dragoons), elder son of Mr. and Mrs. T. Reed, of Sandford House, Swindon, aged 25 years. Elsewhere in the same edition this article appeared;

FOR HIS COUNTRY.
Lieut. Sydney Reed Dies in France.

The war is over, but the last chapter of the Story of Sorrow has yet to be written. To the great grief of his many friends, Lieut. Sydney George Herbert Reed, Machine Gun Corps, eldest son of Mr. and Mrs. Thomas Reed, of Sandford House, Swindon, passed away in No. 62 Casualty Clearing Station, Courtrai, on Christmas Eve. He had been suffering from bronchial pneumonia for about a fortnight, and in the midst of their anxiety his family were naturally hoping for the best, but it was not to be. At the age of 25 he has gone to join the noble army of martyrs. Sydney Reed was educated at Dean Close School, Cheltenham. He afterwards joined his father in business, and was with him for two years prior to the outbreak of the war. The young man was one of the first to answer the call for volunteers for the Wilts Yeomanry but was not then accepted. That was in August 1914, and a month later found him enrolled in the First Reserve of the old county regiment. He joined as a trooper, taking his steps as they came to him. In the course of time he found himself in the Machine Gun Corps and eventually became a sergeant-instructor. As was to be expected in the case of so promising a young soldier, the opportunity of a further promotion was not far distant, and having taken a course of study as a cadet, he obtained his commission early in 1917.

But a short while had elapsed before the young officer was in France, and he fought with Plumer's Army at Ypres. Then came the Caporetto tragedy, and in October of the same year he accompanied the Army which went to the aid of our Allies in their desperate fight against the Austrian forces. Last March saw him back in France to take his share in the "backs to the wall" fight against the Huns, and it was at Ypres that he was "gassed." This was in April, and after being in hospital for some time he came home on leave. On returning to duty in June he was attached to the American contingent as a machine-gun instructor, and at the time of his fatal illness he was with the 104th Battalion Machine Gun Corps, being attached to the Westminster Dragoons.

The late Lieut. Reed was a sportsman of the best type. He was passionately fond of horses, and was a cricketer of great promise. He played for the Swindon Club on several occasions and many followers of the game will remember the match in which a Swindon side of his selection played his old school.

Mr. Reed's younger son is in the Navy, and his daughter has been doing good service as a member of the Women's Legion.

Major Harding, of the Westminster Dragoons, wrote a deeply sympathetic letter to Mrs. Reed: "Although your son had only been with us for about six months," he says, "he was loved by officers and men. Throughout the operations he did extremely well, and was always cheerful and a very fine example to all ranks. It will be some consolation to you to know that he laid down his life for his country – no-one can do more."

Capt. Bostock (officer commanding B Co. 104th Batt. M.G.C.) wrote "Please accept, on behalf of the officers, non-commissioned officers and men of the Company our deepest sympathy with you at your great loss. We paid our last respects, with military honours, to our brother officer on Christmas morning, when he was buried in the cemetery at Courtrai. We feel that we have lost one of our best friends and an officer who can never be replaced. It may be of some comfort to you to know that during the worst fighting he showed conspicuous gallantry and was much admired by all ranks."

The Rev. R. Oakley, C.F., sends some particulars of the funeral ceremony. Lieut. Reed was buried at 9.15 on Christmas morning and the service was a most impressive one. A party of 20 men were present, with eight or ten of his brother officers, four of them bearing his body to the grave. Three buglers played the "last post." The writer adds: "We all thought your son was well on the road to recovery. He had been very ill, but seemed much better and more cheerful. But he had a sudden collapse and the end came very quickly."

1919

Although the war was at an end, it still had misery to inflict. Three men associated with Malmesbury had yet to die who could have been included on our memorials but were not. We are reminded of their sacrifice as their bodies rest here and thanks to the care of the Commonwealth War Graves Commission the graves are prominently marked with their distinctive Portland stone. This brings the total number of casualties buried or commemorated in the town to 81. Like these three there are a number of others mentioned in Part One who might have been added to this list but I have no intention of trying to re-write history at this distance from the events described.

Mobey, Frederick James, Private 5790, age 34, 2/5th Battalion Suffolk Regiment Territorial Force
Died, 21st January 1919, buried in Malmesbury Cemetery plot 714 North (family inscription *BE THOU FAITHFUL UNTO DEATH, AND I WILL GIVE THEE, A CROWN OF LIFE*), but not commemorated elsewhere in town.
Plot 714 North is north west of the Chapel, four rows south of the northern path and two rows east of the western path.
Fred was the third son of William (the blacksmith of Hook) and Ellen Mobey and was born in Old Swindon. He came from a large family with six brothers and four sisters. His youngest brother, Francis from Melksham, died on the Western Front in the Machine Gun Corps on 10th April 1918 and is commemorated in Swindon. In 1901 Fred was working with his older sister Annie as a domestic servant at the Temperance Hotel, 1 Wellington Street, Swindon. He married Ethel Elizabeth Wood in September 1911 in Malmesbury and they lived at 26 Ingram Street, Malmesbury. Ethel was a draper's assistant, the youngest daughter of Thomas (an ironmonger's warehouseman) and Elizabeth Wood, with two brothers Walter & William and four sisters, Emily, Annie, Maud & Minnie. Most of Frederick's military service is unknown, but he served in the 2/5th Suffolks which did not go abroad, transferring to 380th Company of the Labour Corps before 1917 with a new Service Number, 144425. He died in the Fargo Military Hospital, Durrington and the causes of death were (1) Influenza (2) Pneumonia. Because he had not served in a theatre of war he did not receive either the British War or Victory medals.

Spikin, Ernest George, Private, 24839, age 30, 10th (Service) Battalion Hampshire Regiment
Died of wounds, 22nd January 1919, buried in Malmesbury Cemetery, plot 324 South (family inscription *IN LOVING MEMORY, REST IN PEACE*), but not commemorated elsewhere in the town.
Plot 324 South is two rows east of the path leading from the southern part towards the Chapel and about half way between the southern path and the Chapel.
Ernest was born in Gas Works House, St. Peters Street, Maidstone in 1888, the son of Robert (a gas engineer) and Caroline Wood. He had seven brothers, Henry, Frederick, Albert, Sydney, Charles, Frank & Robert and three sisters, Caroline, Ada & Eva. After a spell in the Royal Horse Artillery that ended in 1910 when he bought himself out, Ernest became a ship's steward. In 1913 he married Edith Annie Harris of Malmesbury and their son Ernest Jack was born the following year. On 9th December 1915 he enlisted under the Derby Scheme in the Hampshire Regiment, as they were living in Itchen, Southampton then. He did not disclose his previous service on re-enlistment. On 31st May 1916 he was mobilised and posted to the 3rd Battalion for training. On 4th November he sailed from Devonport for Salonika. A month after arrival he was posted to 10th Battalion. This unit had been one of the first to arrive in this theatre in October 1915. It had been involved in a number of actions including an unsuccessful attack on two farms in the Struma valley during November and December 1916. During the Spring and Summer of 1917 British forces withdrew from of the River Struma. In October the outpost line was to be re-established. Unfortunately the country was a very unhealthy place and many more casualties arose from disease than from enemy action (the ratio was about 20:1). Ernest was sent to a 'Change of Air Camp' at the beginning of October where he was diagnosed as suffering from bronchitis and was quickly transferred first to 28th General Hospital, then to the 60th and on 20th December to the 29th General Hospital (there were 50,000 beds in the theatre, sufficient for one third of the total strength). He did not improve

and a month later moved to the Hospital Ship Formosa where the diagnosis made was Pulmonary Tuberculosis. In January 1918 it was decided to evacuate him to England on H.S. Glenart Castle. Admitted to the Royal Victoria Hospital, Netley on Southampton Water he was found to be medically unfit for further service and discharged on 12th March. He was assessed to be 100% disabled due solely to exposure on service and awarded a pension of 27s. 6d. per week plus 5s. children's allowance. He returned to join his wife at 15 West Street, Malmesbury. Unfortunately on 22nd January 1919 he died at home from Pulmonary Tuberculosis and Haemophysis. There was a short inaccurate report in the Standard of 1st February;

The funeral took place at the cemetery on Monday of Private Spikin, of the Hampshire Regiment. Deceased was gassed on the Western Front and never fully recovered from this injury, which left signs of tuberculosis. He leaves a wife – the eldest daughter of Mr. Alfred Harris – and one child.

Their Deaths column contained;

SPIKIN.- Jan. 22, at West-street, Malmesbury, Ernest George Spikin, aged 30 years.

The Herald's In Memoriam column in January 1920 contained;

SPIKIN.- In ever loving memory of my dear husband, Ernest George Spikin.

> *One year has passed since that sad day,*
> *When one I loved was called away;*
> *His loving ways and smiling face,*
> *No-one on earth can fill his place.*
>> *R.I.P.*
> *Ever remembered by his Wife and little Son Jack.*

This appeared the next year;

SPIKIN.- In ever loving memory of my dear husband, Ernest George Spikin, late 10th Hants Regiment, who passed away at 15, West Street, Malmesbury, Jan. 22nd, 1919.

> *To-day recalls sad memories*
> *Of a dear one gone to rest*
> *But those who think of him to-day*
> *Are the ones that loved him best.*
> *No-one knows the silent heartache,*
> *Only those can tell,*
>> *Who have lost their best and dearest*
>> *That on earth could dwell.*

Sadly missed and always remembered by his devoted Wife and little boy Jack.

Cooper, George Thomas, Sergeant, 8709, age 29, 3rd (Reserve) Battalion the Prince of Wales's (North Staffordshire Regiment)
Died, 20th February 1919, buried in Malmesbury Cemetery 325 South (family inscription *LOVING AND KIND, IN ALL HIS WAYS, FAITHFUL AND TRUE TILL DARK, FRANCE AUG 14 TO SEP 17*), but not commemorated elsewhere in the town.
Plot 325 South is three rows east of the path leading from the southern part towards the Chapel and about half way between the southern path and the Chapel.
George was the only son of Mr. and Mrs. T.G. Cooper of Normacot, Stoke on Trent with three sisters, Cicely, Maud & Emily. In 1908 at the age of 18, having been a potter, he joined the North Staffordshire Regiment to serve seven years with the colours and five on the reserve. At the outbreak of war he was in their 1st Battalion and crossed to France on 9th September 1914. On a short leave in 1915 he married Annie Kaynes which was reported on 13th August 1915;

A SOLDIER'S WEDDING.- The marriage took place at the Abbey Church on Monday of Corpl. George Cooper, 1st North Staffordshire Regiment, and Miss Annie Kaynes, second daughter of Mr. John Kaynes, of St. Johns Street, Malmesbury. The ceremony was performed by the Rev. F.R. Webb (curate). Miss Fanny Kaynes (sister of the bride) was bridesmaid, and Mr. Harry Kaynes was the "best man." Owing to the fact that the bride has several relatives at the front the wedding was a quiet one. Sergeant W. Kaynes, a brother who is in the Wiltshire Regiment, is fighting in France. The bridegroom has been in the trenches almost since the war began, and returned to duty on Wednesday.

In September 1915 he was promoted Sergeant only to be severely reprimanded a month later, fortunately retaining his rank. His niece Mrs Evelyn Denley remembered; *My uncle George was my favourite uncle. I remember sitting on his knee now. He fought in France all through the war, everyone with him was killed but he went the four years without a scratch, all his men were blown to bits, he tried to get himself wounded to be sent back home because the killing was so terrible but while every one else was being killed or wounded he could not get a scratch. At the very end of the war he became ill and six months later died of pneumonia, he is buried near my brother Willy.*

This recollection is not wholly accurate. George was wounded in the right leg on 17th June 1916 and he did not recover until November although he was not evacuated to England. In January 1917 he became one of the instructors at the large depot at Etaples who gained a fearsome reputation. At the end of March he returned to his unit until 29th September when he was posted to the Depot. A month later he became a member of 3rd Battalion and served as a musketry instructor at schools in Heaton, Newcastle-upon-Tyne. At the beginning of January 1919 he was attached to the Dispersal Centre at Clipstone Camp, Nottingham. There he contracted pneumonia and died. On 6th March 1919 the Gazette had a short report;

The funeral of Sergeant G.T. Cooper, 1st Battalion, North Staffordshire Regiment, who died after six days' illness took place on Thursday in the cemetery, after the first part of the burial service having been read in the Abbey. Buglers sounded Last Post at the grave side, and there was a large company of mourners; military and civilians.

The North Wilts Herald had the following entry in its Roll of Honour column;

COOPER.- Feb. 21st, at Mansfield Military Hospital, Sergt. George Cooper, North Staffordshire Regiment, husband of Annie Cooper, St. John Street, Malmesbury, aged 29 years.

The following year a wealth of entries appeared In Memoriam;

COOPER.- In loving and unfading memory of my dearly-loved husband, Sergt. G.T. Cooper, formerly Musketry Instructor at North Heaton Schools, Newcastle-on-Tyne, 1st att. 3rd Batt. North Stafford Regiment, who died of pneumonia at the Military Hospital, Clipstone Camp, Notts., on Feb. 20th, 1919, in his fifth year of active service. Interred at Malmesbury Cemetery.

> *For him high service waits, the earth's last fight is fought,*
> *God did not give that beauteous soul to end at last for nought;*
> *That steadfast soldier's heart was not for this brief life alone,*
> *'Tis as a soldier he will stand before the great white throne.*

Inserted by his loving Wife, Annie Cooper, 17, St. John Street, Malmesbury.

COOPER.- In loving memory of Sergt. George Cooper, 1st North Stafford Regiment.

> *One of the dearest, one of the best.*

Fondly remembered by his Sister Cicely, Brother-in-law Jim, Nephew Tom and Nieces, Clara, Lily, Cissy and Violet, Longton, Stoke-on-Trent, Staffs.

COOPER.- In proud and loving memory of Sergt. G.T. Cooper, N.S. Regiment, who died at Clipstone Camp, Notts., Feb. 20th, 1919.

Fondly remembered by his Sister Maud, Brother-in-law Jim, and Eva, Normacot, Stoke-on-Trent, Staffs.

COOPER.- In loving remembrance of my very dear friend, Sergt. G.T. Cooper.

> *You are not forgotten, George dear,*
> *Nor will you ever be;*
> *As long as life and memory last,*
> *I will remember thee.*

Inserted by Harry Yates, late Sergt.-Major, 1st att. 3rd Batt. North Staffs. Regiment, Hopwas, Tamworth, Staffs.

COOPER.- In remembrance of our dear friend, Sergt. G.T. Cooper, 1st att. 3rd Batt. North Stafford Regiment, who died at the Military Hospital, Clipstone, Feb. 20th, 1919.

> *We feel the loss so very great, him on earth no more to see,*
> *He did his duty to the end, to God, for King and country;*
> *Now he rests in perfect peace from earthly toil and pain,*
> *A comrade truly loved by all, in memory shall remain,*
> > *Gone, but not forgotten.*

Inserted by A. Wye, late Sergeant, 1st att. 3rd Batt. North Stafford Regiment, 4, Lawn Terrace, Frimley, Surrey.

In 1921 these appeared;

COOPER.- *A tribute of love to the sweet memory of my dearly-loved husband, Sergt. G.T. Cooper, 1st attached 3rd North Stafford Regiment, Musketry Instructor at North Heaton Schools, Newcastle-on-Tyne, who died at the Military Hospital, Clipstone, Notts, on Feb. 20th, 1919, in his 5th year of active service; also of Harry and Will.*

> *Do we forget, oh, no,*
> *For memory's golden chain*
> *Has bound your hearts to the hearts below,*
> *Till they meet and touch again.*
> > *Adieu and au revoir – Annie*

COOPER.- *In most proud and tender memory of our dear brother, Sergt. G. Cooper, the devoted husband of Annie Cooper, who passed away at the Military Hospital, Clipstone, Feb. 20th, 1919.*

> *Though death divides, fond memory clings.*
> > *Gone, but not forgotten.*
> > > *From Maud, Jim and Eva.*

If you ever visit any of these war graves or memorials please consider the epitaph which was later amended for the Second World War cemetery at Kohima;

> *When you go home, tell them of us and say*
> *"For your to-morrows these gave their to-days."*
> > John Maxwell Edmonds (1875-1958)

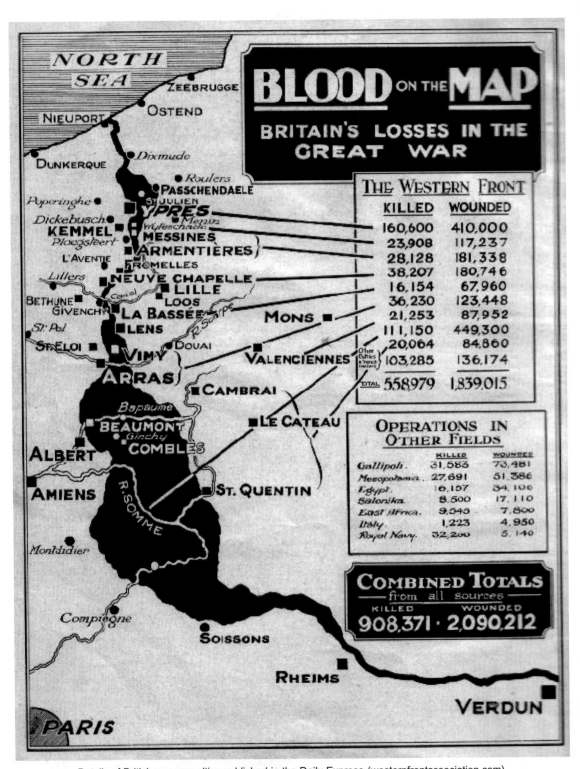

Details of British war casualties published in the Daily Express (westernfrontassociation.com)

Part Three
Malmesbury's Great War Memorials.

Abbey Church of Saint Mary and Saint Aldhelm

Whilst the Abbey did not display the first memorial the Vicar, Canon C.H.D. McMillan, quickly organised the town's first Memorial Service after the November 1918 Armistice on Sunday 8th December. The Order of Service would be familiar to a modern congregation with the Hymns "*O God our help in ages past*", "*Hush! Blessed are the dead*", "*O valiant Hearts*" and "*For all the Saints*". The Vicar read the Roll of Honour, the Last Post was sounded and the Victors' Wreath placed upon the Holy Table. The collection, after expenses, was to be *divided between the Memorial to our Soldiers in this Church, and any Memorial decided upon by the Mayor and Corporation*.

Today as you enter the Church through the main South door there is a wooden memorial in front of you mounted on the wall just to the left. Originally mounted on the Tolsey Gate, this must have been made locally because it was paid for by Captain Elliott Mackirdy Scott Mackirdy T.D., J.P. of Abbey House and is very personal to his family. At the foot of it on careful inspection the names L.G.R.E. Fawcett and C.D.S. Mackirdy can be seen in the carving. These two young men lived at Abbey House prior to the war and originally were commemorated on a brass plaque just above the carving. Captain Mackirdy's daughter Angela recalled;

I was born in the Abbey House and lived there for 25 years until I was married in the Abbey and left home. Cousin Leo was a distant relation but he had been brought up with my uncle Charlie – they lived with us in Malmesbury from the time that they were very young. I last remember seeing them when they were both home from leave from France in 1917.
My mother used to tell me to take flowers from our garden to put on their memorial in the Abbey – I would also polish the brass plates and so of course I was familiar with the inscriptions which were in memory of my dear uncle and a loved Godfather, cousin Leo.

Many years later in 1946 when I returned to Malmesbury from India, I was surprised to see that the brass plate had been taken down and replaced with a new one in memory of 'all the fallen'. Perhaps it is for the better but I remember it as a personal memorial.

The carving at the base is very elaborate but is difficult to decipher – on the left it relates to Capt. Fawcett who is not commemorated anywhere else in town. Under his name is a crown over a double headed eagle with a bell clasped in its left claw, the Lanarkshire Yeomanry's badge.

Leopold George Frederick Elliott Fawcett (Elliott being a Mackirdy family name) served with the Lanarkshire Yeomanry (also the original Regiment of Abbey House's owner) and was killed in action on 6th November 1917. By that time his unit had been transferred to the infantry as 12th Battalion (Ayr & Lanark Yeomanry) Royal Scots Fusiliers. On the day he died this battalion started a successful attack on the main Turkish position at Hureira to Sheria in Palestine which was the precursor of the continuing advance

The Abbey Memorial

northward that led to the armistice with Turkey on 31st October 1918. Leopold was aged 28 and is buried in grave M 84 in the Beersheba War Cemetery, Israel.

In the centre is the Mackirdy family motto *Dieu et Mon Pays* (French for God and my Country) together with their arms, a shield with a bird, conifer tree and sword. To the right beneath C.D.S. Mackirdy's name is his Regimental badge, the 11th (Prince Albert's Own) Hussars. This comprises a pillar bearing the arms of Saxony rising out of a coronet crowned with another coronet out of which rise five feathers and a scroll underneath *Treu und Fest* (German - True and Faithful).

The replacement brass plaque now reads;

THIS SHRINE, SACRED TO THE MEN OF MALMESBURY
WHO FELL IN THE WAR, WAS GIVEN TO THE ABBEY
IN PLACE OF THE PROPOSED CHURCH MEMORIAL;
THE FUNDS COLLECTED FOR THAT OBJECT HAVING
BEEN DEVOTED TO THE COMPLETION OF THE
MALMESBURY BOROUGH MEMORIAL CROSS

The names of the dead are inscribed on two brass plates each headed;

ROLL OF HONOUR

1914   MALMESBURY   1918

69 names are recorded. Unlike other memorials the names do not appear in alphabetical order, it would appear that they are listed in the order that their deaths were confirmed. This gives an idea of the anguish that must have been suffered by some of the families. For example two of the Gallipoli casualties of 1915 (Exton & Selby) are listed amongst deaths that occurred in 1918, so it seems the next of kin had to wait nearly 3 years before their worst fears were confirmed. The left hand plate records the following;

G GREY PTE.
    1ST WILTS. REGT.
ES LOCKSTONE PTE.
    2ND WILTS. REGT.
JW MORRICE MIDSHIPMAN
    H.M.S. "FORMIDABLE"
G ORAM TPR.
    2ND LIFE-GUARDS
F TUGWELL PTE.
    4TH WORC. REGT.
JH BAILEY PTE.
    1ST BEDF. REGT.
GH PAUL SERGT.
    6TH R. MUNS. FUS.
D BISHOP PTE.
    6TH R. MUNS. FUS.
E THORNBURY PTE.
    6TH R. MUNS. FUS.
WS THORNBURY PTE.
    1ST WILTS. REGT.
R PRICE CPL.
    7TH R. DUB. FUS.
A JOHNSON L.CPL.
    6TH WILTS. REGT.
H JAMES PTE.
    6TH WILTS. REGT.

J CURTIS PTE.
    2ND WILTS. REGT.
JH WALLINGTON GNR.
    R.M.A. H.M.S. "QUEEN MARY"
C WOOD PTE.
    1ST WILTS. REGT.
RG NEWMAN TPR.
    R.E. KENT YEO.
AG ANGELL PTE.
    6TH WILTS. REGT.
F SHAW PTE.
    6TH WILTS. REGT.
FF SHARP PTE.
    1ST WILTS. REGT.
W PRICE CPL.
    10TH GLOUC. REGT.
G WESTMACOTT PTE.
    1/7TH MIDDX. REGT.
FH BAILEY SERGT.
    1ST WILTS. REGT.
CT BOND PTE.
    6TH R. DUB. FUS.
VG NEWMAN L.SGT.
    2/5TH GLOUC. REGT.
EW CURTIS CPL.
    7TH LEINS. REGT.

F WOODWARD GNR.
3RD WESSEX BDE. R.F.A.
W BOND PTE.
6TH WILTS. REGT.
AE BAILEY PTE.
1ST COLDSTREAM GDS.
WE WAKEFIELD PTE.
2ND WILTS. REGT.
AJ LEWIS PTE.
12TH GLOUC. REGT.
A PIKE A.B.
H.M.S. "RUSSELL"

JB CURTIS PTE.
8TH SOM. L.I.
EJ HIBBARD 2ND. LIEUT.
1/12TH LONDON REGT.
JS SUMERLAKE GNR.
"Z" BTY. R.H.A.

Their Glory shall not be blotted out .... and their
name liveth to all Generations. Ecclesiasticus XVIV 13-14

On the other plate is;

RG GARLAND LDG. STOKER
H.M.S. "MAIDSTONE"
HT REEVES PTE.
8TH DEVON REGT.
AE BISHOP PTE.
8TH WELSH REGT.
SW EMERY PTE.
8TH SOM. L.I.
AJ PERRY PTE.
1/7TH WORC. REGT.
RR WEEKS PTE.
5TH CANADIANS
JP BRICKELL PTE.
1ST WILTS. REGT.
JE THOMPSON DVR.
R.F.A.
F DEADMAN RIFLEMAN
16TH K.R.R.C.
C BISHOP PTE.
1/4TH WILTS. REGT.
HE JONES 2ND. LIEUT.
R.A.F.
P WOODS PTE.
2ND SCOTS GUARDS
LJ CAREY PTE.
1/4TH WILTS. REGT.
EJ HIBBARD PTE.
2/4TH DORSET REGT.
HJ SAVINE GNR.
R.F.A.
W BARNES GNR.
R.G.A.
HG POOLE PTE.
15TH CYCLIST CORPS
E WOODMAN PTE.
2/5TH GLOUC. REGT.

H WILLIS PTE.
6TH WILTS. REGT.
CDS MACKIRDY LIEUT.
11TH HUSSARS
WJ SELBY PTE.
6TH LEINS. REGT.
R EXTON CPL.
6TH R. MUNS. FUS.
W BAKER PTE.
OXFORD & BUCKS L.I.
G POPE PTE.
R.A.S.C.
JM JONES 1ST AIR MECH.
R.A.F.
HC LIDDINGTON PTE.
1/4TH WILTS. REGT.
HR WESTON SEAMAN
R.N.V.R.
CH BISHOP PTE.
13TH R. WELSH FUS.
WG CURTIS CPL.
7TH LEINS. REGT.
JSW TUGWELL SIGNAL.
1/4TH WILTS. REGT.
A CLARKE PTE.
1/8TH WORC. REGT.
H SHINGLES L.CPL.
6TH WILTS. REGT.
SE LEWIS PTE.
6TH R. MUNS. FUS.
C PRICE PTE.
12TH GLOUC. REGT.

Then we sailed onwards stricken at heart, yet
glad as men saved from death, albeit we had lost our
dear companions. (trans) Homer Odyssey IX 566

Unusually (and usefully for later researchers) not only the man's rank is recorded but also his unit. One name included on this memorial but missing from the recital of deaths above is that of J.S. Sumerlake. This name is not on any of the other town memorials and no trace of anyone of the name or anything like it has been found. However J. Sellwood of the Royal Artillery is missing from this memorial and his date of death fits in this place in the sequence, could they have been confused? Other men's names or initials have been spelt wrongly and some names found on the Triangle Memorial are missing. These errors and omissions have been highlighted in the men's stories earlier.

There are two other memorials inside the Abbey:

On the North wall behind the 'Athelstan' tomb is a brass plaque, erected in June 1920, reading;

IN LOVING MEMORY OF
EDWARD SHARLAND LOCKSTONE
PRIVATE 2ND WILTS REGT.
WHO WAS KILLED IN ACTION IN THE GREAT WAR
AT NEUVE CHAPELLE MARCH 12TH 1915
AGED 25 YEARS

On the South wall amongst the Luce family memorials is one with the following wording;

IN EVER LOVING MEMORY OF
JAMES ROBERT REID
LIEUTENANT 1ST BATT THE ROYAL BERKSHIRE REGIMENT
SON OF JAMES ROBERT REID CIE ICS AND MARGARET HIS WIFE
DAUGHTER OF CAPTAIN JOHN PROCTOR LUCE RN
REPORTED MISSING DELVILLE WOOD 27TH JULY 1916
AGED 19 YEARS
"HE HATH DONE WHAT HE COULD"

Margaret Luce (1859-1950) was the eldest daughter of Captain John Luce (1827-1869), who was in turn the third son of Thomas Luce (1790-1875), the manager of Malmesbury's first bank and owner of a large brewery. Margaret accompanied her two sisters, Ella and Isabel, to India in 1888. She acted as housekeeper whilst her sisters became missionaries. She met and married James Reid who was twenty years older than her and in the Indian Civil Service. They had two sons, the second named after his father. By the late 1890s the family was living at 11 Magdala Crescent, Edinburgh. After her husband's death Margaret moved to 3 Alfred Place, South Kensington, London. James Jnr. joined the Berkshire Regiment and became a casualty in the confused fighting in Delville Wood during the infamous Somme campaign. His body was not identified and his name appears on Face 11 D of the Thiepval Memorial. As he was not Malmesbury born he is not commemorated elsewhere in the town.

Sharland Lockstone's Memorial

James Reid's Memorial

Town Hall

The Borough Council had a great deal of discussion, described later, about the most suitable form for the town's main memorial but the first of the town's war memorials was presented at the Town Council meeting on 8th July 1919;

THANKS TO MAYORESS.
As a memorial of those officers and men from Malmesbury who fell in the war, the Mayoress (Mrs. Duck) presented to the town a handsome tablet with a roll of honour. The tablet contains in letters of gold the names of all the brave dead. It is made of teak from H.M.S. "Britannia." The memorial has a shelf upon which flowers may be placed, has been hung in the Council Chambers.
Mr. Adye, before the ordinary business referred to the generosity of the Mayoress in making the gift. He proposed that the thanks of the Council be given to her for presenting such an appropriate roll of honour.
Mr. Summers seconded, and after being put by the Deputy Mayor (Mr. Thompson) was carried with acclamation.

This comprises a 'mail order' wooden cabinet made from timber from HMS Britannia Cadet Training Ship at Dartmouth 1889-1915 and supplied by Hughes, Bolckow & Co. Ltd. of Battleship Wharf, Blyth and 10 Dover Street, London. It is about two feet wide and four feet high with a pair of doors that open to display the names. At the top the words *FOR GOD, KING & COUNTRY* are printed with *GREATER LOVE HATH NO MAN THAN THIS* arranged on either side of a central plain brass cross. The names were applied in gold leaf by a local craftsman in four columns, one on each door and two on either side of the cross. There are 66 names. The left door reads;

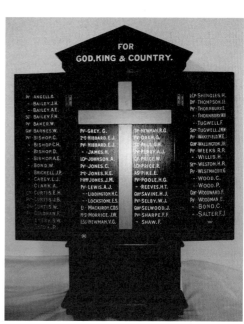

	ROLL
	OF HONOUR
PVT	· ANGELL.G.
"	· BAILEY.J.H.
"	· BAILEY.A.E.
SGT	· BAILEY.F.H.
PVT	· BAKER.W.
GUNR	· BARNES.W.
PVT	· BISHOP.C.
"	· BISHOP.C.H
"	· BISHOP.D.
"	· BISHOP.A.E.
"	· BOND.W.
"	· BRICKELL.J.P.
"	· CAREY.L.J.
"	· CLARK.A.
CPL	· CURTIS.E.H.
PVT	· CURTIS.J.B.
CPL	· CURTIS.W.
RFLN	· DEADMAN.F.
PVT	· EMERY.S.W.
CPL	· EXTON.R.

In the centre on either side of the cross are;

PVT	· GREY.G.	TPR	· NEWMAN.R.G.
2NDLT	· HIBBARD.E.J.	PVT	· ORAM.G.
PVT	· HIBBARD.E.J.	SGT	· PAUL.G.H.
"	· JAMES.H.	PVT	· PERRY.A.J.
L·CPL	· JOHNSON.A.	CPL	· PRICE.W.
PVT	· JONES.C.	L·CPL	· PRICE.R.
2NDLT	· JONES.H.E.	ASN	· PIKE.E.

The right door has the following names;

Unfortunately the passage of years took its toll and in 2008 Malmesbury Civic Trust paid for repairs to be carried out to the woodwork that had split, a new wooden painted cross instead of the badly deteriorated thin brass covering and the names to be regilded. Let us hope it will survive for another 90 years. The names, with ranks, are arranged alphabetically with two names out of order at the end. C. Bond must have been left off by mistake but F.J. Salter probably died whilst the memorial was being lettered.

Originally displayed in the Council Chamber then in the Town Hall before it was removed to the Tourist Information Office in Market Lane until being put into store in the 1990s.

Cirencester Conservative Benefit Society

The Town Hall plays host to another interesting memorial, that of the Cirencester Conservative Benefit Society. Now called the Cirencester Friendly Society Limited but originally known as the Cirencester Conservative Association Working Men's Benefit Society, it was founded in 1890 to provide sickness benefit and life insurance to agricultural workers in the Cotswolds. Organised in Lodges, one was based in Malmesbury which operated from a room in the back of the Borough Council's chambers in Silver Street (now occupied by King's Nursery). After war was declared it was expected that it 'would be over by Christmas' and special rates were offered to members who joined the forces. They would be entitled to six months' benefit from the Society if they were disabled.

The Society sought to look after the welfare of members in hospital or whilst convalescing and found out that soldiers did not receive their service pay whilst in hospital. One of their Trustees, Colonel Bathurst M.P. took the matter up with the War Office which resulted in men receiving up to three shillings and six pence a week at the discretion of the Officer Commanding.

The memorial, unveiled on 20th March 1921, is a large glass fronted wooden cabinet about four feet wide and nearly four feet high made by one of the war veterans, Harold Chew, a local carpenter and lettered by another ex Service member, C Hughes. It has turned columns at either side with the words *Cirencester Conservative Benefit Society* across the top with the word Cirencester curving over a carving of the town's arms. Under the arms *Malmesbury Lodge* is written. The centre panel has the 13 names of those who lost their lives with the five years 1914 to 1918 carved around them;

GOD HELPS THOSE WHO HELP THEMSELVES

ROLL OF HONOUR

G.ANGELL
W.BARNES
G.BOULTON
E.W.CURTIS
W.G.CURTIS
W.H.EVANS
H.JAMES
J.M.JONES
H.D.LABRUM
A.LEWIS
W.PRICE
H.I.RATCLIFFE
S.G.H.REED

WHO IN THE GLORIOUS MORNING
OF THEIR DAYS
FOR ENGLAND'S SAKE LOST ALL
BUT ENGLAND'S PRAISE

E.W.PAGINTON DCM

The Lodge recruited from a wide area and four of those who 'lost all' came from outside the town. George Boulton was born in Long Newnton but is buried in Malmesbury cemetery and his story is in Part Two. William Evans was born in Sherston and is commemorated on their modern memorial in the Lychgate of the parish church. He served as a Private in 6th Battalion Wiltshire Regiment but died of wounds on 11th May 1917, aged 31 and is buried in grave XII B 3 of Lijssenthoek Cemetery, Belgium. He was the son of E. and Mrs. W.D. Evans, of Sherston and husband of Mrs. E.G. Evans, of Station Road, Minety. Hugh Davy Labrum was born in Shaftesbury, Dorset and lived in Warminster. He was serving as a Private in the 1/4th Battalion Wiltshire Regiment. This Territorial Force Unit moved from India to Suez where it arrived in September 1917. Hugh must have formed part of the advance party as he died on 24th May 1917, aged 22 and is named on the Basra Memorial Panel 30 & 64, Iraq. Sydney George Herbert Reed was born whilst his parents Thomas and Kate Reed were living at 32 Cross Hayes so his story appears above. He is named on a stained glass window in Christchurch, Swindon also dedicated to men of the Wiltshire Regiment – see *Tell Them of Us* by Mark Sutton.

Beneath the Roll of Honour is the name E.W. Paginton DCM who survived to tell his tale. Private Ernest Paginton served with the 8th (Service) Battalion Somerset Light

Private Ernest Paginton D.C.M.
(Athelstan Museum)

231

Infantry and was awarded the Distinguished Conduct Medal, the next most important decoration for gallantry after the Victoria Cross. The Citation for his conduct during the night of 24th August 1918 at Biefvillers was;

For conspicuous gallantry and devotion to duty during an advance. He carried messages to forward companies through very heavy fire of all kinds, and after three runners had been knocked out he volunteered and successfully delivered an urgent message to the front company. He showed fine courage and determination.

As well as the list of those who died this memorial helps to put this loss in perspective as on the left and right are the names of 127 who returned (although some of them may have been disabled).

Those on the left are;

		And on the right;	
A.ARCHER	H.ENGLISH	H.KAYNES	J.PONTING
A.W.ARCHER	W.EXTON	W.KAYNES	F.POOLE
J.BALDWIN	A.GARLAND	A.LAW	S.RANSOM
E.BARNES	H.F.GOODWIN	G.LAW	G.H.REYNOLDS
J.BARRETT	H.GOODFIELD	H.LAW	H.REYNOLDS
W.BISHOP	F.GOLDING	J.R.LAW	E.SAVINE
A.J.BOULTON	W.J.GOVE	T.F.LEVENS	S.C.SAVINE
ALF.BOULTON	H.GRANT	F.J.LEWIS	F.J.SCOTT
A.BOULTON	E.GREEN	W.C.LEWIS	A.SEALY
F.BOULTON	T.GREEN	J.LOCKSTONE	W.SELBY

R.BOULTON	F.GREY	P.LOMAX	H.E.SHIPTON
A.F.BOX	W.GWINNETT	E.T.LUCAS	W.J.SHIPTON
E.BOX	P.HARRIS	C.J.MATTHEWS	C.SLADE
C.BUCKLAND	T.B.HAZELL	H.W.NEATE	H.H.SMITH
H.B.CHEW	R.HEATH	T.ODY	W.SMITH
A.CLARK	H.T.HINWOOD	F.W.ORAM	W^m·SMITH
J.CLARK	R.A.HOBBS	C.H.PAGINTON	A.STANCOMBE
R.CLARK	V.H.HOBBS	J.PAGINTON	C.STONEHAM
W.CLARK	B.C.HUGHES	R.H.PAGINTON	A.STRANGE
A.E.CLULEY	C.A.HUGHES	A.PHELPS	G.TABOR
A.COOK	H.ILES	W.PHELPS	J.TAYLOR
H.C.CORDY	C.JACOBS	H.PHELPS	H.E.TIDMARSH
A.P.COX	E.JACOBS	C.PINNELL	E.THORNBURY
W.H.CRESSWELL	A.JEFFERIES	D.PIKE	G.VANSTONE
C.F.CULLEN	F.JEFFERIES	E.PIKE	A.H.WEEKS
J.CULLEN	H.JEFFERIES	F.H.PIKE	G.F.WEEKS
W.P.CULLEN	E.JOHNSON	F.PIKE	F.WESTMACOTT
A.CURTIS	R.JOHNSON	V.PIKE	A.WILLIS
W.H.CURTIS	W.JOHNSON	W.PIKE	J.WILKINS
F.C.DREW	E.W.JONES	A.B.PONTING	W.WILKINS
H.E.DUCK	P.W.JONES	A.J.PONTING	W.WITHYMAN
W.E.DYER	T.JONES	H.E.PONTING	

Malmesbury School

Fourteen former pupils of the Malmesbury and District County Secondary School are commemorated on a marble plaque which has been moved, along with the school, from its original site on Tetbury Hill to the Grammar School at Filands in the 1960s and then to the new Corn Gastons School in 2003. It bears the following inscription;

KEEP EVER IN MIND THE HONOURED
AND GLORIOUS MEMORY OF THE
PUPILS FROM THIS SCHOOL WHO GAVE
THEIR LIVES FOR KING AND COUNTRY
IN THE GREAT WAR 1914-1918

-

GEORGE ANGELL
JOHN BUTCHER
CHARLES EDWARD COVE
FRANK H. CREWE
HERBERT DAY
MONTAGUE JONES
ALBERT LESTER
SHARLAND E. LOCKSTONE
REGINALD NEWMAN
VICTOR NEWMAN
REGINALD RIDDICK
ROBERT SIMMONS
JOSEPH THOMPSON
EDGAR WOODMAN

-

LET THOSE WHO COME AFTER THEM IN
THIS PLACE STRIVE ALWAYS TO LIVE
WORTHY OF THEIR GREAT SACRIFICE
AND EMULATE THE EXAMPLE OF
THEIR COURAGE AND SELF-DEVOTION

-

*"BE THOU FAITHFUL UNTO DEATH AND
I WILL GIVE THEE A CROWN OF LIFE".*

-

𝔇ulce et decorum est pro patria mori

THIS TABLET
WAS ERECTED BY STUDENTS OF THE SCHOOL
AND UNVEILED ON DEC[R.] 16[TH.] 1920 BY
REAR-ADMIRAL JOHN LUCE, CB
OF MALMESBURY, WHO COMMANDED
H.M.S. GLASGOW AT THE BATTLE OF
THE FALKLAND ISLES, DEC[R.] 8[TH.] 1914

The names inscribed on the memorial do not agree with those reported in the North Wilts Herald on 17th December 1920 and my research has not been able to confirm that Charles Cove and Albert Lester died in the war. It would seem that these should be Ernest John Cove and Stanley Victor Lester. Half of those listed came from Malmesbury and what is known about the others is as follows:

John Butcher was born in Crudwell, the son of Thomas and Annie Butcher. He had enlisted in the 1st City of Birmingham Battalion, a New Army unit, in September 1914. He transferred to the Corps of Royal Engineers and served in G & H Special Companies. These units were responsible for the use of poison gas normally released from cylinders or sometimes fired from trench mortars. John served in cylinder companies which would often install their apparatus in the front line and have to wait for wind of the right strength blowing towards the enemy. So they ran the risk not only of accidental leakage during release but also of shelling causing leaks through damage. Later these units used the Livens Projector, a crude type of large bore single use mortar. A number of these were set up together to fire five gallon gas canisters a few hundred yards. John was a Corporal aged 23 when he died of gas poisoning on 1st August 1917 in a General Hospital in Le Treport and is buried in the Mount Huon Cemetery there in Grave IV. M. 3A.

Nothing is known of Charles Cove, but Ernest John Cove was one of five brothers from Garsdon Park Farm. When called up he went into the Wiltshire Yeomanry but was transferred to the 6th Battalion Wiltshire Regiment. Within a month of his arrival at the front he was killed by a trench mortar with three colleagues on 18th February 1917. He was 22 and is buried in Avesnes-le-Comte Communal Cemetery in Grave IV B 11.

Francis Henry Crewe was the son of Henry and Mary Anne Crewe. He joined the 8th Battalion (Manitoba Regiment) Canadian Infantry. He was 33 when killed on 5th August 1917 and must have been one of the first pupils of the School. He is buried in Noeux-les-Mines Communal Cemetery in Grave II G 26 and is also remembered on the War Memorial in his home village of Great Somerford.

KEEP EVER IN MIND THE HONOURED
AND GLORIOUS MEMORY OF THE
PUPILS FROM THIS SCHOOL WHO GAVE
THEIR LIVES FOR KING AND COUNTRY
IN THE GREAT WAR 1914-1918.

GEORGE ANGELL
JOHN BUTCHER
CHARLES EDWARD COVE
FRANK H. CREWE
HERBERT DAY
MONTAGUE JONES
ALBERT LESTER
SHARLAND E. LOCKSTONE
REGINALD NEWMAN
VICTOR NEWMAN
REGINALD RIDDICK
ROBERT SIMMONS
JOSEPH THOMPSON
EDGAR WOODMAN

LET THOSE WHO COME AFTER THEM IN
THIS PLACE STRIVE ALWAYS TO LIVE
WORTHY OF THEIR GREAT SACRIFICE
AND EMULATE THE EXAMPLE OF
THEIR COURAGE AND SELF-DEVOTION.

"BE THOU FAITHFUL UNTO DEATH AND
I WILL GIVE THEE A CROWN OF LIFE."

Dulce et decorum est pro patria mori

William Herbert Day was the elder son of Mrs. Emily Day, the widowed licensee of the Plough Inn at Crudwell. He served for nine years as assistant clerk for Malmesbury Borough Council but was called up into the Royal Field Artillery at the age of 26. He had a cold when he left home to travel to his camp in Hampshire. This developed into pneumonia and he died three weeks later in hospital at Brighton on 21st February 1917. He is commemorated at Crudwell.

Albert Lester was a son of Alfred and Ellen Lester, born in 1890 at Eastcourt but did not die in the Great War. However his younger brother Stanley Victor served at the 4th Depot Royal Field Artillery and died from influenza on 21st September 1918. He is buried in Greenwich Cemetery, grave B 1145 and is commemorated on the Crudwell War Memorial.

Reginald Stewart Riddick was the son of Titus and Emily Riddick and husband of Ellen Riddick who all lived in Church Street, Tetbury. He joined the Gloucestershire Regiment but was transferred to 1/5th Battalion Yorkshire Regiment. In May 1918 this unit was transferred to a quiet part of the French front along the Chemin des Dames where the B.E.F. had been in September 1914. Unfortunately on 27th May the Germans launched a major surprise attack on this sector and Reginald was killed at the age of 30. However his body was recovered and is now buried in the Sedan-Torcy French National Cemetery in Grave XX. 749.

Robert George Simmons, known as Bob, had enlisted in November 1914 and was the eldest son of Theodore and Florence Simmons, of Church Farm, Little Somerford. Whilst at school he won a county minor scholarship and subsequently a senior agricultural scholarship that took him to Armstrong College, Newcastle where he was still a student when war broke out. Subsequently serving in the ranks of 22nd Royal Fusiliers he participated in some tough fighting until returning to the Cadet School at Bushey in January 1917 for officer training. He was a 25 year old 2nd Lieutenant in the 11th Battalion Royal Fusiliers when the first great German attack occurred in the spring of 1918 to win the war before the strength of the United States of America could be brought to bear. Although his unit was in reserve when the blow was struck it was quickly sucked into the battle and he was killed on 22nd March 1918 defending the Crozat Canal near Jussy. By the end of that day the fighting strength of the battalion was two officers and 25 men having suffered hundreds of casualties in just over 24 hours. The news of his death cast gloom over the school where the flag flew at half mast. The Head, Mr. Cameron, commented that of all the boys that had ever attended the school his life was one of the cleanest. His body was not recovered so he is commemorated on the Pozieres Memorial Panel 19 to 21 and on the war memorial in Little Somerford church.

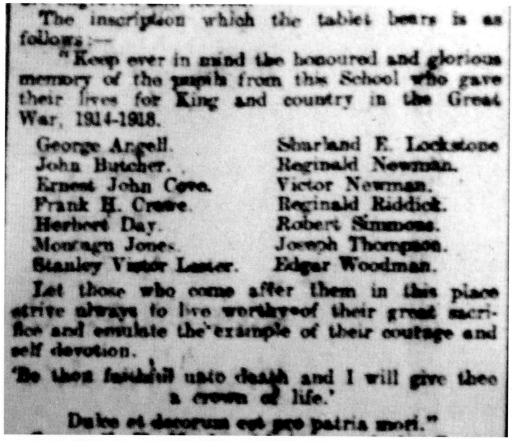

The wording of the inscription reported in the North Wilts Herald's article of 17thDecember 1920. The tablet was the work of C.A. Hughes, formerly a pupil and was originally fixed to the wall of the staircase landing.

United Reformed Church

The Congregational Church, Westport decided in the summer of 1920 that a Roll of Honour together with two special chairs would be a fitting memorial for those from the church who died in the war. Unfortunately they could not decide which names should be included on the Roll and the decision to have one was rescinded. However the memorial chairs were completed and presented along with another pair given as a thank offering by Mr. and Mrs. F.E. Smith (a local solicitor and strong supporter of the church) in November that year. The cost of the chairs was £7 10s. and the inscribed burnished brass plates were £3 15s. This total was raised from the congregation. The inscriptions are;

To the Glory of God and in Grateful Memory
of the following Men in connection with this Church,
who gave their lives in the Great War 1914-1919

Rev. Emlyn Holt Davies BA BD	George Paul
Walter Baker	Frederick Salter
Ernest Curtis	Walter Wakefield
Walter G Curtis	Edgar Woodman

And

Presented as a Token of Gratitude to God
for those in connection with this Church
who returned from the Great War

1914   1919

Triangle

At its February 1919 meeting the Borough Council was told that the Market House Company had accepted the Council's offer of £1,250 for the Town Hall. Mr. J.A. Jones congratulated the Mayor on having taken in hand one of the best pieces of business for which that authority had ever been responsible. The talk then turned to the provision of a war memorial. The Mayor, Monte Duck, was reported as saying: *The question of a war memorial was one which had to be tackled, and he took the opportunity of saying that his mind was perfectly open as to the form it should take. It was rather difficult to suggest anything. They did not want anything "tin-pot" in the Cross Hayes, or a few seats, but something worthy of the town. Now that the Council had acquired the Town Hall the idea had occurred to him that the memorial should take the form of beautifying the hall and making it worthy of Malmesbury or any other town. He thought the best way would be to call a public meeting, which would have to be done in any case.*

The public meeting was held on 20th March;

MALMESBURY WAR MEMORIAL.
What Shall It Be?

The Mayor (Mr. M. Duck) presided at a well-attended meeting in the Council Chamber, Malmesbury, yesterday afternoon, when various suggestions were put forward for the establishment of a war memorial for the town and district. Among those present were Canon and Mrs. McMillan, Col. L.E. Morrice, D.S.O., Mrs. Ramsay, Capt. and Mrs. E.S. Mackirdy, Mrs. Heaton, Mrs. Adye, Mrs. E. Jones, Messrs. H. Farrant, J.G. Bartlett, C.F. Moir, A.L. Forrester, A.W. Chubb, F.G.T. Goldstone, F.J. Compton, J.D. Curtis, H. Wilmot, J.A. Jones, F.H. Summers, J. Moore, W. Tinley, C. Bowman, M. Thompson, A. Adye, F.E. Smith, F.E. Ponting, C.C. Barnes, H.T. Hinwood, F.L. Newman, H.J.A. Beak and J. Walker, the Rev. T. Morrin, the Rev. J.W. Hutler, the Rev. F.A.H. Smith, the Rev. G.W. Ennos, and others. The Town Clerk (Mr. M.H. Chubb) was on the platform with the Mayor.

The Mayor said they were gathered on one of the most important and moving occasions the old borough had ever witnessed. Their purpose was to carry out a solemn obligation to those men who had proved themselves in every way equal, if not, greater, in heroism and self-sacrifice to any soldiers that Malmesbury had ever sent forth, and also to commemorate those men and women who had made great sacrifices for the common good (applause). The Mayor proceeded to outline a general scheme for the efficient provision of a fitting memorial. It must be such as should appeal equally to every section of the community without regard to class or sect, and it must be suited to the honour and traditions of their old town (hear, hear). To attain those objects they proposed to thrash out thoroughly the various schemes – and he hoped there would be many which would be laid before the meeting. After that the proposer and seconder of each scheme would be asked to meet the special committee which would be elected by the meeting in order to elaborate their scheme and prove that they were workable from a practical and financial point of view. He wished to make clear that the committee would have no power to adopt any particular scheme, but would present a report of every practical scheme, giving full details and a brief resume of the arguments for and against, to another public meeting which would be held. That public meeting would then vote, and the scheme which obtained the most votes would be adopted. A committee would also be elected at that future meeting to see that the scheme adopted was properly carried out. He urged them to remember that they were making a memorial to the fallen, to men who had endured more horrors, suffered nobler deaths, than any set of men who had ever lived in the old borough; they were making a memorial to men, and they should make it worthy of them (applause).

Canon McMillan proposed the following resolution – "That a public memorial be provided to commemorate the victory of the Navy and Army of the British Empire in the great war and as a permanent memorial to those men of Malmesbury and district who have given up their lives for their country." In proposing the resolution the Vicar accorded to the Mayor the gratitude of all for giving them the opportunity of meeting and discussing that important proposal. They wanted to establish a memorial which would be worthy of the great victory won by the Navy and Army of the British Empire and the Allies. To realise the extent and importance of that victory they had to remember the interests at stake, the size of the Army and the enormous Navy they furnished to battle with their enemies, the precious blood spilt and treasure so lavishly poured out. Then they would see that it was the most wonderful victory ever known in the long annals of the British Empire (hear, hear). They wanted to establish a memorial as gratitude to Almighty God, for giving them that wonderful victory. They wanted it to be a memorial in every way worthy of their gallant dead. Only five years ago there were over a million men in the Empire who in the ordinary course of events would have lived to full span of life. Now they slept in death because they had laid down their lives for those who remained. They slept in every sea on which the sun shone, in France, in Flanders, in Gallipoli; and they rested for ever in the sacred sod of Palestine until the last great trump should awaken them to the greatest victory of all – the victory over Death. Their memorial must be worthy to commemorate the long-living and self-sacrifice of those men who had come back maimed for life – some sightless, some disfigured. Those men, for what they had endured, had won our freedom, and it should be acknowledged. They thought, too, of those who came back strong in every way. They had made their sacrifice and they wanted to see something which would bring back to their memory what they had won for England. When they thought of the eight million men raised, one million of whom laid down their lives, besides three million other casualties, they ought to put up a great memorial (applause). Besides being a memorial of victory, it was going to be a much more personal matter – a memorial to their own officers, non-commissioned officers and men who went out from Malmesbury and laid down their lives. There were 66 or 67 of them, and they knew them personally. They would never know what they suffered for us – that was only know to the great God Himself; but we did know what they saved us from. We know they saved our womenfolk from nameless atrocities, our homes from utter destruction and ruin, saved our country from being churned up as hundreds of square miles in France and Belgium had been, so that acres were lying useless for long years to come; saved us from being enslaved and deported to foreign lands and worked to skin and bone and cast out hopeless or butchered and bundled into nameless graves. "All this they saved us from," said the Vicar, "so let our memorial be worthy of the greatness of their sacrifice" (applause).

Mr. A. Adye, who seconded, said that whatever they decided he hoped it would be a memorial that the young and rising generation would appreciate as having been established for the brave sailors and soldiers who had done so much for the land they loved. They should all do their best to make it worthy of the names of those who had fallen in battle (applause).

The resolution was carried.

Suggestions were made by various persons.

Mr. J.G. Bartlett suggested the endowment of two beds in the Cottage Hospital.

Mr. C.C. Barnes thought a nice park with a lake with swans and boats, and an institute with reading-room would be desirable for the people.

Mr. Fry suggested a hall or institute seating about 600 people. The town could run its own Cinema and concerts in it.

Mr. E. Jones, in a letter (he was unable to attend) suggested a beautification of the Town Hall with a centre window and brass plate, and also at the entrance mural tablets.

Mr. H. Wilmot made a similar suggestion.

The Mayor said the views of the two latter synchronised with his own.

Canon McMillan advocated the establishment of a Maternity Welfare Centre or Children's Clinic, and Mr. A.W. Chubb supported the idea.

The Rev. J.W. Hutler said they needed a memorial which would benefit the community. They could have a tablet put in the Town Hall, which at present was a disgrace (hear, hear). He favoured the Vicar's suggestion.

Mr. Tinley's idea was the provision of a public play-ground for children.

Mr. A. Adye favoured a recreation ground and swimming bath, a public library and reading-room, and a drinking fountain with the names inscribed thereon of all who fell in the war.

Mr. J.A. Jones favoured the play-ground idea, and also that of an institute. He mentioned what had been done by the Y.M.C.A.

Mr. M.H. Chubb said if there was any place where Malmesbury men would rather have their names on a tablet than anywhere it was the Abbey.

Mr. Thompson held that the Town Hall was the proper place for the memorial.

Mr. F.J. Compton urged the establishment of a reading-room or club-house for the winter months.

Mr. Farrant warned the meeting of the fate of reading-rooms by re-calling what the late Mr. W. Powell, M.P., had done and the effect of his misplaced generosity. He favoured Mr. E. Jones' scheme.

Capt. Mackirdy told of the non-success of the establishment of a park in the town the size of Malmesbury in Scotland. He did not think a public park would be a success.

Eventually the following were appointed as a committee, with power to add; The Mayor, Messrs. H. Farrant, A. Adye and J.A. Jones, Mrs. Ramsay, Miss Luce, O.B.E., Messrs. A.L. Forrester, J. Moore, F.J. Bates, M.H. Chubb, W. Tinley, C.J.H. Pollen, H. Weeks, N. Adye and R. Pike.

Another public meeting was called for 4th June;

Malmesbury War Memorial

A Monument in the Triangle

A meeting to consider war memorial proposals which had been submitted to the committee was held at the Council Chamber, Malmesbury on Wednesday. The Mayor (Mr. M. Duck) presided, and with him on the platform was Mr. M.H. Chubb (town clerk). Amongst those also present were Col. L.E. Morrice, D.S.O., and Mrs. Morrice, Major R. Clarke, Capt. Mackirdy, Dr. and Mrs. Moore, Messrs. C.F. Moir, J. Moore, A. Cameron, C. Bradshaw, J.G. Bartlett, A. Adye, J.A. Jones, H. Matthews, S.A. Adye, A.J. Ponting, J. Riddick, J. Walker, C. Gale, H. Iles, C. Barnes and others.

The Mayor tendered the town's thanks for the excellent manner in which they had dis-charged their duties, and the amount of time they had devoted to their work. Every sug-gestion had been fully considered by them, and in the result their deliberations were unani-mous. He paid a tribute to the late Canon C.D.H. McMillan, stating that he was very enthu-siastic over the proposal. In the last conversation he had with the Vicar the latter said: "Whatever scheme is decided on, you can rely on my wholehearted support, no matter what it may be." That showed the late Vicar's open mind. If the report of the committee was adopted he (the Mayor) had authority to state that the Town Council were prepared to give free of all cost a site in Westport for the erection of a monument (applause).

Mr. Chubb, who is chairman of the committee, presented their report. The recommenda-tion was "that a war memorial be erected in the Triangle containing the names of all those who had fallen in the late war and also of those who had given their services in the war, and that any surplus for the fund be given towards the purpose of providing a recreation ground for the town." Mr. Chubb explained in detail the work of the committee, stating that they had co-opted working men, whose views and services were valuable, and had secured as hon. secretaries two ex-soldiers, Messrs. S.A. Adye and F. Newman, who had fought for their country. It was felt that the monument must be one that would be worthy of the enormous sacrifices made for the country by the men whose names would be inscribed on it, and he had no doubt that Malmesbury would rise to the occasion and provide the neces-sary funds for the purpose. Though he had no expert knowledge, it was estimated that about £500 or £600 would be required, and, whilst that would enable them to put up a monument worthy of the occasion, it would also turn an ugly spot in Westport into a place of beauty and an adornment of the town, for whilst the Abbey at present had no memorial – though there would be one later on – Westport, a parish from which so many had volun-teered for active service, had no monument. He proposed the adoption of the report.

Col. Morrice, in seconding, congratulated the committee on their decision.

Mr. Adye supported. He would have liked to see a recreation field or swimming baths, but when the Town Clerk reminded him of the cost to the ratepayers he willingly dropped the idea and now heartily agreed with the committee's conclusions.

Mr. Moore, Mr. Moir and Mr. Bartlett also spoke in favour of the report.

Mr. Chubb said the site would cost the Council about £100.

The report was adopted with three dissentients.

Mr. Moore proposed that the committee already appointed, with the addition of three representatives of the Federation of Discharged Sailors and Soldiers, be re-elected to complete the scheme.

Col. Morrice, seconded, and it was unanimously carried.

Mr. J.A. Jones thought that if Mr. Chubb had been more explicit with regard to the cost the report would have been carried unanimously. He was not voicing his own views, but people were really asking how such a monument was going to cost £500 or £600. Of course if it was proposed to place seats around the monument he could see where the cost would come in.

Mr. Chubb explained that it would be impossible for him to state what the exact cost would be.

Major Clarke suggested that a prize of £5 should be offered for a design for the memorial.

Mr. Charles Gale (a discharged soldier) pleaded for better representation of discharged, demobilised and disabled soldiers, and complained that the meetings had been held at an unfavourable hour. He had hoped that a public swimming pool could have been provided. The addition of three soldier representatives had already been agreed.

The Borough Council discussed the matter at their next meeting;

THE WAR MEMORIAL SITE.

The Deputy Mayor asked for an explanation of a remark made by the Town Clerk at the War Memorial Meeting the previous week to the effect that the Council had agreed to pay a certain price for the site for the memorial in the Triangle. The Council had arrived at no decision in the matter.

The Town Clerk, quoting the minute relating to the purchase of the weigh-bridge, said that it was "proposed by Ald. Forrester and seconded by Ald. Farrant and carried unanimously that the offer of Mr. Marcus Sealy to sell the weigh-bridge in the Triangle for £105 be accepted." It was considered by the Council desirable that the purchase be effected by June 22nd if possible.

The Deputy Mayor observing that he considered it was very premature the matter dropped.

The Old Corporation held a meeting where the main business was the war memorial;

Malmesbury Old Corporation.
No Donation to the War Memorial.

The High Steward (Mr. M.H. Chubb) presided at a meeting of the Old Corporation in St. John's Court House, Malmesbury, on Tuesday. Also present were Mr. A.W. Chubb (deputy high steward and clerk), Mr. W.T. Clark (clerk to the King's Heath Trustees), Messrs. C. Box, H. Matthews, E. Fry, H. Russell, J. Boulton, A. Bailey and A. Harris (burgesses), Messrs. I. Jefferies, Geo. Pike, H. Sharpe, K. Lewis, S. Grey, H. Poole, W. Adye, W. Hanks, A. Box and Jacob Jefferies (assistant burgesses), and Mr. E. Pike (sergeant-at-mace). There were also present a number of Commoners.

A WAR MEMORIAL DONATION.

Exception was taken by several members to the minute of a previous meeting voting £5 to the Malmesbury War Memorial.

Mr. George May strongly objected to the motion, saying that it was altogether wrong to utilise any portion of the Commoners' funds for such a purpose. By all means, he said, let a war memorial be erected, but let those who were anxious for it put their hands into their own pockets for the funds (hear, hear).

Mr. I. Jefferies expressed himself in agreement with those views.

Mr. Arthur Smith said he repeated now what he had said at the last meeting – that as Commoners they should be only too glad of the opportunity of subscribing to perpetuate the memory of those who fell in the war, and to extol the names of those who were permitted to come back. Only a short time ago representatives of the Wilts War Agricultural Committee visited Malmesbury on urgent business in connection with the Common. As the result of the good offices of their High Steward (Mr. M.H. Chubb), attempts to interfere with the administration of the Common failed, but when the deputation left the room it was with the firm resolve to place a scheme for the future administration of the Common by the Charity Commissioners, and he did not hesitate to say that had the war been prolonged another three months, there would have been no Malmesbury Common ("No, No"). he said "Yes," for it would have been an easy thing to have passed an Act for a different adminis- tration of Malmesbury Common, and for that reason, if for no other, they should agree to this small grant and thus show their appreciation of, and gratitude to, those men who had fallen or those who had come back from the scenes of battle.

The High Steward reminded the members of the number of Malmesbury men who had fallen or participated in the war and submitted that this was a splendid way of showing their appreciation of their services. If the Malmesbury Commoners could afford the £5 it would be a good way of subscribing collectively, for it would not total a large sum individually.

Mr. G. May; I would rather subscribe 2s. 6d. myself than a penny from the Common funds per head.

Mr. E. Lewis suggested that if the Commoners liked to have a war memorial it should be done on their own initiative, and his suggestion met with some response.

The High Steward said he would be pleased to support such a scheme.

The Court, after much discussion, decided by a large majority to rescind the resolution in question, only four voting for the donation.

On 14th June 1919 the Council purchased the weighbridge and hut at the Triangle from Thomas Sealy, the blacksmith. The price was £105 but £25 was recovered when the scrap metal was sold to Joey Wilkins. The Memorial Committee established at the public meeting of 4th June was chaired by the Town Clerk, Montague Chubb with Secretaries Sydney Adye and Frederick Lewis Newman, who had lost his two younger brothers in the war.

The Committee sent a leaflet to every household in the town stating that subscriptions were invited through lists at the two banks (both branches of Lloyds at 10 and 35 High Street) and doorstep collections. In the middle the names of 66 men who died were listed with the request that *Alterations, additions and corrections in spelling or rank are invited and should be sent to the Hon. Secretary Mr. Sydney Adye, High Street*. A number of corrections were made and nine names were eventually added. Although great efforts were taken it seems that some names were missed either due to deliberate inaction by the family or because no relative of the casualty remained locally.

More than £500 was raised and H. de Bertodano, an architect and nephew of Baldomero de Bertodano owner of Cowbridge House, was commissioned to design the memorial. He chose a Celtic wheel cross similar to the Cross of St. Martin on the Isle of Iona. The base com- prises 3 steps made of Pennent stone ten feet square, above being 4 panels of Hopton Wood stone into which the names are set in lead lettering topped by the Portland stone cross carved on all sides. The whole assemblage stands over eighteen feet high.

The War Memorial was unveiled on Sunday 20th March 1921 as reported by the Wiltshire Gazette;

UNVEILING THE WAR MEMORIAL.
DEDICATION AND ADDRESS BY BISHOP FORREST BROWNE.

On Sunday, in typically early spring weather, Malmesbury's memorial to its fallen warriors was unveiled in the presence of a large concourse of people – a larger crowd than we have seen in the borough since Bishop Forrest Browne unveiled the market cross after its reno- vation.

Readers of the Gazette are familiar with all the details and the preliminaries – objections and approvals – leading up to a final decision as to the form the memorial should take; it was a thorny question, bristling with difficult problems. Indeed, it was this which caused the monument to be rather late in its erection; but "all's well that ends well," and though "in the multitude of counsellors there was" confusion, rather than "wisdom," the smaller committee which eventually took the matter in hand have attained their object, and the result is a memorial worthy of the traditions of the borough.

The memorial is a large Ionic cross erected on a foundation of concrete and approached by steps. It is from a design by Mr. H.S. de Bertodano, and was worked by Messrs. Webb and Son, of Chippenham, who have given the utmost satisfaction in the completion of the task. The cross stands 17ft. 6in. high, and is raised on the spot occupied for many years by the

The memorial was concealed by Union Flags draped over the poles before the unveiling. (Athelstan Museum)

old weighbridge in the Triangle. Around the steps appear the names of the 74 Malmesbury men who made the supreme sacrifice.

The ceremony was fixed to take place at three, but long before that time a crowd assembled in the Triangle, which was presently swollen by the children from all the schools, under the care of their teachers, and about 200 discharged and demobilised men who formed a guard around the monument; within the space thus formed were a united choir under the leadership of Mr. W. Brown (organist of the Abbey), and the relatives of the fallen heroes. Just before three came the procession (headed by the town band) of the Bishop, clergy and ministers of the Free Churches, the Mayor and Aldermen (in their robes of office) with the members of the Town Council and their officials, the Old Corporation, the V.A.D. nurses, the Malmesbury Troop of Boy Scouts, the Ancient Order of Foresters, and the Cirencester Benefit Society. The banner of St. George on the Abbey was at half mast, and the Union Jack was similarly hoisted at Castle House.

After the hymn "O God, our help in ages past," the Mayor opened the proceedings by asking Colonel L.E. Morrice, D.S.O., whose son John is one of the names commemorated, to unveil the memorial. Union flags on two flagpoles concealed the cross before the ceremony. The Abbey's vicar, Rev. C.E. Paterson conducted the service and Rev. Dr. G. Forrest Browne, former Bishop of Bristol who had played a large part in raising the funds for the Abbey restoration 15 years before and had rededicated the Market Cross after repair in 1912, gave the address. Local ministers Rev. T. Morrin (Roman Catholic), Rev. P.A.H. Smith (Moravian), Rev. J.W. Hutler (Primitive Methodist) and Rev. G.W. Ennos (Congregational) offered prayers or made speeches. The ceremony ended with the Last Post, two minutes silence and Reveille.

The names, displayed on four panels beginning on the east followed by the northern, western and southern faces, are;

OUR GLORIOUS DEAD

Pte Angell G	Pte Bishop AE	Pte Bye W
Pte Bailey AE	Pte Bishop C	Pte Brickell JP
Sgt Bailey FH	Pte Bishop CH	Pte Carey LJ
Pte Bailey JH	Pte Bishop D	Pte Clark A
Pte Baker W	Pte Bond C	Cpl Curtis EW
Gnr Barnes W	Pte Bond W	Pte Curtis J

Pte Curtis JB	LCpl Johnson A
Cpl Curtis WG	Pte Jones C
Rfn Deadman F	2Lt Jones HE
Pte Emery SW	1stAM Jones JM
Cpl Exton R	Pte Kerr J
LS Garland J	Pte Lewis AJ
Pte Grey G	Pte Lewis SE
2Lt Hibbard EJ	Pte Liddington HC
Pte Hibbard EJ	Pte Lockstone ES
Pte James H	Lt MacKirdy CDS

Mid Morrice JW	Pte Perry AJ	Cpl Price W
Spr Newman HJ	AB Pike E	Pte Reeves HT
Tpr Newman RC	Pte Poole HG	Pte Salter FJ
LSgt Newman VG	Pte Pope T	Gnr Savine HJ
Pte Oram G	Pte Price C	Pte Selby WJ
Sgt Paul GH	LCpl Price R	Gnr Sellwood J

Pte Sharpe TF	Pte Weeks RR
Pte Shaw F	Gnr Wallington JH
LCpl Shingles H	Pte Westmacott C
Dvr Thompson JE	AB Weston HR
Pte Thornbury E	Pte Willis H
Pte Thornbury WH	Pte Wood C
Pte Tugwell F	Pte Wood P
Sig Tugwell JMW	Pte Woodman E
Pte Wakefield WE	Gnr Woodward F

Rev EH Davies BA BD

One man remains a puzzle. All attempts to discover the identity of Private J. Kerr have failed. His was one of the names added to the original list and does not appear on any other memorial in town. One possible candidate is William Frederick Kerr, born in Wroughton and working as a grocer's assistant in Malmesbury. In the spring of 1915 he lived with his wife Maud in St Marys Street where their daughter Dorothy was born. William was called up and enlisted at Malmesbury but his Army record said he lived in Swindon (his wife returned home to Wroughton where he is commemorated). He joined the 2nd Wiltshires and was killed on 21st March 1918.

May he and all those from Malmesbury who served 'Rest in Peace'.

Finally may I remind you of the words recited every Remembrance Day;

They shall not grow old, as we that are left grow old:
Age shall not weary them, nor the years condemn.
At the going down of the sun and in the morning
We will remember them.

Laurence Binyon (1869-1943)

Bibliography

Aspinall-Oglander, Brig. Gen. C.F., *History of the Great War, Military Operations Gallipoli Vol 1*, (reprint 1992)

Aspinall-Oglander, Brig. Gen. C.F., *History of the Great War, Military Operations Gallipoli Vol 2*, (reprint 1992)

Banks, Arthur, *A Military Atlas of the First World War*, (2001)

Barnes, Capt. A.F., *The Story of the 2/5th Gloucestershire Regiment 1914-1918*, (1930)

Becke, Maj. A.F., *Order of Battle of Divisions, Regular Divisions*, (reprint 2007)

Becke, Maj. A.F., *Order of Battle of Divisions, the Territorial Force*, (reprint 2007)

Becke, Maj. A.F., *Order of Battle of Divisions, New Army Divisions*, (reprint 2007)

Becke, Maj. A.F., *Order of Battle of Divisions, the Army Council, GHQs, Armies & Corps*, (reprint 2007)

Beckett, Ian, *Home Front 1914-1918*, (2006)

Bet-El, Ilana R., *Conscripts*, (2003)

Bewsher, Major F.W., *The History of the Fifty First (Highland) Division 1914-1918*, (reprint 2001)

Clarke, Dale, *British Artillery 1914-19, Field Army Artillery*, (2004)

Clarke, Dale, *British Artillery 1914-19, Heavy Artillery*, (2005)

Commonwealth War Graves Commission, *Cemeteries & Memorials in Belgium & Northern France*, (2004)

Cooksley, Peter G., *Royal Flying Corps Handbook*, (2007)

Coombs, Rose E.B., *Before Endeavours Fade*, (1994)

Cooper, Bryan, *The Tenth (Irish) Division in Gallipoli*, (reprint 2003)

Corrigan, Gordon, *Mud, Blood and Poppycock*, (2004)

Edmonds, Brig. Gen. Sir James E., *History of the Great War, Military Operations France & Belgium 1914 Vol 1*, (reprint 1985)

Edmonds, Brig. Gen. Sir James E., *History of the Great War, Military Operations France & Belgium 1914 Vol 2*, (1925)

Edmonds, Brig. Gen. Sir James E., *History of the Great War, Military Operations France & Belgium 1915 Vol 1*, (reprint 1995)

Edmonds, Brig. Gen. Sir James E., *History of the Great War, Military Operations France & Belgium 1915 Vol 2*, (1928)

Edmonds, Brig. Gen. Sir James E., *History of the Great War, Military Operations France & Belgium 1916 Vol 1*, (reprint 1993)

Edmonds, Brig. Gen. Sir James E., *History of the Great War, Military Operations France & Belgium 1917 Vol 2*, (reprint 1991)

Edmonds, Brig. Gen. Sir James E., *History of the Great War, Military Operations France & Belgium 1918 Vol 1*, (reprint 1995)

Edmonds, Brig. Gen. Sir James E., *History of the Great War, Military Operations France & Belgium 1918 Vol 2*, (reprint 1995)

Edmonds, Brig. Gen. Sir James E., *History of the Great War, Military Operations France & Belgium 1918 Vol 3*, (reprint 1994)

Edmonds, Brig. Gen. Sir James E., *History of the Great War, Military Operations France & Belgium 1918 Vol 4*, (reprint 1993)

Edmonds, Brig. Gen. Sir James E., *History of the Great War, Military Operations France & Belgium 1918 Vol 5*, (reprint 1993)

Ewart, Wilfred, *Scots Guard on the Western Front 1915-1918*, (reprint 2001)

Falls, Capt. Cyril, *History of the Great War, Military Operations France & Belgium 1917 Vol 1*, (reprint 1992)

Gudmundsson, Bruce, *The British Expeditionary Force 1914-15*, (2005)

Holmes, Richard, *Tommy*, (2004)

Kearsey, Lt. Col. A., *Strategy and Tactics of the Egypt and Palestine Campaigns*, (reprint 2002)

James, Brig. E.A., *British Regiments 1914-1918*, (reprint 2001)

Liddington, Cilla, *Heroes All, A tribute to the men of Sherston who valiantly served their country*, (2005)

McCarthy, Chris, *The Somme, the Day-by-day Account*, (1998)

Messenger, Charles, *Call to Arms, the British Army 1914-18*, (2005)

Middlebrook, Martin, *The Kaiser's Battle*, (2000)

Miles, Capt. Wilfred, *History of the Great War, Military Operations France & Belgium 1916 Vol 2*, (reprint 1995)

Miles, Capt. Wilfred, *History of the Great War, Military Operations France & Belgium 1917 Vol 3*, (reprint 1991)

Moore, William, *See How They Ran*, (1975)

Nicholls, Jonathan, *Cheerful Sacrifice*, (2005)

North Wilts Herald, (1914-1921)

Passingham, Ian, *All the Kaiser's Men*, (2003)

Richter, Donald, *Chemical Soldiers, British Gas Warfare in World War 1*, (1992)

Spencer, William, *Army Service Records of the First World War*, (2001)

Stedman, Michael, *Great Battles of the Great War*, (1999)

Sutton, Mark, *Tell Them of Us*, (2006)

Swinton, Maj. Gen. Sir Ernest, *Twenty Years After Volume 1*, (1937)

Swinton, Maj. Gen. Sir Ernest, *Twenty Years After Volume 2*, (1937)

Swinton, Maj. Gen. Sir Ernest, *Twenty Years After Supplementary Volume*, (1937)

Terraine, John, *The Smoke and the Fire*, (1980)

The Times, *Diary & Index of the War 1914-1918*, (reprint 2001)

The Wilts & Gloucester Standard, (1914-1921)

Wakefield, Alan & Moody, Simon, *Under the Devil's Eye, Britain's Forgotten Army at Salonika 1915-1918*, (2004)

Western Front Association, *Stand To!*, (1981-2008)

Westlake, Ray, *British Battalions on the Somme*, (2004)

Westlake, Ray, *British Battalions on the Western Front January to June 1915*, (2001)

Westlake, Ray, *British Regiments at Gallipoli*, (2004)

Westlake, Ray, *Kitchener's Army*, (2003)

Westlake, Ray, *The British Army of August 1914*, (2005)

Wiltshire Gazette, (1914-1921)

Wryall, Everard, *History of the Duke of Cornwall's Light Infantry 1914-1919*, (1932)

Wryall, Everard, *History of the Somerset Light Infantry (Prince Albert's) 1914-1919*, (1927)

Wryall, Everard, *Nineteenth Division 1914-1918*, (reprint 1999)

Young, Michael, *Army Service Corps 1902-1918*, (2000)

Index